THE TOMB
IN ANCIENT EGYPT

Royal and Private Sepulchres from
the Early Dynastic Period
to the Romans

AIDAN DODSON AND SALIMA IKRAM

THE TOMB
IN ANCIENT EGYPT

Royal and Private Sepulchres from
the Early Dynastic Period
to the Romans

With 402 illustrations, 28 in color

Thames & Hudson

To the memory of Divisional Sergeant Major Donald Sydney Dodson,
The Queen's Body Guard of The Yeomen of the Guard
19 January 1925 – 23 March 2005

FRONTISPIECE: Anubis holds the mummy of Roy before the stela of his
tomb, while Roy's wife kneels in grief before him (TT255, late 18th
Dynasty).

Designed by Thomas Keenes

First published in 2008 in hardcover in the United States of America by
Thames & Hudson Inc., 500 Fifth Avenue, New York, New York 10110

thamesandhudsonusa.com

Library of Congress Catalog Card Number 2005906274

ISBN 978-0-500-05139-9

Printed and bound in China by Everbest Printing Co. Ltd.

Contents

Preface

Although Egyptology as a science is two centuries old, it is surprising how few volumes provide a systematic coverage of particular types of monuments. This is especially true with the tombs of ancient Egypt, ubiquitous as they are in the popular conception of the country and its culture. While there are many books available on particular types of tomb (for example the pyramids), individual monuments, sites or specific aspects of tomb design (for example Old Kingdom decorative schemes), no modern work attempts to deal with Egyptian tombs as a whole.

Generally, royal and private tombs are rarely considered together, leading to many misunderstandings. Thus one still finds it stated as a 'fact' that private and royal tombs of the New Kingdom differ in that while the former are decorated with scenes of daily life, the latter have scenes of the underworld. This stems from a failure to grasp that the two sets of monuments in question had completely different functions. The private 'tombs' with 'daily life' scenes are actually public offering places, their royal equivalent being not the sepulchres in the Valley of the Kings but the great mortuary temples, such as Deir el-Bahari and Medinet Habu, whose decoration includes equivalent 'daily life' elements. Conversely, the equivalent of the Valley of the Kings monuments are the subterranean pits, passages and chambers that lie below most of the private 'tombs'. On the rare occasions that these are decorated, their adornment is likewise based on compositions dealing with the underworld – sometimes the very same ones.

Thus, this volume aims to tell the story of the Egyptian tomb, its development, construction and study, in an integrated manner. Royal tombs will be considered alongside their private contemporaries and similarities emphasized where they exist, rather than allowing the size and magnificence of the royal tombs to blind one to such areas of convergence. While almost infinitely greater in size and complexity, the Great Pyramid at Giza is actually made up of the same basic components as the very smallest of the private tombs that lie at its foot.

The broad division of labour in the writing of this book has been between the architectural and archaeological aspects of the tombs, which are the responsibility of Dodson and the technological and sociological material, together with decorative schemes, which are from the pen of Ikram, although our pens (or perhaps, rather, keyboards and mice) have not infrequently strayed across these boundaries! The remainder of the volume is generally a joint effort.

We would like to express our thanks to the following friends, colleagues and loved ones for hospitality, help, permissions, photographs, information and assorted kindnesses: Tomas Bács; Ladislav Bareš; Miroslav Barta; Violaine Chauvet; Andrew Chugg; Mark Collier; Lorelei Corcoran; Martin R. Davies; Dana DePietro; Francis Dzokowski; Christine End; Fayza Haikal; Melinda Hartwig; Zahi Hawass; Dyan Hilton; Sheila Hilton; Alison Hobby; Janice Kamrin; Jaromir Malek; Bill Manley; Elizabeth Miles; Karol Myśliwiec; David O'Connor; Sara Orel; Maarten Raven; Janet Richards; Otto Schaden; J.J. Shirley; Ibrahim Soliman; Hourig Sourouzian; Nigel Strudwick; John Swanson; John Taylor; Francesco Tiradritti; Medhat Saad; Miroslav Verner; Nathalie Walschaerts; Leslie Warden; Nicholas Warner; Kent Weeks; Penny Wilson; Alain Zivie; and the Inspectors and *gaffirs* throughout Egypt. To any we have omitted, we extend our sincere apologies.

Bristol and Cairo   Aidan Dodson and Salima Ikram

Introduction

'Little is in life on earth, Eternity is in the necropolis'
(Amen)user (TT131), 18th Dynasty[1]

The tombs of ancient Egypt remain, for many, the defining monuments of that civilization. This is not because the Egyptians were an overly morose and morbid group of people, obsessed by death, but rather because they were obsessed by life and wished it to continue. Tomb construction and decoration were key to the continuation of existence, albeit on another plane.

The burial places of the nobility, artisans and lesser folk of ancient Egypt are fundamental to our understanding of that great civilization. From tombs come both the physical remains of the ancients and their possessions, and the decorations of their walls open significant vistas on life lived on the banks of the Nile. Small or large, they often contain extremely fine examples of two- and three-dimensional art, which are also important objects of modern study.

Owing to the richness and ubiquity of tomb sites and the relatively small number of archaeologically accessible settlement sites, the larger part of our knowledge of ancient Egyptian society and history is still derived from the study of sepulchres. Egyptian tombs were divided into two portions: the accessible tomb-chapel, which was decorated and bore vivid depictions of the world in which the tomb-owner(s) lived, and the burial chamber, usually undecorated, which contained the body and the grave goods. Burial installations of the kings were unusual in that they were not infrequently decorated, especially during the New Kingdom, and give us some of our best evidence for the minutiae of Egyptian religion. Tombs remain fundamental to our understanding of life on the ancient banks of the Nile: one is able to follow the agricultural and domestic life of the country; the industrial processes that created some of the monuments at which the world still marvels; social organization and familial relationships; and funerary beliefs and the ceremonies that accompanied an ancient Egyptian burial.

Tomb-chapels enshrined the name and profession of their owners, but frequently we can learn more about his or her family and life. While the latter aspect is often only a tantalizing glimpse, in a few cases we find extensive autobiographical texts. In the famous example of the 6th Dynasty African explorer Harkhuf (Aswan QH34n), we read of his African explorations and his return to his boy-king, Pepy II, bringing with him a dancing dwarf; in another (QH26), we learn of a journey into the desert by a son bent on avenging his father's murder and bringing home his body for decent burial. Yet more texts describe a man's participation in the ancient mystery-play of Osiris, god of the dead; the construction of the first royal tomb in the Valley of the Kings (TT81); the duties of the Vizier; the way in which General Amenemheb (TT85) saved his king's life when charged by an enraged elephant. Even

---

1 (*above*) Banquet scene from the 18th Dynasty tomb-chapel of Nebamun at Thebes (TTE.2: BM EA37984).

2 The Valley of the Kings, with El-Qurn in the background; the entrance to Ramesses VI's tomb (KV9) can be seen in the right foreground and those of Sety I and Ramesses I (KV17 and 16) on the left.

where there is no autobiographical text, there may be clues in the texts or layout of the decoration that will provide evidence of the events contemporary with the tomb's construction. A good example is the tomb of the Vizier Ramose (TT55), in which a sudden change in the decorative style shows how its owner presided over the transition from the reign of the New Kingdom pharaoh Amenhotep III to that of his 'heretic' son and successor, Amenhotep IV (Akhenaten).

Mortuary temples, the royal equivalents of the private tomb-chapels, usually omit such elements, instead focusing on the pharaohs' cosmic roles as a god in heaven and on earth, with only occasional hints at events during the monarch's reign. The very existence of a royal burial installation, however, is sometimes in itself a fundamental historical document, a number of tombs being the sole evidence that a particular king had ever lived.

However, the importance of Egyptian tombs is not limited to purely historical and sociological aspects: they are also frequently stunning works of art and architecture. Ramose's tomb, for example, besides being a key document for the study of the early Amarna Period, is also adorned with some of the finest reliefs ever executed in Egypt. Other particularly choice monuments include the 5th Dynasty Saqqara tomb of Ti, the 26th Dynasty sepulchre of Mentuemhat (TT34) and the exquisite 19th Dynasty royal tombs of Sety I (KV17) and his daughter-in-law Nefertiry (Nefertari; QV66). Another tomb, that of Petosiris at Tuna el-Gebel, illustrates its period – that of the beginning of the Greek dominion over Egypt – by being adorned with a

composite form of art, which attempts to fuse elements of both Hellenic and Egyptian practice.

Besides the paintings, reliefs and statues adorning their walls, many tombs are significant manifestations of the architect's craft. At one extreme, there is the sheer scale of the royal pyramids of the 4th Dynasty, still the most massive free-standing monuments raised by mankind; at the other is the ingenuity displayed in some of the tombs of the Middle Kingdom and Saite Period, where much skill was expended in protecting the sepulchre from the attentions of tomb robbers.

Unfortunately, in spite of such efforts, the cemeteries of Egypt have been the subject of extensive plundering since the very earliest times. Nonetheless, tombs have revealed vast quantities of funerary equipment, ranging from everyday items to gorgeous jewelry and luxury mortuary items. Amongst these are the furniture of Hetepheres, mother of Khufu (G7000X); the treasures of the 12th Dynasty princesses at Dahshur; of Yuya and Tjuiu (KV46), parents-in-law of Amenhotep III; of Kha and Meryet (TT8), the former being in charge of the construction of the royal tomb during the middle years of the 18th Dynasty; of Tutankhamun (KV62), the richest of all such finds; of Pasebkhanut I (NRT-III) of the 21st Dynasty. Sadly, other items in our museums are monuments to the tombs' destruction. The beautiful fragments of wall-decoration displayed were usually removed at the cost of the utter destruction of the remainder of the scenes that first attracted the cupidity of vandals and self-proclaimed antiquarians.

Vandals, often in the guise of collectors and antiquities dealers, have been responsible for large-scale destruction in tombs. For example, in Theban Tomb (TT) 222, two portions of the wall decoration were removed (and later sold in the international art market), which resulted in the destruction of most of the decoration on the surrounding walls. The tomb was also burnt, out of sheer malice. Some tombs have been bulldozed in order to gain access to the burial chamber. In addition to tomb robbers, many tombs have also been destroyed to a large extent through the vicissitudes of time, visitors, pollution, weather and reuse.

This book is divided into four sections. Part I starts with a discussion of what is known of Egyptian funerary beliefs and

4 The rear wall of the early 12th Dynasty tomb-chapel of Khnumhotep iii at Beni Hasan (BH-III), with the classic Egyptian scenes of fishing and fowling. The lower part of the wall bears the tomb-owner's autobiography.

their influence on the design of the tomb. The next chapter examines the spatial organization within cemeteries, the layout of the tombs and what this may tell us about ancient Egyptian culture and social organization. This is followed by a discussion on the methods of tomb construction, decorative techniques and the builders and artisans responsible for the construction of the tombs. The section concludes with a history of the key figures who have studied the Egyptian tombs, freeing them from the all-embracing sands and clearing and copying them.

Part II gives an overview of the fundamentals of tomb decoration in a high-level way, considering the iconographic approaches taken by the Egyptian designer and then discussing the individual kinds of scene that are to be found within Egyptian funerary monuments. These range from particular motifs such as hunting and weaving to much larger units such as the Book of the Dead and the Pyramid Texts.

The story of the Egyptian tomb is traced in Part III, from the dawn of Egyptian history down to the Roman domination. A range of typical and exceptional tomb designs are described and illustrated, from the multiple points of view of architecture, decorative arrangement, style, location and contents.

The volume concludes with Part IV, providing a conspectus of the main cemeteries of Egypt, maps and a bibliography. The latter and extensive endnotes aim to provide between them references to all the key works dealing with Egyptian tombs in general and the particular monuments discussed in the text.

3 (left) The entrance to the 5th Dynasty mortuary temple of Sahure at Abu Sir.

Part I

Chapter 1

Egyptian Mortuary Beliefs
and the Nature of the Tomb

'When you prosper, found your household…. When you make a place for yourself, make good your dwelling in the graveyard. Make worthy your dwelling in the west.'
INSTRUCTIONS OF HORDJEDEF, 4TH DYNASTY[2]

The preservation and housing of the body on earth so that the individual could be resurrected formed a fundamental part of the ancient Egyptian view of the necessities for the afterlife. Consequently, provision of eternal accommodation for the body in the form of a tomb was granted high priority by the well-to-do Egyptian. Of course, the less well-off were also concerned with their life in the hereafter. In their case, however, economic reality determined that they would have to be content with a hole scooped in the low desert, the only luxury being perhaps burial in some form of coffin, rather than simple wrapping in one's own sleeping mat, or possessing a grave marker in the form of a stela.

Cemeteries tended to be located on the Nile's west bank, the side of the setting sun that marked the end of the day. This was not always practical, so that many burials occur on the east; however, such tombs contain an internal geography that fits with the Egyptian belief system.

5 (*left*) An image of King Ramesses VI before the goddess Maat (KV9: 20th Dynasty).

6 (*above*) The Opening-of-the-Mouth ceremony, as shown in the tomb of Pairi (TT139: 18th Dynasty).

The afterlife that the Egyptians were attempting to attain and maintain was visualized as a more perfect Egypt in which they, as a *maa kheru*, or 'justified one', could pass an ideal life eternally and harmoniously in the company of the gods. This place, which could be either a mirror image of Egypt, subterranean, or even celestial, was often called the Fields of Iaru, or Field of Reeds, and was the domain of the god Osiris (see below). Here the deceased could live eternally at one with the gods.

Our knowledge of the Egyptians' belief in the afterlife is largely derived from New Kingdom and later evidence, although the basic ideas appear to have been in place from the beginning of Egyptian history, evolving over time. Throughout Egypt's long and varied history there remained one essential element that was the cornerstone of the Egyptians' belief in the afterlife: *maat*. This was the divine order and balance that had to be maintained if the universe were to continue. It was every individual's responsibility to contribute to maintaining the balance of the cosmos (*maat*) by living a good and balanced life (one of the symbols for the maintenance of *maat* was a pair of scales), although the burden of responsibility for this fell on the pharaoh and priests. By appeasing the gods through offerings and prayers and by living within the laws of *maat*, life could continue in Egypt and in the afterworld.

The tomb was the point of contact between the worlds of the living and of the dead and provided a space where both worlds could co-exist symbiotically. Tombs were divided into two portions, the tomb-chapel or super-structure and the burial chamber or substructure. The substructure, equivalent to the netherworld, was the realm of the dead, while the decorated tomb-chapel, accessible to the living, was the point where the two worlds intersected, connected by the burial shaft. Generally, with the notable exception of the Valley of the Kings, the portions of the tombs that are visited today are the tomb-chapels, although access to burial chambers through shafts or sloping passages, blocked in antiquity, is now sometimes possible.

The superstructure or tomb-chapel was the 'public' part of the tomb and the focus of the celebration of the cult of the deceased. In the earliest times only a stela served as the focus of the offering place, but this soon expanded to include first a simple superstructure, which later became an elaborate complex, richly decorated with scenes from 'daily life'. A complete funerary chapel thus came into existence and became a clear requirement for any fully equipped sepulchre. Its form varied, depending on the local geography: cut into the flank of a rocky outcrop in some locations; free-standing or incorporated into the core of a bench-shaped structure known as a 'mastaba'³ in others. Various combinations of these types, with their associated decorations, are of course to be found and will be described and discussed below.

The substructure of the tomb was the abode of the corpse. It could consist of a single room or a labyrinth of corridors and chambers, housing one or many bodies. This element was wholly separate from the chapel and the superstructure. While the latter was intended for continued

access – indeed, the regular visits of priests and family to celebrate the cult of the dead was its whole reason for existence – the burial chamber was intended to be secure. Although in most cases constructed close to the chapel – often directly under it – in others it was constructed at some distance. The most extreme examples of this are the royal burial places of the Early Dynastic Period and the New Kingdom, which lay in some cases 3 or 4 km (2–2.5 miles) from their associated mortuary temples or enclosures. The approach to the burial chamber was closed after the interment, options ranging from walling up the door, a simple filling of the shaft with rubble, through large blocking stones to elaborate sealing mechanisms including the use of sand-powered 'hydraulics' in the late Middle Kingdom and Late Period (see pp. 205, 286). The substructure was rarely decorated and when it was, the decorations concentrated on the netherworld, rather than that of the living. In the case of the royal tombs of the New Kingdom, the burial chambers were an elaborate invocation of the world of the sun god, in whose company the pharaoh would see out eternity.

PROVIDING FOR THE BODY AND THE SOUL

'I am strong therein; I am glorious there; I eat there…;
I plough and reap there; I drink and eat there; I make
love there.'
BOOK OF THE DEAD, SPELL 110, NEW KINGDOM

The Egyptians believed that the individual was made up of several parts, some physical, others metaphysical. These parts were: *khet*, the body; *ren*, the name; *shuyet*, the shadow; *ka*, the double or life-force; *ba*, the personality or soul; and *akh*, the spirit. A considerable portion of Egyptian funerary religion was dedicated to ensuring the survival not only of the body by mummification, but of all these components.

The tomb was a house for eternity, the repository of all parts of the personality, but most importantly of the body and the name. The former was mummified, wrapped in bandages and then protected both physically and magically by being placed in coffins and a sarcophagus. It was finally interred in the burial chamber, cut deep into the rock and secured against intruders. Magical texts, inscribed both on the exterior and the interior of the tomb, made the person live forever, especially when the name was spoken or read

7 Section of an Old Kingdom mastaba, showing the key elements of an Egyptian tomb.

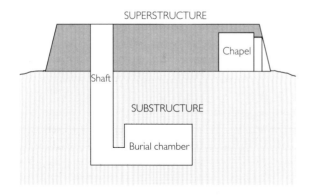

SUPERSTRUCTURE

Chapel

Shaft

SUBSTRUCTURE

Burial chamber

8 Osiris, ruler of the dead, on a fragment of an 18th Dynasty stela (Chiddingstone Castle).

aloud: the articulation of the name magically charged the life-force of the deceased so that he or she could flourish in the afterworld.

The ancient Egyptians believed in the magic and power of both written and spoken words. One of their creation myths refers to how the great god Atum had a thought or conception and then, by voicing it, it came into being. The Egyptians believed that once a word was written down, it was inherently magical and could make whatever was written true, especially when spoken aloud, an act which breathed life into the words. Thus, the representations on the walls could come alive and make real what they depicted and had to be chosen with care lest some dangerous being came into existence in a tomb. This is why sometimes one finds hieroglyphs of potentially harmful animals being disarmed in some way: snakes are shown with a cut in their body, lions are shown without legs and so-on, lest these dangerous beasts come to life and damage the tomb-owner. These precautions were especially common in the Middle Kingdom.

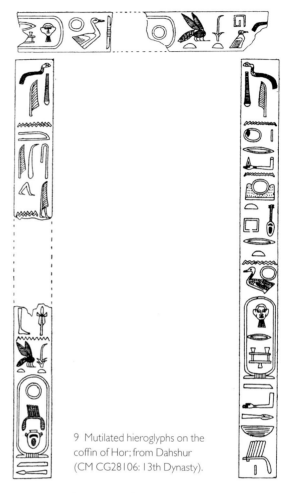

9 Mutilated hieroglyphs on the coffin of Hor; from Dahshur (CM CG28106: 13th Dynasty).

Many tombs contained texts that are called 'Appeals to the Living', which ask the living visitors to say a prayer or even just the name of the deceased so that he or she can thrive in the afterlife. The name was what gave people their identity and its protection and promulgation was therefore crucial to their eternal survival. If one wanted to punish an enemy, the worst thing to do would be to remove his name from his tomb as this one most severe act would render him nameless and beingless in the Fields of Iaru. This *damnatio memoriae* has been carried out in some tombs (e.g. the Vizier Rawer at Saqqara, KV10 and WV23 [both in the Valley of the Kings] and Theban Tombs 39, 42, 48 and 71, to name but a few).

The shadow, appearing in funerary texts, was a reflection of the body through the sun, itself the quintessential symbol of resurrection and rebirth. An image created by the sun, the shadow would vanish and reappear with the help of the sun.

Thus, during life it was a constant reminder and reassurance of rebirth and in death would also be granted the protection it needed to continue and emphasize its role as an agent of resurrection.

The *ka*, *ba* and *akh*, all aspects of the soul and personality, are as difficult to understand as our concept of soul. The *ka* was depicted with a pair of upraised arms on top of the head, while the *ba* was shown as a human-headed bird, sometimes with a pair of arms. The *akh* was rarely depicted, although it was written using the hieroglyphic sign of the Hermit or Bald Ibis, *Geronticus eremita*. The *ka* and the body were created simultaneously by Khnum, the creator-god, on his potter's wheel. Both continued through life and into death, rather like doppelgängers or twins. The *ka* was the animating force for the individual and, according to texts dating from the Old Kingdom onwards, it outlasted the body, while needing the same sustenance as the body had needed during life. Thus, the offerings depicted on tomb walls, or placed in the tomb, were for the sustenance of the *ka*, which absorbed the potential sustenance that the offerings provided and was therefore 'charged' so that it could be active in the afterlife. After the death of an individual, the *ka* resided in the mummified body of the deceased, as well as in the burial chamber and tomb-chapel and any representations of the deceased that they contained.

The bird-bodied *ba* was a more active part of the spirit, being able to move through the tomb, into the cemetery and beyond. According to some texts, in life the *ba* could be released from a sleeping body to travel. Like the *ka* it had all the characteristics enjoyed by a human: an ability to eat, drink, speak, move and, unlike the *ka*, a capacity for travel. Despite this facility, the *ba* was tied to the physical body to ensure the survival of the deceased in the afterlife. The reunion of the *ba* and the mummy was the subject of many portions of the well-known funerary text, the Book of the Dead (see below). The *ba* increased in importance in funerary texts from the Middle Kingdom onwards, although depictions of it were not common until the New Kingdom. The New Kingdom *rishi* or feathered coffin appears to evoke the *ba* with its human head and feather decoration.

The *akh* is the most complicated portion of the individual to understand. It seems to be the result of a union between the *ba* and the *ka*. This *akh* was the manifestation of the transformation of the deceased from a living creature into an eternal and unchanging being made of light who was

10 Inherkhau and his *ba* praising each other in his tomb at Deir el-Medina (TT359: 20th Dynasty).

associated with the stars and the gods. To become *akh* was the ultimate means of securing a successful afterlife. Thus, individuals who had lived lives not in keeping with the rules of *maat* would not achieve the state of being *akh* and would be consumed by Ammit (see below).

It should be remembered that kings, who were divine beings, had a different afterlife and as a consequence different tombs and cultic practices in which to achieve it, from non-royal individuals. The divinity of the king meant that after death he joined with the gods and journeyed with the sun god as part of his entourage.

The *ba* and the *ka* both had human characteristics and human needs, regardless of whether they were royal or not. The tomb was where these needs could be met. Sustenance for the soul was provided in the form of provisions left in the burial chamber, as well as by the images adorning the tomb-chapel's walls that would be magically made real. However, fresh goods were preferable; thus there was a requirement for a place where such offerings could pass between the worlds. In its simplest form, a slab of stone, or stela, placed above ground, could form this interface. Frequently, this stela took the form of a door – the so-called 'false-door' – through which the spirit could emerge, partake of its offerings and then return whence it came. Indeed, in some tombs the false-door actually has a three-dimensional image of the deceased, apparently frozen in its passage between the two worlds. The false-door was arguably the most potent place in the tomb as it was the point where the worlds of the dead and the living came together and, as such, the focus of the cult celebrations of the deceased.

Related to such false-doors are the statues that were placed in *serdabs* (Arabic for 'cellar'), closed rooms connected to the main chapel, if at all, by a narrow hole or slit in the partition wall. This allowed the statues to 'see' out and for incense and prayers to reach them, while remaining safe and hidden in the mysterious darkness.

THE REALM OF OSIRIS

The tomb could be viewed as a passageway to the realm of the dead, the Fields of Iaru, ruled by Osiris. Myth had it that he had been a prehistoric king, son of the earth-god Geb and the sky-goddess Nut, murdered and later dismembered by his brother, Seth. The body's parts were ultimately rescued and reassembled by his sister-wife Isis (with whom he was to posthumously sire a son, Horus), embalmed by the jackal-headed god, Anubis and resurrected to become ruler and judge of the dead. He is almost always represented with a fully sheathed body, which became the characteristic aspect of Osiris as a wrapped mummy. There is, however, an interesting question as to whether this meant that Osiris was being represented as a mummy – or that the mummy was represented as Osiris. In favour of the latter is the fact that the classic fully wrapped mummy only begins to be found after the rise to prominence of Osiris late in the Old Kingdom. Early mummies have a very different aspect,[4] while other sheathed gods exist who have nothing to do with death, such as Min and Ptah. The exposed flesh of Osiris's face is usually painted black or green, both colours of fertility and rebirth, the former recalling the black silt that was annually deposited on the fields by the inundation of the Nile and the latter the resulting crops.

Osiris' royal status is emphasized by his representation with his arms crossed at the breast, holding the royal insignia of the crook and the flail, as well as by his *atef* crown, consisting of a royal white crown flanked by two feathers, alluding to *maat* and a pair of horns which might refer to the ram-headed Khnum and his role as a creator of bodies and souls. In the Ramesside Period the tomb itself, because of the inclusion of depictions of Osiris and other divine beings

and texts, became identified with the realm of Osiris, rather than merely serving as a conduit to it.

While Osiris was the ruler of the dead and especially prominent in funerary iconography from the New Kingdom and later, a wide range of other deities are found in mortuary contexts from the Old Kingdom onwards. Amongst these are Osiris' sisters, Isis and Nephthys, who traditionally guarded the foot and head of the corpse respectively and are often depicted as mourning Osiris. The funeral rituals suggest that some of the chief female mourners or even priestesses took on the persona of these divinities when conducting funeral rites outside and within the tomb-chapel. Thus, during the course of the funeral, as the deceased became a divine *akh*, the mourners and officiants at the funeral took on the personae of different divinities, so moving the funeral into the divine plane.

Two other goddesses, Neith and Selqet, regularly join them in their protective duties, along with four beings known as the 'Four Sons of Horus'. Named Imseti, Hapy, Duamutef and Qebhsenuef, the Four Sons were particularly linked with the internal organs, removed during mummification. However, they also have their place guarding the flanks of the corpse, in conjunction with two aspects of the embalming-god, Anubis, named Imywet and Khentysehnetjer.

Various other divine beings inhabit the world of the dead; some are true gods, to whom temples were built, such as Ptah, Hathor, Anubis and Atum, to name but a few.

11 Isis as a kite conceives Horus with the mummified body of Osiris (temple of Sety I, Abydos: 19th Dynasty).

However, many seem only to exist within the mortuary context – strange beings whose sole purpose seems to be in the cycle of life and death that is exemplified by the daily passage of the sun god through the sky and nightly journey through the netherworld. Different aspects of the sun god also play crucial roles in mortuary beliefs associated with resurrection, as death did not just mean a journey to the afterworld, but becoming omnipresent through uniting with the sun god in the cycle of death and resurrection.

ACCESS TO THE NETHERWORLD

Just as this life was not the same for royalty and commoners, divisions existed in the afterlife as well. At the very beginning of Egyptian history the king was himself a divine being; his posthumous fate was thus to re-join his fellow deities in voyaging the heavens. Ultimately the king was linked most closely to the sun god, with his resurrection manifested as the continual voyage of the sun through the sky during the day and the netherworld, or 'mirror-Egypt', during the night. This solar trek is an important aspect of the decoration of the royal tombs of the New Kingdom and later, but is hardly seen in other contexts as the private individual had a different journey to make, in this case to reach the Fields of Iaru, that even more perfect eternal Egypt.

This was not a straightforward journey; in order to achieve the goal a series of tests had to be passed and gates traversed until the deceased arrived successfully in the Hall of Osiris to be judged. There, the heart, as the organ that

12 Having successfully passed through the trials that followed bodily death, Horus presents Hunefer to Osiris, Isis and Nephthys; before Osiris, on a lotus flower, are the Four Sons of Horus, here shown all with human heads. From the Book of the Dead of Hunefer (BM EA9901: 19th Dynasty).

13 The sun god proceeds on his barque towards his eternal rebirth in the tomb of Ramesses VI (KV9: 20th Dynasty).

identified an individual's 'essence' or individuality, was weighed on a scale against the feather symbolizing *maat*. If the heart and the feather were balanced, it meant that the person had led a good and just life and could enter the realm of Osiris as one who was 'true of voice'. If the heart were heavier, then the person would forfeit the afterlife and his heart would be consumed by Ammit, the female Devourer of the Dead, depicted as a terrifying amalgam of crocodile, lion and hippopotamus.

Aids to this spiritual journey appeared in tombs in the form of a series of texts containing all the necessary information and spells that would bring the spirit to its final destination. These were essentially crib notes that would help the deceased pass the tests that barred his access to 'the West', or the afterlife. The most famous of these is the Book of the Dead, or more accurately called the 'Book of Coming Forth by Day', and usually found in the form of a papyrus roll placed in the tomb or with the mummy. In addition to guiding the dead successfully, the Book of the Dead was also able to predict a successful outcome for the journey. The fact that the papyrus depicted and/or described the dead person's successful passage through the judgment meant that he or she actually had been successful.

The Book of the Dead is, however, by no means the earliest of these 'guides' to the hereafter, incorporating as it does many elements from more ancient sources. The oldest substantial works are contained in the Pyramid Texts, inscribed inside the burial chambers of royal tombs of the late 5th and 6th Dynasties, followed by the Middle Kingdom Coffin Texts and related works. The New Kingdom and later periods saw the development of a wide range of funerary 'books'. Although they employed certain parts of the Book of the Dead, royal burials were provided with a separate set of funerary books that were but rarely found in commoners' sepulchres during the New Kingdom. Unlike that of commoners, the rebirth of kings ensured the continuation not just of their lives, but the continuation of the very cosmos, hence its importance. Once texts such as the Pyramid Texts, initially composed for royal use, are found in non-royal tombs, one is almost always guaranteed that a new composition will appear in royal funerary contexts. Curiously, during the Third Intermediate Period, the Book of the Dead became used much more extensively in royal tombs, reversing the previous emphasis and now including the judgment hall scene, in which the pharaoh is shown being judged like a mortal. Details of this whole corpus are given in pp. 129–31.

FUNERALS AND INTERMENT

The chapel was the focus for the funeral ceremonies, the last point at which the earthly body of the deceased could be viewed and bidden adieu by friends and relations before the soul went to the netherworld. A stela in TT110, belonging to the Royal Herald, Djehuty, of the middle of the 18th Dynasty, provides a vivid account of an Egyptian funeral:

> A goodly burial arrives in peace, your 70 days having been fulfilled in your place of embalming. You are placed on the bier … and are drawn by bulls without blemish, the road being sprinkled with milk, until you reach the door of your tomb. The children of your children, united of one accord, weep with loving hearts. Your mouth is opened by the lector-priest and your purification is performed by the Sem-priest. Horus adjusts for you your mouth and opens for you your eyes and ears, your flesh and your bones being perfect in all that appertains to you. Spells and glorifications are recited for you. There is made for you a 'Royal Offering Formula', your own heart being with you, your heart of your earthly existence. You come in your former shape, as on the day on which you were born. There is brought to you the Son-whom-you-love, the courtiers making obeisance. You enter into the land given by the king, into the sepulchre of the west.[5]

Egyptian funerary ceremonies were long and complicated.[6] The prepared mummy would be retrieved from the embalmers, encoffined and, being placed on a sled pulled, ideally, by oxen, taken in procession with the tomb goods to the cemetery.[7] The procession included the mourning family and friends of the deceased, priests, grave goods and, if the deceased were wealthy, a host of professional mourners who would rend their clothes, beat their breasts and pour ash upon their heads, ululating all the while. Such hired mourners remain a feature of Egyptian funerals. A peculiar object that forms part of the procession from the Middle Kingdom on is the *tekenu*. In the Middle Kingdom it appears as a wrapped figure that is crouching or is in the foetal position, with only the head emerging. In the New Kingdom it is shown as an entirely wrapped bundle, or with the head and sometimes an arm showing. Its role in the funerary ritual is enigmatic.

Special sacred dances, the most famous of these performed by the *muu* dancers, also played a part in the funerary ritual. The ceremonies of burial culminated in the Opening-of-the-Mouth ceremony, in which the dead body was reanimated.[8] Each of the five senses was restored to the deceased in this ritual, which involved the use of implements that on one hand recalled those used in the carving of statuary, in particular the adze. This may have been linked with the fact that artificial images could also be animated through the same ritual. The other tools recalled those used at birth, a key item being the *pesesh-kef* knife, which consisted of a flint blade that broadened to a fork at the end. The knife was probably a model of one used to cut the umbilical cord of the baby and as such was necessary for the soul's rebirth in the netherworld and its ability to eat and drink again, just as severing the umbilical cord means that the child must use its own mouth to eat and therefore live.[9]

The foreleg of an ox was also used in the ritual, coming from a sacrificial animal that no doubt provided a main part of the funeral meal. Once the mummy was reanimated it joined the mourners for one last time in a funerary feast. No doubt many of the fresh food-offerings of the deceased were consumed during the course of this meal, with a share being set aside for the delectation of the deceased. All of these activities took place in front of the tomb's offering place.

Once the deceased had feasted, the corpse was placed in the tomb with accompanying pomp and ritual, with garlands and flowers often being placed on the corpse, as well as on the coffin(s) and sarcophagus. Meanwhile the spiritual aspect of the deceased had set out on its journey to eternity, described earlier in this chapter.

14 Female professional mourners, bare-breasted, weeping and throwing dust in their hair (TT55: 18th Dynasty).

INTERACTION BETWEEN THE LIVING AND THE DEAD

It was not enough to build a tomb if one wanted to live eternally. A mortuary cult/foundation had to be established to provide for the upkeep of the tomb and the celebration of the cult through prayer and food offerings. These cults were endowed by dedicating some land and its revenues to the cult, in order to pay the priest who took care of the tomb. In essence, the offerings derived from these lands would be consecrated for the deceased and then given as payment to the priest in charge of the cult. Passing visitors – ideally for centuries into the future – were also encouraged to enter the chapel to admire it and to recite a prayer, preferably the *hetep-di-nesu*, a traditional incantation that gave the deceased's name and titles as well as the basic offerings,

15 Offering lists were one of the most important components of tomb decoration and could even be personalized to offer more or less of specific items that the deceased favoured. This one is to be found in the tomb-chapel of Ramose (TT55: 18th Dynasty).

thereby magically empowering the deceased (see further p. 86).

Family members would visit the tomb, especially on festivals associated with the dead, such as the New Kingdom Festival of the Valley, which involved visiting the tomb, making offerings of food and incense to the deceased and feasting in the presence of their deceased ancestors. New Kingdom tombs show a scene that takes place in the chapel's courtyard, the festival of the god Sokar, who was also associated with Osiris. A feature of these regeneration festivals involved a grain mummy, a small mummiform figure filled with grain, symbolizing the regenerative powers of Osiris. In modern Egypt visits to the tomb are also a feature of life, with elaborately woven palm-leaves or 'grain-dollies' being left on the tomb.

Once the deceased was safely in the netherworld, the living could approach the dead and ask for supernatural intervention in their affairs, be it for advice, an increase in

16 A typical Middle Kingdom *hetep-di-nesu* formula; it reads, 'A royal offering to Osiris, Lord of Busiris, the great god, Lord of Abydos, so that he may give a voice offering (consisting of) bread, beer, ox, fowl, alabaster, linen and everything good and pure on which a god lives for the *ka* of TITLES AND NAME'. The deity and locations may differ depending on the location of the burial and other factors.

prosperity, or to help heal the sick. The most popular way of doing this was in letter form. Such 'Letters to the Dead' were inscribed on papyrus, or, more often, on pottery bowls. The bowls contained food that would entice the *ka* out of the tomb and provide 'payment' for it to speed along the desired intervention.[10]

Chapter 2

The Tomb and Society

'You have entered your tomb in peace; your grave is eternity.
A place of arising and resting for your noble mummy, a
place of receiving gifts and offerings to your *ka*: your true
repository....'
SARCOPHAGUS OF HAREMAKHET, PTOLEMAIC PERIOD [11]

It is important to recognize that the study of tombs is not
an end in itself: sepulchres, their contents and such factors
as the layout of a cemetery can provide us with key
information about Egyptian society, in the same way that it
did for the ancient Egyptians. The identity and gender of
the tomb-owner, family relationships, religious affiliations
and the social position of the deceased can be gleaned from
tombs, all of which help to construct a picture of ancient
Egyptian society. The elements that enable this are all part
of the tomb complex: size, architectural complexity, location
within the cemetery, the materials used in construction and
decoration, and, in the case of intact tombs, the number
and varieties of grave goods included in the burial.[12] An
interpretation of a tomb-owner's place in society can best
be obtained by analyzing and combining all these criteria
together. Of course, we cannot always determine which of
these was most important to the ancient Egyptians, so that
modern interpretations can at best only be hypothetical.
Practical considerations also came into play, especially with
regard to the location of tombs (the position of earlier tombs
being a hindrance), the general economic climate, as well as
changes in religious beliefs.[13]

Tomb size and complexity are two of the most obvious
criteria that can be used for determining status. Presumably,
the larger and architecturally more intricate the tomb, the
more labour and materials would have been used, thus
reflecting the prominence and wealth of its owner. Certainly,
the pyramid of the king dwarfs the tombs of his nobles, and
the royal mortuary complexes of the New Kingdom are
significantly larger and better decorated than the tombs of
courtiers. They could achieve this as they were built at the
expense of the state. Much of the labour for such projects
was in the form of corvée and/or religious duty, especially
in the Old Kingdom.

Size is also dependent on space within the cemetery
and its general topography, as well as the general prosperity
of the country at a given time. Tombs of the early New
Kingdom were quite small, increasing in size as the 18th
Dynasty became well established and the country prospered.
After the reign of Ramesses II they shrank and continued to
do so until the renaissance of the 25th and 26th Dynasties.

Under King Khufu, areas of the Giza cemetery adjacent
to his pyramid were laid out in streets, with a standard
'nucleus' cemetery allocated to family members or individual
members of the court. These then completed and decorated
them, according to their individual tastes (see pp. 154–5).

17 (*above*) Dancers at a funeral, as depicted on a block which once
formed part of a late 18th/early 19th Dynasty tomb; from the area of
the Serapeum at Saqqara (CM JE4872).

There are records of 4th Dynasty kings providing land, stone, a part of the tomb or labourers for tomb construction; both the site and the labourers were a gift of King Menkaure himself to the nobleman Debhen (LG90) at Giza. Thus, at that time, the size of the tomb was in part dependent on one's relationship with the king. The more favoured the individual, the more probable that the tomb would reflect this in size, location and decoration.

Perhaps the earliest versions of the *hetep-di-nesu* (literally 'gifts that the king gives') offering formulae (see pp. 21–2, 86) that are found on tomb walls are stating an actual fact: that the tomb was provisioned (and provided?) by the king. In contrast, tombs at Giza dating to later periods contain inscriptions that assert that the tomb-owner paid for the construction and decoration of the tomb. An inscription in the 6th Dynasty mastaba of Remenuka (Giza, Central Field) states that he paid the artisans with bread, beer and linen. In his recently discovered tomb in Giza's Western Cemetery, Kai asserts how he himself paid for the construction of his tomb. A similar inscription can also be found in the 6th

Dynasty tomb of Redines (G5032), who stresses how he built his tomb using his own resources. Certainly, by the end of the Old Kingdom it was more usual for the tomb-owner and his family to be responsible for the construction and decoration of the tomb, with the king being less and less involved. The endowment of a funerary cult was also a personal matter. A text from the 4th or 5th Dynasty tomb of Penmeru (G2197) at Giza gives the arrangements that the deceased had made to establish and sustain his cult, and the early 12th Dynasty tomb of the governor Hapidjefa i at Asyut (Tomb 1) contains several inscriptions that deal with his property and the provisioning of his funerary cult.

It is possible that, especially in provincial cemeteries, the local government or some other municipal body carved simple shaft tombs and sold them to potential tomb-owners. This is very similar to the modern tradition of purchasing cemetery plots. It has also been suggested by some scholars that even in royal cemeteries the option of 'purchasing' a mastaba was offered, probably to help finance the construction of the royal burial place. In this instance, the

18 The intact burial chamber of TT8 (Kha), showing the typical funerary equipment (now in Turin) of an 18th Dynasty official and his wife.

19 (*above*) The Giza necropolis seen from the south; Islamic and Coptic cemeteries occupy the foreground. Certainly there is a tradition of locating cemeteries in the same place since antiquity. However, the new cemeteries do not reflect the social organization found around the pyramids, with the clustering of tombs close to the central royal burial.

20 (*below*) A reconstruction of the Giza necropolis as it may have been around the end of the 4th Dynasty, with the pyramids of Menkaure, Khafre and Khufu. The area in the right lower part of the drawing includes modern features.

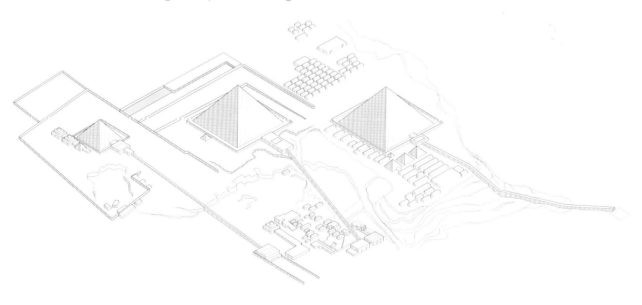

size of the tomb would be dependent on the wealth of the individual, rather than his relationship to the king.

In later tombs, size might also depend on available space in a cemetery; as areas of good stone were used, the cemetery would yield fewer places for new sepulchres. Presumably in these cases the tomb-owners would establish their status through inscriptions, decoration and grave goods.

The complexities of the architecture, as well as the decoration, are also indicative of wealth and status. In rock-cut or built tombs, the additions of porticoes, engaged statuary and courtyards no doubt inflated the tomb's worth. It would seem that relief decoration was more costly than solely painted decoration as it involved far more detailed labour. The quality of the paint used, as well as the atelier, would also suggest a difference in cost. Use of expensive stone elements such as granite, alabaster and basalt would again add to the price. Doors, which for the most part are missing (though the hinge fixtures and swing-back areas are still visible), might also have been a way of displaying wealth. Expensive woods such as imported cedar or juniper might have been used, or the doors could have been carved and enhanced with metals such as gold, copper or bronze. Thus size, complexity and decoration all taken together provide some sort of indication of wealth and status.

Some people seem to have made up for a lack of space, or indicate a change in position, by having two tombs. Examples of this are generally found in the New Kingdom. Horemheb is an obvious example: his tomb at Memphis dates to his years as a general, while his Theban tomb is royal and located in the Valley of the Kings. Some attempts were made to adapt the Memphite tomb to its owner's subsequent status: a small uraeus was added to Horemheb's brow in several images. Other individuals with two tomb-chapels at Thebes include User (TT61 and TT131), Menkheperresonbe (TT86 and TT112) and Djehutynefer (TT80 and TT104). It is unclear what use was made of the 'spare' tomb. Perhaps it allowed a duplication of the deceased's cult, with a consequent enhancement of posthumous status; members of his family might also have been buried in its substructure.

The location of tombs within a cemetery can also elucidate social organization and mores in ancient Egypt. Naturally, the degree to which this was true varied throughout the long course of Egyptian history, being most observable and formal in the 4th Dynasty and becoming more flexible as time progressed. The afterlife was a reflection of normal life and as such, the deceased would continue to exist in a world that was similar in social structure and cultural values to the one that he or she had inhabited during life – the tomb should be in an appropriate 'neighbourhood'. Over time, practical considerations such as lack of space, quality of stone and religious beliefs (including the idea that certain cemeteries were more 'holy' than others due to who was buried there, whether gods or kings), influenced cemetery organization and tomb construction.

The placement of cemeteries, especially royal cemeteries, was on occasion dictated by religious considerations. The earliest royal burial place at Abydos may have been chosen owing to its proximity to a wadi that led west into the desert and might have been seen as a gateway to the underworld. Its later association with Osiris further sanctified it and made it a focal point for funerary rituals. The pyramids of the Old Kingdom, solar symbols promising the rebirth and resurrection of the kings, were probably positioned with reference to the main sun temple of Egypt, located at Heliopolis. The Valley of the Kings may have been chosen for the burials of New Kingdom royalty due to the pyramidal peak that dominates the sky above the wadi, recalling the solar connotations of a pyramid and the primeval mound of creation – as well as for its potential for security.

The king's importance and power are manifest in cemetery organization. In the Early Dynastic Period and Old Kingdom the king was regarded literally as an omnipotent divine being whose word was law. Thus, to be buried near the god-king was a mark of prestige and possibly a greater guarantee of achieving admittance to the afterworld as part of the king's entourage. The closer one was to the king, the more important one's position. The same idea is manifest in the large number of graves centred on cemeteries associated with saints' tombs in modern Egypt, among other countries. Of course, there was an additional reason to be buried near a specific ruler: if the deceased served in the royal cult then he probably had the right to be buried in that king's cemetery. Although this was not always the case, it often held true. The cemetery around the 6th Dynasty pyramid of King Teti is actually surrounded by a wall. Giza also had a wall, now known as the 'Wall of the Crow' separating it from secular areas; perhaps the other sides were protected by the natural geology of the site.

Although the idea of a divine king persisted in subsequent periods, the actuality and limits of his power

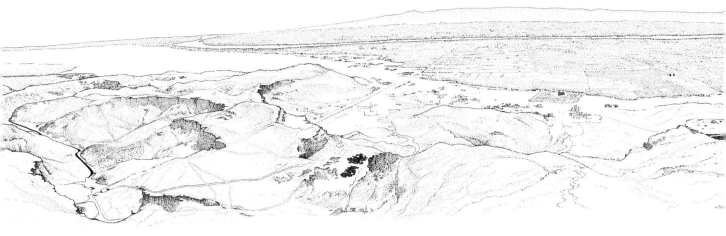

21　View from El-Qurn pyramidal peak over the eastern arm of the Valley of the Kings (at left), looking towards the Nile, with the causeways of Deir el-Bahari in the middle distance, and the Ramesseum to be seen at the edge of the desert, overlooking the Cultivation.

decreased and changed to fit the new social system and dynamic that grew out of the events of the disordered First Intermediate Period. During this time the tombs of the nobility were built in some cases hundreds of kilometres from the king's tomb; indeed, in most cases the king's very tomb remains unknown. Clearly the decrease in the king's power and importance rendered burial next to him unimportant and even undesirable.

In the Middle Kingdom the king regained much of his strength, but due to both political and religious changes, burial near him was apparently not as prestigious as in earlier periods. Indeed, his prominence was dimmed by the strong provincial governors, or nomarchs, who governed much of the country at this time. They built large and well-decorated tombs in the provinces (e.g. Beni Hasan), away from the capital, until the government was reorganized under the 12th Dynasty monarch Senwosret III, whereupon large, lavishly decorated provincial tombs vanish from the archaeological record.

Tombs of the 26th Dynasty and later show a resurgence of the power of kings; however, this is manifested not in a desire to be buried near the reigning monarch, but rather in a desire to be buried near rulers and people who had made Egypt great in earlier periods. Thus the cemeteries of Giza (the site of the Sphinx and the pyramids providing attraction) and Saqqara (the location of Djoser's pyramid and the tomb of his deified architect Imhotep) enjoyed a renaissance during this period. However, it should be noted that the tradition of dependents being buried near or around

the tomb of their patron continued throughout almost the entire span of Egyptian history.

The choice of tomb location also depended on family and job. As one might expect, family tombs are clustered together. In fact, the similarity in decoration of chapels can be linked by the kinship of their owners, as can be seen in several cemeteries. This is especially true of the provinces, where many positions were inherited and the tombs of subsequent generations can be seen in a group.[14] Tombs of people sharing the same major position were also sometimes grouped together. It is unclear whether this was due to rules of official cemetery organization or to chance.

The location of a tomb within a non-royal cemetery was also significant. In non-royal cemeteries, especially in Upper Egypt, where we have a more complete record of funerary remains than from Lower Egypt, the location of one's tomb along the cliffs was indicative of status. At Beni Hasan the most important people, the nomarchs or governors, had tombs located in the highest level of the cliff, where the best-quality rock was located. Individuals of lesser importance and wealth (generally the servants and less important family members) either had much smaller tombs in the same level, or simpler shaft tombs lower down on the slope. Broadly speaking, the lower on the slope was a person's tomb, the lower his/her rank, until the poorest graves were located at the desert edge and consisted of shallow pits dug into the desert gravel, similar in style to tombs of the Predynastic Period. Of course, if a cemetery was used over time, then

later tombs would be squeezed in wherever space could be found, and considerations of rank and status would become secondary. Quality of rock could also reverse this hierarchy. At Thebes, the best rock lies in the lower part of the cliffs and valley floor, so those wishing to carve the decoration of their chapel had to forego a prominent site in favour of one sunk below ground surface.

Space constraints are particularly obvious at Thebes. Tombs dating from the Middle Kingdom through to the middle of the New Kingdom often lie high up the cliff face, with wonderful views over the Nile. Senenmut was probably the first to build his tomb-chapel at the summit of Sheikh Abd el-Qurna. He set a trend, and his tomb, TT71, was shortly followed by several others built during the reign of Hatshepsut and Thutmose III (e.g. Ahmose [TT121], Senimen [TT252], Re [TT72], Tjanuni [TT74] and Amenhotep [TT73]).

The only significantly later tomb at the summit is the diminutive chapel belonging to Anen (TT120), Queen Tiye's brother. It seems that by the end of Thutmose IV's reign, the Sheikh Abd el-Qurna hill was so riddled with tombs that the high officials of his successor's reign (Amenhotep III) had to establish their sepulchres at lower levels, at the foot of that hill (e.g. TT55), or on the low-lying Khokha/Asasif area to the north (e.g. TT48 and TT192). This move may have been reinforced by the desire to access the good stone needed for both the more elaborate tomb-chapels of the period – which closely resemble a cult temple with a hypostyle hall and a series of rooms – and carved decoration.

Other considerations for the choice of a tomb's 'neighbourhood' would include the sacred power of a particular place. As mentioned above, Saqqara attracted tombs due to the presence of Imhotep, Djoser and perhaps also the sacred animal cults, especially that of the Apis bull. Deir el-Bahari, as the centre of the Hathor cult, as well as possessing royal affiliations, must have attracted tomb builders to both it and the adjacent Asasif and Khokha. As the Festival of the Valley gained momentum – an annual event that celebrated the cults of Hathor, Amun and the deceased, particularly the kings (see pp. 220–1) – it is probable that areas along the sacred route would have been favoured for burials as these spots would have been granted added *baraka* or blessings by the gods' passing in divine procession.

The most obvious information found in tombs concerns names, titles and the gender of the tomb-owner. However, it is often difficult for us to gauge the relative importance of different titles save for very obvious ones, such as Vizier or Treasurer. How much more important is the Keeper of the

Secrets of Butchery than the Overseer of Flautists or the Greatest of Seers?

It is clear from the evidence that the majority of Egyptian tombs were built by, and primarily for, men who would share them with their female relatives. Elite women's tombs do exist, although they are fewer than those of men. They vary in size, as do men's tombs, as well as in the amount and quality of their decoration.

The types of scenes shown are generally the same for both genders, except that women's tombs tend to show more female servants than those found in solely male tombs.

Naturally, grave goods also provide other criteria for judging wealth and status. However, tombs that can be assessed on this basis are few and far between and beyond the scope of the present work.[15]

23 The Roman-period cemetery at Marina el-Alamein.

24 The temporal spread of the cemeteries of Saqqara-North, ranging from the Early Dynastic to the Graeco-Roman Periods.

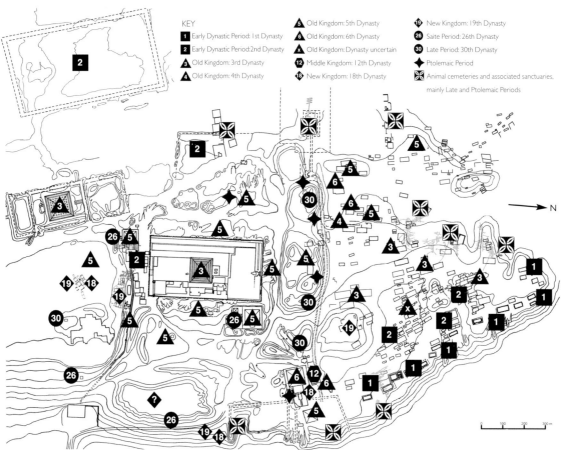

KEY

- ■1 Early Dynastic Period: 1st Dynasty
- ■2 Early Dynastic Period: 2nd Dynasty
- ▲3 Old Kingdom: 3rd Dynasty
- ▲4 Old Kingdom: 4th Dynasty
- ▲5 Old Kingdom: 5th Dynasty
- ▲6 Old Kingdom: 6th Dynasty
- ▲x Old Kingdom: Dynasty uncertain
- ●12 Middle Kingdom: 12th Dynasty
- ●18 New Kingdom: 18th Dynasty
- ●19 New Kingdom: 19th Dynasty
- ●26 Saite Period: 26th Dynasty
- ●30 Late Period: 30th Dynasty
- ◆ Ptolemaic Period
- ✖ Animal cemeteries and associated sanctuaries, mainly Late and Ptolemaic Periods

Chapter 3 — Construction and Decoration

The type of tomb and how it was constructed depended on a number of factors: the geography and geology of the chosen cemetery, the tomb-owner's rank and wealth, and the time expected to elapse before the tomb-owner's demise. The decoration of the tomb also reflected the occupant's rank and wealth, as well as his or her taste, and the prowess of the artists who carried out the decoration of the tomb.

The preparation of Egyptian tombs employed the full range of construction techniques known to ancient craftsmen, ranging from mud-brick, through stone-built to wholly rock-cut structures, and composites of some or all of these. Their interiors also displayed a range of decorative techniques, including all varieties of relief and painting.

The very earliest burial places were simply scooped in the desert surface. Indeed, this method of burial was employed for poor tombs throughout the course of Egyptian history. These might be marked with a low mound made of rubble and brick, with an offering place perhaps focused on some kind of stela, the ancestor of the later false-door.

Tombs of wealthier people were, naturally, more complicated in their construction than those of poorer individuals. In some instances the two principal components, the burial chamber and the offering place, were differently constructed, while in others the same techniques were used for both. In some locales where the rock is friable, the tomb-chapel would be hollowed out of the rock and lined with mud-brick, before being plastered and decorated.

There are two main types of tomb superstructure: free-standing and rock-cut, although many examples have elements of each mode of construction. Free-standing tombs include mastabas, pyramids and those constructed in the form of miniature or full-size temples. All of these could be built of mud-brick and/or stone. Rock-cut examples generally comprise a set of rooms carved out of an escarpment or cliff face, but there are examples of mastabas cut wholly from the living rock.

Most tomb substructures are rock-cut and include simple shafts cut straight down into the rock and opening into a room or rooms, or stairways and passages leading to the principal chambers. Others, however, particularly where the local geology was unsuitable for rock-cutting (as in the Delta), were built from brick or stone in a cutting in the surface of the ground, which would later be filled in and a superstructure erected above.

HOW LONG DID IT TAKE TO BUILD A TOMB?

It is difficult to determine the length of time it took to construct and decorate a tomb. The scope and complexity of both the architecture and decoration, as well as the number of people employed on the project at any one time, determined the speed with which the tomb was completed.

25 (*above*) Masons at work, from the tomb-chapel of Rekhmire (TT100: 18th Dynasty).

26 The distinction between rock-cut and free-standing structures may become blurred, for example in the case of the tomb of Khentkaues I (LG100: 4th Dynasty) at Giza. A unique cross between a mastaba and a pyramid, the lower section has been quarried out of the native rock, with the upper stage built from masonry.

The majority of information concerning the subject derives from royal tombs. It should be remembered that the working week consisted of 8 days with a 2-day weekend.[16]

The construction of a king's tomb would start at his accession. According to Herodotus, it took 20 years to build the Great Pyramid at Giza – plus ten for the causeway – but since he was writing two millennia after the event this can only be a guess. While apparently a credible length of time, the evidence of quarry marks on some of the four pyramids built by Seneferu gives a somewhat different picture. For example, the Red Pyramid at Dahshur, roughly two-thirds the size of the Great Pyramid, seems to have taken little over a decade to build.[17] Yet Menkaure could not quite complete his pyramid in 18 years, despite it being only 13 per cent of the volume of the Red Pyramid. Clearly the number of workers and resources used would, together with other issues, influence the amount of time it took to build a funerary monument.

In the New Kingdom, there are instances when, because the king was advanced in age at his accession, the numbers of workmen used were drastically increased. Ramesses IV enlarged the crew from 60 to 120 men, as well as scaling down the design of his tomb. It was thus essentially finished when he died after only six years on the throne. Others, such as Ay and Ramesses VI, took over the unfinished tombs of predecessors, and in the latter case (just about) finished it on a grand scale.[18] The decade of Sety I's reign was almost sufficient to complete and decorate his tomb, KV17, leaving just one room decorated in outline only.[19] In the tomb of Ramesses IX (KV6), it is possible to see how the quality of decoration changed radically as the artists hastened to complete the monument.

It has been posited that a modest New Kingdom tomb-chapel at Thebes could have been carved, plastered and painted during the 70 days when the corpse was being embalmed.[20] Thus, the unfinished state of many of the smaller Theban tombs seems inexplicable, although it is more understandable for the larger rock-cut tombs. Perhaps financial and other considerations caused delays in the construction of the tombs (see next section). It seems that ultimately a variety of factors influenced the time it took to complete a sepulchre. Until the discovery of sufficient textual evidence one can only speculate about the length of time necessary for building and decorating one's house for eternity.

I (*previous page*) Aerial view of the southern part of modern Luxor. In the foreground are the temples at Karnak, while across the river is the Theban necropolis. Directly opposite Karnak is the most ancient part of the cemetery, El-Tarif, where lay the tombs of the founders of the 11th Dynasty. The principal cemeteries of the New Kingdom lay to the north, with the royal tombs in a valley beyond the curtain of cliffs.

II Nakht seen hunting in a double scene from the north-east wall of the transverse hall of his 18th Dynasty tomb chapel on Sheikh Abd el-Qurna (TT52). Such a scene is typical of chapels down to the late 18th Dynasty, whose decoration focuses on the so-called 'daily life' of the deceased.

III Anubis, the god of embalming and escort of the dead to the Underworld, is often shown in New Kingdom scenes bending over the deceased and carrying out the final phases of the mummification ritual, while Isis and Nephthys flank the funerary couch. This example is on the sarcophagus of Sennedjem (TT1, CM JE27301: 19th Dynasty).

IV (*overleaf*) The *ka* was a spiritual 'double' of a person, created with them at the time of conception. It was symbolized by a pair of raised bent arms, which are seen on this figure of the *ka* of King Hor of the 13th Dynasty. From Dahshur L.LXVII/1 (CM CG259).

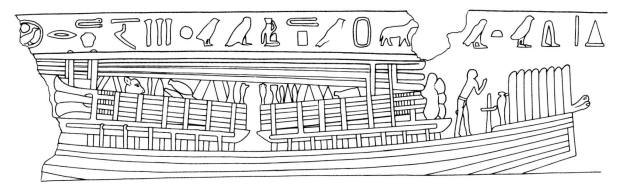

27 Images showing the construction of the pyramid complex were depicted on the walls of the causeway of Unas. Here one can see the granite palmiform columns that were used in the temples being brought from Aswan by boat (Saqqara: 5th Dynasty).

PLANNING THE TOMB

There are several sources that provide information about the construction and decoration of tombs. The tombs themselves, in their various stages of completion, provide evidence for the sequence of work and techniques of the craftsmen. Many tombs, especially the New Kingdom examples at Thebes, are in various stages of completion. There are several explanations for this: insufficient funds, the stopping of work by relatives if the tomb-owner died prior to the completion of the tomb, or perhaps, as has been suggested, even an aspiration to delay death by not having the burial apartments prepared.[21] The tomb-chapel of Ramose (TT55, 18th Dynasty), whose inner chamber is unfinished, as well as the decoration of the outer room, is an especially telling example of the way that parts of a tomb could be all but complete when other parts had hardly yet been quarried.

Remnants of construction aids, such as ramps, like the one found at the southern face of the Great Pyramid at Giza, also provide information about construction techniques. Masons' marks found in tombs, together with graffiti with instructions to builders such as the red and black construction lines found in Mastaba 17 at Meidum, as well as in a number of pyramids at Abu Sir, that of Pepy I at Saqqara and a queen's pyramid (GIa) at Giza, also shed additional light on the way that structures were levelled and laid out.

From the New Kingdom, the extensive texts from the village of Deir el-Medina, home of the workers who carved and decorated royal and noble tombs at Thebes, allow one to reconstruct the organization of the workers and the actual minutiae of tomb construction in Thebes. Other texts, such as the Rhind Mathematical Papyrus,[22] are vital to understanding the mathematics of tomb construction.

Unfortunately, there is little evidence of architectural plans for tombs, especially prior to the New Kingdom. Possibly plans were made on papyrus and are therefore lost to us.[23] As private tombs, especially of the 18th Dynasty, seem to have relatively standard plans, no doubt well known to the ancient Egyptian builders, it is probable that the workers needed no formal architectural drawings. Instead, the builders, like many of their modern counterparts, must have worked from an oral description, periodically elucidated by swift sketches onto pieces of limestone and pottery (ostraka) that were afterwards discarded. Certainly, rock-cut tombs, with their fairly standard plans, would have required less in the way of architectural drawings than the free-standing built tombs that were more common in Lower Egypt. Had more plans been found, there would be less discussion on the 'mysteries' of pyramid construction.

The plans that have been found include the incomplete example of Ramesses IV's tomb, drawn on papyrus, currently in the Egyptian Museum at Turin (ill. 28), a plan of Ramesses IX's tomb on an ostrakon (Cairo Museum, CG25184) and another ostrakon with a plan of a noble's tomb found in TT71 (Cairo JE 66262). An unusual, and perhaps unique, artifact related to tomb construction is a limestone model of the innermost chambers of a 13th Dynasty pyramid, found at Dahshur.[24] However, the

28 Detail of a plan on papyrus of the tomb of Ramesses IV showing the burial chamber, with the sarcophagus and surrounding shrines (Papyrus Turin 1885).

purpose of this model and the other documents (in particular the very elaborate Ramesses IV plan) remains uncertain and it may be that they served some ritual function, rather than an architectural one.

CONSTRUCTING THE TOMB

Naturally, construction methods differed depending on whether a tomb was rock-cut or free-standing and the material out of which it was made: stone or mud-brick. In some instances tombs were made using a variety of materials and, consequently, construction methods.

Rock-Cut Tombs

Almost all Egyptian sepulchres have some rock-cut elements, in particular their burial apartments, except where they lay in areas lacking accessible bedrock, such as the Delta. However, the term 'rock-cut tomb' is normally used to refer to those monuments whose chapels are carved out of the living rock, with minimal, if any, built structure.

The construction of a rock-cut sepulchre required that a passage be carved out of the rock, as was done with a quarry, until the required dimensions of the tomb were attained. Rock faces would be explored to identify sites for good-quality rock, after which the stonemasons would begin to remove the exposed and weathered rock and rubble. Once the good-quality stone was reached, using pointed stone mauls, or metal chisels, the masons would carve the clean face into a series of steps. Then, at the topmost step the

workers would carve out a corridor going deep into the cliff. This later became the basis for the roof of the tomb.

Evidence shows that for many rock-cut tombs and especially New Kingdom Theban examples (e.g. Re's TT201), the main axis was marked by stretching a red painted cord from the entrance to the end of the tomb. Any side halls or pillars were carved opening off the central corridor using this axis. 'In order to ensure perfectly straight walls the surveyor marked out the distance from the red axial line in each section of the tomb by drilling holes along the wall until the bases of the holes were equidistant from the axial line. Completed holes were marked with a touch of black. The roof was levelled off by drawing a horizontal line on the walls and measuring upwards.'[25] This would also be used to determine the height of the tomb. If the tomb had pillars, these would be blocked out, or left as semi-quarried monoliths for later completion. The side-cuttings made from the central corridor could later be turned into chambers. This method often resulted in the front and rear walls of a room being cut out and even partially decorated while the middle part of the chamber was still embedded in the rock. The stone that had been extracted from the tomb was, depending on its quality, either discarded, or dressed and used in other constructions. There are, however, many variations in how the tombs were constructed.

Owing to their unfinished nature, the tombs at Amarna, the new capital built by Akhenaten half way between Memphis and Thebes, are very good examples for studying construction methods. Some of these show that not all tombs were at first carved into the rock to their proposed final depth; craftsmen working at Amarna, in particular in TA13 and 21, carved out the passageway for the first chamber and then indicated the place for the next one, but did not proceed very far into it. The chambers were carved from the ceiling down, though frequently not to floor level. Even in their unfinished state, portions of the stone were dressed and covered by gypsum plaster. It has been suggested that the Amarna tombs were so erratically carved because there were insufficient craftsmen to supply the demand for tombs. Whichever craftsmen were available would work on the tombs, sometimes with a hiatus of a few years. The only Amarna tombs that seem to have had concentrated work done on them are the tombs in the Royal Wadi.[26]

Once a tomb had been cut, it was dressed using chisels and adzes. Any holes or imperfections in the rock would be filled out with plaster and gypsum, or mud-brick, other stone, donkey dung, or even dom-palm nuts and then covered with mud or gypsum plaster.

Rock-cut tombs could pose a problem in planning for subsequent tomb builders as, although their entrances might be known, the subterranean plans of tombs might not be recorded, particularly where a substructure was concerned.

In consequence, tomb builders cutting a passage sometimes broke through into an existing sepulchre. The best-known examples are from the Valley of the Kings; for example, Sethnakhte's KV11 collided with KV10, the tomb of Amenmesse. Sethnakhte abandoned this tomb and instead took over that of Tawosret (KV14). Ramesses III later took over Sethnakhte's abortive attempt and realigned the corridor so that it cleared KV10 and could thus continue onward.

Rock-cut shafts fall into two basic categories. One was simply intended to give access to a chamber or chambers, excavated at the bottom. The other formed part of a broader construction scheme, with a stone-built chamber at the bottom, or allowing (e.g.) a sarcophagus to be introduced into a substructure. Such 'construction' shafts were often of considerable size and may have required scaffolding to permit worker access. In some cases, a secondary shaft or descending passage was added to help with the extraction of debris, which then became the definitive tomb entrance, the 'construction' shaft being filled in after its use and frequently covered over by the erection of the superstructure.

The aforementioned 'sand-protected' shaft tombs (pp. 205, 276) of the 26th Dynasty usually had substantial stone chambers constructed at the bottom of the main

29 Unfinished façade of tomb BH–XI at Beni Hasan, showing the way in which the blocks of limestone were detached from the matrix.

30 The unfinished tomb of Tutu (TA8) at Amarna. The process of carving from the top down is obvious here. The columns are also being shaped as the chapel's chamber is carved out of the rock.

construction shaft and then a subsidiary shaft through which the burial actually took place.

Free-standing Tombs

Free-standing tombs were constructed out of mud-brick and/or stone and were, until the New Kingdom, usually built in the shape of mastabas. From the New Kingdom on, small temples provided the model for free-standing tombs, although mastabas continued to be built at some sites. The fact that they were largely built, rather than carved into the living rock, gave their plans greater flexibility and scope for variation.

The first step in constructing free-standing tombs, regardless of whether they were made of stone or mud-brick, was to level the site. If the building was not placed straight onto the solid rock, then foundations had to be laid down, especially in the case of a stone construction. Generally, for stone edifices, the foundations consisted of a trench filled with sand and topped with a few courses of rough stonework, upon which the main structure rested. The sand may have been symbolic of purity, rather than functional, or perhaps both.[27] Once the foundations were in place, actual building work could begin.

Building in Brick[28]

The earliest built tombs were made of mud-brick. The basic constituents of a mud-brick were Nile mud, chopped straw

31 (right) Mud-brick-making has remained the same since the time of the pharaohs. Mud and straw/temper are mixed together and put into moulds. The bricks are then left in the sun to dry.

32 (below) Scene of brick-making (TT100: 18th Dynasty).

and sand. Relative quantities determined the qualities of the brick, the material being shaped in a wooden mould and then placed in the sun to dry. When this is done, the original mass of mud reduces by around a third. Brick size varied throughout Egyptian history. Bricks of the first dynasties averaged 23 x 12 x 6 cm, although considerable variation is to be seen, with much larger examples coming into use during the Old Kingdom, some at Giza ranging up to 42 x 21 x 15 cm (G2093). Bricks of the Middle Kingdom were smaller and measured 33 x 15 x 10 cm. However, the bricks used to construct Middle Kingdom pyramids were larger, measuring on average 45 x 22 x 12 cm. Brick size remained roughly 33 x 15 x 10 cm during the New Kingdom through the Late Period, with larger bricks being common in Graeco-Roman times (38 x 19 x 12.5 cm, although further upward variations are documented).

Bricks used in pyramid construction tended to be larger than those used for nobles' tombs. During the latter part of the 12th Dynasty, pyramids were composed of bricks averaging 45 x 22 x 12 cm, laid in sand and (in the

case of that of Senwosret II) combined with cross walls of masonry creating compartments into which the bricks were placed.

Bundles of reeds, or even reed mats, were sometimes laid between courses. Timber ties were also used within the structures of some tombs. The exposed surfaces of any mud-brick structure were usually covered with a layer of mud plaster about 2–6 cm thick. The latter was composed of alluvial mud, mixed with sand and chopped straw. Its natural colour depended on the proportions of the components used, but it was often whitened by a final coat of gypsum plaster, or painted with a variety of colours and designs. It is thought that this final white layer, a colour associated with purity, was sometimes intended to represent limestone.

Kiln-fired bricks were uncommon prior to the Roman occupation, although there are a few examples from the Ramesside Period onward. The tomb of Hori iii at Bubastis (20th Dynasty) is amongst the earliest known examples, with fired bricks being used for flooring and the lowest parts of the walls. This was presumably due to the relatively damp conditions in the Delta that were not conducive to the preservation of mud-brick. The roughly contemporary vaulted tombs 21 and 35 at Nebesha were made entirely of burnt brick.

Brick structures were roofed with wooden beams and sometimes mats, above which were built the brick and gravel superstructures. At the end of the 1st Dynasty, however, the first true brick vaults appear (subsidiary graves around Saqqara S3500), larger examples being found within tomb K1 at Beit Khallaf, early in the 3rd Dynasty. Corbelled vaulting, where the roof is spanned by successive courses of bricks, each set slightly further out than the one below until they meet at the apex, is found from the 2nd Dynasty, the best examples coming from Naga el-Deir, with others at El-Amra and Qau and a concentration occurring in Graeco-Roman contexts in the oases. In the 4th Dynasty, domed roofing occurs in the workmen's cemetery (p. 154) at Giza, while domed rooms are found in various later tombs (e.g. pp. 207, 282), as are vaulted ceilings.

Throughout Egyptian history the basic techniques of construction remain broadly the same as those found in the earliest times, vaulting being frequently employed to roof both above-ground chapels and subterranean chambers. Flat roofs, made with palm logs overlaid by matting and mud plaster, were also sometimes used and often served as the model for the skeuomorphic (imitating some other thing or material) roofing of stone-built mastabas, such as that of Ptahhotep i (D62) at Saqqara. Besides the actual tomb-structures, brick is frequently found forming the enclosure wall, regardless of the material of the main monument, and mud-brick remains are often to be seen adhering to the stone surface outside a rock-cut tomb. Brick was thus ubiquitous within cemeteries and always remained the fundamental building material for the Egyptian architect.

Building in Stone[29]

Stone began to be used for details of funerary buildings during the 1st Dynasty, when granite was used to pave the burial chamber of Den and limestone within private tombs at Helwan.[30] Then, from early in the 3rd Dynasty it became increasingly important, until the majority of the highest status free-standing sepulchres were composed of the material. Even more buildings primarily of other materials, such as mud-brick, had architectural elements, such as doorways, in a wide variety of stones. Until the New Kingdom, limestone was most often used in building, after which sandstone became increasingly common, particularly for major temples. Hard stones, such as granite or basalt, were rarely used in non-royal burials, though they were frequently employed to line royal burial chambers and corridors leading to the chambers, the portcullises and thresholds, as well as other portions of royal tombs. Occasionally, they were used as thresholds in non-royal sepulchres. In the Old Kingdom, when the use of granite was particularly a royal prerogative, limestone would be painted so as to achieve a 'faux' granite look – or even magically become granite. The type(s) of stone used might have had symbolic as well as practical value: burial chambers would be constructed out of the white travertine/Egyptian alabaster, symbolic of purity, or elements would be made of reddish-orange quartzite, associated with the solar strength and energy useful for resurrection.

QUARRYING[31]

Much of the building stone employed in funerary monuments was quarried close by. In the Memphite necropolis and as far south as Esna, this was limestone, some particularly good examples of quarrying activity being seen at Giza, where the landscape was fundamentally altered by the extraction of the millions of tonnes of stone needed for the pyramids and mastabas there. At some tombs, local quarrying was taken a step further in that parts of the monument itself were carved from the bed-rock, with additional blocks added to make up the final shape. A number of Giza mastabas are of this form, as are others at Lahun, where the lower portion of the pyramid of Senwosret II (and much of the superstructures of other tombs at the site) was also shaped from a rocky knoll. There are many other examples of such uses of existing rock massifs.

The local limestone so used was sometimes of fairly poor quality and although suitable for core masonry was not regarded as appropriate for the exteriors of the very highest status sepulchres, nor for receiving decoration. For these, as well as some mud-brick monuments, the outermost layers were often supplied in northern Egypt from the Muqqatam Hills, just to the east of modern Cairo, in particular the quarries of Tura and El-Masara. Here, a very fine-grained white limestone can be found, that was capable of taking on a high polish, as well as receiving fine relief carving.

Different quarrying methods were used depending on the location of the quarry and whether hard or soft stone was being extracted. Stone could be extracted from large open excavations (used for both hard and soft stone), or by removing portions of the horizontal or vertical cliff faces (used for both hard and soft stone) and proceeding with an open quarry, or by excavating deep galleries (never used for hard stones; for details see above in rock-cut tombs).

In open-cut quarries the rubble would be removed, then the cleaned surface was marked with lines or a series of chisel-cuts in order to show the stonemasons where to cut the blocks. Trenches (20 to 60 cm or 8 to 24 inches wide) were created between the blocks so that the workers could stand in these whilst cutting.

When stone was quarried far from the building site, it was transported by water. This was aided in the case of granite by the upstream location of the quarries relative to most building sites. It is likely that the carrying of Tura limestone across to the Memphite cemeteries on the opposite bank was facilitated by the annual Nile flood, which led to the inundation of much of the river valley, right up to the edge of the desert. Canals, leading from the Nile to the building site, also helped reduce the need for land transport. On land, movement of stone relied on human muscle-power, in some cases with the aid of sledges

33 Remains of the quarry around Khafre's pyramid at Giza. The initial levelling and quarrying of the site created a false cliff into which rock tombs were carved. The surrounding quarry was again exploited in the time of Ramesses II, and presumably again in the Late Period when the necropolis enjoyed a renaissance.

and the sprinkling of water, milk or oil to ease the passage of the block. The building of dedicated transport roads with specially prepared surfaces provided further aid.[32]

Stonework and quarrying seem to have been carried out using tools of stone, copper, and later bronze, aided by, on occasion, levers. Tools included pointed picks or axes in the Old and Middle Kingdoms and then a pointed chisel used in conjunction with a wooden mallet was employed from the New Kingdom onward. Until recently, it had been assumed that granite was removed by cutting holes into the rock, inserting wooden wedges into the holes and wetting these. The expansion of the wood supposedly fractured the granite. However, this idea is no longer current as, for the most part, the wood would have been insufficiently strong to split the rock and also, the wedge holes all date to the Ptolemaic Period, when iron was available. It seems that in the Pharaonic Period proper, the task was accomplished in a very time-consuming manner by using hammerstones of dolerite to break down the granite. A fine example of a granite quarry that is 'frozen' in time is the quarry of the unfinished obelisk at Aswan, where the broken, half-finished obelisk still lies in situ. The detritus[33] would be removed in leather bags and baskets made of palm or reed.

Finishing was often carried out in situ, a good example being the undressed and unfinished granite casing stones on the lower portion of the Third Pyramid at Giza. Experimental work suggests that some finishing may have been carried out with stone implements and sand as an abrasive, although copper/bronze tools were certainly employed in some cases.

TECHNIQUES

Our knowledge of ancient building techniques is almost wholly derived from the examination of the structures themselves. It is certain that the use of ramps was an important way of raising blocks to a higher level. Remains of ramps have been found adjacent to the first pylon at Karnak, at the pyramids at Meidum and Sinki, as well as at that of Sekhemkhet at Saqqara, a number of Giza mastabas, and, according to recent work carried out by Zahi Hawass, on the southern side of the Great Pyramid at Giza. However, it is by no means certain exactly how they were employed, nor whether the same system was used consistently, or was varied over time. As well as in large-scale building, ramps were also

34 The methods used for quarrying the hardest stones are well illustrated at Aswan, where this 18th Dynasty obelisk still lies in its quarry.

35 Undressed and dressed granite in the lower part of the casing of the Third Pyramid at Giza (4th Dynasty).

used inside some tombs to place the sarcophagus lid atop the coffer and are still to be seen in place in (for example) the tomb of Mereruka at Saqqara (ill 196).

Wooden scaffolding was generally used for the carving and painting of a monument, rather than its construction. For lifting and manoeuvring blocks, levers were a key tool; indeed, one that is still used with skill in Egypt today. In essence, a lever (or levers) are used to raise one side of a block, which is then chocked up. The other is raised to the same level and chocks inserted, the process being continued until the required level is reached.

The introduction of heavy items, such as sarcophagi, into deep burial chambers presented major problems. In tomb-chambers approached via vertical shafts, two tactics could be used. First, the shaft could be filled with sand, the block placed atop the sand and the latter slowly but surely dug out from around and under it, so that the block ultimately arrived at the bottom. The other common option was to use ropes looped over wooden scaffolding poles: pulleys do not seem to have been prevalent. Ropes were also employed in controlling the descent of items into sepulchres with sloping access passages and there are a number of tombs with sockets in opposing walls which had held the beams and could also be used as hand- and foot-holds.

A number of different approaches are found as far as the masonry of stone buildings is concerned. There was a tendency towards economy, particularly in the reuse of

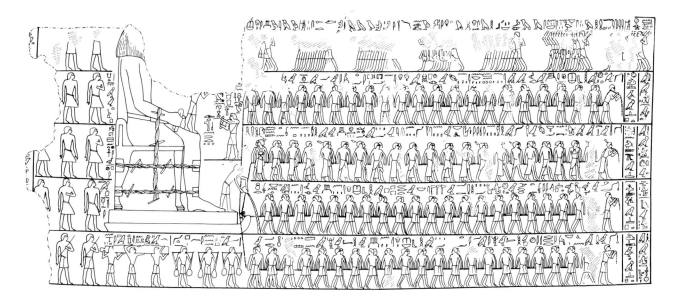

36 Very little information on Egyptian engineering survives in the decoration of the monuments. One partial exception is the 12th Dynasty tomb of Djehutyhotep ii at Deir el-Bersha, showing the transport of a colossus of the owner from the nearby alabaster quarries at Hatnub.

37 As well as employing ramps for heavy construction work, scaffolding also had a part to play, especially in the decoration of walls and the carving of statues. Here, in Rekhmire's 18th Dynasty tomb TT100, one may see sculptors putting the finishing touches to a series of statues belonging to Thutmose III, using scaffolding to reach the higher areas. In the upper register (not pictured), a mason builds a ramp to be used in the construction of a building.

blocks derived from demolished or remodelled buildings, e.g. the causeway blocks from Giza being reused in the pyramids at Lisht. In addition, core blocks were frequently far rougher than those towards the exterior, in some cases comprising little more than rubble. When looking at the pyramids, the best quality workmanship is to be seen in the earlier monuments, core blocks becoming smaller and less well made as the 5th and 6th Dynasties progress. This contrast is reflected in their states of preservation today: despite the loss of their Tura limestone casings, the 4th Dynasty pyramids at Dahshur and Giza still retain their form; some of those of the late 5th/6th Dynasties are now little more than amorphous mounds. Likewise, while some mastabas are solid masonry, others are, like many brick examples, composed of masonry retaining walls enclosing a rubble core.

When building, butting planes of the stone were dressed before use, but ultimate finishing carried out only after they were in situ. The blocks used were not always uniform in size or shape. The Egyptians carved and jointed their stones to maximize the usefulness of every block. Mortar was used sparingly; it generally provided lubrication to slide blocks into position. In extremely large constructions wooden butterfly clamps were inserted in order to hold the blocks tightly together.

The techniques of stone building evolved from the Early Dynastic Period onwards. A number of periods display distinctive features, a good example being the vogue for corbelled roofs at the beginning of the 4th Dynasty. They are found in the pyramid and private tombs at Meidum, as well as the stone pyramids at Dahshur and in the so-called Grand Gallery of the Great Pyramid at Giza. However, in pyramids, they henceforth disappear from the record, replaced by pointed roofs made from two massive slabs (or layers of such slabs) leaning against one another. Although vaulted roofs in brick had been used since the Early Dynastic Period, most apparent stone vaults were actually carved out of the blocks of a conventional pointed roof. Only a handful of true stone vaults are known prior to the 25th Dynasty, when examples are found in the tombs of the God's Wives at Medinet Habu (pp. 277–8). Subsequently, a series of vaulted burial chambers were constructed in shaft-tombs at Saqqara, Abu Sir and Giza, but they remain an exception from regular Egyptian practice. Flat stone roofs, constructed in the post-and-lintel tradition, remained popular for free-standing tombs throughout Egyptian history.

PROTECTING THE TOMB

Films about ancient Egypt often feature complex mechanisms in tombs that are meant to prevent theft. Although such devices did exist, their number and variety are by no means as diverse as Hollywood movies may suggest.

38 Butterfly clamps, generally made of wood, were used to hold two pieces of stone together. Although the wood has disappeared, the plaster and cavity for the clamp remains; Elephantine.

39 Model of the substructure of an early 4th Dynasty tomb in the Great West Cemetery at Meidum, showing the plug-block slid down the descending passage after the funeral. Another interesting aspect of the tomb is the niche at the far end of the chamber, apparently one of the earliest known niches for a canopic chest (formerly in Bristol Museum).

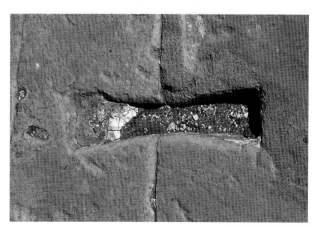

Basic precautions included deepening the location of the burial chamber, plug-blocks, hardstone portcullises blocking the passage to the burial chamber (e.g. in later Old Kingdom pyramids), as well as constructing both the passage and/or burial chamber out of this hard material (e.g. the quartzite chambers of late Middle Kingdom pyramids). However, tomb-robbers quickly learnt to circumvent these simply by excavating a parallel passage in the softer stones surrounding the obstructions, or even painstakingly chiselling through the apparently impregnable quartzite.

Pyramids of the Middle Kingdom show evidence for many of the devices that have inspired film-makers: reversing the direction of passages, false passages, dead ends, dummy shafts and hidden accesses to the burial chamber all feature, together with the use of sand after the manner of hydraulic fluid to lower blocks that closed the entrances to burial chambers (see p. 205). Sadly, despite these various precautions, the royal tombs were invariably plundered.

From early in the New Kingdom, royal tombs were located in the Valley of the Kings, a distant and inaccessible valley, in an effort to stop robbers. The sites for the tombs themselves were initially in inaccessible clefts in the rock,

where rock falls and floods might obliterate their entrances. Later, however, tombs were given monumental entrances, closed by no more than a sealed door and in full view. In this case, security was in the hands of the guards who were assigned to protect the royal wadi. Nevertheless, all precautions came to naught and plunderers entered every single tomb in the Valley, although a handful, including that of Tutankhamun (KV62), escaped relatively unscathed.

The other major attempts to protect the burial chamber are to be found in the 26th Dynasty, when an innovative use of sand succeeded in protecting a number of high-status monuments from desecration (p. 286). This included a revival of the Middle Kingdom system of 'sand hydraulics' and marked probably the high point in the ancient Egyptian technology of tomb protection. The most elaborate examples left the sarcophagus buried under thousands of tonnes of sand, almost every grain of which had to be removed if anyone wished to gain access to the body: even working under ideal conditions, the archaeological excavation of such a tomb can take many weeks. A measure of the success of the type is the fact that over half of the known examples have been found intact.

40 The well room of New Kingdom royal tombs was often designed to look like the terminal chamber of the tomb to prevent plundering. Thus the decoration would pass over the entrance to the next series of passages and rooms. Here, in Horemheb's KV57, only part of a scene featuring Osiris survives the breakthrough into the next chamber.

41 Horemheb's tomb in the Valley of the Kings (KV57) was never properly finished and is thus a source of invaluable information concerning tomb construction and decoration. Part of the grid and the drawing, including corrections, appear on the left side of the scene of marching deities, while the right side has already been carved away. Such examples show that the sequence of tomb decoration was not immutable, and probably was the result of expediency rather than ritual (18th Dynasty).

Curses (p. 131) inscribed on tomb walls can also be said to protect the tomb and its owner.[34] These, however, are relatively mild and try to shield the tomb from the entry of impure people, as well as those who would desecrate the tomb – or embezzle the endowments left to support the dead person's cult. Curses are found inscribed in tombs of all periods and generally threaten the violator with punishment in the afterlife when he or she will be judged by the tomb-owner, as well as the gods.

DECORATING THE TOMB

The type of decoration depended ultimately on finances as well as the quality of the rock. If one could afford it, the tomb was carved in raised relief and then painted; if one could not, then it was only plastered and painted. Sunk relief became more commonly used from the end of the 18th Dynasty onwards. It is probable that when choosing a tomb's location, its site and the quality of rock used or exploited, if rock-cut, also determined its price. Time might also have influenced the choice between carving and painting, as the latter type of decoration was quicker than the former. Some tombs use both relief carving and painting, such as the tomb of Ramose (TT55) at Thebes. The unfinished state of many Egyptian tombs (e.g. TT55, TT175, KV57) allows us to see the work 'in progress' and so study the different techniques employed.

Relief Decoration

Tombs were generally decorated in raised (also known as low or *bas*) or sunk (also known as high) relief if the stone was of good quality. Frequently mistakes or accidental chips in the stone were repaired with plaster. In some instances, especially in Thebes, where the stone quality was relatively poor, thick layers of plaster were applied to the friable rock and this plaster was then carved. Presumably the plaster was carved before it had completely hardened, as it is easier to work when it is damp and there is less chance of it chipping off and breaking.

Paint could be directly applied to the smoothed walls if the quality of stone was fine. Otherwise, holes and fissures were filled with plaster or fitted chunks of stone and a thin layer of plaster was laid over the walls, which was painted. Frequently, in the New Kingdom tombs in Thebes, the rock

was covered with a layer of mud plaster mixed with straw and sometimes dung and applied by hand. This in turn was covered by a thin layer of gypsum, applied with a coarse brush made of plant material, which was covered by a wash of lime carbonate and size to avoid the colours being absorbed by the plaster, after which the paint was applied.[35]

The Mechanics of Decoration

Whether a tomb was painted or carved, the basic preparation for the wall decoration was the same. First a grid was laid down by stretching strings tautly from roof to floor and along the length of the walls.[36] The strings were dipped in red ink, pulled tight and released to leave the grid lines. Splatters from this process are still visible in many tombs, as are, in some instances, the grids themselves, as can be seen in the tomb of Horemheb (KV57) and Amenhotep III (WV22), to name but two examples. The scenes were then drawn upon the grid, generally in red paint (an exception to this is the tomb of Ramesses XI (KV4), where yellow ochre was used for the initial sketch) and corrected by the master draughtsman in black, before being finally painted. The tomb of Horemheb (KV57) is unusual in that the design was in parts drawn in black ink and corrected in red. Many tombs were never completely finished, so evidence of the corrections is easily visible. In other instances the corrected paint or plaster has fallen off, revealing the corrections below. Neferrenpet's tomb (TT249) shows corrections made to drawings of figures, faces and a harp. In some instances, when the tomb decoration was carved, mistakes can be seen in the carvings, such as are visible in the depiction of two crocodiles in the tomb of Kagemeni at Saqqara, or in the placement of the crocodile's limbs in the tomb of Mereruka at Saqqara. In ancient times these mistakes would have been plastered or/and painted over and thus made invisible, but with the loss of the disguising painted cover, the errors are very obvious.

Although not always actually drawn out, grids reflecting a standard canon of proportions underlay the laying out of key elements of a wall scene. Concerned in particular with the human body, the grids utilized vary over time.[37] From the Middle Kingdom onward a standing male figure measured 18 squares from the soles of his feet to the hairline. Seated figures measured 14 squares. Changes in these proportions begin during the reign of Thutmose III and continue into the Ramesside Period, when 19 squares

42 A grid is visible on this female figure in the tomb of Sirenput ii (QH31) at Qubbet el-Hawa (Aswan: 12th Dynasty).

became the norm for standing images. Radical changes occurred in the 26th Dynasty when standing individuals measured 21 and the seated figures 17 squares.[38]

Different techniques were used to carve raised relief. In the most common method, as can still be seen, for example, in the tombs of Ptahhotep (Saqqara D62 – 5th Dynasty), Horemheb (KV57 – 18th Dynasty) and Nespaqashuti (TT312 – 26th Dynasty]), the background is cut away, leaving the solid outline of the various elements of a wall's decoration. These were then refined and smoothed using chisels and abrasives, with details of hands, feet and objects that the figures were carrying executed with care. The reliefs were then painted, sometimes after being first covered with a very thin layer of plaster.

Another method that was used in some Theban tombs and is seen in the tomb of Ramose (TT55) entailed outlining the relief decoration in black and cutting the background away by a few millimetres. Then the paint and chisel marks were removed by abrasive stones and sand and the reliefs refined with smaller chisels. Details were then modelled and refined and then the completed scene might have been covered with plaster prior to painting. A third method of relief decoration is known primarily from the Ramesside Period and is found in tombs cut in poor-quality stone. The stone was covered with a thick layer of gypsum plaster and carved before the plaster dried. The Egyptians must have applied the plaster to limited areas and worked on carving it quickly before moving on to the rest of the scene. Paint adhered very well to such plaster-carved representations.

In built tombs, it is likely that the innermost rooms will have been constructed, and thus decorated, first. This is borne out well by Ptahhotep's Saqqara tomb (D62), where the entryway is unfinished, while the main offering room is complete. The reverse will inevitably have been the case for rock-cut tombs and is seen both in (e.g.) the chapel of Ramose (TT55) and the tomb of Horemheb (KV57), where the outer parts are far more advanced than the inner parts.

Logically, one would expect the decoration to start at the top of a wall and then proceed downward, thereby sparing the lower areas from any damage. This is the case in Ptahhotep's tomb, but is not always so. In Horemheb's sepulchre, the carving was proceeding from bottom to top when suspended. In some of the unfinished portions of certain tombs sometimes only the hands or eyes are carved, thereby suggesting that a specialist in those areas would start working regardless of whether or not the rest of the scene was receiving attention at that time. Thus it would seem that there were no strict rules as to how the artists proceeded with the decoration once the initial stages had been completed and that the Egyptians decorated their tombs depending chiefly on convenience.

Painted Decoration

Once the masons, plasterers, draughtsmen and relief carvers had visited the tomb, it could finally be finished by the artists' application of the polychrome decoration. Some tombs did not have the benefit of relief decoration and

43 Black ink final sketches, with some preliminary carving, in the tomb of Ramose (TT55), dating to the reigns of Amenhotep III and IV.

44 The well-chamber of Thutmose IV's tomb was only ever partly decorated. On the end wall can be seen the *kheker*-frieze and sky-sign that was painted in advance of any further adornment.

would just be painted. Paint could be applied to a variety of surfaces, including gypsum and mud-plastered walls. Different techniques of painting are sometimes used in the same tomb: in some areas, the colours are applied in a thin layer, rather than the usual thicker layer, and colours appear to have been mixed differently in the same tomb (e.g. TT175).[39]

Artists used very basic materials: string, vegetable fibre brushes (including the Egyptian rush *Juncus maritimus*), water and different types of paint.[40] The palette of the painter was limited. Until around the 4th Dynasty, the paints used were naturally occurring ochres; thereafter a greater diversity was achieved, although still using natural compounds. Black was made of soot or ground charcoal.

Brown was made of ochre or iron oxide, or a combination of red painted over black. White was either chalk or gypsum, found in the cliffs around Egypt. Red and yellow came from the ochre that is found in the desert in lumps. It was broken up and ground to a fine powder to produce the bright colours that have lasted so well on tomb and temple walls. Red iron oxide was also used for red paint. Orpiment pigment, a natural sulphide of arsenic, also provided yellow; it has been identified in tombs dating to the Middle Kingdom, but is more commonly found in New Kingdom sepulchres. It was imported from Persia or perhaps Asia Minor, although some sources have been reported in Egypt.

Blue and green were the most difficult and costly colours to reproduce. Blue was made of azurite, or from an artificial frit made of silica, copper and calcium. Special blues were also made from lapis lazuli, a blue stone imported from what is modern Afghanistan. Green could be produced through an artificial frit like blue, or was made, less frequently, from powdered malachite, a natural ore that is found in the Sinai and the eastern desert, frequently at copper or even turquoise mines. Chrysocolla, a natural copper ore, was also a source for green paint. Other colours were produced by mixing together primary colours: pink was made by mixing red ochre and white gypsum, while grey was made from mixing soot and gypsum and orange was a combination of red and yellow.

Egyptian paint was tempera and it is thought that different adhesives were used, including local resins and beeswax. Analyses of painted tomb walls continues in an effort to determine precisely what materials were used as vehicles for the paint, as well as to see if varnishes or beeswax were used to set the colour. There is some evidence that beeswax was used as a thin covering on some painted tombs in Thebes (e.g. the tomb of Inyotef [TT155], as well as others dating to the early New Kingdom [TT39, TT82, TT86, TT93, TT179 and TT251]).[41]

Illumination was provided near the entrance by the sun. As the workers descended, sunlight would be reflected into the tomb by mirrors of polished metal, much as is done even today. Once beyond the reach of sunlight, simple ceramic lamps with linen twists as wicks were used. These burned locally produced oils, such as sesame oil. Salt was often added to prevent the lamps from smoking unduly. Despite this precaution, however, workers commonly complained of eye problems. A letter, written by the draughtsman Pay of Deir el-Medina to one of his sons, importunes him to bring salves and eye-paint to soothe and improve his sight. No doubt the smoke, dust and poor quality of illumination led to serious eye-diseases and even blindness amongst the tomb workers.

Scene Choice: Ateliers, Artists and Patrons

Although there was certainly a basic canon of scenes to be included in a tomb, the tomb-owner clearly exercised some personal choice. Some scenes, relevant to his position would no doubt be included, as well as vignettes reflecting his

tastes, e.g. hunting, fishing, etc. This leads us to the question of how these scenes were chosen. Were there pattern books to select from, or was each scene invented and reinvented by an artist? Although no such pattern books survive, sketches on ostraka and the repetition of scenes on the walls of different tombs suggest that certain images, vignettes and entire scenes were indeed copied. In some tombs new grids are placed over older paintings (e.g. in Menena's TT69) as an aid to the copyist.

Perhaps each atelier had some sort of pattern book from which the patrons would choose the scenes that were to be pictured in their tombs. Thus an atelier would provide a selection of different hunt scenes or fishing scenes for the client's decision. Certainly groups of tombs exist where one can see evidence of this practice: the 6th Dynasty mastabas in the Teti Pyramid Cemetery at Saqqara contain hunting scenes that are clearly made by the same artist or at least atelier (the tombs of Mereruka and Iunumin); there is also evidence of certain motifs, such as the force-feeding of hyenas that occurs repeatedly in that cemetery, that might

45 An ostrakon showing the head of Senenmut that was drawn using a grid. The initial sketch was done in red, while the corrections and final drawing were in black. This appears to be the prototype for a similar head found in a passage in the substructure of his tomb (TT353: MMA 36.3.252).

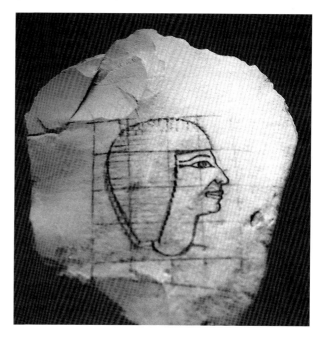

46 a&b Different parts of a single tomb may display different styles: this scene (*above*) in the tomb of Mahu at Saqqara contrasts with this element (*below*) elsewhere in the chapel.

have been derived from the 5th Dynasty tomb of Ti (Saqqara 60) and a group of mastabas whose presentation scenes are very similar, located at Giza (G7249, 5150, 4970 and 2155).

This practice is also evidenced from later periods. The 18th Dynasty painted tomb of Wensu (TTA4) at Thebes and the carved burial place of Paheri at El-Kab (EK3), some 55 km (35 miles) away, contain identical scenes related to granaries. Other scenes, such as those dealing with foreigners, are also transferred from tomb to tomb. Interestingly, some vignettes, or even individual figures, are sometimes copied from one tomb and placed in another, irrespective of suitability. The chariot workshop scenes in Mery's tomb (TT95) contains an image of a carpenter that is copied from the tomb of Rekhmire (TT100). The figure is typical of carpentry scenes, rather than chariot-making vignettes, but was transferred into this scene.[42] This transference might also have its roots in pattern books.[43]

The tombs of Menena (TT69) and Pairi (TT139) also show evidence of having been painted by the same artist/atelier, or at least having been influenced by one another or the same 'pattern book'. Pairi's artist appears to have copied, somewhat crudely, many of the scenes found in the tomb of Menena. Scenes from the Middle Kingdom tomb of Senet and Inyotefiqer (TT60) at Thebes were also copied in the New Kingdom tomb of Amenemhat (TT82) and Heqanefer's tomb at Toshka copies from Amenhotep-Huy's TT40, who was Viceroy of Kush, while the decoration of TT38 copies from TT52 and TT75.

The 25th and 26th Dynasties were a time of archaism in art. Indeed, it was quite common for 26th Dynasty tombs to contain vignettes copied from older tombs, even from some that were found in far-distant cemeteries.[44] Within the Theban necropolis several New Kingdom scenes can be seen repeated in Saite contexts. For example, the woman nursing a child first occurs in TT69, the tomb of Menena and then is repeated in the 25th Dynasty tomb of Mentuemhat (TT34). The apiculture scene from Rekhmire's TT100 is repeated in the 25th Dynasty sepulchre of Harwa (TT37). Pabasa (TT279) and Ankhhor (TT414) may have either mimicked Harwa, or gone directly to TT100's original. Another group of Saite tombs might also have borrowed from one another: Shoshenq (TT27), Basa (TT389) and Ibi (TT36).[45]

Royal tombs of the New Kingdom are decorated with a number of broadly standard texts that will certainly have been taken directly from papyrus masters. The tombs of

Thutmose III (KV34) and Amenhotep II (KV35) suggest that the scribe who was decorating the tomb was copying directly from a damaged papyrus roll, as at the points where the text was missing he wrote 'found damaged'!

There are some unusual instances where a tomb's decoration has been modified. In the tomb of Ptahemhat (TT77, 18th Dynasty), a roughly drawn monkey has been added under the earlier, better-drawn depiction of a seated man and his wife.[46] The reason for this addition is unknown. In TT52, the Ramesside usurper of the tomb reflected changes in social mores by giving Nakht's naked dancing girls clothes – which have since flaked off, restoring them to their former glory. Other changes, however, are more understandable, as is the case with *damnatio memoriae*. Apart from examples of animosity against tomb-owners, other vestiges can be found during the Amarna Period, where Amun's name, together with his totemic animal, the duck, was erased from several monuments.

Specific artists' styles can be recognized in certain tombs and one cannot help but wonder if these might have been requested by discerning patrons. This is especially true for the New Kingdom Theban artists, as their work has been examined the most closely.[47] Thus, the hands of some of the artists who worked in the tomb of Sety I (KV17) can also be discerned in the tomb of Ramesses II's sons (KV5), the tomb of his queen, Nefertiry D (QV66) and the tomb of Sennedjem (TT1) – who was probably himself one of the team of artists working in these tombs.

ARTISTS AND ARTISANS

It is clear that tomb building was a major industry in ancient Egypt, although detailed information is only available on those who constructed the greatest of the sepulchres – the pyramids and the royal tombs in the Valley of the Kings and those at Amarna. Two large communities of pyramid-builders are known, one at Giza and one at Kahun, near the Lahun pyramid of Senwosret II, although others no doubt existed and may still yield their secrets to the excavator's trowel.

The Giza settlement lies around a kilometre south of the Great Pyramid and covers a very considerable area.[48] It contained a large industrial complex, with food-producing

47 The area of the settlement of the 4th Dynasty pyramid builders at Giza lies south of a massive wall, known as the 'Wall of the Crow' (in the background), that separated it from the necropolis. It was accompanied by its own cemetery, which is in the foreground of this photograph.

48 Deir el-Medina: at the left is the enclosure of the Ptolemaic temple, while in the centre is the New Kingdom workmen's village.

facilities, a metal workshop, as well as houses and store-rooms. Senwosret II's pyramid town at Kahun included a walled section containing 220 small houses, no doubt intended for the workers.[49] The majority of information concerning tomb builders and artists comes from the archaeological remains and textual evidence (dating primarily from the Ramesside Period) from the New Kingdom walled village of Deir el-Medina on the western bank at Thebes.[50]

From the 18th Dynasty onwards, the workers in the Theban royal necropolis lived at Deir el-Medina, subsidized if not totally supported by the state and the system of redistribution. In return for their work they received all sorts of commodities, which, when in surplus, could be traded. In slack periods, they also worked on the tombs of the nobles, as well as their own very elaborate tombs in a necropolis adjoining the village. The differences in pay scales are reflected by the workers' titles. It has also been suggested that another group of workers was responsible for decorating the majority of private tombs as the Deir el-Medina contingent was primarily devoted to working on royal sepulchres.[51] This is still a matter under investigation.

The workers were divided into teams or gangs, the membership of which became hereditary: families are traceable from generation to generation. This was only natural as sons tended to learn their metier from their fathers and thus carry on a family tradition. A stela in the Louvre, belonging to the craftsman Mertisen, says that he only shared his knowledge with his son.

The basic work gang was divided into 'left' and 'right' 'sides', each under its own foreman, with a single 'Scribe of the Tomb' in overall charge of administration. The foremen were responsible not only for their members' work and actions, but also for the tools and other items provided by the administration. The workers laboured for 8 days at a stretch, 8 hours a day, unless there was an emergency and a tomb had to be completed in haste. The skilled workers included stonemasons, outline draughtsmen, painters and carpenters.

Chapter 4 The Study of the Egyptian Tomb

Although closed by pious hands, few tombs have survived the millennia intact. In the vast majority of cases, they were plundered within a few years – and in certain cases, hours – of the funeral. Some burial chambers have been found sealed, with no sign of post-interment penetration, yet with the funerary equipment smashed and the denuded corpse lying in pieces around the room![52] Interestingly, it was not only gold and jewels that attracted the robbers; more homely items such as beer and oils were also stolen from tombs. Although robberies were endemic throughout Egyptian history, it would seem that they were particularly common during periods in which central authority was weakened and thus necropolis guards less well organized or honest. The most notorious episodes of this kind come late in the 20th Dynasty, when a number of papyri shed a lurid light on the web of corruption and greed that led to the wholesale robbery of the cemeteries at Thebes.[53] At least one royal tomb is known to have been robbed during the Amarna Period, while it is clear that the Intermediate Periods saw much looting of cemeteries. For example, the 10th Dynasty text 'Instruction for King Merykare' alludes to Herakleopolitan troops plundering the Abydos necropolis during their war with the 11th Dynasty Thebans.

Following the final collapse of ancient Egyptian civilization and religion in the face of the forces of Christianity and Islam, the old cities of the dead lost what little sanctity and physical protection still remained, with many tombs falling victim to the monotheistic iconoclasts

49 (*top*) Façade of a now-destroyed tomb at Asyut, as depicted by Bonaparte's scholars.

50 (*above centre*) Part of the Leopold II papyrus, one of the documents recounting the tomb-robbery trials of the 20th Dynasty (Brussels E6857).

51 (*above*) Graffito in the tomb of Thutmose IV (KV43), recounting the tomb's restoration after robbery during the reign of Horemheb.

52 Prince Khaemwaset, the fourth son of Ramesses II, might well be called one of the first Egyptologists. Living in the Memphite area as High Priest of Ptah, he spent a great deal of time and effort cleaning and restoring the monuments of earlier periods. He left inscriptions on a number of structures detailing his restoration work, in this case on the pyramid of Unas at Saqqara.

and treasure-seekers, with others converted to become churches or parts of monasteries. Medieval Arabic accounts tell, often with wondrous embellishments, of ventures into pyramids and tombs to recover their riches.[54] However, by the 16th century, the first real signs of European interest in ancient Egypt were becoming apparent, beginning the process that would culminate in the scientific resurrection of its monuments in the 19th, 20th and 21st centuries.

THE EARLIEST INTEREST

The earliest explorers and visitors of Egyptian tombs were the ancient Egyptians themselves. The monuments of their ancestors were of interest to them and played a part in the funerary culture that was a pillar of Egyptian society. Egyptians visited tombs to pray for the spirits of their dead, to invoke their blessings, elicit help and to pacify those who seemed to be unquiet and vengeful. Royal tombs were centres of cultic activity and were a primary focus of visitors. Tombs were also visited as a source of inspiration for the construction of other tombs: attractive designs, scenes and vignettes were sometimes copied by artists and tomb-owners who had visited a certain tomb (cf. p. 52).

Graffiti help trace the path of both ancient and modern visitors in tombs. The tomb of Senet/Inyotefiqer (TT60) at Thebes contains 18th Dynasty graffiti praising its beauty and recording the names of those who visited the tomb. Khaemwaset, the fourth son of Ramesses II, restored a number of royal tombs, such as those of Shepseskaf, Unas and Senwosret III, leaving a carved record of his activities. Djoser's Step Pyramid complex still contains examples of visitors' ink graffiti.

The 25th and 26th Dynasties saw an upsurge in interest in earlier monuments, the art of the period being frequently modelled on ancient prototypes. As noted in the previous chapter, they even went so far as to make direct copies of wall-scenes in tombs of the distant past. That 'archaeological' clearances were sometimes carried out is shown by the new access passage dug under the 3rd Dynasty Step Pyramid; the objective in this case is suggested by the grids drawn over some of the reliefs in the substructure to allow copying.[55] Similarly, the Late Period nobleman, Hapymen, had a sarcophagus made whose decoration was a direct copy from that of Thutmose III.

Other ancient designs were more indirectly borrowed; for example, in TT33 is a curious rectangular rock-cut massif directly above the burial chamber, with goddesses with outstretched arms on each corner (see p. 284–5). This seems to have been directly inspired by a royal sarcophagus of the late 18th Dynasty, something seemingly only possible through direct inspection of an original – presumably either that of Ay or of Horemheb.

Egypt was a destination for the tourists of the Greek and Roman world, amongst the earliest being Herodotus of Halicarnassus (5th century BC). He visited a number of Lower Egyptian sites, including Sais, Giza and Hawara, leaving interesting, but often frustrating, accounts in his great *Histories*. These tourists also left their graffiti on many of the pyramids, as well as in the royal sepulchres in the Valley of the Kings. However, with the Arab conquest of AD 642, Egypt became essentially cut off from Europe. The new masters of the country had little concern for the ancient monuments, save as convenient quarries, although a number of Arab historians took an interest in the pyramids, in particular Abd el-Latif, who gives a good description of the interior of the Great Pyramid at Giza.[56]

A few devout Christian pilgrims did, however, reach Egypt, en route to Jerusalem, including Bernard the Wise in 870.[57] Although they saw the pyramids, most failed to recognize their sepulchral purpose, calling them the 'Granaries of Joseph', while the challenges that they encountered show that casual travel to the country was difficult. Travel conditions started to improve following the end of the Crusades late in the 13th century, increasingly so after the Ottoman takeover in 1517, but apart from repetitious descriptions of the pyramids, western travellers did little to advance knowledge of the ancient monuments.

Gradually, however, more information is to be found: Johannes Helffrich (fl. 1570s) relates his visit to a communal tomb at Giza, as well as to the Giza pyramids and sphinx, which were drawn in the early 17th century by George Sandys (1578–1644), while John Greaves (1602–52) in 1639 carried out the first real survey of the Great Pyramid, publishing the results in 1646 as the *Pyramidographia* (London: George Badger). A few years later, Jean de Thévenot (1633–67) explored the 'mummy-pits' of Saqqara, while in 1668 Father Charles François mentions 'the place of

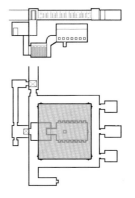

53 Directly above the burial chamber of the tomb of Pedamenopet at Thebes (TT33) is a curious rock massif with the figures of the protective goddesses at the corners. For a plan of the whole tomb, see ill. 323.

mummies called Biban el Melouc' – the Valley of the Kings. In 1672, Johann Vansleb (d. 1679) entered the catacombs of the Sacred Animal Necropolis at Saqqara.

The 18th century saw a number of travellers exploring Egyptian tombs and leaving important accounts of these.

54 A nobleman of the Late Period, one Hapymen, had his sarcophagus made with its external decoration copied from that of Thutmose III, created a thousand years earlier (BM EA23).

Paul Lucas (1664–1737) visited the country twice and entered the Sacred Animal catacombs at Saqqara, apparently being one of the first to enter the Serapeum (tomb of the sacred bulls) in modern times.[58] His contemporary, Claude Sicard (1677–1726), a Jesuit missionary to Egypt, was perhaps the first European to identify modern Luxor with the Thebes of the Classical authors. He drew a map of Egypt on which he recorded 24 monuments, 50 decorated tombs and 20 pyramids. Another prelate-turned-mapmaker was Richard Pococke (1704–65). In 1738 he drew fairly accurate plans of two Saite tombs on the Asasif (TT33 and TT37) – the first decorated private tombs to be described in print – as well as more fanciful maps of other sepulchres. In the Valley of the Kings, he identified 18 tombs, of which nine were accessible, and drew plans of those that were open. Further useful drawings were produced around the same time by Frederik Ludwig Norden (1708–42).

James Bruce (1730–94) also examined the Valley of the Kings. Although he was really searching for the source of the Nile, he did pause on his southward journey at the Valley. There he entered the tomb of Ramesses III (KV11). At the entrance to the tomb were two harpers. Bruce copied these, but when published they appeared in a very European-orientalized way – whether the blame lay with the copyist, the engraver or both remains uncertain. Despite their rather fantastical depiction, these harpers captured the

55 (*left*) George Sandys and his companions approach Giza in 1610.

56 (*below*) The Theban necropolis as depicted by Richard Pococke in 1737–38.

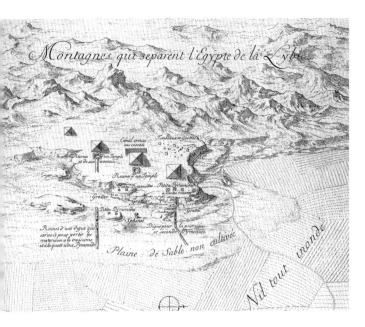

imagination of Europe and the tomb became known as the Harper's tomb, or Bruce's tomb. The Englishman William Hamilton (1777–1859), secretary to Lord Elgin of the Marbles fame, also visited Thebes and wrote about the tombs in some detail in his 1809 volume entitled *Aegyptiaca*.

THE DAWN OF EGYPTOLOGY

A key event in the growth of popular interest and scientific investigation of ancient Egypt was Napoleon Bonaparte's invasion of Egypt on behalf of the French Republic in 1798. In addition to his soldiers, the emperor-to-be took with him a commission of scholars to record the monuments, geography, fauna and flora of the country. Nearly all the ancient material collected soon passed into the hands of the British after the French capitulation on 30 August 1801. However, the commission's multi-volume illustrated account of the country, the *Description de l'Égypte* (1809–22), was instrumental in pushing Egypt to the fore in the consciousness of the educated elite. Amongst the standing monuments recorded were a large number of tombs. Sites whose sepulchres received fairly close attention were Giza, Asyut, the Asasif, the Valley of the Kings and El-Kab.

Bonaparte's expedition was responsible for a major upsurge in interest in ancient Egypt amongst the general public of Europe. The growth of the great public collections brought things Egyptian before the educated public as never before. Against this background, the early years of the 19th century saw the launching of a frenzy of excavation and plundering that was to continue into the next century.

This was facilitated by the assumption of the Ottoman governorship of Egypt by Muhammed Ali in 1815. Avid for Western technology and diplomatic and commercial relations, he was responsible for a large influx of Europeans. Particularly important individuals were the Consuls and Consular Agents of the various European powers. Apart from their broader diplomatic roles, many also took it upon themselves to gather collections of antiquities for national, and more importantly personal, enrichment.

Two of the most prominent figures in this Consular activity were Giovanni Battista Belzoni (1778–1823), working for the British Consul, Henry Salt (1780–1827), and Bernardino Drovetti (1776–1852), Consul-General for France. Belzoni was by far the more careful worker – although by no means a scientific archaeologist – publishing

57 (*above*) Norden's map of the Giza necropolis.

58 (*below*) A member of the Napoleonic commission working in the tomb of Paheri at El-Kab.

a very fair book on his adventures. Apart from exploring communal tombs, his discoveries brought to light some of the most important examples of New Kingdom royal sepulchres, including the tombs of Ay, Ramesses I and Sety I (WV23, KV16 and 17). Belzoni was amongst the first people to make facsimiles of a tomb (that of Sety I). He worked in Lower Egypt too, most spectacularly clearing a way into the Second Pyramid at Giza. To commemorate the event he scrawled his name in lamp-black across one of the walls of the chamber, where it can still be seen today.

A military appointee of Muhammed Ali, Prisse d'Avennes (1807–79), also took a great interest in Egyptian monuments and copied (and photographed during his 1858 expedition) several scenes from Theban tombs that have subsequently been destroyed or stolen. Another important

59 Part of one of the scale copies of the tomb of Sety I prepared by Belzoni and his collaborators. This was perhaps the first known attempt to copy an entire Egyptian monument, and gives the lie to Belzoni's long-standing reputation as a mere plunderer (Bristol's City Museum & Art Gallery).

figure working in the necropoleis of Thebes was the former horse-dealer, Giuseppe Passalacqua (1797–1865), who discovered a number of Middle Kingdom/Second Intermediate Period tombs. He ultimately sold his collection to the King of Prussia, becoming curator of the new Berlin Museum until his death.

The superbly painted tomb-chapels at Thebes were the subject of visits by a number of travellers and investigators, many of whom took up residence in some of the tombs themselves. Their copies are of crucial importance, as so many scenes have since been destroyed by the vicissitudes of time and nature, but particularly at the hand of plunderers. Two copyists were the naval officers Charles Irby (1789–1845) and James Mangles (1786–1867), who in 1817 also visited other sites, at Deir el-Bersha making the first record of the famous scene of a colossus being dragged by workmen (see ill. 36). Of others present at Thebes, such as Frederic Cailliaud (1787–1869), Yanni Athanasi (1798–1854) and William Bankes (1787–1855), some restricted themselves to copying the depictions, but others took the far more drastic step of removing areas of plaster from the walls, as a result of which many of the finest tombs were destroyed, only a few pitiful fragments surviving in museum collections.[59]

Unfortunately, such vandalism was to continue for some time, and to this day tombs are still being denuded of decoration to satisfy the demands of unscrupulous collectors. Nevertheless, by the early 1820s progress was being made in the serious study of the Theban tombs, particularly through the agency of (Sir) John Gardner Wilkinson (1797–1875). He spent over a dozen years in Egypt, deriving from his researches the material for his celebrated *Manners and Customs of the Ancient Egyptians* (1837), for many years the key textbook on the subject. Much of its contents was derived from the decoration of the private tomb-chapels, demonstrating their value to Egyptology. In addition to collecting and interpreting scenes of daily life from private tombs, Wilkinson located many 'new' tombs in Thebes and eventually made the first archaeological map of the area. During his researches he lived in one of the tombs on Sheikh Abd el-Qurna, TT83, the sepulchre of Ametju, to which he added extensive mud-brick elements, a few of which still survive.

Others who spent their time copying the monuments were James Burton (1788–1862) and Robert Hay

(1799–1863), like Wilkinson independent researchers, much of whose material remains unpublished. In contrast, during 1828, a large team sponsored by the French and Tuscan governments had arrived in Egypt to undertake a major survey. It was led by Jean-François Champollion (1790–1832), decipherer of hieroglyphs, and Ippolito Rosellini (1800–43), and brought into the public domain far more of the decoration of Egyptian sepulchral monuments. In 1848 Maxime du Camp (1822–94), accompanied by the author Gustave Flaubert (1821–80), made a photographic record of many monuments.

The 1830s saw the first systematic archaeological work at Giza, by Colonel Richard Howard Vyse (1784–1853) and the engineer John Perring (1813–69). During 1836–37 they opened the pyramid of Menkaure and cleared a very interesting Late Period tomb (LG84), which was named after a colleague of Vyse, Colonel Patrick Campbell (1779–1857). Perring then carried out a survey of the pyramid sites to the north and south of Giza. Despite the pair's enthusiastic use of explosives, the information that they gathered was sound and Perring's survey is still fundamental.

The middle years of the 19th century saw Egypt swept by many in search of antiquities. The great Prussian expedition, under the leadership of Karl Richard Lepsius (1810–84), covered the whole of Egypt and Nubia in 1842–45. The elephant folio volumes of the *Denkmäler aus Ägypten und Äthiopien* (1849–59) published plans of monuments and drawings of their decorations, while collections of antiquities were shipped back to Berlin. This Prussian work made available the widest and most accurate digest yet of information on the structure and decoration of Egyptian tombs and remains of value, in particular where the monuments recorded have been damaged or destroyed.

TOWARDS TRUE ARCHAEOLOGY

Unlike the great state-sponsored expeditions, the Scotsman Alexander Henry Rhind (1833–63) worked alone. He had come to Egypt for his health, but soon became interested in antiquities, with a scientific approach that was ahead of its time.[60] Although he undertook some work in the Valley of the Kings in 1855, his principal activities were on the Sheikh Abd el-Qurna hill. Two of his discoveries are of particular interest. Both were reuses of earlier sepulchres, one being the

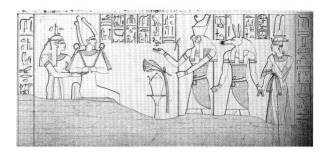

60 This plate from Lepsius's *Denkmäler* volumes illustrates the continuing importance of these old works. This is a funerary scene of the Ramesside Queen Baketwernel, added to KV10 when it was reused for her and another royal lady. Today, the whole scene is lost, except for part of the queen's face.

last resting place of one Mentusebaef, who lived under Cleopatra VII and Augustus, and the other holding a group of 18th Dynasty princesses reburied after robbery during the reign of Pasebkhanut I.[61]

Some order began to be imposed on the antiquarian free-for-all in 1858, when Auguste Mariette (1821–81) was appointed the first head of the Egyptian Antiquities Service. He had previously found fame in 1851 through his (re?)discovery of the Serapeum at Saqqara. Under his direction, unofficial digging was suppressed and official excavations were begun around the country. Unfortunately, supervision was poor and little thought was given to the preservation of monuments once they had been uncovered, thereby leading to their destruction and loss.[62]

Mariette's tomb-discoveries were vast, but unfortunately only partly published, some records being lost in a flood in 1877. Saqqara was a particular focus; the tombs investigated there ranged in date from the dawn of the 3rd Dynasty to the Late Period. The former was represented by the sepulchre of Hesyre, its adornment including some exquisitely carved wooden panels (pp. 144–5). At the other end of Egyptian history was a tomb that contained the burials of two men named Psametik and, probably intrusively, the 30th Dynasty queen Khedebneithirbinet II. Altogether, some 200 sepulchres were examined at Saqqara alone. Elsewhere, large tracts of Abydos were investigated and, beginning in 1858, work at Deir el-Bahari revealed a number of crypts constructed under the pavements of the temple of Hatshepsut for priests of Mentu during the 25th/26th Dynasties.

61 The inner tomb chapel of Nefermaat at Meidum, drawn in 1878, already suffering badly from the attention of vandals. When found seven years earlier it had been all but perfect. Three decades years later, its pitiful remains would be dismantled by Flinders Petrie and moved to the museums of Cairo and other major centres to save them from final destruction.

After the pyramid explorations of Belzoni, Vyse and Perring, little was done with these great monuments until late in Mariette's regime. Under the (apparently justified) assumption that pyramids were 'mute' (uninscribed) and unlikely to reveal historical/religious texts, Mariette had given little priority to the unexplored examples that dotted the Saqqara necropolis. Nevertheless, in early 1880, a French grant was given to the Antiquities Service for the specific purpose of their excavation.

In May 1880, a Saqqara villager penetrated the burial chamber of the pyramid of Pepy I, a monument so devastated that the roof of the burial chamber was exposed: hieroglyphic texts adorned the walls within. With the help

of Service workmen, Emile Brugsch (1842–1930) entered and made preliminary copies of the texts. These were sent to France for study by Mariette, who was on leave there, and Gaston Maspero (1846–1916), then Professor at the Collège de France. At the end of the year, the Antiquities Service *reis* (head worker) Mohammed Shahin opened the nearby pyramid of Nemtyemsaf I, which was examined and partly copied by Brugsch and his elder brother, Heinrich (1827–94), together with the previously opened pyramid of Pepy I. They were able to announce to Mariette that the existence of the famous Pyramid Texts was proved, shortly before he died in Cairo-Bulaq on 18 January 1881.

As Mariette's successor, Gaston Maspero oversaw the true internationalization of excavation in Egypt, with concessions given to a range of individuals and institutions. Together with Egyptian official work, the next three decades would see some of the most important discoveries in the history of Egyptology.

Perhaps the most spectacular was the clearance in 1881 of a tomb found a decade earlier by local plunderers near Deir el-Bahari. It proved to be the tomb of Pinudjem II (TT320: p. 273), which had served as the hiding place for over 50 mummies removed from their own tombs for safety during the first part of the Third Intermediate Period. Although rapidly emptied of its contents, the tomb itself was not properly examined and planned until 1999/2000, when a Germano-Russian team under Erhard Graefe undertook the work. Another key find, by Maspero in 1886, was that of the Deir el-Medina burial chamber of the workman Sennedjem (TT1), wonderfully decorated and still containing, intact, 20 mummies and their funerary equipment.

The same decade saw the advent of William Matthew Flinders Petrie (1853–1942), often held to be the 'Father of Egyptian Archaeology'. He began with a survey of the Giza pyramids and then worked in successive seasons at a vast range of sites throughout Egypt, many of them funerary. In 1888, at Hawara in the Fayoum he found a large Roman-era cemetery, still of fundamental importance for the study of burial customs of the period. Over the next three-and-a-half decades he would undertake work that still provides the skeleton for the study of the evolution of the Egyptian tomb, from Predynastic times onwards.

In 1891, Eugène Grébaut (1846–1915), Maspero's successor, opened a pit at Deir el-Bahari (dubbed the Bab el-Gasus) to find a pair of galleries filled with over 150 coffins, placed there at the very end of the 21st Dynasty (p. 273). His successor, Jacques de Morgan (1857–1924), planned a systematic archaeological survey of the Nile Valley, but this was cut short after one volume had been published. His excavations at hitherto virgin sites, however,

62 (*top right*) Maspero and his workmen at the entrance to TT320, a photograph taken some time after the actual clearance of the tomb.

63 (*right*) Flinders Petrie at Abydos in the early 1920s.

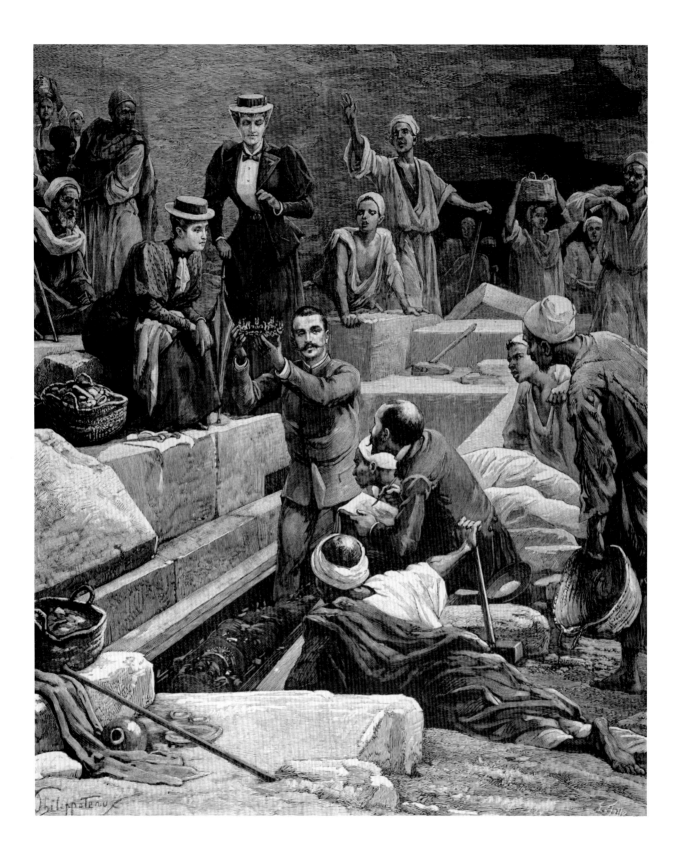

brought to light a number of important sepulchres. At Dahshur he devoted his efforts in 1894–95 around three of a series of badly ruined Middle Kingdom pyramids along the edge of the desert. The pyramids themselves were completely robbed, but the surrounding tombs yielded some of the finest treasures of ancient Egypt, including the partially intact tomb of a 13th Dynasty king, Hor, and the untouched tombs of four daughters (?) of Amenemhat II. De Morgan also dug at Saqqara, finding the tombs of Mereruka and Kagemeni, adjacent to the pyramid of Teti, two of the largest mastaba tombs of the 6th Dynasty.

The earliest phases of the evolution of the Egyptian tomb were revealed during the late 1890s. First, at Naqada and Ballas, Petrie found graves dating to the Predynastic Period. Then James Quibell (1867–1935) and Frederick Green (1869–1949) discovered the oldest decorated tomb in Egypt at Hierakonpolis (Tomb 100, datable to Naqada II), which perhaps was the burial place of one of the 'proto-kings' of Upper Egypt. Around the same time, De Morgan cleared at Naqada a large panelled mastaba (the so-called 'Royal Tomb') dating to the very beginning of the 1st Dynasty, while Émile Amélineau (1850–1915) began working on the Early Dynastic Period royal cemetery at Abydos – Umm el-Qaab. The latter excavation was badly executed and the full value of the site was only appreciated after Petrie re-cleared the site in 1899 under the auspices of the London-based Egypt Exploration Fund (now Society), founded in 1882 by Amelia Edwards (1831–1892).[63] Meanwhile, during 1893 to 1907, Édouard Naville (1844–1926) cleared the temples of Deir el-Bahari, bringing to light many sepulchres, including a royal cemetery of the 11th Dynasty.

ONCE MORE INTO THE VALLEY

In 1897, De Morgan was replaced as head of the Antiquities Service by Victor Loret (1859–1946). Loret undertook excavations in the Valley of the Kings, where he found a number of tombs, both royal and noble, including that of Thutmose III (KV34) and the largely untouched tomb of Maihirpri (KV36). In 1898 he discovered a second cache of royal mummies in the tomb of Amenhotep II (KV35).[64]

64 Jacques De Morgan lifts one of two crowns from the mummy of the 12th Dynasty Princess Khnemet; her tomb was found in the enclosure of the pyramid of Amenemhat II at Dahshur in 1894.

65 Petrie recleared the royal tombs of the Early Dynastic Period at Abydos, after the blundering work of Émile Amélineau. This shows part of the tomb of King Djer, with the 13th Dynasty 'Osiris bed' found there. From the Middle Kingdom onwards, Djer's sepulchre was regarded as that of the god Osiris.

After Loret's resignation in 1899, Maspero returned to the Directorship-General of the Service, which he reorganized, with the installation of a new series of Inspectors in Upper and Lower Egypt. The key appointments were of Howard Carter (1874–1939) at Thebes and James Quibell at Saqqara. Carter had earlier worked as an epigrapher at Beni Hasan (see below), Deir el-Bahari and other sites. He now oversaw the monuments and excavations of southern Egypt. From 1903, this included the work being financed by the American Theodore Davis (1837–1915), but executed under the auspices of the Service. Working with him, Carter discovered the robbed tombs of Thutmose IV (KV43), Hatshepsut (KV20) and others in the Valley. He was later succeeded as Inspector first by Quibell and then by Arthur Weigall (1880–1934), who also oversaw the discovery of several important tombs while funded by Davis.

The first of these finds, in 1904, was the burial place of Yuya and Tjuiu (KV46), parents-in-law of Amenhotep III. Although partly ransacked, it still contained much of its fabulous furnishings. Until 1922 and the discovery of the tomb of Tutankhamun, it was the richest tomb found in Egypt. Another was KV55, a curious deposit that held an

66 The damaged coffin from KV55 as found: the identity of its occupant has long been a subject of debate (CM JE39627: 18th Dynasty).

anonymous mummy that has been claimed to be both Akhenaten and his co-ruler, Smenkhkare.

The final major tomb discovered in the Valley before 1914 was that of the pharaoh Horemheb (KV57). Badly robbed, it contained the bones of four individuals, but these remains now appear to be lost and whether any might have belonged to the king (whose mummy is missing from the caches) is unknown.

THE GROWTH OF EPIGRAPHY

Alongside the explosion of excavation that accompanied the end of the 19th century, there was a major growth in the recording of standing monuments, many having lain open for generations, vulnerable to deterioration and destruction. The copying of individual scenes in tombs had been common since the days of the Napoleonic expedition and excellent work had been done, particularly by the Prussians. However, the idea of the copying of every part of a monument came to the fore only in the 1890s, when the Egypt Exploration Fund founded the Archaeological Survey of Egypt.[65] Under the overall direction of Francis Ll. Griffith (1862–1934), the early work was carried out at Beni Hasan by Percy Newberry (1869–1949) in 1890–94. Later assisted by a

young Howard Carter, Newberry continued with the tombs at El-Bersha, but rivalries with other members of his team led to a temporary suspension of activities.

Copying re-started in 1898, when Norman de Garis Davies (1865–1941) began work at Saqqara in the tomb of Akhethotep and Ptahhotep (D64). Davies and his wife Nina (1881–1965), were amongst the finest epigraphers of all time and over the next 40 years would produce wonderful records of tombs throughout the length of Egypt. Amongst Davies' greatest pieces of work was the recording of the private tombs of Tell el-Amarna (the publication of the royal tombs was to wait until Geoffrey Martin's work in 1968 and 1980/2). Later, working for the Metropolitan Museum of Art, New York, the couple were to draw and paint large numbers of the private tombs at Thebes. Nina's colour facsimiles of Theban tomb scenes are still on display at the Metropolitan Museum of Art and other institutions. After the death of Norman de Garis Davies, Torgny Säve-Söderbergh (1914–98) continued with the project of recording the Theban tombs.

The preservation of the Theban tombs, so badly damaged since the time of Wilkinson, was greatly enhanced by the work of Arthur Weigall while Inspector-General of Antiquities for Upper Egypt during 1905–14. He instituted a programme of restoration and the fitting of security gates, a practice that had been started in 1903 when Howard Carter had held the same position. By 1908, 70 of the Theban tomb-chapels had been given iron gates. In 1913, along with the philologist (Sir) Alan Gardiner (1879–1963), Weigall published the first major listing of the Theban tombs,[66] enumerating 252 tombs. This cataloguing exercise continues to this day, with 409 of the over 1,000 known now bearing official numbers.

Much of Weigall's funding came from private sources, in particular from the chemist Sir Robert Mond (1867–1938), who also financed the excavation and publication of monuments in the area into the 1920s. As part of the documentation process, Mond had designed a special carriage for the camera to enable it to move smoothly on one plane, allowing a whole wall to be photographed uniformly. He also experimented with colour photography and tried to match the colours of the facsimiles with the photographs, perhaps the earliest attempt at colour matching. Mond was very keen on restoration as well as documentation and had a plan to make casts of the missing portions of tombs that

67 An example of one of Nina Davies' facsimile paintings: part of the east wall of the tomb-chapel of Nakht at Thebes (TT52: 18th Dynasty).

were now in museums and return them to the tombs. This scheme continues sporadically today.

Walter Wreszinski (1880–1935) was an epigrapher who used photography as the basis for his work. His five-volume *Atlas zur Altägyptische Kulturgeschichte* (published between 1913 and 1936) contains copies of many tomb walls that are now lost.

The epigraphic tradition of Newberry and Davies continues to flourish, although the great majority of Egypt's known tombs are still inadequately published, if at all.

However, new volumes appear regularly, especially under the auspices of the German Archaeological Institute in Cairo. The potential rewards of such work and the accompanying cleaning and conservation of decorated surfaces were shown in 2002. The removal of grime from a doorway of the long-known tomb of Sobknakhte at El-Kab allowed Vivian Davies to locate an autobiographical text that reveals a whole new chapter in the struggles of the Egyptians against Nubian foes during the 17th Dynasty.[67]

Tomb scenes had been copied since travellers started visiting Egypt, although there is a marked difference between artistic and archaeological copying methods, especially in terms of accuracy. The earliest copyists had to accustom themselves to an unfamiliar art style and it was only once that hurdle had been crossed that greater accuracy could be achieved. Ideally, Egyptologists strive for a complete and faithful record, although they do not always succeed, due to unfavourable copying conditions, including poor light and dirt-covered decoration.

However, there are some cases when mis-copying has been deliberate due to ideas of propriety prevalent at the time. The tomb of Khety at Beni Hasan (BH-XVII), as published by Newberry in 1893, shows a lacuna on a pilaster. However, when one visits the tomb, even today, there are no gaps in the decoration – rather, there is an image of a man and a woman lying on a bed together. Clearly this was not regarded as 'proper' subject matter for a scholarly volume on ancient Egypt and as such was suppressed.

The earliest and most basic method of copying was by eye; this very much depended on the skill of the copyist and his/her attention to detail. Sometimes grids were placed over the wall to aid precision. In the 19th century artists also used the camera lucida to help with copying. This tool consists of a prism set on a stand and aimed at the tomb wall. An image from the wall is projected onto a piece of paper, allowing the artist to trace it.

The second most common way, and one still in use today, involves placing a transparent sheet on the wall and tracing directly onto it. Over time the type of the paper (and later plastic) and the quality of pens and pencils have changed, although the essential method remains the same. While commonly used, this is often not the best way to copy a tomb wall, as it is difficult to fix the sheet to the wall and both the adhesive material and the pressure of the tracing can damage the monument. Furthermore, it is difficult to decide how to depict different sorts of relief and painted decoration.[68] However, this method is infinitely preferable to the squeezes that were so popular in the 19th century and used by antiquaries and tourists alike. Squeezes are made by moulding wet paper (newspaper, blotting paper or special squeeze paper) over a relief. Although this provides an accurate negative image of the relief, it causes considerable

68 Epigraphy can be carried out in a variety of ways. One of the most standard has been and remains placing some type of tracing paper directly on the wall, as is being done here by Beth Thompson at Saqqara, and tracing the drawings below. Conventions for raised and sunk relief as well as details are worked out by the artist for the final publication.

damage to the surface, first by wetting it and second, by removing the paint from the wall. Dry squeezes are also possible, but these still have the drawback of requiring the exertion of pressure on the wall.

The advent of photography has contributed significantly to epigraphic work. Straightforward photography often provides a good record, with modern photogrammetric methods enhancing its accuracy. Photographs can also be used in the 'Chicago House Method', one of the most complicated and exact copying techniques, used by the University of Chicago's epigraphers, based at Chicago House in Luxor. The walls are carefully photographed from a single plane (as Mond had first done); artists then draw over the photographs in ink. After this, the photographic images are bleached away, leaving the line drawings, which are then copied onto paper and taken to the wall to be checked in different lights. Both artists and experts in hieroglyphic writing check the drawings for accuracy before final collation and eventual publication. This method is very precise and does not damage the monument, although it is extremely time consuming and expensive.

Slides can also be used: the tomb is photographed using slide film and then the slides are projected onto paper and the epigrapher can draw around the projected image, although gauging the proportions can be difficult. This method likewise has the benefit of not touching the monument.

Innovations in digital imaging are now bringing new possibilities into the recording of tomb walls. Experiments are being carried out with devices that can scan whole areas with minimal human involvement and damage. However, no matter the method of undertaking the basic copying of a tomb, for an accurate facsimile the epigrapher must check and re-check the images against the original. Thus, the human eye will remain for the foreseeable future the final arbiter in epigraphy.

EXCAVATION NORTH AND SOUTH

Although by the early 20th century the copying of open monuments was regarded as an important imperative, conventional excavation continued apace. In the north, some key discoveries were made by Alessandro Barsanti (1858–1917). At Saqqara, he found the tomb of the founder of the 2nd Dynasty, Hotepsekhemwy and, from the other end of Egyptian history, cleared the first example to be discovered of the great shaft tombs of the Late Period (see pp. 286–7), which was found intact. A few kilometres away he was the first man in modern times to enter the two pyramids at Zawiyet el-Aryan.

In 1906, Ernesto Schiaparelli (1856–1928) found the intact tomb of the architect Kha at Deir el-Medina (TT8: ill. 18). The same Italian team was responsible for the finding of some beautifully decorated tombs in the Valley of the Queens, the greatest of them being that of Nefertiry D (QV66), consort of Ramesses II. Schiaparelli also dismantled the tomb of the Theban draughtsman May

(TT338) in 1906 and reconstructed it in the Egyptian Museum in Turin, where it can be seen today.

Less spectacular, but of at least equal archaeological value, are the discoveries made in a number of Middle Kingdom private cemeteries in Middle Egypt. In particular, the labours of John Garstang (1876–1956) at Beni Hasan recovered the contents of nearly 900 middle-class tombs. Together with the decorated tombs of the nobles copied by Newberry, they make Beni Hasan the quintessential Middle Kingdom necropolis. Other Middle Kingdom cemeteries worked on during this period included Gebelein, Qau el-Kebir (Schiaparelli), Asyut (Ahmed Kamal [1851–1923]) and El-Bersha (Kamal and Boston Museum of Fine Arts), although these represent only a selection.

For Old Kingdom funerary archaeology, the instigation of systematic excavations at Abu Sir (Ludwig Borchardt [1863–1938]) and Giza was of key significance. Giza was initially split between the Italians, Austrians and Americans in 1902; the latter two teams, led respectively by Hermann Junker (1877–1962) and George Andrew Reisner (1867–1942), worked on into the post-First World War era, clearing the cemeteries east and west of the Great Pyramid. Between the wars, Selim Hassan (1886–1961) began clearing Giza's Central Field as well.

Finally, the Early Dynastic Period and early Old Kingdom were illuminated by the work of Quibell at Saqqara, parts of the extensive early noble cemetery being cleared and recorded. Finds also, however, extended into the Late Period, a tomb near Teti's pyramid revealing no fewer than nine sarcophagi, including that of the dwarf Djehor. Quibell's work around the Teti pyramid continued after the war. In 1931, although long retired, he took over direction of the excavation of the Step Pyramid complex, the oldest of all such monuments, and was still so engaged at his death.

AFTER THE GREAT WAR

Excavations from 1914 onwards were greatly affected by the changes that came about both as the result of the final retirement of Maspero and the upsurge in nationalism that culminated in the establishment of a nominally independent Egyptian monarchy in 1922. The latter closely coincided with Howard Carter's discovery of the tomb of Tutankhamun (KV62), the controversies surrounding which played a major role in a tightening-up of excavation

69 (*above*) George Reisner and his team at the excavation of the tomb of Hetepheres (G7000X) at Giza in 1925.

70 (*left*) Howard Carter opens the shrines in the burial chamber of Tutankhamun in 1923.

regulations and which definitively placed the balance of power on the side of the Egyptian authorities.

While opposition to these reforms led to the abandonment of Egypt by Flinders Petrie, other teams continued work, many of the most important tomb-finds being made by the Metropolitan Museum expedition under H. E. Winlock (1884–1950) at Deir el-Bahari and on the surrounding hillsides. Also at Western Thebes, the French Institute expedition under Bernard Bruyère (1879–1971) excavated both the tomb-workmen's settlement at Deir el-Medina and their adjoining cemetery, including a number of intact sepulchres.

The Metropolitan had also held a concession at Lisht since 1906, and their efforts there provided important data on the royal cemeteries of the early Middle Kingdom;

unfortunately, like most of the museum's work, relatively little was published at the time apart from high-quality preliminary reports in the institution's *Bulletin*. The need to work up the surviving archival records for the definitive publication of the pyramid of Senwosret I led to renewed excavations in 1984–87 – nearly 50 years after the previous season had ended.

The Early Dynastic Period once again came under the spotlight when in 1935 Bryan Emery (1903–71) took over Quibell's old site north of the Teti pyramid at Saqqara, finding the first of a series of large 1st Dynasty mastaba tombs. The area south of the Step Pyramid also produced Early Dynastic material, when another 2nd Dynasty royal tomb, that of Ninetjer, was found by the Antiquities Service in 1937–38; a German team has resumed work on this tomb in recent years. Alongside Old Kingdom tombs that included those of the wives of Unas was the intact Late Period shaft tomb of Amentefnakhte, found by Zaki Saad (1901–82) in 1939. The English archaeologist Cecil Firth (1878–1931) had previously found another intact example adjacent to the pyramid of Userkaf in 1929.

Saad was also responsible for the excavation of the Early Dynastic cemetery at Helwan, opposite Saqqara, where some of the earliest-known stone-built tombs were found. New excavations at the site were begun by Christiana Köhler at the beginning of the 21st century. Those buried at Helwan ranged from the middle classes to minor royalty, making the site one of very considerable importance for the study of this early period.

The southern part of the Saqqara cemetery was the subject of investigations by Gustave Jéquier (1868–1946) between 1924 and 1936, during which time he cleared the Mastabat Faraoun, two 13th Dynasty pyramids and the complex of Pepy II, together with its associated cemeteries.[69]

Alongside work on such glamorous 'national' cemeteries, the necropoleis of lesser individuals in Middle Egypt were investigated by Guy Brunton (1878–1948) at Mostagedda and Matmar during 1928 to 1931.[70] Amongst his discoveries was an untouched Third Intermediate Period lower-class cemetery at Matmar.

Most known Egyptian tombs lie in the Nile Valley; necropoleis were certainly present in the heavily populated Delta, but the high water table and the activities of the *sebakheen* who quarry the mud-brick of ancient sites for fertilizer have meant that relatively little is known of many

places. However, at Bubastis, the tomb of the Viceroy of Kush, Hori iii, was found accidentally in August 1925 by railway workmen.[71] Then, in April 1944, Labib Habachi (1906–84) discovered the family tomb of Hori's like-named father (p. 268).

Tanis (San el-Hagar) has been worked by a French team since 1929 and in 1939 Pierre Montet (1885–1966) discovered what turned out to be the partly intact royal necropolis of the 21st/22nd Dynasties.[72] Unfortunately, assessment of these tombs is marred by a robbery of the expedition storerooms in 1943 and inexplicable contradictions between various written accounts of the work by Montet and his colleagues.

During 1939–45, archaeological work was unavoidably cut back, while reduced supervision and the presence of large numbers of servicemen led to severe damage to a number of monuments, particularly tombs at Thebes. Other monuments were pressed into use for the war effort, a radar aerial being placed on the summit of the Great Pyramid at Giza. Nevertheless, the Antiquities Service made some

71 Pierre Montet descends into one of the royal tombs at Tanis, explored in 1939–40.

important sepulchral finds, including the necropolis of the Third Intermediate Period High Priests of Ptah at Memphis, found by Ahmad Badawi (1905–80). A few kilometres to the west, Abdelsalam Hussein (d. 1949) excavated the valley building of Unas, part of which had later been turned into the burial chamber of the late Old Kingdom Prince Ptahshepses.[73] Hussein had begun excavating the eastern part of the Unas complex in 1940 and in following the line of its causeway had come across a number of Old Kingdom tombs. He also excavated the pyramid of Isesi, some way to the south, in 1945, in conjunction with Alexandre Varille (1909–51).

A NEW EGYPT

After the Second World War the progressive replacement of European museum and Service officials by Egyptians, begun in the 1920s, was completed. The Director General, Étienne Drioton (1889–1961), the last foreigner, was replaced in the wake of the 1952 revolution, first on a temporary basis by Abbas Bayoumi (1904–83), Director of the Egyptian Museum, and then by Mustafa Amer (1896–1973). At the same time, new regulations came into force that stipulated that all excavations had to be on behalf of governments, universities or learned societies and must be under the ultimate control of the Antiquities Service, with whom copies of all excavation records had to be lodged.[74]

During the preceding years, Antiquities Service staff had made a number of significant finds. The 26th Dynasty tomb of Queen Takhuit was excavated by Shehata Adam (1917–86) at Athribis in 1950, with a major study of the pyramids initiated in 1947. The latter, the 'Pyramids Study Project', fully cleared the Bent Pyramid complex at Dahshur between 1946 and 1955, firstly under the direction of Abdelsalam Hussein and then after his premature death by Ahmed Fakhry (1905–73). The best-known Egyptian discovery in this period, however, was the unfinished pyramid of Sekhemkhet, located at Saqqara by Zakaria Goneim (1911–59) in 1952. After the latter's death, work in the enclosure was continued by Jean-Philippe Lauer (1902–2001), who had been working on the Step Pyramid complex since 1926 – and was still engaged there as the 21st century began.

Yet another royal discovery was made in 1956 when Nagib Farag and Zaki Iskander (1916–79) opened the intact burial chamber of the 12th Dynasty princess Neferuptah at

Hawara. The years immediately following were, however, relatively uneventful, French and British work (including Emery's continuing efforts at Saqqara) being halted in the wake of the Anglo-French attack on the Suez Canal in 1956, and attention then shifted to rescuing the monuments of Nubia threatened by the building of the High Dam at Aswan.

The drawing to a close of this Nubian campaign in 1964 was followed by an unprecedented upsurge in archaeological work in Egypt, by teams from across the world as well as Egypt. Emery once again resumed his Saqqara excavations, adding Late Period sacred animal catacombs to the mass of Early Dynastic and 3rd Dynasty tombs already found. More recently, Paul Nicholson has returned to the catacombs, mapping further stretches of these incredibly elaborate underground galleries, packed with millions of mummified birds and mammals.[75]

In the 1970s, long-term programmes of excavation were underway at Abu Sir (Charles University, Prague) and in the New Kingdom necropolis at Saqqara (National Museum of Antiquities, Leiden/Egypt Exploration Society [later replaced by Leiden University]). The latter revealed the long-lost tombs of such important late 18th Dynasty individuals as Horemheb (later king – found in 1975) and the Treasurer Maya (1987), both of which had been seen in the 19th century and from which material had been removed, but which had subsequently been lost from view.[76]

The Czech excavations have produced a range of tombs and pyramids that have been crucial to the study of the funerary monuments of the 5th and 6th Dynasties, together with a Late Period necropolis of great shaft tombs, including the sepulchre of Iufaa, found intact in 1995.[77] The area linking Saqqara to Abu Sir has also been surveyed by the Czechs as well as by Ian Mathieson and has revealed tombs not only of the Old Kingdom and Late Period in this area, but also an unexpected cluster of Early Dynastic burials.

The Unas causeway area was once again investigated from 1965, when Mounir Basta and Ahmed Moussa located a number of tombs, including that of the manicurists Khnumhotep and Niankhkhnum and the singer Nefer, the latter containing one of the oldest known mummies still intact. Work carried out by a Polish mission, headed by Karol Myśliwiec, to the west of Djoser's pyramid has revealed a large cemetery of late Old Kingdom tombs.

Further south at Saqqara, in 1965 French teams began the re-investigation of the late Old Kingdom pyramids that had hardly been touched since their opening over 80 years before. This work has continued to the present day, uncovering and reconstructing the very badly damaged monuments. The pyramid of Pepy I has been most completely investigated, including the adjacent smaller pyramids of his queens.[78]

Another French expedition, under Alain Zivie, began work in 1987 on the escarpment to the southeast of the pyramid of Teti, where tombs had long been known, but never investigated. One belonged to the Vizier Aperel, the burial chamber of which proved to be only partly plundered.

A whole series of other tombs of the late 18th/19th Dynasty have also been revealed, including that of the Lady Maya, the wet-nurse of Tutankhamun.

Following the completion of Fakhry's work at Dahshur and the discovery there of the pyramid of Ameny-Qemau by Charles Muses (1919–2000) in 1957,[79] much of the site came under military control, the only substantive work being Dieter Arnold's definitive examination of the pyramid of Amenemhat III from the 1970s onwards and Rainer Stadelmann's work at the Red Pyramid of Seneferu. Since then, however, much of the area has been opened up. Nicole Alexanian has worked on the Old Kingdom private tombs,[80] and a Japanese team discovered a hitherto-unsuspected New

72 Czech archaeologists opening the sarcophagus of Iufaa at Abu Sir in 1997.

Kingdom necropolis at the northern end of the site in 1999. In addition, re-excavation of the pyramid complex of Senwosret III by Arnold, on behalf of the Metropolitan Museum of Art, has resulted in important reassessments of the monument and the discovery of the intact tomb of the Lady Sitweret.[81]

In Middle Egypt, Australian work under the leadership of Naguib Kanawati at El-Hagarsa produced two intact First Intermediate Period family tombs in 1989, along with other sepulchres of this time and the Middle Kingdom. Another Antipodean team, under Boyo Ockinga, documented near Sohag in 1988–91 the important but long-ignored tomb of Sennedjem, an official of Tutankhamun. At Oxyrhynchus (El-Bahnasa) a Spanish team has found a Third Intermediate Period cemetery, including several high-status interments.

Since the clearance of Tutankhamun's tomb, the Valley of the Kings had seen very little archaeological activity. The 1970s, however, saw work resuming there, not in the hope of finding new tombs, but with the aim of properly clearing and recording those long known. Thus, John Romer cleared the tomb of Ramesses XI in 1979; Otto Schaden cleared the tomb of Ay and adjacent monuments in the 1970s and has been working in the tomb of Amenmesse (KV10) since 1992. Hartwig Altenmüller has undertaken similar work in the tomb of the Chancellor Bay (KV13) and a Swiss team led by Hanna Jenni cleared the tomb of Ramesses X (KV18) in the late 1990s. In 1989, Don Ryan began the reinvestigation of a number of the smaller tombs first discovered by Belzoni, Carter and Edward Ayrton (1886–1914) many years previously, and belonging to especially favoured nobles and royal retainers.[81A] Most spectacularly, in 1987, Kent Weeks started the clearing and recording of KV5, the burial place of some of the sons of Ramesses II. Well over 130 chambers had been reached by 2005, making it the biggest and most singular tomb in Egypt. More importantly, Weeks' team has published a large-scale atlas with accurate plans of all the tombs in the Valley. Finally, the first full-scale excavations since the 1920s were begun in 1998 by Geoffrey Martin and Nicholas Reeves, removing the last areas of untouched ancient debris in the Valley, finding a number of Ramesside workmen's huts and revealing indications that further tombs might lie in this, the lowest part of the wadi.

A shaft tomb was found in this very place during the 2005–6 season by the University of Memphis, Tennessee,

73 Cleaning and conserving tombs is of paramount importance so that they can be accurately copied and preserved for posterity. Here, Lotfi Khaled works in KV5, the tomb for the sons of Ramesses II.

expedition led by Otto Schaden, who had now extended his work around the entrance of KV10. Lying some 15 metres from the tomb of Tutankhamun (5 metres from KV10), this proved to be a simple shaft tomb with a single chamber – intact! It contained seven wooden anthropoid coffins of a type apparently belonging to the latter decades of the 18th Dynasty together with 27 jars. It proved to be the burial place of large quantities of left-over material from the embalming process, plus other left-over elements from the outfitting of a tomb. It is as yet unclear from whose mummification the material derives, but the tomb (KV63) was probably originally made for a member of the nobility or royal household.[81B]

Other work in the 1990s identified the latest surviving royal tomb in Egypt. Over a century earlier, a large sarcophagus lying exposed in the ruins of Mendes was found to contain some bones and a shabti figure of the 29th Dynasty King Naefarud I. It was not until 1992–93, however, that excavations by Donald Redford uncovered the remains of the walls of the chamber that had once surrounded the sarcophagus, bearing the funerary texts of the king.

By a coincidence, only a few years earlier in 1988, Günter Dreyer had found at Abydos perhaps the earliest tomb of a named king, 'Scorpion'. Numbered U-j, it provided a rich harvest of material and stood at the heart of a large cemetery that forms the vital link between the funerary practices of Predynastic times and those of the historic era (see p. 134). Current work at Abydos under the direction of David O'Connor and Matthew Douglas Adams is yielding further information about the earliest royal burials.

At close to the opposite end of the social scale, however, is a group of tombs found by Zahi Hawass and Mark Lehner in the southeastern quadrant of the Giza necropolis in 1990, which proved to belong to the workers responsible for building the nearby pyramids (pp. 53–4, 154). These were accompanied by more elaborate sepulchres of the officials overseeing their work, and their nearby settlement. Taken together, the area has proved to be the source of much important data on the administration of a pyramid site and those employed there. Elsewhere at Giza, in 1998, Hawass managed to penetrate the lowest chamber of a tomb found by Selim Hassan during the 1930s. Formerly filled with water, it proved to be of a curious design that has been described as the 'Tomb of Osiris' (p. 291).

Hawass has also been responsible for the investigation of a series of tombs at Bahariya Oasis. Originally located in 1996, a huge complex of Roman Period communal burial places has been cleared since March 1999, the decoration of some of the bodies found leading to its being dubbed the 'Valley of the Golden Mummies'.[82] At another site in the oasis, Sheikh Sobi, Hawass had been re-excavating three 26th Dynasty tombs previously found by Fakhry in 1947 when, in October 1999, another was located. It proved to be that of the local governor, Djedkhonsiufankh, and during the excavations in April–May 2000 the intact sarcophagus of the tomb-owner was discovered and opened.[83] Other oases, such as Siwa, Dakhla and Kharga, have also yielded several significant cemeteries of the Graeco-Roman Period.

Excavations are not the only way in which new information concerning tombs has recently come to light. Lise Manniche has been engaged in the task of 'rediscovering' lost tombs by studying the numerous fragments of decoration of Theban tombs that have found their way into private and public collections. Some have been identified as parts of extant monuments, while others have been assigned to sepulchres now destroyed, allowing their schema of decoration belatedly to be studied.[84]

Also outside the Nile Valley proper, 100 km (60 miles) west of Alexandria, is Marina el-Alamein. The site has been excavated by a Polish team since 1987, uncovering a wide range of tombs dating to Greek and Roman times. Interest is currently growing in the funerary practices of the times of the Ptolemies and Roman emperors, contrasting with the situation in some past decades, when such 'late' levels were simply demolished on the way down to more 'ancient' remains. As part of this work, reassessments are being made of earlier discoveries and more is becoming known of the way in which earlier tombs were appropriated and new ones constructed, for these final examples of the age-old burial customs of Egypt.

Fieldwork continues apace in Egypt, as it has done for some two centuries, and the foregoing has been intended merely to give a flavour of some of the more significant discoveries and projects that have elucidated our knowledge of the development and meaning of the Egyptian tomb. While it is often implied that the great discoveries lie in the 'heroic' days of the past, it is important to recognize that large areas of Egypt are still essentially unknown archaeologically. Although most will have long since been plundered, basic structures frequently survive, while some of the discoveries described above show that major intact burials are still to be found in apparently well-known areas. The study of the Egyptian tomb is thus still far from complete, with many links in the chain of its evolution missing, or but weakly formed. The delineation of the whole picture can only come about with the steady accretion of data from the many teams, Egyptian and foreign, that are revealing more of the ancient cities of the dead.

Part II

Chapter 5 # The Decoration of the Tomb

ICONOGRAPHY

Egyptian tomb 'art' was not just for aesthetic pleasure; rather, like most Egyptian formal art, it served a specific purpose. Within the tomb its function was to create an ideal afterworld, delimited by *maat*, for the deceased to inhabit for eternity. The images found in tombs were fundamentally magical things, which, however, served the practical purpose of facilitating and guaranteeing the posthumous destiny of the deceased. This was done not only through explicit depictions of the underworld and religious texts, but even more through the depictions of offerings and their production of offerings and other 'daily life' activities. These images served as 'insurance' for the tomb-owner in case the family or mortuary priests ceased to carry on the cult, or if the burial were disturbed. If the images survived, then all the deceased's needs for the hereafter would still be magically within his or her grasp. As these images of life were projected for the afterlife, they did not always have to be a reflection of true reality, but rather, an ideal reality that fulfilled the tomb-owner's wishes for eternity.

The Egyptians believed that if things were represented, written and spoken out loud, they actually had been created and would be reified and exist in eternal worlds: those of the dead and of the gods. Thus the images on tomb walls were actually active participants in the deceased's afterlife. Indeed, the word for sculptor or carver, *s'ankh*, is translated from Egyptian as 'the one who makes (it) living'. To damage and destroy these images, or, more potently, the name of the deceased, would result in annihilation or an unsuccessful transition to the afterlife. Thus, by eradicating the name, titles, or image of someone would render them non-beings deprived of eternity. Examples of *damnatio memoriae* (e.g. KV10, TT39, TT42, TT48, TT71, WV23) in tombs are a powerful manifestation of this belief.

The images in tombs follow the basic canon of Egyptian art in order to convey meaning in a certain way and have a specific vocabulary that is suited to the function of these representations. Thus, as one might expect, the largest figure is that of the tomb-owner (or, in later periods, gods and kings), as he or she is the focus of the monument. Texts and activities focus on the tomb-owner and actions tend to move towards him, especially if he is facing out to receive the cult. The tomb-owner is always shown in a formal pose, standing or seated, with the head and legs in profile and a frontal torso. This is not always true for minor figures, which can be seen in more relaxed poses: three-quarters view, sleeping, fighting, etc. However, everyone was neatly organized into registers, separated by lines, so that it is obvious that *maat* is maintained in this world and the next.

74 (*opposite*) West wall of the burial chamber of the workman Sennedjem at Deir el-Medina (TT1: 19th Dynasty). The tomb-owner and his wife Iyneferti are shown adoring the gods of the underworld.

75 (*above*) Part of a fishing scene in the mastaba of Kagemeni at Saqqara (6th Dynasty).

76 (*above*) South wall of the offering-room of the mastaba of
Ptahhotep ii at Saqqara (D64: 5th Dynasty). Two figures of the
deceased observe activities on his estate, including harvesting of
papyrus; dancing; games; wine-making; hunting; fishing; rope-making;
drying fish; catching birds; and looking after livestock.

77 (*below*) Sunk relief figures of Mereruka flanking the entrance to
his tomb at Saqqara (6th Dynasty). Over the door is the imitation of
a roller-blind, bearing his name and titles.

'Reading' a monument is not easy for us, as Egyptian
iconography is extremely complex and difficult to
understand. Some of our interpretations will be (more or
less) accurate, while others may be very wide of the mark.
The experience of interpreting an ancient Egyptian
monument can be likened to visiting a medieval church, a
building not too far removed from modern experience.
Church decoration generally shows scenes from the Bible,
thus anyone who has read or heard the stories illustrated
would most probably understand the scenes, just as they
could identify some of the statues. Additionally, the images
are rife with iconographic allusions: lions represent St Mark,
eagles stand in for St John, fish are symbolic of Christ and
the persecuted Christians, and lambs and shepherds allude
to God, Christ and all Christians. However, if one is not
conversant with the Bible and its iconography, much of
what is shown will be meaningless, or could have a different
meaning brought to it, dependant on the viewer's cultural
background. Thus, one should bear in mind that when
looking at Egyptian tomb decoration, what you see is not
always just what you get.

The hieroglyphs and the images work together with the
architecture, displaying a message or series of messages that
would have been understood by the literate, as well as the

semi-literate or illiterate ancient viewer. Some, if not all, of the scenes on tomb walls are metaphors or allegories, or contain allusions to aspects of the afterworld. These are the most difficult to interpret for the modern visitor.

The main genre of scenes found in tomb-chapels is those that depict daily life; in the late New Kingdom these were joined and, to some extent, supplanted by scenes of divinities or vignettes from funerary texts. Unlike the latter, the daily-life scenes found in Egyptian tombs seem superficially to be divorced from the act of resurrection of the tomb-owner and could be thought merely to focus on the idea of the continuance of the best things in this life into the afterlife and the projection of the personality of the deceased (by showing his work and activities in this life) into the hereafter. However, it is quite possible that the images are not only a representation of an ideal life for eternity, but contain encoded messages and allusions to resurrection and spells associated with this crucial event.

One should be aware that ideas as well as icons changed over time. In some cases there is an accretion of religious imagery within one symbol, so that it has layers of meaning. In other instances, an icon can change its meaning and its message entirely over the course of time. For example, images of offering tables placed in front of the deceased and associated with the offering list are found throughout Egyptian history. In the Old and New Kingdoms one such image showed the table covered with tall loaves of bread. In the First Intermediate Period and Middle Kingdom, however, the 'loaves' retained their shape, but were sometimes painted green. Was this originally a misinterpretation by the artists who thought the bread was actually representing reeds, based on similarity in shape, or was this due to a change in religious beliefs when the deceased went to the green fields of Iaru? Some examples do clearly show reeds rather than bread, but it is unclear what the Egyptians intended in each case.

It has frequently been argued that Old Kingdom tomb scenes of 'daily life' are not showing metaphors related to the transformation and rebirth of the deceased, but rather, just an exaggeration of a perfect life, while the images dating to the New Kingdom are primarily metaphors. Perhaps there is some truth in this, but it is doubtful that we will ever be sure what the ancient Egyptians intended and thus our interpretations must remain in the realm of 'what is probable', but not necessarily 'true'.[85]

78 A key part of the decoration of a tomb-chapel was the owner's self-presentation to posterity. In particular any links with the pharaoh were emphasized; thus, Paheri, mayor of El-Kab, wished to highlight the fact that he was also a royal tutor. This image shows him with his charge, the prince Wadjmose, seated on his lap (EK3: 18th Dynasty).

One should also take into account that several elements might be involved in the choice of which scenes were selected for display and how they were chosen. One cannot underestimate factors such as wealth, convenience, a desire to 'keep up with the Joneses', as well as personal religious beliefs and tastes in determining the components of tomb decoration. It is quite possible for one image to represent a plethora of ideas, thoughts and emotions. Doubtless, tomb scenes were interpreted on different levels by different people: the more educated and literate a person, the more allusions could be derived from one image.[86]

Probably some elements of tomb decoration were fairly straightforward, especially those depicting the activities of the tomb-owner in life (particularly in the New Kingdom) so that his identity and personality would survive into the hereafter. The anonymous Overseer of Unguent Production's TT175 had scenes of unguent manufacture painted in his tomb, while Irukaptah-Khenu, the Master

Butcher, had a concentration of butchery scenes in his tomb at Saqqara and the Overseer of the Garden in the Ramesseum Nedgemger (TT138) showed the temple gardens. In some instances, the illustrations might serve a dual purpose: they might depict a job, but the job might also include activities that are generally part of the schema of decoration and have religious overtones. Thus, granary officials depicted activities associated with their jobs, including measuring the fields and calculating taxes, the agricultural cycle of harvesting the grain and processing it, its transportation and harvest festivals. The agricultural cycle, however, is also part of the general schema of decoration and is a way in which resurrection and rebirth can be maintained.

However, other images had additional interpretations. One should note that the Egyptians tended to avoid depictions of negative or harmful things in tombs, unless they had a standard cosmic role to play in the world of the dead and the divine. Indeed, in the late Old Kingdom and throughout the Middle Kingdom (and later), there are myriad examples of hieroglyphs being shown in a truncated state so that they could not harm the body of the deceased: birds are shown without legs, lions are featured only in half, serpents are severed in two and the use of inanimate hieroglyphs are favoured over the animate. Hippopotami, manifestations of Seth, were often depicted being hunted with harpoons; annoying insects, such as mosquitoes, which were rife in Egypt, never feature in Egyptian tombs. After all, why suffer such inconveniences in a perfect afterlife? Insects such as grasshoppers, dragonflies and butterflies, which were harmless or even positive for life are featured in tombs, but inconvenient creatures are never shown unless they are being hunted, killed or consumed.

Images that seem to depict daily-life activities can indeed be interpreted in other ways. The calf that is saved from being devoured by crocodiles in the water might be interpreted as a metaphor for saving the spirit from the perils of death, especially if taken in conjunction with texts found in the various funerary books. Images of viticulture can be interpreted simply as images showing wine-making, a product that was appreciated by all in this life and the next. However, they can also be seen as images associated with Osiris, who took the part of Lord of Drunkenness at the *Wag* Festival, a celebration attached to the grape harvest that came just before the inundation at the end of June. As such, the viticulture scenes have the added meaning of rebirth and

79 A young woman sniffing an open lotus in the 5th Dynasty tomb of Nefer, Saqqara. She is also holding a hoopoe, the significance of which is still not clear in ancient Egyptian iconography. It is frequently shown as a pet, as well as in the wild. Some scholars believe that the bird is not a hoopoe, but a lapwing, a symbol for the common people.

resurrection brought to the land by the inundation, as well as the resurrective qualities inherent in plant life that reappears annually after withering and dying.

Many images have been interpreted as having sexual and regenerative imagery inherent in them, especially in the New Kingdom. Metaphors for sexuality and fertility are indeed a celebration of life and point to a desire for its continuation in the hereafter. To some extent, the iconography of sexuality and fertility appears not only in the choice of imagery, but also in the accompanying hieroglyphic text. The Egyptians were inveterate punsters, and a language that was both phonal and visual gave them enormous scope for punning. Hence, the choice of hieroglyphic signs used in certain situations could be full of double entendres (e.g. p. 91). However, the context should also be taken into consideration, because at times a lotus is just a lotus, rather than an erotic symbol indicative of alluring perfume, although it is probably always a symbol of resurrection. Naturally, certain connotations and puns are lost to us due to our ignorance of the language and culture of ancient Egypt, as well as, in some instances, the cryptographic writing used by the Egyptians.

Allusions to sex and regeneration are particularly associated with New Kingdom tomb scenes, although also proposed for vignettes dating back as far as the Old Kingdom. Some scenes show the deceased and his wife seated side by side, or clasping one another around the shoulder, waist or leg. These images of closeness can be thought to represent intimacy and reproduction. Some scholars would even go so far as to say that they symbolize the actual act of love (e.g. TT96),[87] rather than public manifestations of affection. Images of beds, the tomb-owner and spouse sitting on beds, or the preparation of a bed by servants, have also been interpreted as suggesting the sexual act, as well as referring to Isis and Osiris who conceived Horus on a bed, albeit a funerary one.

This sexual undertone might be extended to images of head-rests, used as pillows in ancient Egypt. However, another equally or more feasible interpretation can be attached to them: several spells in the corpus of funerary literature refer to fears of heads falling off. An additional function of the head-rest amulet is to keep the head of the deceased in place, as to lose one's head meant to lose one's identity. Thus, these items might be of even more basic importance to the deceased than as images of fertility.

Other scholars associate anything to do with wigs and make-up as erotic, as donning these items is suggestive of preparation for mating.[88] Some researchers also believe that monkeys are suggestive of erotic or sexual events, perhaps due to the fact that monkeys are often seen mating in the wild.[89] The sun disk, an image of regeneration, can also be linked to the round mirrors depicted in tombs, which also

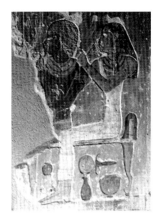

80 The mirror below the woman's chair is indicative of rebirth and resurrection, with the mirror's disk symbolizing the sun, and the handle a papyrus plant, symbolic of regeneration and creation; tomb of Reneni at El-Kab (EK7: 18th Dynasty).

symbolize the afterlife due to the fact that they reflect this life. Perhaps their circularity might also be likened to the rounded belly of a pregnant woman, the quintessential symbol of birth? The word for mirror, *ankh*, is the same as the word for life.

Colour symbolism must also have played a part in Egyptian art, as it did in medieval and Renaissance art and even, to some extent, continues to do in contemporary art. Thus, the yellow background colour used in the Ramesside period sets the activity in the divine realm as yellow or gold were indicative of the imperishable or divine, or perhaps of an existence blessed by the sun god. However, it is then slightly puzzling as to how the grey-blue background of some 18th Dynasty tombs is to be viewed: perhaps as the crepuscular moments prior to rebirth, or the blue that was linked to the skin of Amun and the entirety of Nut, goddess of the sky. Black and green symbolized fertility since they refer to the rich, black Nile silt and the green plants that it produced following the Inundation, itself regarded as metaphorically linked to the first act of creation. These two colours were particularly associated with Osiris. White indicated purity, joy and celebration, while red was symbolic of power, the desert, blood and, together with yellow, the sun. In fact, white and red were both associated with different aspects of the sun, one destructive, the other productive. No doubt, the idea that white was pure also led to bleached linen being used in mummification, as well as to the whitewashing of tombs and false-doors.[90]

Whether or not one can completely understand the colour symbolism or the iconography of Egyptian art, one can at least appreciate its beauty and the window it provides us into ancient Egyptian life.

THE LOCATION OF DECORATIVE COMPOSITIONS IN THE TOMB

No two tombs in Egypt are completely identical in their decoration; indeed, there is an almost infinite variety to be seen along the Nile Valley. However, there is generally a set of underlying patterns, subject to the exigencies of space, rock quality, wealth and time. A dynamic movement from the entrance inwards was always present: in the chapel towards the climax of the actual offering place – either a stela or a statue of the deceased – or the body itself where the substructure is concerned. The visitor was thus taken along a hypothetical east–west axis from the land of the living (outside and more secular) to the land of the dead (interior and more sacred). It is important to emphasize the nominal nature of many orientations, particularly where a rock-cut structure is concerned, with its reliance on local topographical and geological considerations. It should be noted that the Egyptians oriented themselves facing south, the source of the Nile; accordingly the left side tends to be associated with the east and the right with the west, although this is not always the case if practicalities contradict this alignment. In tombs, generally speaking, facing towards the Nile was regarded as being along an east–west axis, with the Nile providing the north–south axis.

81 Although there are no strict rules for the location of many scenes, this diagram shows some general guidelines for the placement of the decoration. 1 Image of tomb-owner; 2 images of the tomb-owner or statues of him/her in the thickness of doorway; 3 the tomb-owner fishing and fowling; 4 scenes of outdoor activities in non-domestic contexts; 5 & 6 crafts and outdoor activities in a domestic context (e.g. agriculture, etc), images of activities directly pertaining to the tomb-owner; 7 offerings; 8 cult focus (statue or false-door).

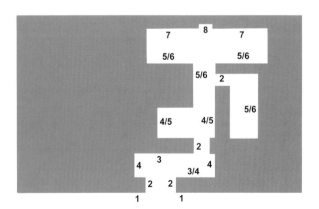

Clues as to which wall represented each cardinal direction can sometimes be found within the scenes; these are especially easy to read in royal tombs where the heraldic plants of Egypt, lotus for the south and papyrus for the north, immediately give guidelines as to the internal geography of the tomb. In private tombs this is also the case, albeit more subtly. Frequently northern walls, representing the north of the country, are adorned with marsh scenes, reflecting the environment of the Delta (e.g., the tombs at El-Hamamiya), while the eastern and western directions are provided through appropriate solar images.

Superstructures[91]

The decoration of the public part of the tomb was fundamentally concerned with its role as the interface between the world of the living and that of the dead, with the area near the cult focus being the most sacred, and the more exterior spaces being more secular. Ideally, the outermost doorway of a chapel would be adorned with the name and titles of the deceased, together with a basic offering formula (often the *hetep-di-nesu*), so that the tomb and its owner could immediately be identified and be made to live in the hereafter by any passer-by who could recognize and read the name. Indeed, a visible stela might contain the so-called 'Appeal to the Living', which explicitly asked anyone passing the tomb to recite the offering formula.

Images of the deceased always flank the entryway or appear on the jambs, greeting both visitors and the rising sun. This was a convention regardless of whether the tomb actually faced the sun or not. For tombs that were aligned differently due to practical constraints ideal directions were assumed and can be recognized by the symbols used to decorate the different walls (cf. p. 260). Following usual Egyptian artistic conventions, the tomb-owner is always the largest figure in a tomb, unless the king or a god is depicted. The latter two rarely, if ever, appear in private Egyptian tombs prior to the New Kingdom. The owner is generally shown as a young person in their virile prime, but is occasionally also shown as an older, more corpulent individual. In this case, plumpness is indicative of wealth and a successful middle age.

The minor figures on walls are oriented towards images of the tomb-owner or to the false-door. A sense of symmetry is always attempted by balancing large-scale figures and

82, 83 Mereruka as a young and vigorous man, wearing a short kilt and a long wig (*above left*) and as an old man (*above right*), whose body shows the rolls of fat indicative of prosperity (Saqqara: 6th Dynasty).

scenes on opposing walls. Sometimes there is a dialogue between walls and pillars that stand nearby, thus integrating the decoration. An example of this is found in the courtyard of the tomb of Harwa at Thebes (TT37, 25th Dynasty) where a fishing scene on the wall carries over to the pillar that faces it. For the most part, images of the tomb-owner face outwards, towards the entrance of the chapel, rather than in the direction of the false-door or chapel focus, as if waiting to receive visitors and offerings, both real and metaphysical. However, in some instances, particularly at doorways, the tomb-owner is shown going in on one side (generally the left or western side, depending on the tomb's orientation) and out the other, presumably as a reborn spirit. He might also be shown facing in when he is involved in the action.

Broadly speaking, the rooms closest to the exterior tend to be decorated with scenes showing outdoor activities that deal first with nature in its wild form and secondly with tamed nature, a world where *maat* reigns supreme. These are frequently followed by scenes associated with the deceased's

position, as well as scenes showing food production and the manufacture of goods.[92] These production scenes are to show the orderliness of the world, to provide for the hereafter and in some cases, are associated with the tomb-owner's job. As the visitor progresses inward to the cult centre of the tomb – manifested as a false-door or statue – the scenes become increasingly concerned with funeral rituals and the journey to and arrival in the afterlife. This is particularly apparent in the New Kingdom when such images were commonly expressed in an obvious way (e.g. Khaemhat's TT57). In earlier periods this is implied through the choice of motifs decorating those areas and their accompanying texts, namely an intensification in scenes of offerings and the **Voyage to Abydos** (**bold** type signifies that the motif is discussed in detail later in this chapter). Thus, as the scenes move from the exterior to the interior, they reflect a progression from secular to sacred. Within a tomb certain scenes, whenever possible, would be placed on appropriately oriented walls.[93] Thus, there was a preference for showing

84 The entry to the cult focus of the double tomb of Niankhkhnum and Khnumhotep, with the two owners flanking the doorway. A *hetep-di-nesu* offering formula is carved on the door's lintel, while the roll, indicative of a rolled up mat, is inscribed with their names. Family members, at a much smaller scale, stand in front of the dominant figures of the tomb-owners (Saqqara: 5th Dynasty).

two- and three-dimensional images of the deceased on the western side of a wall or on western walls in preference to the other locations in the tomb. Scenes of the **netherworld** and **funerary rituals** would also be placed on the west, with the east balancing the composition by showing scenes of life, or indeed, as it is sometimes difficult to differentiate, an ideal life in the afterlife. At Amarna, the flow of the decoration leads towards the east, where one finds an image of an Aten temple. The movement of traditional tombs, especially in the New Kingdom, not only affirmed the tomb as an eternal house for the soul, but also as the passageway leading to the door to the underworld. However, practical considerations

relating to the world-view also formed part of the basis for scene positioning. Scenes showing similar activities (e.g. **marsh scenes**, **agricultural scenes**) are grouped together, with scenes depicting resulting activities: beer and bread production, **boat-building**, etc.) flowing off from them.

The doorways within a tomb (as well as in temples) are particularly charged with religious significance. Passing through a doorway is a metaphor for change, transitions and moving between levels. This is particularly apparent in the New Kingdom royal burial chambers where architectural doorways tie in to the funerary texts and correlate passing through the physical door with going through the gates in the underworld in the company of the sun god on his nightly voyage to his resurrection the following day. Although Old Kingdom elite tomb-chapels were not adorned with the same texts as the New Kingdom royal sepulchres, the door jambs may show the censing of a statue of the deceased as it made its way to the burial chamber, or images of the deceased entering and leaving (on opposite jambs) the tomb. Perhaps his entry was in his earthly manifestation and his exit in his spirit guise. Thus, these were marked out as significant passageways in the voyage to the Fields of Iaru.

A nice conceit, found on the door jambs of Theban tombs where the deceased is pictured worshipping the sun, is that on the east the hieroglyphic inscriptions face towards the rising sun and to the west, the signs face towards the setting sun, into the tomb. These depictions do, however, vary over time. In 18th Dynasty tombs, from the reign of Hatshepsut (TT73) until that of Tutankhamun, scenes of the king enthroned flank the door from the transverse hall into the passage. It is almost as if the royal image acts as a divine guardian to the passage into the afterlife. In the Ramesside period private tombs show scenes of the deceased adoring different gods flanking the tomb entrance.

An 'Appeal to the Living' commonly appears in New Kingdom Theban tombs in the transverse hall, where even the most casual visitor can read it and thus benefit the tomb-owner's spirit. These texts, together with the traditional *hetep-di-nesu*, were the standard public offering texts that empowered the dead through the living.

Although the east–west orientation was an important axis for the lands of the living and dead, this was not always as significant throughout the Old Kingdom in the Memphite necropoleis. In mastabas of the 4th and early 5th Dynasties, the key portion was the left, or southeastern quadrant. This is clearly a carry-over from the earliest offering places of 1st Dynasty mastabas, which were placed in one of the southernmost niches of the eastern panelled façade (p. 136) and is also seen in the Step Pyramid complex where the only working entrance is in the southeast. The first proper mastaba chapels were also located in this position. The east is understandable as it is the direction of the rising sun. The south is less easily understood; perhaps it bears some relationship to the fact that the sun's arc moves southwards in its daily journey from east to west, or that the Nile flows from south to north.

Within the tomb, the scenes are arranged in a variety of ways in the registers. Certain scenes tend to appear together as they would occur in the same area in reality, such as brewing and baking and fish processing and fishing. Some scenes generally have a set position. For example, in the Old Kingdom, butchery scenes are always on the lowest register of the main offering or cult chamber. They might be very elaborate and continue up the wall, but their standard location is the bottom register. They appear in the cult centre as they not only show meat production for daily life, but also provide it for the continual celebration of the deceased's cult, as well as referring to the funerary feast. In the same way, pairs of scenes of the deceased fishing in the marshes and fowling in the same environment are shown on opposite walls, or symmetrically on one wall. They occupy an upper register – or take up the entire wall.

Scenes were often contained within a border, or topped by a frieze. The various types of friezes are discussed below.

Substructures

The rules for decoration in the burial chamber are different from those applicable to the public portions of the tomb and vary considerably through time. Indeed, the vast majority of substructures are undecorated, suggesting that the possession of a decorated burial chamber was of considerable social significance. The first regularized schemes appear during the latter part of the Old Kingdom, with the Pyramid Texts in royal tombs and offering lists and images of offerings in private ones. The decoration of royal substructures is much more complex than that of private individuals as the former tend to have more rooms, while the latter are generally limited to one chamber.

From the New Kingdom, vignettes and texts from the Book of the Dead appear in certain non-royal sepulchres, while royal tombs contain increasing numbers of the various Books of the Underworld that are first seen in the time of Thutmose III. Some typical distributions of these are set out on p. 262.

Extracts from the Books of the Underworld are later also found in private contexts, not only in their 'natural' habitat of the burial complex, but sometimes in the superstructure as well (see pp. 227–8, 255 and 284–5). In later times, eclectic mixes of all these sources were utilized, in particular in the massive tombs of the Saite Period.

It is beyond the scope of this book to include every scene type or vignette found in Egyptian tombs. Thus, a selection of the most common types found throughout Egyptian history is provided below, with interpretations of their iconographic meaning. There is some overlap in scene type. For example, scenes of agricultural activity that occur as part of the 'daily life' sequence should be separated from the scenes that are part of the 'autobiographical' section of the tomb. The location of these scenes is sometimes key in making this distinction. The scenes discussed below are arranged as they might be met with in the tomb-chapel: outdoor and wilderness activities followed by controlled nature or crafts and ending with purely funerary motifs.

The *hetep-di-nesu* formula[95] and 'Appeal to the Living'[96]

In many ways, the various vignettes in a tomb-chapel could be seen as a reinforcement of the magical *hetep-di-nesu* formula that underpinned the whole posthumous survival of the deceased. It could appear on almost any object from a tomb, but was particularly to be found on the false-door or at the entrance to the tomb. Its name derives from the first Egyptian words of the formula *hetep-di-nesu*, literally 'an

85 An unusual offering scene in the 12th Dynasty tomb of Senet / Inyotefiqer at Thebes (TT60), with a red-crowned mummy receiving offerings upon a papyrus boat.

offering that the King gives'. The exact meaning of this phrase is not wholly certain, but seems to be based on the concept that all offerings ultimately derived from the king.

The formula continues to state the god to whom the offering is directed and then states that the god passes on a list of foodstuffs to the *ka* of the deceased. A representative early example is given on p. 22 (ill. 16), and is based on the concept that the king would give an offering to a god, and that this offering would then be passed on in some way to the deceased. By this a set of broadly standard 'staples' – bread, beer, beef, poultry, alabaster jars of ointment and clothing – would miraculously be provided for the dead person.

The precise formulation and length of the formula varies with time, beginning in the Old Kingdom, while the god invoked can depend on the site from which the text comes – for example, texts from Abydos usually call upon Osiris. The inclusion of different divinities is more common after the 4th Dynasty.

The formula is linked with the 'Appeal to the Living', whereby a visitor to the tomb is confronted by a text along the following lines:

> O any person who shall pass this monument in going downstream or upstream: as you love your king, as you praise your city-gods, as your children remain in your place, as you love life and ignore death, you shall say: 'A thousand of bread and beer, beef and fowl, all things good and pure on which a god lives, to the *ka* of the revered N, true of voice.'

Hunting

Hunting scenes of various sorts appear throughout the history of Egyptian tomb decoration. The earliest comes from the Naqada II-period Tomb 100 at Hierakonpolis, which shows men hunting animals with weapons as well as trapping them. Conflict between man and nature, with man triumphing over the wild and chaotic aspects of nature, are an integral part of the Egyptian belief system. The maintenance of *maat* and balance represented by the victory of the ordered world over the chaos of the wild is the responsibility of the tomb-owner if a continued existence is to be expected. There are a variety of hunting scenes: hunting hippopotami in the marshes; hunting in the desert; hunting birds and spearing fish. Minor variations

86 A hippopotamus hunt in the Saqqara tomb of Ti, showing men in skiffs spearing the snarling animals that are symbolic of chaos and Seth (5th Dynasty).

occur in these scenes throughout the course of Egyptian history (see below).

Hunting Hippopotami in the Marshes

Scenes of the hippopotamus hunt appear in the Early Dynastic Period and continue thereafter. It has been suggested that in the earliest periods, this scene represented a rite expressing the victory of the uniting dynasty over the conquered people of the Delta and was associated with kingship. It certainly features in Old Kingdom royal mortuary temples, such as that of Pepy II at South Saqqara. The male hippopotamus is a symbol for the negative and destructive aspects of the god Seth and thus hunting the animal became a symbol of Horus' triumph over Seth and the establishment and maintenance of *maat*. The meaning of this scene changed after the Old Kingdom and it became transformed into a symbol for the protection of the sun god and his rebirth and, by extension, the rebirth of the deceased,[97] with the green papyrus alluding to Osiris, as well as Horus' emergence from his hiding place in the Delta, prior to engaging Seth in combat.

The hippo-hunting scene was very popular in the Old and, to some extent, Middle Kingdoms, but was rarer in New Kingdom and later representations, when it is featured in temples as the triumph of Horus over Seth.[98] Generally, in Old Kingdom private tombs, a group of men harpoon the animal, while in Old Kingdom royal contexts this is the prerogative of the king who single-handedly harpoons the snarling beast. Very few examples come from the Middle Kingdom, though at Beni Hasan (BH-III) and Meir the scene is combined with the fish-spearing scene, with the fish being speared and the hippopotamus appearing before the boat, in the same pose as is found in Old Kingdom royal contexts. Despite the absence of an active spearing of the animal, the hieroglyphic legend refers to throwing the harpoon on the day of 'harpooning the hippopotamus', presumably a religious festival. In the New Kingdom the scene only occurs sporadically in tombs dated to the reigns of Thutmose III and Amenhotep II, primarily TT39, 82, 53, 125 and 164. At this time, however, the tomb-owner actively participates in the hunt, rather than watching the outcome. Small vignettes of a more general nature also form part of these scenes: crocodiles and hippos struggle with one another (perhaps in this context the crocodile is an image of the sun god engaged in battle with the dark Sethian forces

represented by the hippopotamus?) and crocodiles wait to devour the hippos' young (or possibly the afterbirth) after the animal is born.

Hunting in the Desert

Although representations of hunting in the desert appear in tombs throughout Egyptian history, the types of hunting and the involvement of the tomb-owner differs significantly through different periods. This provides information concerning the dating of tombs and is indicative of changes in religious and cultural attitudes during the course of Egyptian history. However, the main symbolism of the scene throughout Egyptian history is the triumph of order over disorder, the establishment of *maat* over chaos. The red desert was the land of Seth and its denizens belonged to him. Thus, capturing the people or denizens of Seth's realm embodied Horus' triumph over chaos and Seth himself.

Additionally, the scenes included vignettes of wild animals in their natural habitats, which emphasized the continuity of the natural cycle, fertility and the importance of the sun in its continuum. This promised an eternal resurrection for the deceased, just as the sun was continually reborn and provided life and sustenance for nature. Delightful vignettes highlight the Egyptians' intimate knowledge of the animal world and provide a picture of the different animal species found in Egypt. It has been suggested that as time progressed, some of these animals became rarer, but, due to the convention of the hunt scene, they continued to be shown.

In the Old Kingdom the tomb-owner is never shown taking an active part in the hunt; he merely observes the results as they are brought to him. The actual hunting (or collecting of animals) is carried out by minions who use lassos and hunting dogs. A possible exception is the damaged scene of Akhmerutnesut (G2184) at Giza, where the deceased is hunting with a lasso. In Old Kingdom royal contexts the king displays his physical prowess by being the hunter; this motif of the king as a hunter, subduing and taming nature (and the metaphoric enemies of Egypt that inhabited the desert margins, just as the animals did) continues throughout Egyptian history. In Middle and New Kingdom versions, the tomb-owner takes on the role of the king and becomes actively involved in the hunting, thus embodying the forces of *maat*.

87 (*above*) By the New Kingdom the tomb-owner (here Userhat, in TT56) was shown hunting from a chariot with a bow and arrow; this emulated royal activities, and this scene is most commonly found in tombs dating to the reigns of Thutmose III and Amenhotep II.

88 (*below*) A hunt in a fenced area. Hunters, equipped with bows, as is the tomb-owner, take aim at antelopes and gazelles in the tomb of Senbi at Meir (B1).

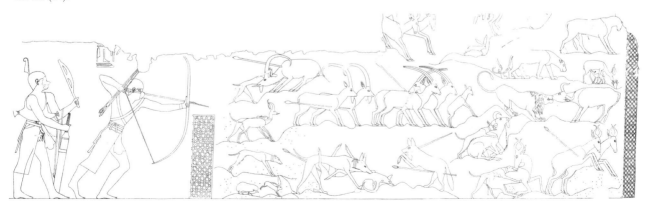

The hunt, especially in the Old Kingdom, served not just to kill animals, but also to trap them for later consumption or use. This can be seen as a metaphor for capturing captives and bringing them back to Egypt for exploitation. The animals would have been fattened up and consumed (see below).

Fishing and Fowling in the Marshes by the Tomb-Owner

The scene of the tomb-owner engaged in fishing and fowling in the marshes appears throughout Egyptian history, starting in the 4th Dynasty and continuing into the Graeco-Roman Period, with occasional hiatuses. These activities extend the control of *maat* over water, land and air, as well as hinting at eternal regeneration, as these were activities in which Osiris engaged when he became overlord of the underworld and had the use of his senses and limbs restored to him (see Coffin Texts 429, 473 and especially 475). These scenes are symmetrical and are generally shown together on one wall, or balanced on facing walls. From the mid-5th Dynasty onwards, they sometimes appear in the exterior portico of the entrance. Fowling scenes show the tomb-owner on a papyrus skiff in the marshes, hurling throwsticks at birds, once again establishing *maat* over the disorder of nature. These scenes, set in the verdant papyrus swamps where Horus was raised, also convey the idea of regeneration. The papyrus and lotus plants also emphasize this association (see below). This is further stressed by the fact that the throwsticks are also a visual pun: in Egyptian, 'to throw' such a stick is *qema*, which recalls a word with a similar sound meaning to 'create' or 'beget'.[99] Actual throwsticks have been found in tombs: Tutankhamun had several. Ducks and geese that sometimes appear balanced on the prow of the boat (most common in the 18th Dynasty) have variously been interpreted as hunting-decoys, or symbols of the god Amun, alluding to eroticism and fertility.

The fish-spearing scene shows the tomb-owner in a papyrus skiff with water conveniently rising up so that he does not have to bend down and can balance the fowling composition. Although a plethora of fish are shown in the water, the scene proper focuses on two fish: *Tilapia* and *Lates*. *Tilapia*, or *bulti*, are mouth-brooders.: they keep the eggs, and later their young, in their mouths for safety. Once

89 From the Old Kingdom onwards parallel scenes of the tomb-owner fishing and fowling are found in tombs. These indicate the acquisition of eternal life and the establishment of order over the chaotic natural world; tomb of Sabni at Qubbet el-Hawa (QH26: 6th Dynasty).

hatched, the young do swim in the water, but they retreat to their mother's mouth at the first sign of danger. Once the danger is past, the young fish emerge almost magically from the mouth of the mother. This habit fits in very well with the ancient Egyptian idea of the sun being swallowed and being reborn on a daily basis.[100] *Tilapia* are supposed to protect and accompany the sun god on his daily voyage and are mentioned in Spell 15 of the Book of the Dead; their presence summons up the image of the rebirth of the deceased. The Egyptian word for this fish, *in*, relates to a word for offerings, *inw. Lates nilotica*, or Nile Perch, is the other fish that shares the harpoon in fishing scenes. These fish can grow to huge sizes, often well over a metre (3 feet) in length and are noted for being fierce fighters. There is also a further pun found in the word for spearing fish, *seti*. This is a homonym for 'to impregnate',[101] and once again conjures up images of fertility and rebirth in the most literal sense, while alluding to the birth of Horus.

Fishing and Fowling

People other than the tomb-owner are also shown catching fish and birds in different ways (traps, nets) in the course of food acquisition, or for pleasure. These scenes continue to adorn chapel walls until the 19th Dynasty and then again, although less intensively, from the end of the 25th Dynasty onwards. Birds are captured using clap nets and traps and killed with sling-shots. Throw sticks, with their ritual connotation, are used only by the tomb-owner. Fish are caught in nets that are either dragged between two boats (a process that is still used very commonly on the Nile in Sudan), by linen nets laid down in the river, by cunningly constructed fish traps made of reeds and through angling. Spearing of fish is restricted to the tomb-owner. Vignettes of mending nets are also a part of this scene type.

These scenes not only serve to procure food for the tomb-owner in the afterworld, but also serve to show the cycle of life and the maintenance of *maat* by the Egyptians. The trapping of birds and fish can be seen as the equivalent of trapping enemies and is also found in temples (e.g. Edfu). The fish were generally immediately processed for consumption or storage (see below), while the fowl were frequently kept in pen or poultry yards for fattening up and breeding. Images of poultry yards date from the 5th Dynasty onwards, though scenes of poultry-rearing in yards occur rarely after the end of the Old Kingdom; a very few

examples are documented in Middle and New Kingdom tomb-chapels. In the case of the latter, the scenes are generally related to the position of the tomb-owner.

Food Production and Preparation[102]

Scenes of food production and preparation continued to be included in tombs, with the odd gap, throughout Egyptian history. Food was of fundamental importance as it provided sustenance for the deceased and also reflected wealth and prosperity. The food in a tomb was especially potent as it, like the tomb-owner, was metamorphosed into an eternal verity. All manner of food was shown being acquired, grown, prepared and served: bread, beer, wine, meat, fish, poultry and fresh fruits and vegetables.

Agriculture

Entire agricultural scenes or portions of them appear in Egyptian tombs from the 4th Dynasty onwards, with a concentration in 5th and 6th Dynasties and again in the 12th and 18th. The scenes can have slightly different meanings in different contexts: if they relate to the deceased's work, as seen in his titles, they may be at least partly autobiographical in their connotation; otherwise, they are purely intended to sustain the deceased in the afterlife and to underline the rebirth motif inherent in the plant world. For example, Khaemhat (TT57), an Overseer of the Granaries, has two scenes of agricultural activities in his tomb, which reinforce his identity for eternity.

Agricultural scenes can be broken into smaller groups: the growing, harvesting and processing of grain, flax, fruit and vegetables and viticulture. Either entire cycles (sowing through harvesting) or portions of cycles (perhaps with the parts representing the whole) are depicted on tomb walls (pl. V). The process of grain cultivation in all its stages – hoeing (5th Dynasty onwards), ploughing, sowing, harvesting, processing the harvest (threshing and winnowing) and its transport to the granary – is one of the most popular cycles and appears even during time periods when there are few daily life scenes in tombs. The rendering of the accounts also makes up part of the final stages of this scene-type. Sowing vignettes are of particular interest because pigs (e.g. tomb of Paheri [EK3] and Nebamun [TT24]) as well as ovicaprids (sheep and goats) were used for this activity. Magically, these representations would constantly provide sustenance for the

90 Scene showing the use of a *shaduf* for lifting water, in the tomb of Ipuy (TT217: 19th Dynasty).

tomb-owner, as well as symbolizing the cycle of birth, death and rebirth that the tomb-owner hoped to go through in order to achieve an eternal existence. The vignette of Spell 110 of the Book of the Dead, found (e.g.) in the burial chamber of TT1 invokes this agricultural existence, with the dead person carrying out the cycle.

Gardens and Plants

By their very nature, plants were associated with rebirth and resurrection. Two types of gardens are shown in Egyptian tombs, vegetable gardens and gardens of leisure. Vegetable gardens show the cultivation of food plants, such as onions

and lettuce. The scenes depict plots of land divided into small squares, each containing a plant, that were easy to irrigate. Men bring water in jars from a nearby pool and pour it into the small divisions. In some examples, mainly from the New Kingdom, a *shaduf* or water-lifting device is pictured. Temple gardens are sometimes shown in Egyptian tombs of the New Kingdom, but these only appear in chapels belonging to people whose work was associated with these areas and are primarily found in the Theban necropolis.

Images of vegetable gardens appear throughout Egyptian history. The most commonly shown plant is the Egyptian lettuce, akin to a cos lettuce. This plant is sacred to the ithyphallic fertility god, Min. It is associated with him as it grows straight and tall and when harvested, exudes a pale milky sap. It is clearly a symbol of fertility and rebirth, in addition to providing food for the deceased.

Onions, a mainstay of the diet, were associated with death as well: bulbs from small onions were placed under the eyelids of Ramesside mummies in order to give the impression that their eyes were still present. Onions were also associated with the afterlife, perhaps because of their many layers which suggest the wrapping of a mummy, as well as the idea of different worlds being hidden, one inside the other. Occasionally a canopy of vines was shown covering the vegetable gardens and providing shade; use of this image starts in the Middle Kingdom.

91 Garden and pool as depicted in the tomb of Nebamun (TTE2, BM EA37983: 18th Dynasty).

Pleasure gardens, attached to houses, were slightly different in character. They appear primarily in New Kingdom tomb-chapels and contain ponds and loggias as well as flowers and trees. The flora and fauna found in these images clearly have symbolic meaning in addition to their obvious identities.[103] Flowers were also produced on a large scale, in a similar environment to that of vegetables, for use in bouquets and garlands. Certain flowers had a funerary symbolism, especially the lotus. The blue lotus lies under the water until the sun rises. As the sun climbs higher in the sky, the lotus rises up on its stem away from the water and opens up. As the sun starts upon its descent in the later afternoon, the lotus closes its petals and slowly sinks back into the water to be reborn at the next sunrise. It is no wonder that there was an Egyptian myth relating that the sun god was born out of a lotus flower. Lotuses are also supposed to possess mild hallucinogenic qualities, especially when they are mixed with wine.[104] This no doubt contributed to the idea of a change in the state of consciousness that was achieved by the deceased as he transitioned from this life to the next. There is even a spell in the Book of the Dead (Spell 81A) to transform oneself into a lotus. Poppies, cornflowers and mandrakes were also associated with both life and death and appear in funerary as well as daily-life contexts.

Palm trees were associated with Re and Min, the bifurcated dom-palm with Thoth, tamarisks with Osiris and the sycamore fig with Hathor. A particular tree, known in ancient Egyptian as the *ished*-tree, is also pictured in tombs. The gods wrote the deceased's name on its leaves in order to ensure his or her eternal life. Traditionally this image was used in a royal context in temples, though by the 19th Dynasty it also appears in private tombs (e.g. TT1). Trees also alluded to the sacred groves associated with ancient funerary rituals, as well as to the tomb of Osiris, which was supposed to be marked by a grove. Perhaps this is why groves were planted around the royal mortuary temples of the New Kingdom.

The earliest depiction of a pond actually appears in the context of a poultry yard in an Old Kingdom tomb. However, that is an exception as ponds are more usually a feature of 18th Dynasty and later tombs. The majority of ponds shown in gardens are rectangular, but many also take a 'T' shape, reminiscent of the shape of the New Kingdom rock-cut Theban tomb-chapels. Perhaps this shape had a special significance, incorporating the Nile and its Delta?

Orchards and Fruit Picking

Scenes of fruit picking occur most commonly in the Old Kingdom at Saqqara, but are also known from Middle Kingdom chapels at Beni Hasan, where baboons are showing assisting in the harvest. Figs are most commonly shown being harvested; sycamore figs were attached to Hathor in her guise of Lady of the Sycamores, who in New Kingdom tombs is pictured holding out a tray of offerings to the deceased. Sycamore figs are unusual as the fruit has to have a cut administered to it while it is still on the tree so that it ripens and does not fall prey to wasps; only then does it grow to its full extent and can be harvested for consumption. When cut, the tree, as well as the fruits, give off a milky liquid, which is associated with the divine milk of the goddess. Consuming the goddess' milk, or the tree's fruit, helps bring about a state of divinity that becomes permanent in the afterlife. Some vignettes show a mother and child under a tree, sitting before a basket of figs, with some images showing the child suckling. The figs might allude to the Lady of the Sycamores who provides sustenance to the re-born deceased, just as a mother feeds her newborn child. Scenes of orchards often include vignettes of scaring birds (also found in grain-growing scenes). Other identifiable fruit trees pictured are date and dom palms.

Papyrus Harvest

Harvesting papyrus is a part of the sequence of marsh scenes that include fishing and fowling. Papyrus gatherers first appear in the 4th Dynasty and continue until the New Kingdom. Papyrus-harvesting scenes show the workers at the edge of a papyrus thicket pulling or cutting out long stems of papyrus, which are bound into bundles and then carried on their backs. The papyrus is transformed into paper, baskets, boats (pl. VII), ropes, mats and other woven objects. Portions of the papyrus can also be eaten. Many of the people shown who are involved with these marsh activities have receding hairlines; this might be to show age, or, more likely is a side effect of bilharzia or schistosomiasis, a parasitic disease caught from water snails that results in distended bellies, enlarged genitalia, hair loss, discharge of blood in the urine and, eventually, death. Fishermen, papyrus workers and some agricultural workers who spent time in slow-moving water would all have been prey to this disease and are therefore pictured showing some of its effects.

Bread and Beer Production

Scenes of brewing and baking are frequently linked in both two- and three-dimensional art as they share similar needs – the most important and basic one being yeast. The elements found in these scenes include granaries, grinding of grain, kneading of dough, filtering of beer, heating pots and baking. Brewing first appears in the 4th Dynasty tomb of Meresankh III (G7530+7540) and is quickly picked up by subsequent tomb-owners for inclusion in their chapels. The scenes tend to occur in the intermediate part of the tomb-chapel, away from scenes of untamed nature and closer to agricultural scenes or offering and banquet scenes. This division is logical as it is the raw material of the agricultural scenes that is used to produce the bread and the beer, which

92 (*left*) A man involved with papyrus harvesting. He is shown with the receding hairline and enlarged genitalia that are the typical symptoms of bilharzia and often found amongst people who spent a great deal of time in still water where the parasite and its snail-host are found (Saqqara, tomb of Nefer: 5th Dynasty).

93 (*below*) Bread-making in the tomb of Niankhkhnum and Khnumhotep at Saqqara (late 5th Dynasty).

are both consumed at feasts and by the tomb-owner throughout eternity. In fact, beer and bread were the cornerstones of the Egyptian diet as well as the economy – significant amounts of pay were measured in these commodities.

Butchery and Meat Processing[105]

Scenes of butchery were commonly shown in Egyptian tombs. At their most elaborate, the scenes show the bringing down of the animal, sometimes using a lasso, trussing it, slitting its throat and then jointing it, with the choice pieces being offered to the deceased. Their preferred location was the west wall, especially in the Old Kingdom, although they do sometimes stray. These scenes generally occupied the lowest registers of a wall, although in some instances they continued upward. They also appear in the thickness of the doors at entrances and in the most active cult areas in the tomb. Butchery was regarded as highly religious, especially in the Old Kingdom, as it related to the funerary ritual; perhaps depicting the funerary feast that was celebrated at the tomb in association with the Opening-of-the-Mouth ceremony, when the mummy was revivified. It also ensured a constant supply of meat in the afterlife, as well as illustrating the triumph of order over chaos, where the domesticated (and in several instances, wild) animal was subjected/tamed to man's will and *maat*. The importance and meaning of this sequence of scenes changed over the course of Egyptian

94 An ox being slaughtered; from the tomb of Iti at Gebelein (Turin Suppl. 14354h: First Intermediate Period).

history. The Opening-of-the-Mouth ritual was more often explicitly shown in the New Kingdom, while in the Old and Middle Kingdoms it was implicit in the amount of offerings being produced and offered in the main cult chambers.

Further scenes cover the processing of the butchered meat. This consists of either preserving the meat or cooking it. Butchers' shops and kitchens frequently figure in these images. Scenes show that after butchery, joints and pieces of meat were disposed of in a variety of ways: salted and dried, cooked with fat and salt for storage, cooked in a stew, or grilled over the fire. These magically provided sustenance for the deceased for specific funerary and religious rituals, as well as for eternity.

Poultry

Poultry processing is often shown with fish processing, especially in the New Kingdom. In Old Kingdom tombs this vignette frequently appears in conjunction with clap-net or poultry-yard scenes. Birds are shown being strangled, eviscerated, plucked and then salted and dried, or else cooked. It is curious that there are no representations of birds being beheaded with a knife, although they are pictured thus in tomb scenes and actual offerings are also similarly trimmed. New Kingdom scenes show the preserved birds being placed into amphora-style jars; such jars and contents have been recovered from contemporary tombs, such as that of Kha at Deir el-Medina (TT8).

Fish

Fish are shown being gutted, cleaned and then dried. The workers are most generally found seated at the edge of the water on a mat or low stool, wielding a knife or scraper. The proximity to water ensures the freshness of the fish and an abundance of water to wash up during the processing. After gutting the fish are opened up, sometimes with their heads and sometimes without, salted and air-dried. Mullet roes, perhaps the earliest form of caviar, were also dried using salt and air and are shown in fish-processing scenes, especially in the Old Kingdom Saqqara necropolis. Scenes of fish being cooked are extremely rare, although they were consumed enthusiastically in antiquity. Certain fish are not shown being consumed, such as the Oxyrhynchus fish, which was supposed to have eaten Osiris' penis, following his dismemberment and was thus deemed taboo in funerary situations. Fish very rarely appear on offering tables (e.g. in

95 Fish and fowl being processed for storage and later consumption. The fish are beheaded, gutted and washed. The poultry is strangled, eviscerated and plucked. It is probable that both the fish and the poultry were salted and dried before being placed in storage jars; tomb of Paheri (EK3: 18th Dynasty).

the New Kingdom tomb of Nakht [TT52]) and then only species symbolic of resurrection, such as *tilapia* and *bulti* (e.g. in TT52).

Viticulture

Wine presses appear in tomb-chapels of the 4th Dynasty at Meidum, but a complete viticulture scene does not appear until the 5th Dynasty at Giza. A complete scene shows the grape arbour, collecting the grapes and putting them in baskets to take to the treaders, treading on them, extracting the must and then bottling the wine.

Viticulture becomes a popular motif and one that appears to have carried over through the Graeco-Roman Period with its association with the god of wine, Dionysus, who was identified with Osiris as a god of resurrection and rebirth. This association then carried over further into the Christian era, with Christ being associated with vines, their fruit and their product. The red of the wine identifies it with blood and drinking wine makes one's blood flow, as is attested by the resulting flushed cheeks. Furthermore, the alcohol in wine alters one's perception and in many cultures this altered state is associated with divinity and existence on a different plane, a state of being quite in keeping with a reborn and therefore semi-divine soul. Vines probably became so closely identified with rebirth because they turn brown and dry in the winter and then miraculously become green and put out fresh shoots and tendrils and another crop of grapes in the spring. The clusters of grapes that hang

96 Grapes being harvested and then trampled and the juice being collected during the wine-making process; Tuna el-Gebel, tomb of Petosiris. (Dynasty of Macedon).

down stress the idea of plenty. Occasionally, clusters of grapes are used in alternation with pendant lotus blossoms in friezes (TT249). Faience grape clusters were also suspended within the garden kiosks at Tell el-Amarna.

One scholar has suggested an alternative allegorical interpretation of the wine-making scene: the wine god Shesmu protecting the justified dead. In order to eradicate their enemies and those of the sun god, he used his wine press to squeeze the head of his murdered enemies. Thus, trampling on grapes and putting them through a press might be equated with the victorious rebirth of the sun god and the successful arrival into the afterlife by the deceased.[106]

Apiculture

Although honey was the most highly prized sweetener, scenes of bee-keeping and honey production appear infrequently in Egyptian art. The first such scene appears in the 5th Dynasty sun temple of Niuserre at Abu Ghurob. One of the most famous scenes dates to the New Kingdom tomb of Rekhmire (TT100), which was copied in tombs of the 25th and 26th Dynasties (e.g. TT279 and TT414). Some scholars regard bees as being symbolic of kingship, although the insect that appears in the *nesu-bity* title (𓆤𓏏) was more probably the wasp that is often found hovering near papyrus plants.

Animals

All sorts of animals are shown in tombs in different contexts. They appear as part of the marsh scenes, in the desert hunts, in scenes of agriculture, livestock and pasturage, as offerings and as pets.

Hunted and Trapped Creatures

Scenes of hunting, fishing and trapping often contain wonderful vignettes of animals. These representations illustrate the Egyptians' intimate and detailed understanding of the natural world, as, for the most part, accurate animal behaviour patterns are shown. Hunt scenes show hedgehogs emerging from burrows, antelope and gazelle mothers fleeing with their offspring, lions fighting with the hunting dogs, otters awaiting fish, birds protecting their nests, scenes of copulating animals and the resulting births. The mating scenes emphasize the aspects of tomb decoration connected with fertility and ensure the continuation of the natural world. Occasional vignettes show animals giving birth with jackals or dogs hovering nearby. It is more probable that the carnivores are waiting to eat the afterbirth, rather than consume the newly born creatures. Hippopotamus birth scenes show crocodiles lurking nearby – these might be more

97 (*above*) A wall in the tomb of Nefer at Saqqara; amongst the scenes is a depiction of mating animals, at the left-hand end of the upper register.

98 (*right*) The monkey under the chair of Paheri and his wife not only indicates its owner's wealth and status (the monkey is imported from sub-Saharan Africa), but also suggests sexual activity (EK3).

likely to eat the young and probably give no or little thought to the afterbirth.

Pets

Pets are shown under the chair of the tomb-owner, as well as being walked by a servant, who is frequently a dwarf. Dogs, monkeys and birds (particularly hoopoes) are shown as pets from the Old Kingdom onwards. From the Middle Kingdom onwards they are joined by cats and water-fowl, the former being useful for catching vermin, as well as alluding to several divinities (Re, Hathor, Sekhmet, Bastet, Mut), and the latter being associated with Amun, potentially with erotic overtones (see p. 90). Gazelles (e.g. TT73 and TT78), geese (e.g. TT18, 100, 112, 155) and monkeys (e.g. EK3 and LS27) appear from the New Kingdom onwards, although there is a decrease in representations of pets during the later Ramesside period, when fewer secular or secular-seeming scenes featured in tombs. In some instances pets are named so that they can be clearly identified in the afterlife. This is especially true in the case of dogs, most famously Inyotef II's hunting hounds from his tomb.

Livestock and Offering Animals

Scenes of livestock (poultry, cattle, sheep and goats) prior to their being offered show animals in several situations. They are depicted in herds, in poultry yards, sometimes being used to pull a plough, trample in the newly sown grain (ovicaprids and pigs), threshing, mating (cattle and ovicaprids), giving birth (with dogs waiting to eat the afterbirth), cows being milked and herds of cows fording the river. The fording scenes are particularly interesting as they also show images of crocodiles lurking below the surface, trying to seize the cattle. The cattle are cleverly manoeuvred by a herdsman, who takes a calf across in a boat, thus forcing its mother and the rest of the herd to follow.

Often such scenes or other riverine scenes also feature spells to repel the crocodiles that lurk beneath the water's surface. These spells are just supposed to be simple repelling/protection spells; however they are reminiscent of the later Coffin Text Spell 342 and Book of the Dead Spell 31, which repels crocodiles to prevent them from stealing magic from the deceased. Perhaps the simpler protection spells are precursors to those found in the Book of the Dead?

Pigs are rarely featured in tomb art. In their infrequent appearances they are shown both as domestic creatures that are used to trample in the grain as it is sown, as well as wild creatures that emerge from the marshes. Certainly the rarity of their depictions is no reflection of their popularity as a food in ancient Egypt.[107]

Force-feeding animals prior to consumption is also a part of this genre of scenes. In the Old Kingdom scenes showed both wild and domestic creatures being fattened for table. Force-feeding involves first tethering the animals at their troughs, then feeding them by hand. Oryx, gazelle, hartebeest and even hyaena were fed with delicacies to improve their flavour. No doubt consuming such animals was a delicacy due to their rarity. Eating them also gave the consumer dominion over chaos and was a metaphor for establishing *maat* and control. Poultry of all sorts, from ducks to cranes, were also shown being force-fed. Perhaps the ancient Egyptians were the original inventors of foie gras.

Rows of animals are also shown being led to the tomb-owner. These are offerings for eternity. Sometimes they appear independently, in single file, or driven by a herder. It has been suggested by several scholars that the word *ren*, meaning 'name', written above the animal, together with the name of the animal (e.g. ibex, bull/cow, oryx) means that the creature in question is being consecrated as an offering; however, this idea has not been conclusively proven.

Fighting Bulls

The scene showing two bulls fighting, presumably over a cow, is generally found in tombs in provincial cemeteries (e.g. Meir, El-Hagarsa,[108] El-Hawawish,[109] and Aswan) dating to the 6th Dynasty on through the Middle Kingdom. Generally, a nearby vignette pictures a bull and cow mating, after which the cow is shown giving birth. This sequence is clearly tied in to the rebirth and fertility motif that is an inherent part of tomb decoration and also might link the deceased to Hathor. The text accompanying some of these scenes (e.g. El-Hawawish) indicates that the tomb-owner and others are clearly watching a planned bull-fight. An unusual vignette in a New Kingdom scene of cattle inspection shows a pair of fighting bulls (TT123). The bull was the quintessential symbol of male fertility, associated with Min and the pharaoh; indeed, one of the king's titles was 'Mighty Bull'.

99 Captured cranes in a poultry yard being force-fed prior to consumption; Saqqara, tomb of Kagemeni (5th Dynasty).

V (*previous page*) East wall of the burial chamber of Sennedjem at Deir el-Medina (TT1: 19th Dynasty). This shows the deceased and his wife in the Fields of Iaru, the agricultural paradise that played a large part in the posthumous destiny of the dead Egyptian. The whole scene comprises the vignette to Spell 110 of the Book of the Dead.

VI (*opposite*) In the Old and New Kingdoms offering tables may be shown covered with tall loaves of bread. In the First Intermediate Period and Middle Kingdom, however, the 'loaves' retained their shape but were sometimes painted green. This may have been as a result of artists mistaking the bread for reeds, based on similarity in shape, or was perhaps due to a change in religious belief. South wall of the tomb of Khety at Beni Hasan (BH-XVII: 12th Dynasty).

VII (*above*) Detail from the wall seen in full in ill. 76, showing of the construction of a papyrus canoe in the tomb-chapel of Ptahhotep ii (Saqqara D64: late 5th Dynasty). The register below includes the trapping of birds in a clap-net.

VIII (*previous pages*) The burial chamber of the tomb of Sennefer on Sheikh Abd el-Qurna (TT96A: 18th Dynasty) is very unusual in its extensive and eclectic scheme of decoration. This includes the adornment of part of its ceiling with grape-vines, taking advantage of the rock's natural undulations to give a realistic effect.

IX (*above*) Part of the lower registers of a banquet scene from the tomb-chapel of Nebamun on Dra Abu'l-Naga (TTE2, BM EA37986: 18th Dynasty).

X (*opposite*) Mereruka's statue shows him as a young man, striding out of his niche. In antiquity a pair of doors would have stood before the image, and these would have had to have been ceremoniously opened by the funerary priests prior to making offerings to Mereruka (Saqqara: early 6th Dynasty).

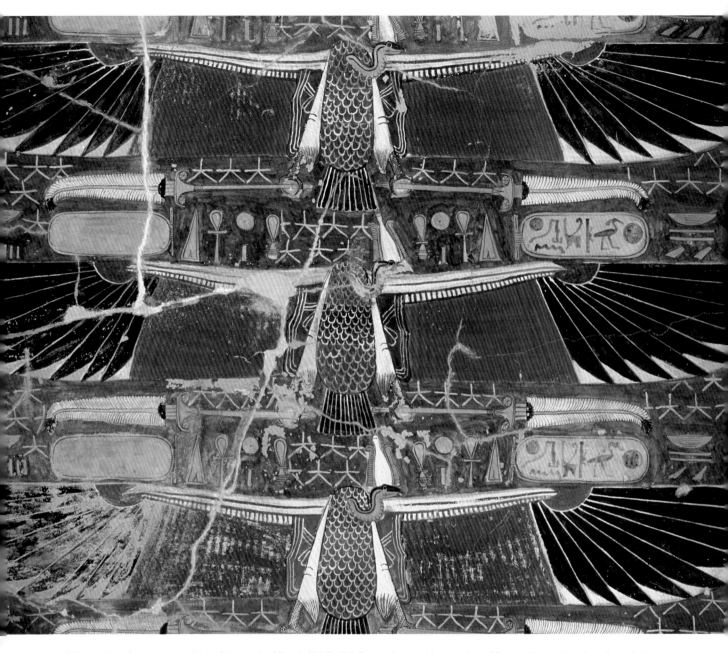

XI The ceiling of the outer corridor of the tomb of Siptah (KV47: 19th Dynasty) was, as in a number of Ramesside royal tombs, adorned with vultures, their wings outspread in protection.

Workshops and Crafts[110]

While the substructure of a tomb would be equipped with many manufactured items, it was also felt necessary to depict such items being made in workshops. No doubt, in some instances it was financially not viable to place all that one might want in the tomb; paintings were thus magical substitutes. Or the images may have served as 'insurance'. Although some of these images occur in 4th Dynasty tombs, they only become common from the 5th Dynasty onwards. They are not all shown in every tomb; frequently only a selection feature in tombs, sometimes dependent on space and/or the taste and status of the tomb-owner.

Jewelry and Metal Workers

Jewelry-making scenes show the weighing out of the gold, its working and the end products. Dwarfs are frequently shown labouring in these workshops; presumably their smaller and nimbler hands were particularly skilful in producing jewelry. Even in the Western tradition dwarfs are associated with jewelry-making, as well as with acquiring the raw materials necessary for its manufacture.

100 A scene of jewelry production, depicting the measuring and melting of the gold before making the broadcollars and other adornments for the tomb-owner. Dwarfs were frequently depicted as jewellers, perhaps as their diminutive size made their fingers particularly dextrous (Saqqara, tomb of Mereruka: 6th Dynasty).

Other types of metalwork are also shown, including the weighing of the metal, heating the fires with bellows, using blowpipes, using moulds and hammering vessels out over forms. Engraving or otherwise enhancing vessels is also depicted.

Boats, Boat-Building and the Transportation of Goods

Navigating the Nile was a normal part of life and is frequently depicted on tomb walls. Additionally, boats were regarded as highly important in religious contexts as they were the main means of transport for the sun god. Several references and spells relating to boat-building can be found in the Coffin Texts (e.g., 189, 194, 113), as well as in other religious and funerary writings.

Boats are shown in several contexts, including funerary, ritual and practical. Their connotations depend on their placement, as well as the larger scene in which they feature. Boats are often shown carrying the deceased on his voyage to the afterworld (in these instances, they are frequently shown travelling in a westerly direction, or appear on the western wall), or to make a pilgrimage to Abydos (below). They are also shown as craft being used practically (although the scenes generally have religious undertones) in fishing and fowling scenes, scenes of picnics on the river and the general transportation of objects and livestock.

Boat-building is also a typical feature of Old Kingdom tombs from the 5th Dynasty onwards. Both papyrus (pl. VII) and wooden boats are shown being manufactured. Sometimes a baboon is shown helping the boat-builders; this might be an allusion to Re since baboons were sacred to the sun god and appear in later funerary texts on his boat. However, baboons and other monkeys are used in several cultures to help with tasks, including sailing and fruit harvesting, particularly coconut collection. Papyrus boats also connote Osiris, as the green papyrus is one of that god's symbols. Boats also allude to the sun god as his daily journey was accomplished by sailing his boat through the sky. Perhaps this is why, as well as for practical reasons, many Old Kingdom burials (primarily royal) were accompanied by boats.

The river was the main 'road' through Egypt (and was mirrored in the afterlife). Thus, boats were the main method of transporting goods and people and are shown carrying livestock, produce and goods from the Old Kingdom onwards and particularly in the New Kingdom.

Spinning, Weaving, Leather-Work, and Rope- and Mat-Making

Although making mats and rope from papyrus is shown from the 4th Dynasty, spinning and weaving scenes are rarely found in the Old Kingdom. They only become popular in the Middle Kingdom and later. The scenes, in their most complete forms, show the processing of the flax, spinning it and then weaving on looms. The Middle Kingdom looms tend to be horizontal ground looms, while the New Kingdom ones are vertical. Although the linen is primarily intended for clothes, the sub-text suggests that the mummy bandages are also being fabricated. Wrapping things in pure white linen indicated their holiness and separateness from this world. The cultivation of flax for linen (and perhaps oil) is also shown, albeit infrequently. Flax can be identified as it is green at the time of harvest and is collected by pulling, rather than cutting. Leather-working is shown in tombs from all periods, but rarely.

Carpenters, Stonemasons, Potters and Brick Makers

Carpenters are shown fashioning shrines and coffins, as well as mundane objects such as beds and chairs. They are also sometimes shown making oars. Oars were obviously necessary for the boats shown in the chapel, but they also refer to texts in the Book of the Dead, which mention the 'four rudders of heaven', so these images have a sacred undertone and images of rudders often appear independently, especially in the 19th Dynasty.

Stoneworkers, depicted from the Old Kingdom on, make vessels, as do potters (who are rarely shown and then most frequently from and after the Middle Kingdom). Masons are also shown carving sarcophagi, shrines, the false-door or even a portion of the tomb. They are thus engaged in sacred work for eternity. Scenes of brick-making are extremely rare and tend to be found in New Kingdom chapels.

Trade

Although the ancient Egyptians did not use money until the Persian 27th Dynasty, trade was carried out through barter. Scenes of bartering of goods appear in both royal (causeway of Unas) and non-royal contexts, starting in the early 5th Dynasty. The Old Kingdom scenes all date from the 5th Dynasty on and come from the Saqqara/Abu Sir area. Scenes in later periods are distributed more widely. One charming Old Kingdom vignette from the tomb

of Tepemankh, now in the Cairo Museum (CG 1556), shows a baboon being used by the authorities to 'police' the market.

Games[111]

Games of different sorts are depicted in Egyptian tombs from the 5th Dynasty onwards. The most commonly depicted game is the board game *senet*, akin to draughts. This appears in offering rooms starting in approximately the mid-5th Dynasty and generally shows family members playing the game, or most often, especially in the New Kingdom, the deceased playing the game with an invisible opponent. This suggests that at least in the New Kingdom and later, when the deceased is shown in a pavilion playing *senet* against an invisible opponent, the game is a metaphor for the voyage to the afterworld; emerging victorious from the *senet* match is equated with a safe arrival and acceptance into the afterlife.

101 (*above*) Craftsmen making rope and using a bow drill (TT100: 18th Dynasty).

102 (*below*) Nebenmaat ii playing *senet* with his wife, Meretseger. In later representations the deceased is shown playing against an invisible opponent with the stakes being eternal life (TT219: 19th Dynasty).

Senet boards have 30 squares, representing the different regions in the realm of the dead, while the throwsticks (precursors of dice) are compared to the jackals that pull the sun god's barque. References to this game appear frequently in the Book of the Dead (e.g. Chapter 17).[112] In Thebes, from the 21st Dynasty onwards, an offering table is substituted for the *senet* game. Other board games, such as the snake game (*mehen*), are also depicted in tombs, especially during the Old Kingdom and then in the 26th Dynasty. Snakes are frequently depicted as enemies, as well as friends of the deceased during his journey to the afterlife.

More physical amusements are also shown, such as acrobatics, ball games (generally in the Middle Kingdom), leap-frog, stick fights, shooting arrows (mainly New Kingdom, e.g. TT109 and 143), or tug-of-war. A game akin to an elaborate form of leap-frog called *khuzza lawizza* in Arabic and still played today is also shown in tombs of the Old Kingdom. Sometimes boxing would be shown as well, occasionally associated with the celebration of a royal festival, such as the *sed*-festival, as can be seen in the tomb of Kheruef (TT192) and wrestling, which is found at Beni Hasan.

A specific vignette, one showing duelling boatmen in papyrus skiffs, might also be considered part of the 'game' group of scenes, although these men were probably responsible for transporting provisions for the deceased as well. This scene is common from the 4th Dynasty onwards, through the Middle Kingdom and perhaps into the very early New Kingdom and is one of the liveliest scenes in the tomb. Perhaps these scenes of struggle and victory related to the ultimate victory of *maat*, as well as the desire for the deceased to enjoy and be entertained in the afterlife.

Carrying Chairs[113]

The tomb-owner is often shown being transported to inspect the tomb in a carrying chair or palanquin. The idea is that the owner is going to inspect his tomb, so the notion of repeated visits is encapsulated on the wall through this image. These vignettes start in the 4th Dynasty and continue until the end of the Old Kingdom. A rare example of a carrying chair placed on a donkey appears on the door-jamb of the 5th Dynasty double tomb of Niankhkhnum and Khnumhotep at Saqqara.

Bed-Making and Beds

Scenes of bed-making and beds in tombs appear intermittently in tombs from the 4th Dynasty onwards,[114] but remain rare in Egyptian art. These are not only records of daily rituals, but are also loaded with significance implying rebirth. Beds are places where one sleeps, and, one hopes, reawakens. In the mythological realm, Osiris was laid on a bed that doubled as his bier prior to his resurrection. It was also where Isis came to him to conceive Horus, thus underlying the sexual and procreative elements in its symbolism. This might be why couches such as the ones found in Tutankhamun's tomb were included as part of the funerary equipment. Also, coffins are sometimes shaped as though lying on beds and in the later periods of Egyptian history, mummies were frequently laid on beds and buried. Beds are shown being prepared in tombs of all periods, albeit not commonly. Frequently mirrors, kohl pots and unguents are placed under the bed (see also toilette, below). All these are elements of beautification and erotica, which might be

103 (*left*) Leatherworkers and carpenters producing goods (TT100: 18th Dynasty).

104 (*right*) Fighting boatmen are found in a number of Old Kingdom tombs, in this case on the lower register of a wall of the Saqqara tomb of Mereruka.

105 Ipi carried in a palanquin, accompanied by attendants and carriers of sunshades; from South Saqqara (CM CG1536-7: 6th Dynasty).

tied into the idea of resurrection, as well as erotic moments on earth, as is attested by several love poems.

Statuary

Images showing statues of the deceased occur frequently in tombs, either on door-jambs or in the tomb proper. They are shown being made, dragged and censed. These images probably depict the statues that were placed in the tomb, either in the *serdab* (mainly in the Old Kingdom), or in the tomb proper as a focus of cult practice or as insurance for the *ka* should the mummy be damaged. The images start to appear at the end of the 4th Dynasty.[115] Statues are often shown being taken into a tomb, with a ritual of incensing taking place before them. This ritual serves to animate the statue of the deceased and is similar to that used for statues of divinities. In the Old Kingdom they are shown being transported on sleds and appear mainly on door-jambs and near doorways, i.e. points of transition and transformation.[116]

Different aspects of the individual can be embodied by the statues: some are shown as young, wearing short kilts and elaborate wigs, while others depict individuals in their more mature years, shown as plump and carrying many more impedimenta of office. Such statues are depicted as part of the focal points of the funerary cult, so time depth can be achieved through images of statues being produced, transported and revered.[117] The transportation and revering of statues is most commonly shown in Old and Middle Kingdom tombs, while New Kingdom tombs focus more on their production. Often, in the latter context the statues are of kings who the tomb-owner served, rather than of the tomb-owner himself (e.g. TT100).

(Auto)biographical Elements

All tombs contain elements that might be called autobiographical: names, titles, familial affiliations. These are further augmented by texts and images that relate to the tomb-owner's work and position in society that he (or she) chooses to show. In New Kingdom 'T'-shaped tombs they occur in the transverse hall and continue into the passage. These texts and scenes provide an insight into the tomb-owner's wealth and the responsibilities attached to certain positions, as well as telling us about the particular people who owned the tombs. Due to their nature some of these images are very specialized and appear in only a few tombs. This personalization of tombs was more common in the New Kingdom than in any other period.

Depictions of overseeing taxation and the rendering of accounts are amongst the first 'professional' scenes to appear

106 Tax defaulters are beaten in the upper register of this wall in the 18th Dynasty tomb of the Overseer of the Fields Menena (TT69), while winnowing continues below.

in tombs, starting in the Old Kingdom. They are most commonly found in the tombs of viziers. When taxes are in arrears, vignettes within the larger scene show the punishment of the laggards. Vizier Rekhmire's tomb-chapel (TT100) also includes a long text that explains the duties of the vizier, and is fundamental to our understanding of the responsibilities of that position in the 18th Dynasty. His duties included receiving tribute, with images of foreigners bringing diverse items ranging from giraffes and elephant tusks to Cretan vessels being shown thus in TT100. Foreigners are rarely shown (except at Beni Hasan) in tomb-chapels prior to the New Kingdom. Then they are invariably featured when the tomb-owner's duties in life necessitated interaction with foreigners.

Officials responsible for provision, such as Userhat (TT56), show the registering and branding of cattle, in addition to scenes of grain production. As Userhat was the equivalent of a quartermaster for the army, soldiers are also featured in the tomb, awaiting their rations. The sub-scenes show them lounging around, as well as getting their hair barbered – presumably these were the recruits. Military scenes are rarely shown in tombs (see below).

In some instances, extraordinary acts or services to the king were commemorated. Thus, Harkhuf had the text of a letter sent to him by King Pepy II reproduced on the exterior of his tomb at Aswan. He had completed a successful mission to Central/Western Africa and brought the king a pygmy (or possibly dwarf) as a companion, for whom the then child-king expressed his gratitude. The architect Ineni (TT81) records how he constructed a tomb (the first in the Valley of the Kings) for his monarch, Thutmose I. Amenemheb (TT85) records in text, but without illustrations, how he sliced off the trunk of a marauding elephant that was attacking Thutmose III.

Outstanding personal events commemorated include Djehutyhotep ii's transportation of a colossal alabaster statue (Tomb 2 at El-Bersha). On a different tack, Hapidjefa ii, in his tomb at Asyut (Tomb 2), records ten contracts setting out the wages received for his various offices. Ankhmahor's Saqqara tomb contains a curious scene of circumcision, as well as other surgical procedures, none of which are directly linked to his principal titles of priest and Vizier. Thus, very personal narratives not only elucidate the culture and history of ancient Egypt, but also bring the personal history of the deceased to life.

In addition to these 'real' autobiographies there are certain formulaic 'quasi-autobiographical' texts, found in most tombs, including the 'Negative Confession' (a list of evil things contrary to *maat* eschewed by the deceased), or the inscription recounting all the good deeds (e.g. 'I gave to the hungry', etc.) of the deceased.

Warfare

Images of warfare are rarely depicted in tombs, perhaps as the continuation of a violent struggle throughout eternity, carried out by private people, was unappealing. Exceptions to this do, however, occur in a handful of 6th Dynasty tomb-chapels, as well as a group of sepulchres at Beni Hasan, and at Deir el-Bersha. Soldiers are depicted, but generally in peaceful contexts: being rewarded, waiting as recruits, etc. Inscriptions from the tombs of individuals who defined themselves by martial prowess, such as Ankhtify of Moalla (First Intermediate Period), tell of military exploits, which provide us with historical data. The early 18th Dynasty tomb of Ahmose, son of Ibana, at El-Kab is also rich with texts concerning naval battles that took place at the start of the dynasty and are an invaluable source of information concerning the events of that period.

Images of the Deceased

Images of the deceased dominated the tomb. He (or she) is shown entering the tomb, fishing and fowling, carrying out duties in life, overseeing various events, relaxing, seated in gardens or houses, participating in religious festivals, hunting, attending banquets and receiving offerings. A curious scene-type shows the toilette of the deceased. This occurs infrequently in the Old Kingdom and then slightly more frequently in subsequent periods, especially in the 11th Dynasty. The scene appears in tombs of both men and women, though it is more commonly found in female chapels of the Middle Kingdom.

The toilet scenes show hairdressing, anointing with oils and unguents, as well as applying make-up. Make-up exaggerates ones image, creating a new, improved version, and also has religious overtones. For example, kohl or galena were symbolic of the divine eye that judges, as well as being associated with several divinities.[118] The make-up in the toilette scenes ensured that the deceased, in an idealized

107 It is not always clear why certain motifs were included in a tomb. For example, a scene of circumcision is depicted in the 6th Dynasty tomb of Ankhmahor at Saqqara.

state, would look his best throughout eternity. Perfumes and oils also have sacred functions in mummification and cult rituals, as well practical applications: they have a pleasant smell, and, in some cases, have insect-repellent properties (see below under 'Banquet Scenes'). There is also a spell in the Coffin Texts (CT282) that states how the deceased can use scent to drive off the harmful serpent Rerek.

Mirrors, which become common in representations from the First Intermediate Period onwards and are placed under chairs and sometimes appear as funerary goods, also have a symbolic meaning. Their circular shape alludes to the solar disk and the fact that they provide a reflection suggests the afterworld, which is a mirror image of this one. The word for 'mirror', *ankh*, has the same sound as the word for 'life'. Mirrors are associated with the goddess Hathor, as one

of her manifestations is goddess of beauty, as well as being 'Mistress of the Sycamore', providing sustenance to the deceased and a personification of the western mountains of Thebes. Some mirror handles bear her likeness, while others take the form of papyrus plants, symbolic of the resurrective powers of Osiris and also allude to Hathor's residence in the marshes where she safeguarded the young Horus.

Families

Images showing the deceased and his wife (generally on a smaller scale) start in the Old Kingdom and appear throughout the course of Egyptian history. Children are also frequently shown, accompanying their parents, attending banquets, offering to their deceased parents, as well as acting as the *sem* or funerary priest and therefore, heir. A proliferation of images of the extended family occur during the New Kingdom, when the idea of ancestor cults became linked with the idea of royal ancestor worship.

Banquet Scenes

Scenes of feasts are a key decorative element in the tomb-chapel of the New Kingdom,[119] although they do appear throughout Egyptian history (pl. IX). It is difficult to separate images of funerary banquets from other festivities, so they will be treated as a group here. Banquet scenes show rows of richly dressed and bejewelled men and women, sometimes on separate registers and sometimes grouped together, attended by servants and being entertained by musicians and dancers (see below). This event can allude to the funerary festivities, akin to a modern wake, with the added message of celebrating the rebirth of the deceased in the other world. They can also represent religious and secular festivities attended by the deceased and others, especially the Festival of the Valley (see below, p. 220). The motif stresses the message: eat, drink and make merry. Hairstyles, clothes, jewelry and furniture help provide dating criteria, as well as indicating rank.

A curious feature of most of the banquets is that food is not the focus: rather, the concentration is on drinking. Some late 18th Dynasty tombs even show men and women suffering the ill-effects of overindulgence in a corner of the room and being carried away afterward (e.g. TT53 and 49).

108 Part of certain banquet scenes is a depiction of a female guest vomiting, presumably through a surfeit of alcohol (Western Thebes: 18th Dynasty).

Various elements used in the scenes, including puns, serve to underline the rebirth/resurrection motif. The word for the garlands that are placed around the necks of revellers is *ankh*, which sounds the same as the word for life. The Egyptian word for 'to pour', *seti*, is spelled in the same way as the word meaning impregnate. As Lise Manniche writes, '[t]he … banquet scene … hinted again and again at the proper atmosphere for creating new life'.[120] The presence of the blue lotus also serves to remind us symbolically of rebirth. Small cones, resembling party hats, also appear on the heads of banqueters in New Kingdom tombs. These have been identified as cones of fat, impregnated by perfume or incense, which gradually melted during the course of the festivities, releasing a pleasing aroma. Recently, however, some doubt has been cast on whether these were actually ever worn, or if they were merely an iconographic device, to show that these people were perfumed and oiled.[121] Although oils and perfumes were an element of everyday life, they had religious overtones since gods and rulers were anointed (see Pyramid Texts 879–881 and 936–37), and of course oiling the body was an important part of the mummification process.

In fact, the Pyramid Texts state that oils were necessary for the resurrection of the deceased, as they knitted the bones together and re-clothed them with flesh. Presumably the seven sacred oils that were part of the tomb equipment were for this reanimation process. In mythology, the oils had divine origins: some came from the eye of Horus, while others came from Re, or from the sweat of the gods. A sweet odour was thought to be a sign of divinity. Indeed, many people commented on Alexander the Great's sweet smell, which was interpreted as a manifestation of his godhead. Additionally, several New Kingdom Theban tombs include scenes or references where the anointing of the deceased is an important part of the celebrations at the end of the year (e.g. TT50, TT82 and TT112).[122] Did these celebrations merely entail bringing ointments as offerings, or involve actually entering the burial chambers and pouring oils and unguents over the coffin or even the body of the deceased? Certainly in modern Coptic monasteries the carefully preserved bodies of their founders are annually anointed.

Musicians, Singers and Dancers

Entertainers appear in different contexts in Egyptian tombs of all periods, most commonly at the banquet scene. While

the musicians are of both genders, the majority of the dancers are women, although there are also dances exclusive to men (*muu*) and stick dancing at Beni Hasan. Dancing was both secular and sacred, and certain dances, performed by the *muu* dancers (see below), were a part of the funerary ritual.

Music, song and dance provided entertainment through eternity, as well as providing imagery that would aid the deceased's voyage to the Fields of Iaru. Certain lyrics, especially in the New Kingdom, such as the Song of the Harper,[123] praised the afterlife, while instruments, such as the sistrum, were associated with Hathor. Musicians and dancers are also depicted celebrating festivals, such as the king's *heb-sed* jubilee (TT192), or in religious processions. In some instances the tomb-owner or his wife are shown with musical instruments of a ritual nature, notably the sistrum. These vignettes generally underline a priestly role, or a dedication to a particular divinity.

109 (*above*) A harpist, lutist and singers entertain guests in Rekhmire's tomb at Thebes (TT100: 18th Dynasty).

110 (*below*) Dancing and tug-of-war were popular entertainments (Saqqara, tomb of Mereruka: 6th Dynasty).

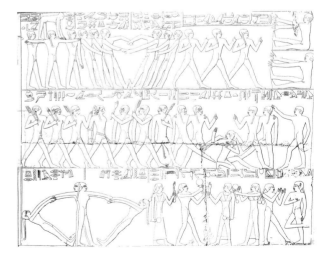

Divinities

Although divinities are a natural part of the decoration of funerary monuments, they rarely figure on the walls of elite tombs until the New Kingdom. In royal contexts gods and kings are shown in offering scenes, scenes of giving life (*ankh*) to the king, watching the king, etc., as well as being protagonists in the Books of the Underworld in both royal and private contexts.

From the New Kingdom on, especially starting in the 19th Dynasty, gods and demi-gods regularly feature in private tomb-chapel decoration, either alone or in vignettes of the Book of the Dead, in particular those associated with the judgment of the deceased. The deities shown include the stock funerary gods: Osiris, Isis, Neith, Nephthys, Selqet, the Four Sons of Horus, Hathor, Maat and Thoth. Certain gods, including Amun, are not shown in tombs, but hymns and offerings are addressed to them, so that their presence is implicit in the tomb-chapel.

Harvest deities are also shown in tombs of the New Kingdom. No doubt they stressed the idea of fertility and plenty in this world and the next. The most frequently depicted goddess was Renutet in her serpent form (e.g. TT112, 143, 172, 217, 256, 261, 284), who was often shown close to scenes of viticulture as well as grain production and processing.

Offering Ritual and the False-Door

The scene of offering is the most sacred image in the Old Kingdom non-royal decorative repertoire and is a standard feature in tomb decoration throughout Egyptian history. In its iconic form, it consists of a table of offerings being presented to the deceased and appears on the false-door, as well as on the walls of the tomb proper. This ensures that the deceased will be well provided for in the afterlife. The ritual accompanying this scene is one that is supposed to have been carried out on a daily basis – indeed, perhaps more than once a day. This is similar to temple rituals, where the image of the divinity would be given offerings, after which the offerings would revert to the priest. Presumably this was also the case for the actual offerings given to both royal and non-royal individuals. As insurance, if offerings were not provided on a daily basis, the images in the chapel would magically provide the necessary sustenance. This scene,

111 A diagram showing the different parts of a false-door. These doors were the focal point of the cult, and sometimes an individual had more than one false-door in the tomb. Occasionally some were external for ease of offering.

often repeated in tombs, was a key scene throughout Egyptian history, although it enjoyed the most prominence in the Old Kingdom when other ritual or religious scenes were rarely depicted. Offering scenes and false-doors appear in both sub- and superstructures.

Offering lists appear at the start of the Old Kingdom, but a standardized form is first found in the 5th Dynasty and consists of over 90 items, each shown together with its name within individual cells of a grid. Many of the items listed are foodstuffs, but include material required by the cult of the deceased, including incense and the seven sacred oils.[124]

The false-door was, from the 4th Dynasty, the focal point of the cult, developing from the slab stelae of earlier times. It was generally located in the superstructure, as directly above the burial chamber as possible, so that the deceased's *ka* could access the offerings directly. It comprised several discrete elements mirroring the elements of a real door, including jambs, lintels and bolts, and was generally ornamented with torus mouldings and a cavetto cornice. The door was almost always carved in sunk relief, a technique most frequently employed in carving exterior spaces so that the images would be visible even in bright, direct sunlight. This charming conceit emphasized how the door was exterior to the afterlife. The door was extensively inscribed with the name and titles of the deceased, as well as offering formulae. The tablet above the central section was usually inscribed with an image of the deceased sitting before an offering table with the offerings listed above him or below the table. There are wide variations in the details of false-doors over time and between sites, such as the number of jambs, types of offerings listed, presence or absence of other family members on the door, etc.; these can also provide dating criteria for the monument.

Offerings: Bearers, Estates, Priests and Family Members

Bringing the deceased offerings of food (both processed and raw), drink, cloth, incense, perfumes, oils, flowers, bouquets, furniture, jewelry and other objects were some of the most, if not the most, important images inscribed in tombs. This scene type is most common in the Old and Middle Kingdoms, as well as the Saite Period. It is present, but less prominent, in New Kingdom funerary monuments. Offering scenes can be separated into different groups: products of marshlands, products of fields and farms, Opening-of-the-Mouth offerings, and offerings and libations made directly in front of the deceased or his statues. The most significant offerings are those made by priests who were responsible for the continued celebration of the mortuary cult, especially the *sem* priest, a role that was traditionally assigned to the eldest son.

This scene type tends to occupy several registers, but is most frequently placed in the lower register, with a preference for the west wall. Often, with multi-chambered tombs, these rows of offering bringers form a link between rooms. The offerings are always taken in the direction of the deceased. They are brought by a variety of individuals, including offering bearers, friends, family members and human figures representing personified estates. By the Middle Kingdom the latter abstract personifications were replaced by figures of real servants.[125] Most of the items being brought to the deceased feature in the offering list inscribed near the false-door or tomb focus. Occasionally some unusual offerings, such as the caged hedgehogs in the tomb of Mereruka at Saqqara, are presented to the deceased.

The offerings magically ensured the permanent provisioning of the deceased in the afterlife. In some instances a scroll, inscribed with offerings or lists of goods, is shown being presented to the deceased. Furthermore, some

112 Estates bringing their produce for the use of the tomb-owner in the 6th Dynasty tomb of Mereruka at Saqqara.

objects might have had additional significance, such as linen offerings which would provide clothing for eternity and also suggest the idea of mummy bandages and the practice of wrapping sacred or precious objects in linen. Food would naturally provide sustenance, as well as underline the fact that the chaos of nature had been harnessed to the rule of order and productivity imposed upon it by man's will. Bouquets provide allegorical offerings in the flowers that they contain, as well as make a pun: the word for 'bouquet', *mes*, shares the same root as the word for 'birth'.

Although most of the scenes of offerings show the deceased as the recipient, there are a few occurrences where the deceased makes offerings. Generally these are made to kings, deities or ancestors (semi-deified, due to their deceased status). However, there are rare depictions of the tomb-owner offering to the architects and artists who constructed and decorated the tomb, as well as to a sculptor who produced the statues that were placed in the tomb (TT82). Although it is relatively rare to find named individuals other than family members in tombs, those who are named are frequently priests or artisans who were presumably quite well known and were responsible for producing some of the grave goods (e.g. A2 at Meir).

Funerals, Mourning and the Funerary Procession

Although there are 4th Dynasty examples of elements taken from the mourning cycle of the dead (e.g. in the tomb of Meresankh III at Giza), funerals and funerary processions do not become common until the 6th Dynasty. The funerary cycle in full (good examples of which are found in TT20 and 29) includes mourning, the funerary procession (by land and/or water) and rites performed before the mummy.

In tomb-chapels from earlier periods, only the last stages of the funeral are shown. The cycle is most complete in the 18th Dynasty, when it becomes a significant scene in the decorative schema. As one might expect, the preference is to place such scenes on the west wall, or whichever wall has been designated as the ritual 'west' if geographic orientation cannot be followed due to practical constraints. In some cases, such as in the tomb of Ramose (TT55), the funeral scenes are shown directly over the entrance to the substructure. These representations are frequently linked to those depicting the Voyage to Abydos (see below).

The mourners are depicted fainting with grief, weeping, wailing, pulling at their hair and heaping dust on their head. Some are professionals, although many are family members and friends. New Kingdom scenes tend to be more dramatic than those of the Old Kingdom, although a woman in the tomb of Mereruka at Saqqara is shown fainting with grief .

The procession, from the embalming house to the tomb, shows the coffin or the mummy on a bier that is placed on a sled pulled by oxen. The parade includes offering bearers carrying grave goods, priests, priestesses in the guise of Isis and Nephthys and the deceased's friends and family. An enigmatic object called the *tekenu*, which is pulled on a sled, is also a part of the procession. The *tekenu* is shown in representations dating from the Old Kingdom onwards and looks like a man in a foetal position, covered by an animal skin or fabric. However, its origins remain obscure. Some scholars believe that it was a representation of the dead body, wrapped in an animal skin that was used prior to the use of coffins, while others have thought it might refer to human sacrifice, or even the wrapped placenta.

113 (*left*) The top register of this wall of the 18th Dynasty tomb of Pairi (TT139) had offering-bringers above a depiction of the funeral procession. Below we see the Opening-of-the-Mouth ceremony and the Voyage to Abydos.

Part of the funerary rite refers to the 'Buto Burial' and the trip to Sais. This was an ancient ritual supposedly derived from one performed for the Predynastic rulers of the Delta at the sites of Buto and Sais, consisting of stopping at these sites and the performance of certain ritual acts there. Later, these towns became symbolic religious destinations rather than literal ones. After the 4th Dynasty these rites were taken over by the elite and stopped being the sole preserve of royalty. They are difficult to understand as their origins are shrouded in the mists of time. They include purification rituals and the dance of the enigmatic *muu* dancers, incarnations of the ancient kings of Buto. Censing, offerings, the *tekenu* and the erection of two obelisks are also part of this ritual.[126] The final stages of the funeral were meant to take place in front of the tomb (shown most often in the New Kingdom), including the Opening-of-the-Mouth ceremony.

The Opening-of-the-Mouth Ceremony

This funerary ritual was performed either on the mummy itself, or on a statue of the deceased at the tomb's entrance or courtyard, as it faced the land of the living for the last time. In its full state, it consisted of 75 separate episodes. These included purification, censing, butchery and offering and the recitation of specific funerary texts, with accompanying gestures and accoutrements that restored the five different senses to the mummy, thereby enabling its rebirth and resurrection. This was carried out by the *sem* priest, clad in a leopard skin, a role that was generally taken by the eldest son and/or heir of the deceased. This scene, which is most commonly shown in 18th Dynasty tombs, becomes rarer after the end of Tutankhamun's reign, although it enjoyed a renaissance in the 26th Dynasty.

Voyage to Abydos

The pilgrimage to Abydos to visit the burial place of Osiris was one of the most important religious duties for an Egyptian because the trip symbolized their own resurrection and rebirth. This image first appears in tomb-chapels of the Old Kingdom and continues throughout Egyptian history. The scene develops out of a funerary journey carried out from Buto to the Re temple at Heliopolis that is pictured in 4th Dynasty tombs. As the importance of Osiris increased in the 5th Dynasty, the pilgrimage to his temple replaces the earlier prototype. A boat or flotilla of boats is shown wending its way to Abydos and back, the direction of travel clearly indicated by the sails: downriver the sails are furled as the current is being used for momentum and upriver the sails are unfurled to use the 'sweet breeze of the north'. The scene is generally shown on the west side of the tomb. New Kingdom variants show the trip to Abydos with a coffin on board one of the boats; on the return trip there is no coffin, intimating that the deceased has been accepted into the realm of Osiris. The boats emphasize the rebirth motif: towards Abydos they face into the tomb, while on the return journey they face outwards, to the land of the living, with the emphasis on a successful rebirth. This scene is sometimes shown in association with the funeral procession. Rites associated with it might actually have been re-enacted in the necropolis on special occasions. According to Lise Manniche, 'the symbolic significance of the representation is emphasized in the rites performed during one of the annual festivals in the necropolis, when model boats were placed in the tomb to help the deceased undertake his journey. At midnight the boats were turned round so that he could travel home again.'[127]

Decorative Motifs

In addition to the specific images of activities and individuals, other decorative elements feature in tombs of all periods. These include friezes at the top of walls, ceiling decoration and engaged statuary that is carved as part of the tomb itself. These elements change somewhat over time; a synopsis of their types and occurrences is given below.

Friezes

The most common element used as a frieze is the *kheker*, resembling tassels of a carpet and used as a decoration on the highest part of a wall. Particularly common from the Middle Kingdom onwards, it is actually known from the 3rd Dynasty complex of King Djoser. The term *kheker* is derived from the word for ornament in Egyptian and is just that: a decorative motif that is used as a frieze to fill up awkward wall spaces. Its origins, however, are surprisingly practical. It is thought to have its genesis in the knotted tops of reeds that were used for construction during Egypt's earliest history, including the temples associated with the Buto Burial, as well as funerary constructions, and to have evolved into a purely decorative

motif, occurring even when the construction is actually of stone or brick, rather than of reeds.

In the Old Kingdom it is used predominantly in royal contexts, although an example has been found in the mastabas of Seshemnefer (LG53) and Tjeti at Giza.[128] It becomes increasingly common in the Middle Kingdom, a time when other previously royal motifs have been taken over by the elite. The Old Kingdom upper frieze areas tended to be enhanced by trident-like shapes that are also derived from flora. In addition to the *kheker* frieze, Middle Kingdom tombs also used decorative bands made up of different colours to frame scenes.

Friezes from New Kingdom contexts are the most diverse, with examples of different frieze-motifs being used in the same tomb (e.g. TT43, 78, 151, 189, TT272). This probably reflects personal choice associated with religious beliefs, as well as an aesthetic decision. The shapes of the *kheker* vary during the course of this period, with the addition of a sun disk to its centre during the reign of Amenhotep III.

Other motifs used to decorate friezes include lotus flowers (these increase in popularity during and after the reign of Thutmose IV) and Hathor heads, first introduced in TT71, the tomb of Senenmut and appearing in several other Theban tombs (e.g. TT45, 58, 163). A unique frieze appearing in TT72 consists of the cartouches of Thutmose III, topped by one of the titles of the deceased. In the tombs at Amarna a *pt* symbol, the hieroglyphic sign for the sky (⬭), or coloured bands adorn the frieze area. Ramesside tombs have particularly elaborate friezes: Anubis couchant (e.g. TT14, 58, 149, 166), snakes (e.g. TT99, 284 and 354), *djed* pillars and *tyt* amulets (TT65), and combinations of all these motifs. Clearly Egyptians in the Ramesside period saw an increase in the need for explicit religious protection for the tomb, as manifested in the frieze.

Ceiling Decoration

The soffits of tombs were also enhanced. The few that have been found from Old Kingdom mastabas were carved and

---

114 (*right*) Images of the Voyage to Abydos by boat were common in tombs of all periods. When Egyptian boats travelled northwards they are shown with their sails furled as they used the current to move; when they are going south their sails are unfurled so that they could take advantage of the north wind (TT100, Rekhmire: 18th Dynasty).

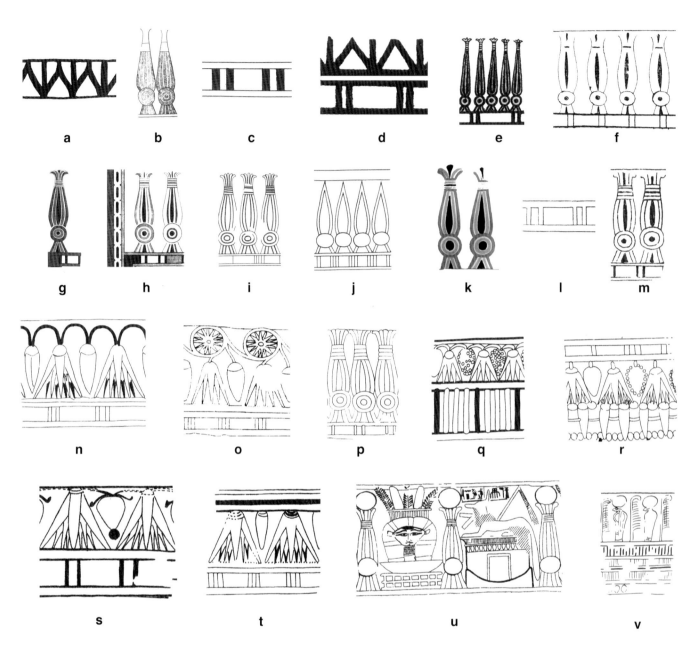

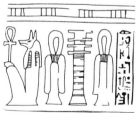

115 Friezes developed over time, with simple coloured borders appearing throughout Egyptian history: a. Ptahhotep i (Saqqara D62: late 5th Dynasty); b. Mereruka (Saqqara: early 6th Dynasty); c. Ibi (Deir el-Gebrawi 8: 6th Dynasty); d. Baqet i (Beni Hasan BH-XXIX: 11th Dynasty); e. Baqet jii (Beni Hasan BH-XV: 11th Dynasty); f. Inyotefiqer (TT60: t. Senwosret I); g. Netjernakhte (Beni Hasan BH-XXIII: 12th Dynasty); h. Khnumhotep iii (Beni Hasan BH-III: 12th Dynasty); i–j. Ukhhotep (Meir C1: t. Senwosret II); k. Djehutynakhte vi (Deir el-Bersha 1: early 12th Dynasty); l. Puiemre (TT39: t. Thutmose III); m. Qenamun (TT93: t. Amenhotep II); n. Djeserkeresonbe (TT38: t. Thutmose IV); o. Amenhotep-sise (TT75: t. Thutmose IV); p–r. Nebamun (TT90: t. Thutmose IV/Amenhotep III); s. Nebamun & Ipuky (TT181: t. Amenhotep III/IV); t. Huy (TT40: t. Tutankhamen); u. Userhat (TT51: t. Sety I); v–w. Nefersekheru (TT296: 19th Dynasty).

116 Detail of the ceiling of the tomb-chapel of Nakht (TT52: 18th Dynasty).

painted to look like the roofs of houses that were made of palm logs (e.g. D64 at Saqqara). Middle Kingdom tombs that are better preserved show brightly coloured textile patterns on the ceiling; different designs sometimes appear in different parts of the chapel. These might also have been present in Old Kingdom sepulchres. This mode of decoration continues into the New Kingdom, with other motifs also being present.

The tomb-chapels of Nakht (TT52) and Userhat (TT56) are inspired by the ceilings of private houses as they are painted to show imitations of wooden beams and mats. This also underlines the identification of the tomb as a house for eternity. More variations date from the time of Amenhotep III onwards. No doubt this change mirrors royal taste, as can be seen in the painted ceilings of Amenhotep III's palace at Malqata and the later changes that are so apparent at Tell el-Amarna. Birds, butterflies and plants appear (TT6, 30, 31, 49, 65, 159), as do ox-heads supporting the sun disk and separated by spirals, akin to the motif found at the palace of Amenhotep III at Malqata. Unfortunately few preserved ceilings have been found from other New Kingdom cemeteries, so it is difficult to determine if this tradition varied in other locations.

Engaged Statuary

Statues of the tomb-owner were part of the standard tomb equipment since these served as focal points for the cult, as well as insurance for the *ka*, should any mishap befall the actual corpse. An additional statue type was also introduced into tombs, possibly from the 4th Dynasty onwards (LG90): images that were carved from the rock that formed the tomb. This genre of statuary naturally appears only in rock-cut tombs from all periods thereafter throughout Egypt, although they are more commonly found in certain cemeteries, especially in Upper Egypt where the rock is most suitable for such images. The presence of such figures did not preclude the additional inclusion of free-standing statuary.

Frequently not just one, but several images were cut from the living rock. These included images of the deceased and his/her *ka*; several images of the deceased, perhaps showing him manifest in his different positions; statues of the whole family; statues of the deceased and his wife. The tomb of Kakerenptah (Giza G7721) contained as many as 29 statues and only one wall adorned with two-dimensional decoration.

In the Old Kingdom most of these images are standing, although there are a few variants showing seated figures. A handful of unusual images appear during this time, primarily in the Memphite necropoleis. Giza has the largest number of such engaged statuary. The 5th/6th Dynasty tomb of Idu (G7102) shows the deceased, framed by his false-door, emerging from the ground (the area of his burial chamber), with his arms opened in a position to accept offerings (ill. 186). He is shown as a plump mature man, rather than as a youth striding forward, as is the case with the statue in the false-door of Mereruka (pl. X). The image is reminiscent of the 'Reserve Heads' found in the Memphite cemeteries and the truncated statue of Ankhhaf from Giza. Squatting statues appear in the tomb of Ankhmare (G7837+7843).[129] Certain false-doors from the Abu Sir/Saqqara area show fully frontal standing images of the deceased emerging from the door portion of the false-door (e.g. that of Netjernefer, now in Cairo).[130] Engaged statues in the rock-cut tombs at El-Hamamiya have offering basins cut into the chapel floor near the statues so that the offering focus was constructed together with the rest of the chapel.[131] Clearly the Old Kingdom was a time for experimentation.

Engaged statuary is commonly found in the Middle Kingdom rock-cut tombs of Middle Egypt. These, however, tend to be seated rather than standing. For the most part they are located in the small cult room at the back of the tomb, deep in the cliff.

New Kingdom tombs contained this genre of statuary, although in Thebes it was more common in the Ramesside Period than the earlier part of that era, which favoured free-standing statues, sometimes placed in especially constructed niches, over the engaged variety (e.g. TT71, which shows the tomb-owner and his royal ward and in TT100). One of the reasons for this might be the relationship between the location of the earlier tombs and the quality of the rock. Certainly this statue type was very common at el-Amarna. The statues appear not only in the tomb-chapel proper, but in its court (e.g. TT56, 66, 82, 123). They tend to be located in niches cut into the deeper and more sacred part of the tomb, facing the entrance, as they are the focus of the cult. Texts of the *hetep-di-nesu* formula jostle with Opening-of-the-Mouth texts, as the latter might have been carried out on these engaged images during key religious festivals. Subtle stylistic changes, as well as changes in dress and adornment help in dating these statues (e.g. fat cones tend to appear on the heads of statues only from the 19th Dynasty onwardss, although there might be a few random occurrences prior to that time, e.g. TT49).

In the Ramesside Period statues of (generally) seated gods also appear (e.g. TT10, 23, 32, 106, 263, 296), frequently taking the central position, with engaged statues of the deceased and his family carved on walls that were at right angles to the central axis. Usually the deity featured is Osiris, often flanked by two goddesses. This god even appears on the tomb façade in the Ramesside Pseriod (e.g. TT26, TT35, TT41, TT158, TT178, TT263, etc.). A few tombs, such as TT356 and TT296, also contain images of Osiris, that mirror the images found in the burial chambers of Ramesses II (KV7) and his sons (KV5) in the Valley of the Kings and are also found in the Saite TT33 and 34. A few tombs even have Osiride pillars (TT157, 156).

One particularly Ramesside image, found in tombs of that era both at Thebes (TT387) and at the tomb of Netjerwymose at Saqqara (Bubasteion I.16) show the Hathor cow protecting the image of Ramesses II. This focused part of the tomb's cultic activity on the king, rather than the tomb-owner.

117 Anonymous females stand as rock-cut statues in the Old Kingdom tomb of Meresankh III at Giza.

Engaged statues of the deceased and various deities are especially popular in tombs of the Graeco-Roman Period. There the deceased is generally shown in a conventional standing position, as well as reclining. This tradition is complemented by the Hellenistic tradition of funerary busts.

Funerary Books[132]

Pyramid Texts

The Pyramid Texts represent the oldest known Egyptian corpus of religious texts. They do not form a continuous narrative, but comprise over 700 individual elements. While all relate to the posthumous destiny of the dead king, they contain many divergent or even blatantly contradictory concepts, many of which were clearly of considerable antiquity even at the time they were first inscribed, on the walls of the pyramid of Unas at Saqqara. Many spells speak of the king joining the gods in the sky and journeying with the sun god across the sky.

In the burial chambers of the pyramids of the late Old Kingdom the spells are organized for the convenience of the dead king. Those around the sarcophagus chamber protect the body of the king, while the north wall of the sarcophagus chamber is inscribed with the Offering Ritual with libation, censing, Opening-of-the-Mouth, provisions for a meal and his toilet, all things necessary for the king's renewed existence. The antechamber and corridor spells are written so that the king's spirit can use these to aid his passage to the next world: the king emerges from the underworld (*duat*) and gains access to the gateway of Nun, with the texts relating to his travelling through the pre-dawn sky. Thus the king goes from the sarcophagus chamber, equivalent to the Duat, located in the west, eastwards to the *akhet* or horizon between dawn and night and out through the north, where his soul was guided by the north star to the heavens, where he became an *akh*.[133]

Subsequent to the Old Kingdom, the Pyramid Texts are found in private contexts as well and feed into many of the subsequent funerary texts. They undergo something of a resurrection during the Saite Period, when they appear in fairly pure form in many tombs.

Coffin Texts

Although not generally inscribed on the walls of tombs, the Coffin Texts form an important corpus of mortuary material

118 Detail of the Pyramid Texts in the substructure of the pyramid of Unas at Saqqara (5th Dynasty).

that bridge the gap between the royal-focused Pyramid Texts and later compilations, such as the Book of the Dead. They are usually found on the interiors of coffins, but also occur on canopic chests, papyri and other items of funerary equipment.

The Coffin Texts by no means form a consistent set of formulae, spells, prayers and other elements, varying in content from site to site and even between coffins within the same burial. For example, coffins from Deir el-Bersha feature a composition known as the Book of Two Ways, which includes what is in essence an annotated plan of the underworld. The idea of providing the deceased with intelligence needed to successfully attain the next world runs through many parts of the Coffin Texts, a feature that continues on into many later funerary compilations.

Book of the Dead

More correctly called the 'Book of Coming Forth by Day', this composition is first found during the Second Intermediate Period and starts to become common in the 18th Dynasty, particularly under Thutmose III. Initially restricted to private contexts, certain parts are found in royal tombs from the time of Merenptah. As with the Pyramid Texts, it does not form single narrative, but has spells which allow the deceased to prevail through the various ordeals that face him or her on the way to face the judgment of Osiris and undergo the various transformations required by the spirit.

119 The fourth hour of the Amduat text was found in royal burial chambers of the 18th Dynasty – and of one private person (tomb of Thutmose III: KV34).

During its development, the Book of the Dead acquired vignettes to accompany many of its spells and these frequently appear as part of tomb decoration as well as the bare text. One of the more popular ones is the image of a pair of lions, back-to-back. These represent yesterday and tomorrow, spanning significant lengths of time between worlds. Others include images of the sun god as a cat killing the serpent Apophis and scenes of gods and demi-gods questioning the deceased.

Books of the Underworld

These texts originate in New Kingdom royal tombs, although elements subsequently became incorporated into private sepulchres as well. They are mainly concerned with the sun's nocturnal journey and rebirth, in which the dead would participate. Principal examples are as follows:

Book of Amduat: First found in the tomb of Hatshepsut (KV20) and shortly afterwards in those of Thutmose III (KV34) – and most unusually the Vizier User (TT61) – the Amduat describes and illustrates the journey of the sun god through the twelve hours of the night.

Book of Gates: The earliest example of the Gates is found in the tomb of Horemheb (KV57). It has a similar structure to the Amduat, but gives a more significant role to the king and also, uniquely for one of the Books of the underworld, incorporates a scene of the judgment hall of Osiris. The king is not, however, subject to judgment here.

Book of Caverns: Introduced under Merenptah in the cenotaph of Sety I at Abydos (the Osirion: p. 256), the first use on the walls of an actual royal tomb comes under

Ramesses IV (KV2). Only parts were generally used in the 20th Dynasty, the fullest versions being in the Sety cenotaph, the tomb of Ramesses VI (KV9) and in the Saite TT33. Once again, the Caverns is concerned with the sun's nightly voyage, but with greater prominence given to Osiris.

Book of the Earth: Parts of what became this book are seen for the first time in the tomb of Merenptah (KV8), the fullest version being found in Ramesses VI's burial chamber in KV9. The basic concepts are similar to the Caverns, although a journey through the body of the earth god Aker is now incorporated.

Litany of Re: The first elements of the Litany, which is wholly unrelated to the structure of the other Books of the underworld, appear in KV34 and TT61. From the 19th Dynasty it becomes the standard decoration of the outer part of royal tombs. It also has quite extensive use during the Late Period. The text begins with the repeated invocation of the sun god in his various forms, after which the inhabitants of the netherworld are exhorted to prepare the way for the deceased in the following of Re.

Book of the Divine Cow: This composition stands apart from the true Books of the underworld in being in part a mythological narrative, but is found in KV62, KV17, KV7

120 Portions of the Book of the Earth, showing different forms of the sun god and other divinities, in the tomb of Ramesses VI (KV9: 20th Dynasty).

and KV11. As preserved in the last three tombs, it relates how Re resolved to destroy humanity, but changed his mind after his Eye (Hathor) had begun the mission. To stop the blood-crazed goddess, red ochre is mixed with beer and spread over the world. Hathor drinks this, thinking it to be blood and becomes too drunk to complete her work. The rest of the Book (the only part found in KV62) comprises complex explanations of the origins of deities, places and customs.

Curses

Tombs were carved and decorated to protect the deceased's soul and body. In addition to the practical measures of closing and guarding the tomb, religious means were also used in the form of apotropaic tomb decoration and 'curses'. Contrary to popular belief, curses were not overly common in tombs and when they appeared, they were clearly not that terrifying, as most Egyptian tombs were looted in antiquity.

The 'curse' texts that do appear generally promise punishment for desecration in a fairly standard manner, as can be found in the mastaba of Khentika-Ikhekhi at Saqqara (6th Dynasty):

> All who enter my tomb in an impure state, having eaten abominations … they shall not be pure to enter into [it] or there will be judgment against them in the Council of gods … I shall seize his neck like a bird … I shall put fear of myself in him … so that the living may fear those who go to the West ….

At Giza, the tomb of the Overseer Petety contains a similar curse, which is intensified in his wife's tomb. She threatens the violator of the tomb with being attacked by crocodiles and hippopotami in the water and serpents and scorpions on land. Tutankhamun's tomb was reputed to contain a clay tablet inscribed with a curse, but there is no evidence for its existence, the whole story having been apparently made up by journalists soon after the tomb's discovery. As one might point out, had the tomb been cursed, Howard Carter, the tomb's excavator, would surely have been struck down immediately, rather than over a decade-and-a-half later (in 1939). Moreover, the anatomist Douglas Derry, who dismembered the mummy to examine it, lived on for a three and a half decades, dying in his 87th year, having been working in his garden until the previous day!

Part III

Chapter 6 # Predynastic and Early Dynastic Periods

The centuries surrounding the unification of Egypt at the beginning of the 1st Dynasty saw the transition from simple graves in the sand to elaborate stone-built monuments with substructures cut in the living rock. They thus laid the foundations for the outstanding achievements of the succeeding Old Kingdom.

PREDYNASTIC PERIOD

The burial places of the Predynastic Period are generally very simple and marked by little more than low mounds of sand or gravel above the burial pit. The latter comprised a scooped hole in the desert gravel, in which the flexed corpse was laid on its side, surrounded by various possessions. Graves of the Badarian and Naqada I Periods are generally oval or circular, with the body placed in a foetal pose, often wrapped in goat skins or mats and facing east, with the head to the south. Funerary equipment is largely restricted to pottery vessels, together with some examples of ivory and bone combs, slate palettes and perhaps pottery figurines.

By Naqada II, the design of the grave becomes more rectangular, with the locations of the more plentiful and varied funerary equipment more standardized. However, the orientation of the body is generally reversed to face west, in historic times the location of the home of the dead. The head remained at the south end. The graves are sometimes elaborated with wooden linings and roofs, while some very high-status examples are lined with brick and divided into two compartments by a wall. Amongst these is the first-known decorated tomb in Egypt, Hierakonpolis 100.[134] The mud-brick walls of the tomb were covered with a layer of mud plaster and then by a coat of yellow ochre. Only one wall was wholly covered with decoration, although hints of decorated areas survive on the other walls. A dado separated the decorated from the undecorated zone. The scenes depicted therein contain elements of what later became part of the Egyptian iconographic canon, such as hunting, smiting enemies and a series of bound prisoners. The overall theme depicted is one of combat and victory, perhaps images that foreshadow the victory of *maat* over chaos. The majority of the scenes show hunting through various means, combat between humans and scenes of boats. The battle depictions might reflect actual historical struggles or perhaps were merely stereotypical images of martial prowess. Such scenes of overt hostility between individuals were not the norm in Egyptian funerary art.

Hierakonpolis appears to have been the focus for the grouping of southern Egyptian polities that seem to have begun to coalesce around 3300 BC. Later chieftains moved their cemetery of brick-lined tombs 2 km (1 ¼ miles) to the

122 (*opposite*) Osiris as shown on a wall of the burial chamber of Sennedjem at Deir el-Medina (TT1: 19th Dynasty, reign of Sety I).

121 (*above*) Drawing of part of the main decorated wall of tomb 100 at Hierakonpolis (Cairo Museum).

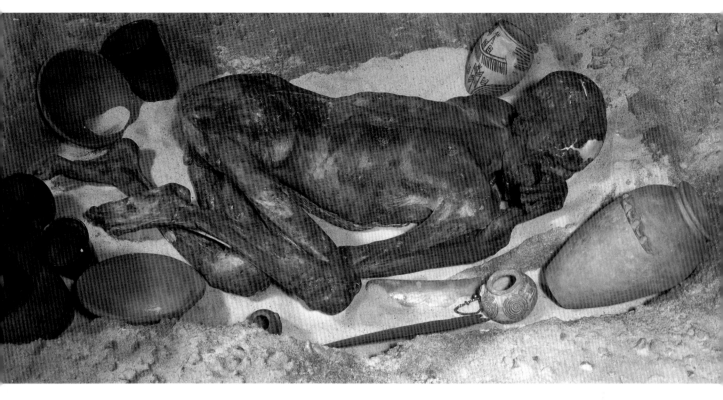

123 Reconstructed burial of a naturally-mummified male of the Naqada II Period, from Gebelein (BM EA32751).

west of tomb 100, up the Wadi Abu'l-Suffian, where had lain an earlier (Naqada I) cemetery. The tombs here were considerably larger than earlier examples and occupied areas of between 9 and 22 sq. m (100–240 sq. ft).[135] One tomb, number 23 of Naqada IIa/b date, is the largest of its date anywhere in Egypt and preserved traces of a superstructure of wood and reeds. It is entirely possible that other such superstructures existed, although they have not survived.

Tombs with very similar substructures lie in Cemetery U at Abydos. They form part of the Umm el-Qaab necropolis, first used in Naqada I/IIa times, with elite tombs beginning in Naqada IId2 and running through until historic times. These were almost certainly the tombs of the men whose immediate descendants would unite the country for the first time.

The succeeding Naqada III culture saw a more general elaboration of burial places, the rectangular form now becoming standard. There was also far greater distinction between the sepulchres of the highest status individuals and those of lesser folk. One of the most impressive of the

former lies at Umm el-Qaab; now designated U-j, it dates to perhaps up to a century prior to the unification of Egypt.[136] The tomb measures 9.1 x 7.3 m (30 x 24 ft) and probably belonged to a ruler whose name is written with a drawing of a scorpion (King 'Scorpion' I). It comprises a dozen rooms, including a large burial chamber; material recovered included an ivory sceptre (or adze handle?), a wooden shrine and examples of some of the very earliest known hieroglyphs in Egypt.

EARLY DYNASTIC PERIOD
1st Dynasty

Superstructures

Royal Tombs: The tombs of the earliest kings at Umm el-Qaab at Abydos preserve limited evidence regarding their superstructures. What stood directly above the burial chamber remains uncertain, as any structure had been destroyed before the first scientific excavation took place. However, it appears that a low mound was

124–5 View and plan of the Umm el-Qaab cemetery at Abydos, the burial place of Egypt's earliest kings.

constructed directly above the roof of the substructure, perhaps representing the primeval mound upon which the Creator first manifested himself when the mound emerged from the waters of Chaos.[137] This mound may not have been visible above the ground surface and the only certain markers of the tomb were a pair of stelae, each bearing the name of the king, between which were presumably placed offerings to the dead king's spirit.

In addition to these modest memorials back in the desert, a new element was added from the reign of Hor-Aha in the form of large rectangular brick enclosures nearly 2 km

126 The earliest stelae marking burials were very simple round-topped stones with the name of the deceased (here Queen Meryetneith) carved in bas relief (CM JE34450; 1st Dynasty).

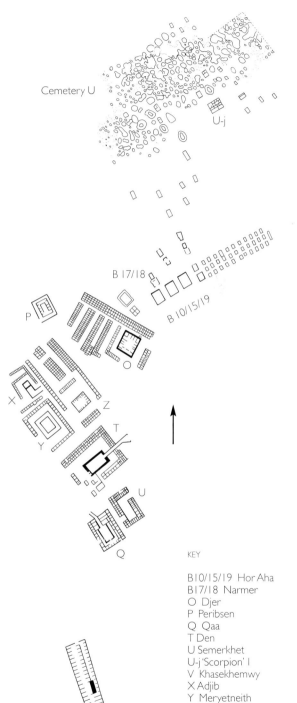

Cemetery U

U-j

B 17/18

B 10/15/19

P Peribsen

X Adjib

Z Djet

Y Meryetneith

T Den

U Semerkhet

Q Qaa

KEY

B10/15/19 Hor Aha
B17/18 Narmer
O Djer
P Peribsen
Q Qaa
T Den
U Semerkhet
U-j 'Scorpion' I
V Khasekhemwy
X Adjib
Y Meryetneith
Z Djet

(1 ¼ miles) away, close to the desert edge.[138] The outer walls of these mortuary complexes were decorated with brick panelling and at least some had a small chapel in the southeast quadrant. They may have contained temporary ritual buildings – although no traces of post-holes have been identified – and formed the prototypes for a long series of royal mortuary chapels that continued through the New Kingdom and beyond. On the other hand, the enclosures do not seem to have been intended as permanent monuments, as at least some show signs of having been dismantled within a fairly short time of the funeral.

Twelve wooden boats, found in individual mud-brick tombs, appear to have been associated with the enclosure of Djer, third ruler of the 1st Dynasty.[139] Actual boats are intermittently associated with royal burials until the Middle Kingdom.

Private Tombs: Analogous panelled monuments were also being built as parts of the sepulchres constructed for great officials at Saqqara, near the new capital at Memphis. However, here they lay directly above the burial chambers, the first manifestation of the 'mastaba'. Within the mastaba, a mound was erected directly above the burial chamber, in at least one case with a stepped casing. Private tombs thus combined the two separate Abydene elements in one monument.

The earliest such superstructures, at Naqada and Saqqara,[140] have a thick, panelled outer retaining wall, within which was constructed a network of lower walls delimiting wood-roofed store-chambers. Rubble was subsequently piled atop the roofs up to the level of the retaining walls. The full roofing of the tomb could not be carried out until the burial had taken place, since the earlier tombs lack any form of entrance other than through the roof of the burial chamber. Funerary equipment was stored in both the sub- and superstructures.

Probably owing to concerns as to the security of the above-ground magazines, later 1st Dynasty superstructures became devoid of chambers and comprised a thick brick outer section enclosing a mass of rubble; funerary equipment was thus now restricted to the substructure. The problem of admission to the latter was solved by adding a stairway accessed externally from the tomb's east side.

Little is known about the offering arrangements at the earliest 1st Dynasty private tombs. It is not until the very end

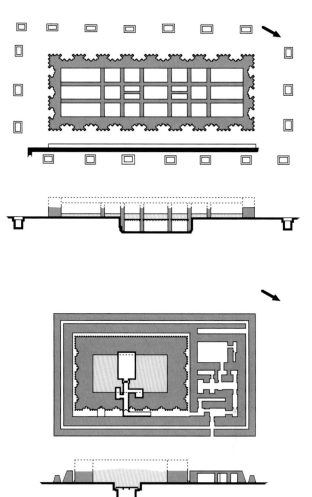

127 Plans and cross-sections of large private tombs of the 1st Dynasty at Saqqara: S3503 (unknown: time of Queen Meryetneith) and S3505 (Merka: reign of Horus Qaa).

of the dynasty, into the reign of Qaa, that a stela is to be found at an elite tomb at Saqqara (S3505). It shows the tomb-owner, Merka, seated, with his name and titles carved above him.[141] This was embedded in the southern niche on the tomb's east side, a location that became standard for mastaba offering places.

In addition, the tomb had an extensive building at its northern end, which preserved the feet of a pair of statues, the earliest evidence for cult-figures in an Egyptian tomb. Although the plan of the building anticipates some aspects of the 3rd Dynasty mortuary temple of Djoser, there are no known parallels from the Early Dynastic Period.

Substructures

Royal Tombs: The design of the sepulchral chambers of the royal tombs at Umm el-Qaab followed the earlier pattern of being brick-lined cuttings in the desert gravel, roofed with wood. The substructure of Hor-Aha (B10/15/19) took the form of three roughly equal separate compartments, but by the next reign, a basic standard had been established. The sepulchre of Djer (tomb O) was approximately square, with a wooden central chamber surrounded on three sides by store-rooms. A major step forward came with the tomb of Den (T). Earlier tombs had no means of access other than through the roof of the substructure; that of Den, however, added an entrance stairway, together with a sliding portcullis slab. This was further elaborated under Qaa, last king of the dynasty, with store chambers opening off the descending stairway of his tomb Q.

The royal tombs and their great mortuary enclosures were surrounded by smaller brick-lined compartments, used for the burial of minor members of the royal household. From their positions, some had certainly been occupied at the same time as the king had been interred; in other cases, this is less clear. Comparable instances of the king's followers dying with their monarch are known in a number of cultures, but in Egypt are restricted to the Early Dynastic Period, in particular the middle years of the 1st Dynasty, after which their numbers decline rapidly.

It appears that the interiors of the royal tombs may have been adorned with patterned reed mats hung on their walls, fragmentary remnants of which survived.[142] Doubtless, such mats were hung on the walls of houses at that time, just as they are in Egypt today, thus stressing the identity of the tomb as the eternal house for the deceased's spirit.

128 The tomb of Den at Umm el-Qaab (T) is the first royal tomb to have an entrance stairway, allowing the superstructure (of unknown form) to be completed prior to the king's interment.

Private Tombs: Private tombs also grow in size and elaboration during the 1st Dynasty. The smaller tombs continue Naqada III norms, with wood and brick linings and wooden roofs and sometimes one or more subsidiary chambers behind partition walls. An alternative approach, also beginning in Naqada III, comprises a shaft culminating in a chamber cut into the side. The opening of the chamber was closed with wattle, brick or stone and this tomb type marks the beginning of a long series of such shaft graves in locations where the local geology permitted structures of this form.

The substructures of the sepulchres of the great officials were also originally open brick-lined and wood-roofed cuttings; funerary equipment was stored in the sub- and superstructures. However, changes appear with the ending of the practice of placing store-rooms in the superstructure and the addition of an access stairway on the east side of the tomb. Where the stone was suitable, as at Saqqara, some or all of the substructure might be tunnelled, rather than cut as an open pit. Further refinements included the addition of a portcullis-block in the descending passage and on occasion a degree of decoration, for example the titles of the deceased on the lintel of the burial chamber in tomb S3506 of the middle of the dynasty.[143]

The reign of Den marks an important point in the development of Egyptian funerary practices. Not only was there a major step forward in the architecture of the royal tomb, but the number of high-status tombs known increases greatly, with a new cemetery established at Abu Rowash (Cemetery M),[144] and others at Abu Sir and Helwan. The latter necropolis included a vast number of tombs of the middle and upper levels of Early Dynastic Period society. A number of the tombs have tunnelled substructures, while stone-lining is a feature of three tombs of the 1st Dynasty at Helwan.[145] This marks important progress in the architectural development of private tombs, albeit representing less than 0.05 per cent of the burial places at the site.

2ND DYNASTY

Superstructures

Royal Tombs: At the beginning of the 2nd Dynasty, the royal cemetery moved from the ancestral Umm el-Qaab to Saqqara, albeit to a location remote from the noble cemetery that had begun early in the 1st Dynasty. The superstructure of the Saqqara tomb of Hotepsekhemwy, founder of the 2nd Dynasty, had been wholly demolished when the 5th Dynasty funerary complex of King Unas was erected on the site. However, enough has been traced of that of Ninetjer, lying 150 m (500 ft) due east, to show that it had two distinct parts. The northern part seems to have been an open, clay-paved, court some 20 m (65 ft) deep, lying above the outer passages and chambers of the tomb. This was bordered to the south by a rock 'step', which may mark the place behind which rose the main part of the superstructure.[146] It is possible that a complete 2nd Dynasty royal superstructure survives a little to the north, where a huge (*c.* 400 x 100 m [1300 x 330 ft]) tripartite cased-rubble structure covers what may be the tomb of a king of the dynasty. This building was later incorporated into the 3rd Dynasty Step Pyramid complex.[147]

The great rectangular enclosures that formed a key part of the Abydene royal tombs may also be present at Saqqara, albeit in a translated form. Two extremely large enclosures lie to the west, in the desert behind the 2nd Dynasty royal sepulchres. The larger, known as the Gisr el-Mudir, covers some 25 hectares (60 acres). Although they have not yet been fully excavated, they have revealed material that suggests that they are of the 2nd Dynasty.[148] Although apparently behind, rather than in front of their associated tombs, this is

129 Tomb 3504 at Saqqara, probably belonging to Sekhemkasedj, showing the store rooms in the superstructure, and the wood-roofed substructure (reign of Djet).

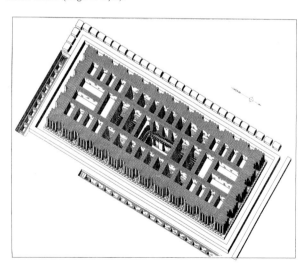

in fact illusory, as the ancient approach to the cemetery was along a wadi from the northwest. From this direction, the enclosures lie en route to the royal tombs.

While the Gisr el-Mudir is stone-built, the other example (known as the 'L-shaped Enclosure') is composed of desert gravel scraped up to form embankments. It is likely to be the earlier of the two, on the basis of both its construction and its position. This would seem to have placed any southeastern entrance in line with a rock-cutting that runs east–west and defines a platform upon and within which the tombs of Hotepsekhemwy and Ninetjer were built.

Although Saqqara had now been established as the royal cemetery for over a century, the sixth king of the dynasty, Peribsen, abruptly abandoned it in favour of the ancient necropolis of Umm el-Qaab at Abydos. Like the earlier tombs there, the superstructure of his tomb is totally obliterated, only the pair of stelae that had flanked the

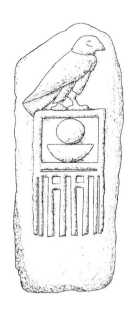

130 (*left*) Stela from the lost tomb of King Reneb (MMA 60.144: 2nd Dynasty).

131 (*below*) The Shunet el-Zebib, the funerary enclosure of King Khasekhemwy at Abydos (2nd Dynasty).

offering place survive. However, the second element of the king's tomb, the monumental enclosure, can be traced close alongside the 1st Dynasty monuments. The reasons behind Peribsen's move are obscure, but may be linked to tensions that led to civil war in the years following his demise.

The final king of the 2nd Dynasty, Khasekhemwy, was also interred at Abydos: his monuments are the biggest of their respective types there. His funerary enclosure, known today as the Shunet el-Zebib, is by far the best preserved of its genre at Abydos. Its panelled walls still stand nearly 11 m (35 ft) above the desert surface and enclose an area of some 4,500 sq. m (48,000 sq. ft). A small building, probably a chapel, has long been known in the southeast quadrant of the enclosure, corresponding to a similar structure in the enclosure of Peribsen. Unlike earlier examples, most of the exterior wall still survives, as do traces of buildings within, together with a series of basins of uncertain use, which might be intrusive 26th Dynasty features associated with the

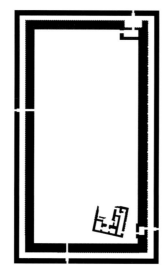

132 (*right*) Plan of the Shunet el-Zebib, Abydos.

133 (*below*) The 2nd Dynasty tomb of Ruaben (S2302: reign of Ninetjer).

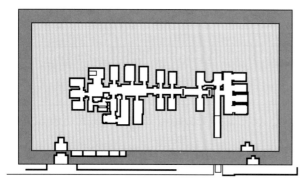

enclosure's subsequent use as an ibis cemetery. The traces of one of these were for a time misinterpreted as the remains of a brick-sheathed mound.[149]

Private Tombs: The idea of cult installations at both north and south ends of the superstructure seen in Merka's tomb took on a standardized form in 2nd Dynasty tombs at Saqqara, with a panelled niche at each end of the eastern façade. A good example, from the reign of Ninetjer, is the tomb of Ruaben (S2302).[150] Interestingly, the mastaba was enlarged during construction, the original niches being hidden behind new brickwork and fresh ones created on the new front/façade. Around the end of the dynasty, these niches began to develop into a cruciform shape, a typical feature of the succeeding 3rd Dynasty. The first datable example is S3043, which contained a sealing of Khasekhemwy, last king of the 2nd Dynasty. Panelled mastabas, albeit on a much smaller scale, are also found above tombs of this dynasty at Helwan.[151]

The offering niches were increasingly equipped with stelae showing the tomb-owner in front of a table with offerings, the stela becoming generally wider than it was high and mounted roughly at the eye-level of the viewer. Such 'slab-stelae' remain the basic elements of tomb-chapel decoration into the 4th Dynasty, when they become incorporated into more elaborate false-door stelae.

Substructures

The substructures of 2nd Dynasty tombs are generally wholly different from those of 1st Dynasty tombs, featuring complex tunnelled construction, rather than the extensive open trenching seen earlier. One of the best examples is Ruaben's S2302, whose burial complex is approached by a stairway and has no fewer than 18 chambers. It has been suggested that some of these were intended to replicate elements of a house, including a latrine.[152] The body appears to have been placed in the room at the right-hand side of the last vestibule of the tomb, the whole sepulchre being protected by two portcullises.

Such elaborate substructures are also found in the royal tombs of the new dynasty. Compared with the fairly simple Umm el-Qaab tomb of Qaa, that of Hotepsekhemwy has a sloping passageway that leads to an extremely complex series of galleries and chambers. The outer passageways were roofed with limestone blocks and protected by stone

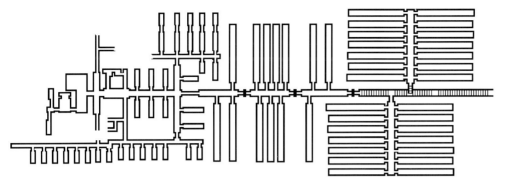

134 (*left*) Plan of the tomb of Hotepsekhemwy at Saqqara (2nd Dynasty).

135 (*below*) Plan of the tomb of Peribsen at Umm el-Qaab, Abydos (2nd Dynasty).

portcullises, lowered on ropes from above through the superstructure. A substructure of the same type, but much less regular and deeper, lay under the tomb of Ninetjer.[153] A similar, but smaller, tomb was later adapted as the substructure of the late 18th Dynasty tomb of Meryneith (H9, p. 232);[154] like Ninetjer's it had become a communal catacomb in the Late Period. Unfortunately, the original owner remains uncertain, while another remarkable complex of galleries, whose superstructure now lies under the western side of the Step Pyramid complex, has never been properly cleared. However, they may represent the tombs of the other 2nd Dynasty kings known from inscribed material to have been buried at Saqqara: Reneb and Sened.

The Abydos burial place of Peribsen is wholly unlike these tunnelled tombs and follows the basic pattern of 1st Dynasty royal tombs, built of brick and sunk in a pit in the desert surface. Similarly constructed is the underground tomb of Khasekhemwy, although its form is wholly different from that of earlier Abydene royal sepulchres and is by far the largest, being no less than 68 m (225 ft) long, by 12 m (40 ft) broad. Yet these dimensions are insignificant compared to those of the tomb of Hotepsekhemwy, whose substructure occupies an area of 123 x 49 m (400 x 160 ft). On the other hand, the rows of store chambers that are such a feature of both sepulchres clearly suggest a commonality of concept.

Most Saqqara private tombs of the 2nd Dynasty tended to follow the patterns seen in the sepulchre of Ruaben, albeit on a more modest scale. Distinctive features are a multi-room tunnelled substructure, approached by a stairway in a trench cut in the top of a two-niched mastaba. Of course, in addition to such relatively elaborate monuments, smaller

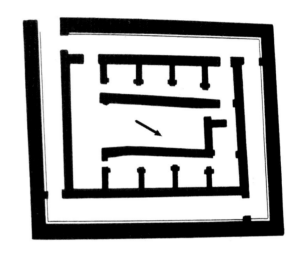

single-roomed tombs were also built, although generally with a stair-entrance and a double-niched superstructure. Such structures are also found in such southern Egyptian cemeteries as Naga el-Deir. In these, however, corbelled roofing is sometimes found in the substructure in place of wooden roofs, needed where a fully-tunnelled burial complex was not possible.

The Helwan necropolis continued in use through the 2nd and 3rd Dynasties and included the burials of a number of royal children. Designs range from simple stairway tombs to more elaborate structures, including a handful of stone-lined monuments. Certain tombs conformed to a curious design in which a narrow shaft, parallel to the main one, led down through the ceiling of the burial chamber, at which point a stela showing the deceased in front of a table of offerings was placed. Other tombs had stelae placed on the west side of the burial chamber, for example in tomb 480 and tomb 810.[155]

Chapter 7

The Old Kingdom

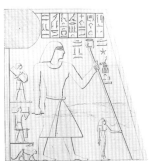

The Old Kingdom marked the consolidation of the Egyptian state following civil war towards the end of the 2nd Dynasty. It was also the pivotal epoch for the evolution of the Egyptian tomb. During this time, all the classic forms of Egyptian sepulchre came into existence, as did their modes of decoration, producing monuments that continue to define the popular perception of ancient Egypt.

3RD DYNASTY

Superstructures

Royal Tombs: The great innovation of the 3rd Dynasty was the construction of the very first pyramid: Djoser's Step Pyramid at Saqqara, the earliest monumental stone building in the world.[156] It took the mud-brick panelled enclosure of the Shunet el-Zebib and transformed it into stone. Likewise transformed were the temporary buildings that may have been placed within the Shunet,[157] to judge from the way in which many of the Step Pyramid's buildings imitate organic materials. The royal burial apartments and the mound above them were moved into the centre of the enclosure, thus combining the elements previously found separated in royal tombs, both at Abydos and Saqqara. The mound was regularized into a square stone structure.

The size of the stone blocks employed in the Step Pyramid complex clearly recalls those of mud-bricks, marking its place close to the beginning of the history of stone masonry. The buildings included within the enclosure embrace a wide range of forms, with their purposes the subject of much debate. Many of their columns and architectural details were clearly modelled directly from wood and other plant prototypes. It seems clear that these structures are linked with the rituals of kingship, including the *heb-sed* jubilee and might be a skeuomorph of buildings associated with this ritual that existed at the capital city of Memphis. The *heb-sed* was a ritual associated with the renewal of kingship, indicating that the king would continuously renew his rulership and dominion over Egypt throughout eternity.

Little decoration survives from these buildings. The few carved motifs adorning the buildings include *kheker* friezes and *djed* pillars, symbolic of Osiris and the union of the dead king with that god. In addition, a number of items of statuary were placed within the complex, most of them carved from the block against which they appeared to stand. It is not known if any of the buildings within the complex were painted, as no vestiges of paint remain.

Aside from the sheer scale of the Step Pyramid complex – at 15 hectares (35 acres), it covers 360 per cent of the Shunet el-Zebib's area, although only 60 per cent of that of the Gisr el-Mudir – and the massive embrace of stone technology, the most radical innovation of Imhotep, Djoser's architect, concerned the burial place itself. It was placed in the middle

---

136 (*above*) Doorjambs from the rock-cut tomb of Debhen at Giza (LG90: late 4th Dynasty).

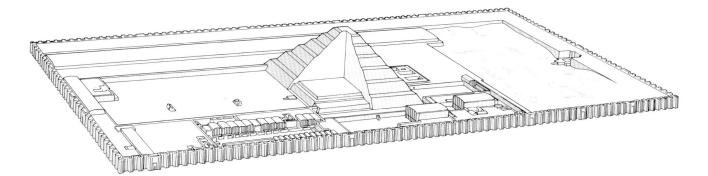

137 (above) Reconstruction of the Step Pyramid complex at Saqqara, revealing the earliest phases of the central monument.

138 (below) The entrance colonnade of the Step Pyramid complex, opening from the left-hand end of the eastern enclosure wall in the same way that the chapel of a mastaba opened from the corresponding end of the mastaba's eastern façade.

of the enclosure and was topped with what became the lowest of the six steps of a pyramid. The reasons behind this transformation remain unknown, but the result formed the first link in a chain of pyramids that, large and small, would be built along the Nile for the next three millennia.

Against the inner face of the southern enclosure wall lies a long, narrow, limestone mastaba, decorated with the niched palace façade motif and surmounted by a row of uraei on the east side, perhaps to greet the rising sun. Known as the 'South Tomb', this structure is the prototype for a long series of such miniature sepulchres, in this case with a central chamber too small to hold a body. Later topped by small pyramids, these subsidiary tombs always lie to the south of the main pyramid or its temple and are of obscure significance. None of the suggestions for their use are convincing; for example, the proposal that they were intended for the royal viscera is disproved by the large number of pyramids that have both a subsidiary pyramid and also a canopic chest in the main burial chamber. A cenotaph alluding to the king as ruler of the south as well as the north of the country has also been suggested, but with no accompanying evidence.

The patterns established by Djoser were followed during the immediately subsequent reigns.[158] However, while stepped pyramids continued in use until the early years of the next dynasty, the great rectangular enclosures are no longer certainly attested beyond the middle of the 3rd, the latest certain example being Sekhemkhet's, which covers 10 hectares (25 acres). Sekhemkhet's likely predecessor, Sanakhte, may have reverted to brick for a little-known enclosure at Abu Rowash, known as El-Deir. It measures 330 x 170 m (1080 x 560 ft), with a 20 m (65 ft)-square central massif of the same material.[159]

139 The huge mastaba K1 at Beit Khallaf, dating to the reign of Djoser.

The size of the blocks used to build pyramid complexes increases over time, although the last ruler of the dynasty, Huni, seems to have switched back to mud-brick for his sepulchre. He has been tentatively identified as the owner of the Brick Pyramid at Abu Rowash, a monument intended to be some 215 m (700 ft) square – as big as the much better-known Second Pyramid at Giza. However, it may never have been completed: the last remnants of brick were removed in the 19th century, leaving nothing more than the rock core.[160]

Private Tombs: Brick mastabas continued to be the favoured form of private tomb-marker, although a panelled exterior gradually fell out of use. A group of tombs at Beit Khallaf, north of Abydos, dating to the reigns of Djoser and Sanakhte, include two gigantic plain mastabas, K1 and K2, whose dimensions once led to suggestions that they might actually be the burial places of these monarchs.[161] The identities of the true owners remain uncertain, but they may have been of the local gubernatorial class – or possibly of the royal family.[162] Their construction employs solid mud-brick, rather than the rubble core faced with brick, as had been the case with the earliest mastabas. Solid brickwork had appeared in the 2nd Dynasty and became common in the 3rd, although both techniques survived alongside one another into the late Old Kingdom. Nothing of the cult elements of the Beit Khallaf tombs is known, but at Saqqara a number of new approaches are to be seen in the contemporary tomb of Hesyre (S2405).[163]

Like many tombs of the era, S2405's superstructure had undergone a number of alterations and includes some hitherto-unknown features. Originally, its cult installation comprised two panelled niches in the northern part of the east face. However, these were replaced by a new, wholly panelled, façade, enclosed by a wooden roof and a curtain wall opposite it, thus forming a narrow corridor and entered

140 Plan and section of the tomb of Hesyre (S2405: reign of Djoser); the final form of the tomb was the result of a series of enlargements that seems to have been common with tombs of the early Old Kingdom.

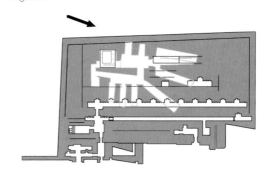

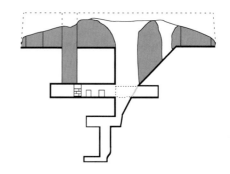

141 View of the tomb of Hesyre under excavation; the 'corridor' in the centre is the walled-in original façade with the wooden panels.

by a doorway at its southern end. The panelled niches were made of the same mud-brick as the rest of the mastaba and plastered and painted with various geometric patterns in bright colours. Embedded in the back of each niche was a wooden panel, bearing an image in raised relief of the deceased, of which the six southernmost survive (pl. XIII). The opposite wall of the corridor was also plastered and painted with framed images of domestic items set against a background imitating matting. As well as such objects as furniture, barrels and gaming items, the outer corridor also boasted images of people and animals, creating a unique ensemble.

The preservation of the paintings and wooden panels owed much to a further change of plan that resulted in the corridor being entirely filled with solid mud-brick. Another corridor, with only two niches, was constructed parallel with

the first, with access via a group of antechambers at the southern end.

Although internally elaborate, the exterior of Hesyre's tomb seems to have been plain, except probably for a coat of whitewash, as were most sepulchres of the dynasty. However, examples of the old fully panelled mastaba exterior are still found, a good example being tomb T at Giza. No special offering place is identifiable, but the 'corridor-chapel' of the type found in S2405 was used in a number of other tombs of the 3rd Dynasty and early 4th Dynasty, both at Saqqara and elsewhere, an example of the latter being R70 at Reqaqna.[164] Two most interesting tombs at the former site are S3518 and S3073, belonging respectively to an anonymous noble of Djoser's reign and Khabausokar who lived around the end of the dynasty.[165] Both show developments in the form of the offering place, S3518 having a remarkably complex chapel at

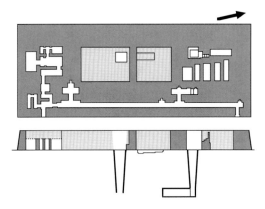

142 (*above*) Tomb S3518, potentially the tomb of Imhotep, architect of the Step Pyramid.

143 (*left*) A wooden panel from the tomb of Hesyre. Such items were probably a more common feature of Egyptian tombs than the current level of preservation would suggest (CM CG1426: 3rd Dynasty).

the southern end of the mastaba, plus a southern niche of cruciform shape. In view of its complexity and massive size (52 x 19 m [170 x 60 ft]), the tomb clearly belonged to a particularly prominent member of the court, conceivably the great Imhotep, architect of the Step Pyramid, whose orientation it shares.

Khabausokar's mastaba includes a niched corridor very similar to Hesyre's, but has a pair of cruciform chapels opening from it, into the core of the mastaba. The central niche of each was stone-lined and decorated in relief, thus initiating a move away from simple stelae to far more elaborate carved decoration. The following dynasty would see a massive expansion in such figurative elements.

Substructures

While 3rd Dynasty tombs continued to employ extensive tunnelled subterranean galleries, approached by stairways, increasing use was made of open shafts for the construction of the burial chamber. Such a shaft was employed in Djoser's Step Pyramid, whose substructure centred on a burial chamber 28 m (90 ft) below ground level, approached by a stairway and tunnel from the north. Until the Middle Kingdom this was to be the standard orientation of a royal tomb entrance. Around this lay a number of galleries; most were store-chambers, but those on the east included a set of four decorated rooms; near duplicates were found under the

South Tomb. Their adornment featured simulacra of reed mats formed of faience tiles set into limestone, carved in the form of the rope that held the reeds together. Some of the rooms also had additional decoration in the form of carved doorjambs and lintels and limestone *djed* pillars. Most impressively, one room had carved limestone panels set into the walls depicting the pharaoh running the *heb-sed* race – the first depiction of a king in the substructure of a tomb and the last until the middle of the 18th Dynasty, over a millennium later.

This part of the substructure is clearly the final development of the 2nd Dynasty concept of including rooms imitating the deceased's home in his tomb, while the inlaid imitation of matting on the walls presumably recalled the 1st Dynasty tombs at Abydos. These rooms make the Step Pyramid unique amongst royal tombs of the first

144 (*above*) Image of Djoser taking part in the *heb-sed* festival, from one of the tiled rooms under his South Tomb; the tiles (see also pl. XIV) imitate hangings of mats.

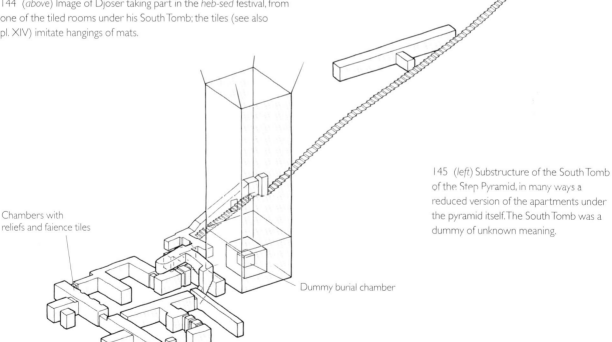

Chambers with reliefs and faience tiles

Dummy burial chamber

145 (*left*) Substructure of the South Tomb of the Step Pyramid, in many ways a reduced version of the apartments under the pyramid itself. The South Tomb was a dummy of unknown meaning.

six-and-a-half centuries of Egypt's unity in having a decorated substructure; it is not until the very end of the 5th Dynasty that another example is known.

Private sepulchres were generally approached by stairways from the top of the associated mastaba. This arrangement is found at Beit Khallaf, where K2 is interesting in having two separate, but similar, substructures, clearly for husband and wife. The substructures of both K1 and K2 were protected by a series of portcullis-slabs, lowered from the top surface of the superstructure, a scheme also found in the pyramid of Sekhemkhet, whose unfinished galleries show a number of affinities with the Beit Khallaf tombs. This pyramid and the Layer Pyramid at Zawiyet el-Aryan have tunnelled corridors and chambers, plus an extensive set of store-rooms; the latter elements were abandoned for subsequent royal tombs. In contrast, the substructure of the probable last pyramid of the dynasty, the Brick Pyramid of Abu Rowash, comprised a simple corridor and burial chamber.

The substructure of the tomb of Hesyre is also of the stair-approached type, with a set of lower rooms accessible

146 Section and plan of the Layer Pyramid at Zawiyet el-Aryan. The 'dog-tooth' storage galleries are a feature shared with the immediately preceding pyramid of Sekhemkhet.

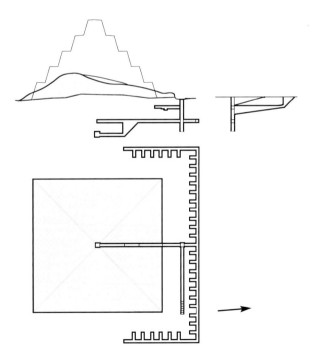

via a shaft in the floor of the antechamber. Similarly, Giza tomb T has an elaborate set of rooms reached by a stairway, supplemented by a further room at a lower level. S3518, however, is interesting in having a much simpler design for one of its two burial complexes,[166] both being approached by a shaft only. However, stairways to link up with them had been begun, but were soon abandoned. This transition from stairway to shaft substructures is an important motif of the transition from 2nd/3rd Dynasty tomb types into those of the 4th Dynasty and it is instructive to find it as early as this.

THE 4TH DYNASTY

Built Superstructures

Royal Tombs: The earliest of Seneferu's many pyramids[167] was begun as a seven-stepped structure at Meidum; this was later enlarged to eight steps and then converted, late in his reign, into a 'true', straight-sided pyramid. This change seems to have resulted from a shift in religious beliefs, whereby the king ceased to ascend to heaven by a stairway, but rather mounted a ramp laid down by the sun's rays and made concrete by the sloping sides of the pyramid.

The monument also marks the first certain move away from the great rectangular mortuary enclosure that had been a key feature of royal tombs since the beginning of the 1st Dynasty until at least the middle of the 3rd Dynasty.[168] Instead, at Meidum we find an enclosure that is approximately square and lies only a modest distance beyond the perimeter of the pyramid itself.

The mortuary temple was placed on the east side of the pyramid, a location that may have solar significance. Its focus consisted of an offering table, flanked by a pair of stelae, placed against the face of the pyramid. From the mortuary temple, a causeway led down to the edge of the desert, where lay the valley temple, which formed the ceremonial entrance to the whole pyramid complex. Many valley temples had one or more quays, providing boat access via a canal and/or during the annual Nile flood – the Inundation – which covered everything up to the desert edge.

All these basic features became standard in subsequent pyramids, as did the placement of a miniature, 'subsidiary' pyramid to the south of the main monument, which is found for the first time at Meidum. This is clearly a development of the 'South Tomb' of Djoser's complex and is just as obscure in purpose.

147 (*right*) At Meidum, a pyramid was begun as a step pyramid, but was ultimately converted to a straight-sided one. The partial collapse of the outer part allows the original structure to be seen. In addition, the pyramid marks the abandonment of the rectangular enclosure in favour of one with a small temple and causeway on the east side (4th Dynasty).

148 (*below*) The mortuary temple of the Meidum pyramid centred on a pair of stelae to bear the titulary of the king.

In parallel with his construction work at Meidum, Seneferu had commenced building the first true pyramid to be designed as such, at Dahshur. Failure of the bedrock seems to have resulted in changes of plan, most crucially the construction of a whole new set of burial passages and a reduction in the whole structure's height, changing the angle half-way up and giving it its modern name, the 'Bent Pyramid'. Further consideration clearly led to an assessment that the pyramid was still unsafe, since yet another pyramid (the 'Red Pyramid') was begun at Dahshur and completed with the same lower angle as the upper part of the Bent Pyramid.

The spectacular pyramid-building of Seneferu, which also included one and perhaps another six, small pyramids of uncertain purpose along the Nile,[169] is unmatched. However, to his son, Khufu, belongs the credit for the construction at Giza of the most massive free-standing structure ever built, universally known as the 'Great Pyramid'.[170] Its enclosure marks an evolution from the prototypes provided by Seneferu, with a considerably enlarged mortuary temple, but also a set of pits for boat burials,[171] reminiscent of those found near the Shunet el-Zebib. Another change was the placement of the subsidiary pyramid just south of the mortuary temple, a location that was to become standard during the 5th Dynasty. Adjacent to the subsidiary pyramid stood three further miniature pyramids, intended for the interment of Khufu's womenfolk. These are the first pyramids to belong

149 (*above*) As in the slightly later Meidum complex, the mortuary temple of Seneferu's Bent Pyramid also featured a pair of stelae (one on either side of the structure in the centre), now broken.

150 (*below*) The queens' pyramids at the foot of the Great Pyramid at Giza, with one of the boat pits that lay adjacent to Khufu's mortuary temple; Cemetery G7000 lies beyond.

to persons other than kings and are of simple design, with a small chapel on the eastern side.

The Great Pyramid and the two large pyramids subsequently built at Giza by Khafre and Menkaure, show the continual development of the mortuary temple, causeway and valley temple. By the end of the 4th Dynasty, the stelae in the inner part of the mortuary temple had been replaced by a single stela and additional elements were added beyond the innermost apartments. Typically, a room with five niches for statues lay just outside the sanctuary, as did various corridors and store-rooms. A courtyard, surrounded by a peristyle, fronted this inner complex. In front of the courtyard stood a solid walled entrance hall as the gateway to the temple.

Owing to the destroyed state of the royal monuments of the period, it is unclear when and how royal funerary monuments of the 4th Dynasty were decorated. Apart from their stelae, the mortuary temples of Seneferu appear to have been plain, while those of his successors apparently relied for their adornment on the various coloured building stones employed – granite, basalt, limestone and calcite (also known as travertine and Egyptian alabaster) – and statuary.

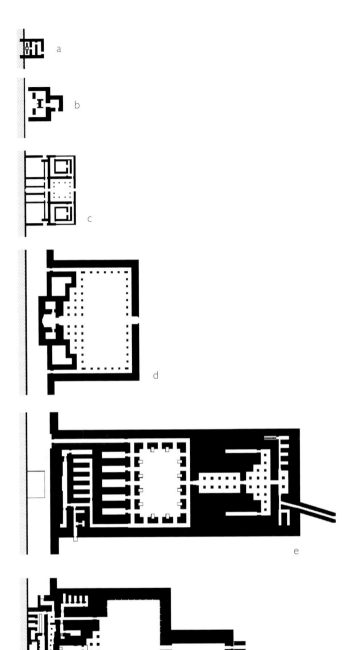

151 The evolution of the royal mortuary temple: a. Seneferu (Meidum); b. Seneferu (Dahshur – Bent Pyramid); c. Seneferu (Dahshur – Red Pyramid); d. Khufu (Giza – Great Pyramid); e. Khafre (Giza – Second Pyramid); f. Menkaure (Giza – Third Pyramid).

In contrast to the mortuary temple, the valley temple of Seneferu's Bent Pyramid was decorated with extensive reliefs of offering bringers and of the king in the presence of the gods, as well as scenes showing the king running the *heb-sed*, together with the additional celebration of the 'Running of the Apis Bull', a ceremony associated with the fertility of the herds and fields. Three-dimensional images of the king himself were also found here. The same may also have been the case for the valley building of Khufu, fragments possibly deriving from which contained reliefs of the bringing of offerings by personified estates, a procession of oxen being brought to the king and inscriptions relating to him. One curious scene that comes from Khufu's complex and which survived through its re-use in Cairo's Bab el-Futuh gateway, shows a ritual involving the king and a white hippopotamus. The adjacent causeway also seems to have been decorated from the reign of Khufu onwards, with scenes related to offerings executed in painted raised relief.

The royal pyramids that followed that of Khufu mark a further move towards the 'standard' pyramid complex.[172] The widely differing forms of mortuary chapels seen previously were replaced by much larger mortuary and valley temples, which provided prototypes for the standard plans that developed later in the Old Kingdom. These buildings, in particular the valley temples, were provided with large numbers of statues. The temple attached to the Bent Pyramid had a number of statues with their own specific cults, while the main hall of Khafre's had 23 statues, each apparently with its own identity.

Private Tombs: The Meidum pyramid has a number of associated cemeteries. The tombs of the main private cemetery at Meidum, situated to the north of the pyramid, mark an important stage in the development of the mastaba, in particular that of the offering place.[173] Leaving aside the 'experimental' 3rd Dynasty tombs such as those of Hesyre and Khabausokar, the standard approach since the 2nd Dynasty had been based on niches close to the ends of the eastern tomb façade. At Meidum one finds important examples of the further developments that occurred early in the 4th Dynasty.

These are to be seen in particular in two of the largest tombs of the cemetery, which underwent alterations that completely changed the form of their cult areas. M16 (Nefermaat) was the largest in the whole necropolis, measuring no less than 120 x 68 m (390 x 225 ft) in its final form. Before reaching such dimensions, however, it had been enlarged twice. In the first phase, each of the two offering places consisted of a recess, the back of which was faced with stone and from the middle of which a short stone-lined decorated corridor led back into the brickwork, ending in a false-door. The first enlargement added an extra layer of brickwork, necessitating the construction of a passageway to allow the stone-lined elements to be reached from the exterior. This resulted in the creation of two cruciform chapels, a design used sporadically since at least the beginning of the 3rd Dynasty. Although superbly decorated, the entire chapels were made inaccessible when the mastaba was enlarged for a second time, new niches being constructed and an external court added outside the northern one. A similar, but even more elaborate series of alterations occurred at the tomb of Rahotep (M6). Here, the sealed southern chapel housed painted limestone statues of Rahotep and his wife, Neferet, two of the finest portrait

pieces surviving from ancient Egypt (pl. XVI), making it the earliest known private *serdab* (closed statue room). *Serdabs* became an integral part of tomb-chapel design as the 4th Dynasty continued.[174]

The decoration of these Meidum tombs in many ways set the principal patterns for tomb-chapel decoration seen through the remainder of Egyptian history.[175] During the 4th (and to some extent, 5th) Dynasty the decoration centered on the active service of the tomb-owner with regard

152 (*right*) Section of decoration from the chapel of Itet in Meidum 16 (Nefermaat), showing the inlaid pigment (Ny Carlsberg ÆIN1133 a–b; Munich Gl.103 e–f).

153 (*below*) Plan and section of the mastaba of Rahotep and Neferet at Meidum (6). The tomb was enlarged a number of times, the penultimate one blocking off the original stone-lined funerary chapels at either end of the façade. In its final form, the tomb had a southern chapel against the face of the mastaba and a northern one within the outermost layer of the mastaba. The substructures were reached via shafts in the top of the superstructure. Rahotep had a corbelled burial chamber, with relieving chambers constructed above (4th Dynasty).

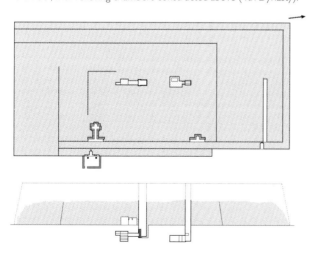

154 The three main pyramids at Giza (the Great Pyramid of Khufu at left), with the Western Cemetery on the right.

to the monarch, while also introducing daily-life scenes into the repertoire. The tombs were decorated with paint as well as raised and sunk relief. The tomb of Nefermaat and his wife Itet also displays a unique decorative technique, comprising blocks of pigment let into the surface of the stone. The tomb-owner seems to claim credit for this innovation, which was not, indeed, used in any other tomb.

At Dahshur, private cemeteries were established at considerable distances from the royal pyramids, comprising a mixture of brick and stone mastabas, the latter being amongst the earliest of their kind. The time-hallowed arrangement of offering places at either end of the eastern façade continued, the surviving examples being of a simple niche plan.[176] In contrast, at Saqqara, stone cruciform chapels, embedded in a brick mastaba, had become standard early in the 4th Dynasty (e.g. Metjen [LS6], Akhethotep [A1=S3076], Akhetaa, Pahernefer and S3078).

East of Khufu's pyramid at Giza was a massive cemetery intended for lesser members of his family. Other cemeteries were placed west and south of the pyramid and mark an important shift from the wide separation of royal and other

tombs seen from Early Dynastic times down to the reign of Khufu's father. Now, rather than the pyramid standing in splendid isolation, the members of the court huddled around its base, in many ways emphasizing even further the gulf between the ruler and ruled.[177]

The tombs in these cemeteries had all been laid out and their cores built as part of a single project. Known as 'nucleus cemeteries', their cores were allocated to and finished by, their ultimate owners. As originally built, these cores were solid, initially composed of rubble, but soon succeeded by large blocks of stone. The tombs in the nucleus cemeteries had been envisaged as accommodating single burials only. However, some mastabas had been extended to embrace a second shaft for the deceased's spouse and, in the Eastern Cemetery at Giza, pairs of individual mastabas were joined together by a single casing and appropriate cult structures created for couples. The original cores had no internal or exterior provision for offering places, other than a small 'slab stela' towards the southern end of the east side. As a minimum, a mud-brick chapel would have been built to protect this modest interface between the worlds. Some

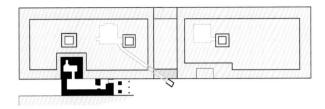

155 The tomb of Kawab (G7110+7120); it comprised two of the nucleus mastabas that were built by Khufu for subsequent allocation. The internal 'L'-shaped chapel was supplemented with a built external section. Substructures were once again accessed via shafts from the mastaba roof, although an unusual sloped passage was subsequently added to Kawab's burial chamber (4th Dynasty).

tombs subsequently received a proper casing, together with a stone chapel and a fully fledged false-door, but others were rebuilt with much more elaborate chapel structures.

In certain cases, a thick casing was placed around the mastaba core, with a chapel within it or in an annex built on one end; in others, the core was penetrated and new structures constructed inside. These were generally based upon an 'L'-shaped arrangement, with false-door(s) placed in the long rear wall. Although many variations are known, this shape of offering place is the dominant type down to the time of Neferirkare, with two false-doors usual by the end of Menkaure's reign. Compared with those begun under Khufu, overall chapel designs in the later part of the 4th Dynasty were more elaborate and innovative and paved the way for further developments in the following period.

The adornment of such chapels at Giza include large figures of the tomb-owner and family viewing the presentation of offerings and animals. Other scenes are often linked with the funerary meal, as well as a limited repertoire of daily-life scenes.

156 Plan of the tomb of Meresankh III (G7530+7540) at Giza, showing the unusual subterranean chapel at its north end.

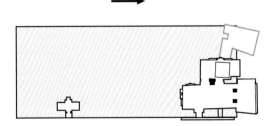

In addition to the offering place itself, *serdabs* (see opposite) now began to be placed behind the false-doors. Statues played an increasingly important part in the mortuary cult during the Old Kingdom, although the presence of such images of the dead is attested as far back as the end of the 1st Dynasty in the tomb of Merka (S3505) (p. 136, above). *Serdabs* were often connected to the main body of the chapel by small slits through which the statue could 'see' the offerings and incense could reach it. It was in these statues that the *ka* was believed to manifest itself to receive offerings.

At the opposite end of the spectrum from these noble tombs are the mastabas of the skilled artisan class found in the so-called 'Workers' Cemetery' at Giza. Their superstructures comprised twin-niched mastabas of the usual form, but constructed on a much smaller scale,

157 (*above*) Detail of the 'Workers' Cemetery' at Giza; in the foreground are mud-brick miniature mastabas of the artisan class.

158 (*bottom*) Amongst other tombs at the site are some unusual domed or conical examples. The doorway in the east side ultimately gives access to the burial pit.

159 The *serdab* – a closed room containing statues – of Akhethotep held four images, including one of the tomb-owner and one of his wife (Saqqara: 6th Dynasty).

perhaps only a metre or so high. Another type of tomb found in the same area is of domed or conical shape, perhaps intended to be a model of one of the pyramids upon which the community laboured.

The majority of substantial tombs dating to the 4th Dynasty have been found in the Memphite necropolis. However, a number have been identified at more remote sites. One example is El-Tarif, at the northern end of the Theban cemetery, where two brick mastabas have been found.[178] They are of simple form, with an offering niche at the southern end of the east side, although their internal structure reveals a somewhat complex building history. Another Upper Egyptian site with 4th Dynasty mastabas is El-Kab,[179] in this case with panelled exteriors and simple offering places on the east side.

Rock-cut Superstructures and Offering Places

Until the middle of the 4th Dynasty, the offering place of a wealthy tomb was a built structure, either free-standing, or set within the core of a mastaba. However, the cemeteries that date to Khafre and Menkaure's reigns contain a mixture of free-standing mastabas and rock-cut tomb-chapels. Hitherto, cemeteries had typically been built on flat areas of desert; other sites, however, including the central part of the Giza necropolis, shelve fairly steeply and in such cases it is generally most practical to cut the offering place out of the rock, with the superstructure otherwise limited to an ornamental façade. While there are examples of whole mastabas having been cut out of the living rock – including

160 Cemetery MQ at Giza, containing rock-cut tombs of the late 4th Dynasty.

the very unusual Giza tomb of Queen Khentkaues I (LG100) of the end of the 4th Dynasty – the vast majority of such tombs conformed to the simple pattern.

A large number of rock-cut tomb-chapels were built in a former quarry area between the pyramid complexes of Khafre and Menkaure and are probably the earliest examples of such sepulchres. The forms of the chapels of rock-cut tombs follow the same patterns as those of contemporary mastabas, but with at least two rather larger rooms. Externally, their eastern elevations are reminiscent of that of a mastaba and at some sites built elements were also present. The new tomb-type was used at Giza for a number of members of the royal family, including both royal wives and sons. A composite form is G7530+7540, the massive double mastaba of Queen Meresankh III, which had an additional subterranean chapel quarried out below it (ill. 156). In contrast to the limited repertoire seen in mastaba chapels at Giza, a significant number of 'daily-life' scenes appear in rock-cut chapels, with the chapel of Meresankh III providing important examples of a number of vignettes. Texts, pertaining to the deceased's life or the building of his tomb, also start appearing at this time, for example in the tomb of Debhen at Giza (LG90, 4th/5th Dynasty). Another feature of this tomb is the ranks of three-dimensional figures carved into the walls. Similar images are found in a range of contemporary and later rock-cut chapels, for example those of Irukaptah-Khenu at Saqqara and Kakerenptah (G7721, 5th Dynasty) and Idu at Giza (G7102, 6th Dynasty).

Rock-cut tombs appear in Upper Egypt at around the same time as they do at Giza, some of the very earliest being the so-called 'Fraser Tombs', at Tihna.[180] Their designs vary, that of Nikaankh having a mastaba containing a chapel with false-doors and niches and behind it, in what is now the cliff-face, three doors leading to small rooms (ill. 183d). However, all centre on a transverse passage, with offering places located on the same side as the entrance doorway, as these tombs are on the east bank and thus face away from the realm of the dead in the west. This somewhat awkward arrangement is found in other east-bank tombs as well, for example that of Iymery at Gebel el-Teir,[181] and those of the Middle Kingdom at Beni Hasan (p. 193).

Substructures

The early part of the dynasty may be distinguished by the extensive use of corbelling in the roofing of chambers and

161 (*top*) The two rock-cut mastabas of Tihna (the 'Fraser Tombs'), as seen from the east (early 5th Dynasty).

162 (*above*) The tomb of Nikaankh (Tihna 13), the right-hand tomb in the previous image. Its western façade faces into the cliff from which it is cut, and thus access to the chapel within is via what is little more than a trench in the rock.

163 (*right*) Ceiling of the burial chamber of the pyramid of Meidum. Tombs at the site were amongst the first to employ such corbelling.

164 (*above*) Tomb 17 at Meidum (4th Dynasty: reign of Seneferu).

165 (*right*) Granite sarcophagus in the burial chamber of tomb 17, the earliest of its kind.

corridors. All three of Seneferu's burial pyramids employed the technique.[182] None were designed to hold a stone sarcophagus, although the Red Pyramid, Seneferu's apparent final resting place, may have had one constructed in the masonry flooring of its burial chamber.

Meidum tombs M6 (ill. 158) and 16 each had two burial shafts, driven through the superstructure into the bedrock, without any apparent stairway approaches. The shafts of Rahotep and Nefermaat themselves had stone-built, corbelled, chambers at their bottoms, while the sepulchres of their wives, in the northern halves of the tombs, had smaller, wholly rock-cut chambers. These two basic approaches to the construction of the burial chamber were standard in the early 4th Dynasty, although a number of Meidum tombs had substructures of a distinctive type. These comprised an open, sloping, trench at the bottom of which was constructed the burial chamber. The male burial chambers in M6 and 16 each had a niche in the south wall, apparently intended for a canopic chest; the latter item is first attested in Seneferu's reign. Similar niches are to be found in a number of the smaller tombs at Meidum, in the Great West (see ill. 39) and Far West Cemeteries; in the latter, the burial chambers were frequently blocked with portcullis slabs, sliding in grooves at the bottom of the shaft, in the former by plug-blocks.

Unlike those of the late 3rd Dynasty pyramids, the chambers of Seneferu's pyramids lay, with one exception, within, or partly within, the superstructure. Khufu, for his Great Pyramid at Giza, initially reverted to a sepulchre

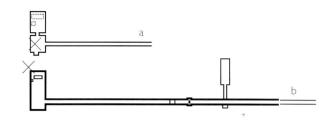

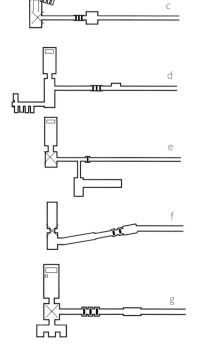

166 The development of the substructures of the royal tombs of the 4th to 6th dynasties: a. Djedefre at Abu Rowash (4th Dynasty); b. Khafre at Giza (4th Dynasty); c. Menkaure at Giza (4th Dynasty); d. Shepseskaf at South Saqqara; e. Userkaf at Saqqara (5th Dynasty); f. Niuserre at Abusir, similar to Sahure, Neferirkare, Neferefre and Menkauhor (5th Dynasty); g. Unas at Saqqara, similar to Isesi, Teti, Pepy I, Nemtyemsaf I and Pepy II (5th–6th Dynasty).

167 The burial chamber of Khufu in the Great Pyramid at Giza (4th Dynasty).

tunnelled deep underground. However, the tomb's final form placed galleries and chambers within the pyramid itself. These are generally interpreted as representing one or more changes in plan, although some scholars would prefer to see the pyramid as having been designed from the outset with its ultimate layout. If indeed a change, this might have been the result of a decision to use a stone sarcophagus, which would not fit down the entrance passages of the pyramid and thus needed to be introduced through the roof of the burial chamber – which thus had to be relocated above ground-level, enclosed within the pyramid structure.

The need to be able to introduce material such as sarcophagi thus led to new approaches by subsequent kings. The tombs of Djedefre and Seth?ka had their burial chambers built at the bottom of deep cuttings instead of being tunnelled out of the rock. Since this added greatly to the work of construction, the internal passages of the pyramids of Khafre and Menkaure are of a much more simple form, with the roofs of the burial chambers at ground level, an approach used by all subsequent pharaohs.

The substructures of the queens' pyramids comprised a descending passage, a tiny antechamber and a right-angled turn leading into the burial chamber; one has the same layout as those adjacent to the Great Pyramid, but the other (GIIIb: GIIIc was Menkaure's subsidiary pyramid) had a simple axial plan, with the sepulchral chamber at the end.

Approaches to the burial chambers of most Giza mastaba tombs were via shafts sunk through the superstructure and bedrock, with a short passage (sometimes blocked by a portcullis) leading to a burial chamber on the south side, although orientations become less consistent later in the 4th Dynasty. The room usually had a canopic cavity sunk in the floor, while there were many minor variations in its design, such as a stone lining, or a stair/slope beyond the doorway at the bottom of the shaft.[183] All are devoid of decoration, with the solitary exception of a false-door in the burial chamber of the tomb of Meresankh III (G7530+7540).[184] A roughly contemporary provincial tomb at El-Hagarsa also has some decoration in the burial chamber.

In rock-cut tombs, substructures generally open out of the interior of the chapel, in contrast to the situation in mastabas. Both shafts and sloping passages are employed, although the former are perhaps more common. Burial chambers rarely lie particularly far underground in this kind of sepulchre.

168 (above) The last attempt to provide a deeply buried substructure seems to be at the Unfinished Pyramid at Zawiyet el-Aryan of Seth?ka. The cutting is here seen from the top of the entrance trench.

169 (below) The burial chamber of Menkaure in his pyramid at Giza, showing the now-lost sarcophagus.

XII (*previous page*) Aerial photograph of the Saqqara necropolis, with the causeway of the pyramid of Unas running down the centre. In the foreground is the northern extremity of the New Kingdom necropolis of temple-tombs, with sepulchres of the reign of Ramesses II, in particular that of the Vizier Neferrenpet (ST0). On the opposite side of the causeway are many tombs of the late Old Kingdom, with the substructures of two royal tombs of the 2nd Dynasty occupying the area between the boat-pit in the middle distance and the Unas pyramid. Beyond is the Step Pyramid complex of Djoser and in the distance the pyramids of Abu Sir.

XIII (*above*) Wooden panel from a niche in the original façade of the early 3rd Dynasty mastaba of Hesyre at Saqqara (S2405). Such items were probably a more common feature of such tombs than the current level of preservation would suggest (CM CG1430).

XIV (*opposite*) Detail of one of the panels of faience tiles that decorated the substructure of the South Tomb at the Step Pyramid at Saqqara, 3rd Dynasty. These were intended to imitate mat-work hangings.

XV (*overleaf*) Panorama of the Dahshur necropolis from the south-east, looking across Dahshur Lake. Visible from the left to the right are Seneferu's Bent and Red Pyramids, and the Black Pyramid of Amenemhat III. The mound between the Red and Black Pyramids represents the location of the 13th Dynasty pyramid of Ameny-Qemau; just to its right is an Old Kingdom private cemetery.

XVI (*above*) Statues formed an important part of the furnishings of the chapels of the Old Kingdom. Amongst the earliest are the superb near-life-sized figures of Prince Rahotep, a son of Seneferu, and his wife Neferet. From Meidum 6 (CM CG3, 4: 4th Dynasty).

XVII (*opposite*) The innermost part of the 12th Dynasty tomb-chapel of Sarenput ii at Qubbet el-Hawa (QH31) contains a stone *naos* which will once have held a statuette of the deceased. The rear wall is adorned with a painting of Sarenput in front of an offering table.

XVIII The second register of this painting in the tomb of Khnumhotep iii at Beni Hasan (BH-III, 12th Dynasty) shows members of a delegation of brightly clad foreigners from Syria-Palestine. Their leader – not visible in this coloured drawing – bears the title *heqa-khaswet*, the prototype of the later term, 'Hyksos'.

Superstructures

Royal Tombs: All 5th/6th Dynasty pyramid complexes are similar in size and basic plan, each having less than half the volume of even the smallest 4th Dynasty example,[185] with one exception (Neferirkare's). Apart from that of Userkaf, they are built with relatively small blocks of stone and today are all badly ruined.

The temples attached to the pyramids, although displaying variations in detail, follow the basic layout established by the end of the 4th Dynasty that continues to the end of the Old Kingdom and even beyond. The subsidiary pyramid remained an important feature and its location now became fixed south of the innermost part of the mortuary temple; earlier subsidiary pyramids had occupied various positions on the south side of the main pyramid during the 4th Dynasty.

The underlying idea of the decorative organization of the pyramid temples of the 5th and 6th Dynasties seems to be a movement from secular to sacred, with a concentration of images of divinities and the resurrection of the king located in the parts of the temple closest to the pyramid. The ceilings of these temples were adorned with five-pointed stars, smaller versions of which, linked together, also served as register lines, thus moving the actions depicted into a divine and eternal plane. Three-dimensional representations placed in the temple included images of the king and of kneeling bound captives that were placed in locations where they would clearly show their subjugation by the monarch.

Although it is difficult to determine the precise programme of decoration due to the damaged nature of the monuments, it is possible to broadly reconstruct a generic model by combining evidence gathered from the funerary complexes of Sahure (ill. 3), Niuserre, Neferirkare, Userkaf, Unas (particularly the causeway), Isesi, Pepy I and Pepy II, the last-named possessing the best preserved-complex of them all.

It should be noted that these temples contain scenes that sum up and eternalize kingship and the cosmic role of the king, explaining in part the fact that a considerable number of scenes are directly copied from one temple to another. For example, a scene of smiting Libyans that appears in Sahure's complex is also found in the mortuary temple of Pepy II, and a scene of starving people, once thought to be unique to

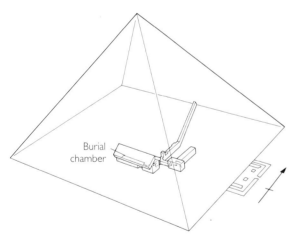

Burial chamber

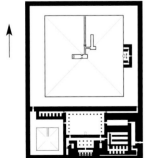

170 (*above and left*) Axonometric section and plan of the pyramid of Userkaf (Saqqara: 5th Dynasty).

171 (*right*) Plan of a typical royal mortuary temple of the 5th/6th Dynasty.

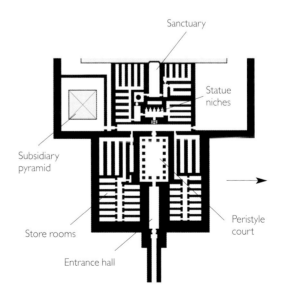

Sanctuary

Statue niches

Subsidiary pyramid

Store rooms

Entrance hall

Peristyle court

172 (*above*) View up the causeway of Unas towards his pyramid (end of the 5th Dynasty).

173 (*left*) Block in Isesi's mortuary temple at Saqqara, showing the king, to whom a divinity symbolically proffers life in the form of an *ankh*. The king's eye was formerly inlaid (5th Dynasty).

174 (*below*) Images of the king as a sphinx, a divine form, conquering Egypt's foes were a standard part of the decorative scheme of royal funerary temples, especially the causeways; mortuary temple of Pepy II (Saqqara-South: 6th Dynasty).

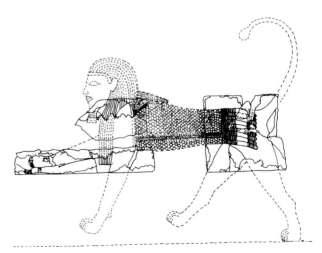

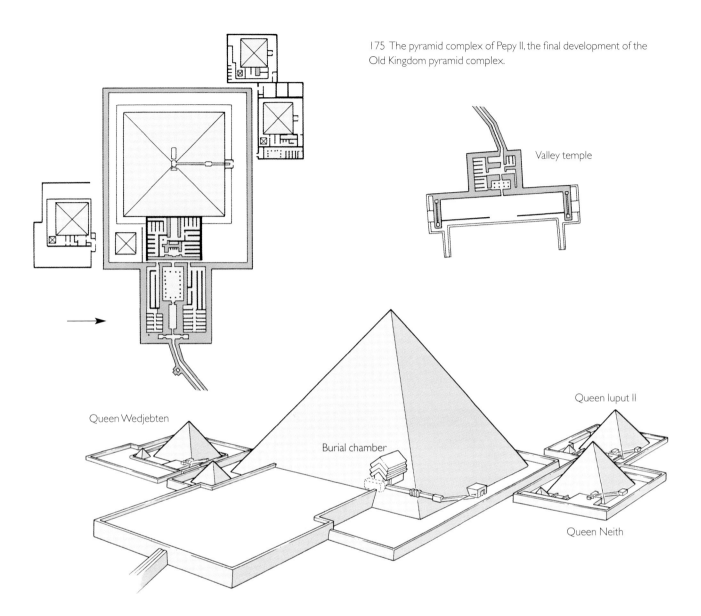

Valley temple

Queen Iuput II

Queen Wedjebten

Burial chamber

Queen Neith

Unas' causeway, also appears on that of Sahure. An interesting feature of these temples is that the images of the king are frequently shown attended by his *ka*, perhaps symbolic of all the royal *ka*s.

Pepy II's valley building yielded fragments of reliefs that show the king hunting in the marshes and being attended by divinities and officials. Fragments of similar scenes have been found in other temples, as well as additional scenes showing the recording of booty or tribute. Niuserre's valley building might have also shown scenes of the seasons in this area.

The causeway was covered with a variety of scenes and texts. For the most part, these related to the prowess and greatness of the king as protector of the land and provider through conquest. These were standard kingly acts and images of the king carrying them out successfully appear on objects from the end of the Predynastic Period onwards. The decoration on the lower portion of the causeway showed the king as a sphinx and a griffin trampling the enemies of Egypt, while the upper portions were divided into sections showing bound prisoners, counting of booty, tribute being brought and images of the king being approached by rows of gods and offering bearers. The causeways of Unas and Sahure also show scenes of nature, with animals living, mating and giving birth in the wild. Additionally, the causeways of these two kings bore scenes of the construction of the funerary complex. Sahure's showed the positioning of the capstone, while Unas' depicted the transport of the granite columns to the site. Vignettes of daily life are also depicted in the causeway, including images of markets, soldiers training and boats.

The passage leading into the courtyard of the temple proper showed the king being embraced by gods. The vestibule that led from there into the court showed the king moving from the prosaic secular world slowly into the divine. Here, with his attendants, he battles with the wild, chaotic and dangerous aspects of nature, emerges victorious and is applauded by the queen and divinities who embrace him and otherwise show their approbation. The king is pictured fowling and spearing hippopotami. A fowling scene appears early in the 4th Dynasty in the valley temple of Seneferu and a fishing and fowling scene is also found in the court of Userkaf's mortuary temple. At the end of the ritual hunt, the hippopotamus is shown being dragged on a sled after his ignominious capture by the king; chaos has been bound and contained and *maat* can reign supreme. The bound animal evokes the bound captives that were brought to their knees by the king. It is interesting to note that in general, when registers of gods and people approaching the

king are shown, the gods appear in the higher celestial registers and the people in the lower earthly ones.

The central transverse corridor that leads out of the court to the enclosed and increasingly sacred spaces of the temple is decorated with scenes of the king, followed by his *ka*, smiting Egypt's enemies, being embraced by the gods and watching or being engaged in rituals associated with the *heb-sed* jubilee. This emphasizes the king's success in ruling Egypt and maintaining *maat* eternally and the acceptance and blessings of the gods, not just for the king, but for the whole country and its denizens. Other scenes in the interior of the temple continue to show the king's dominion over the powers of chaos and his loyalty to the gods. These include a fowling scene and a hunt in the desert, which climaxes, in Pepy II's temple, in the slaying of an antelope, symbol of the untamed desert, before the gods. The antelope-slaying motif is a standard feature in later Egyptian temples of all types. Sahure's hunt scene is particularly famous as it shows the king using a bow and arrow in the desert; after the end of the Old Kingdom this motif is usurped by private individuals. At the end of the hunt, the gods show their appreciation of the king by offering him life in the form of the *ankh* sign.

177 The erection of the *sehent-pole* was possibly a part of the *heb-sed* festival; mortuary temple of Pepy II.

176 The king hunting a hippopotamus, symbolic of Seth, was a key scene in mortuary temples as it emphasized the king and *maat*'s dominion over Seth and chaos; Saqqara, mortuary temple of Pepy II.

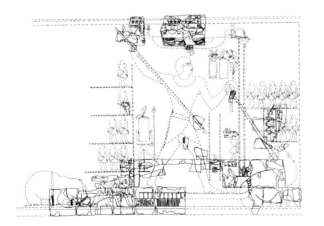

Further into the temple, in a niche, the king is shown being suckled by a goddess. By ingesting the divine milk he further acquires divinity and becomes one with the gods. This scene also serves as a reminder that the king will be reborn and live amongst the gods.

The antechamber that leads to the sanctuary of Pepy II's temple is decorated with images of the gods of Upper and Lower Egypt, on separate walls, indicating the different parts of the country. Butchers slaughter and joint cattle below. They are clearly providing the offering for the royal cult. The location of this scene, close to the cult centre, is followed in elite tombs. Below the register of butchers is a row of officials; this layout is peculiar to royal tombs. Probably the officials featured were divided between the two walls depending on whether they served in the north or the south.

Images of butchery continue into the sanctuary, where they are joined by piles of offerings and endless rows of offering bearers, all making for the central focus of the chamber: the seated figure of the king at table with his *ka* behind and the *sema-tawy* – a metaphor for the uniting of Upper and Lower Egypt by tying together their respective heraldic plants, the papyrus and sedge – below. The king is separated from the offering bearers by an extensive offering list that was being provisioned by the bearers.

Additional scenes, perhaps specific to the events of each reign, might also appear in the funerary temples. However, for the most part, stock scenes had to be shown in order to magically ensure the maintenance of *maat* and the continuation of the country and its rulers.

Private Tombs: In contrast to the royal standardization, private tombs of the 5th Dynasty varied very considerably in design, with some evidence for different architectural traditions at each cemetery. A major problem in studying their development is the difficulty in reliably dating many sepulchres of the later Old Kingdom, with the result that many can only be dated to the '5th/6th Dynasty'. Criteria of size, layout, decoration, details of false-doors and formulae of offering lists have all been employed with varying degrees of success.

Although stone was now the preferred material for such sepulchres, many brick examples were still constructed at both Giza and Saqqara. Their designs were frequently fairly conservative, making them sometimes difficult to distinguish architecturally from 3rd/4th Dynasty tombs. Similar conservatism is also seen in some stone structures, for example that of Nihetepkhnum at Giza, which has a multi-niched corridor chapel; many, however, follow 4th Dynasty norms. Nevertheless, steady developments are generally to be seen, particularly around the middle of the dynasty when there was a fundamental change in the orientation of the main offering room, perhaps reflecting the influence of royal practice.

178 A group of 5th Dynasty mastabas at Giza: from the left G6010 (Neferbauptah); G6020 (Iymery); and G6030 (Iti).

179 The tomb of Perneb (Saqqara S913); now in New York (MMA 13.183.3; late 5th Dynasty).

Up until then, the axis of the room ran north–south, with the offering place on the long (western) wall. By the second half of the 5th Dynasty it generally (but not exclusively) ran east–west, with the stela at the far end of a long, narrow, room. At the same time, there were changes in the design of the false-door, which became increasingly complex, while the outer chambers and passages of the chapel became more elaborate. This led in some cases to the occupation of almost the whole interior of the mastaba with chambers, halls and courts, creating space for much more elaborate decoration. Outer entrances were sometimes also elaborate, with ramped approaches, pillars and flanking statues or obelisks. Like those of the earlier part of the Old Kingdom, a number of tombs show signs of having undergone one or more enlargements.

A good example is the very large mastaba of Ptahshepses at Abu Sir (reign of Niuserre). The original mastaba had five rooms, plus a *serdab*. First a porticoed structure was added to this, which subsequently received a new entrance with another pair of pillars. Finally, a large colonnaded court and subsidiary rooms were added to the south. Such courts are found in a number of private tombs of the 5th/6th Dynasties, as well as being a standard feature of royal mortuary temples.

Another interesting tomb-complex is that Senedjemib-Inti and his family (G2370-2378, Isesi-Unas). It centred on the square mastaba of Inti himself, entered via a two-pillared portico, with a three-room chapel, which was later extended to include an eight-pillared hall and extra *serdab*. G2378, belonging to his son, Senedjemib-Mehi, was built to the right of and at right angles to Inti's, with the tomb of another son, Khnumenti, fitting G2374 into the gap between the two. This accretion of family monuments is common, as is the further filling in of gaps by later individuals, leading to distinctly confusing layouts.

The 5th Dynasty also saw considerable elaboration in *serdab* arrangements, with a number of separate cavities and occasional representations of doors on the walls that separated them from the main body of the chapel.

The decoration of mature Old Kingdom elite tomb-chapels emphasized the natural cycle, whether it was in wild or in domestic contexts and presented an ideal world with everyone living in *maat*. The establishment and maintenance of *maat* was of paramount importance in the tombs of this era. Scenes relating to the tomb-owner's position are also commonly depicted, often with accompanying explanatory texts. Although deities are never shown in private tombs prior to the New Kingdom, the prominence of Re is clearly implicit in the natural cycles that form the nexus of representations in the tombs of this period. In fact, it may well be the royal solar temples of the 5th Dynasty that are the source of inspiration for many of the scenes that are found in private tombs of the late 5th and 6th Dynasties. The vital force of the sun and its effect on nature and fertility were of crucial importance to the beliefs in an afterlife, both in royal and elite contexts.

180 Plan of the tomb-complex of the Senedjemib family at Giza (G2370, 2374 and 2378: late 5th Dynasty).

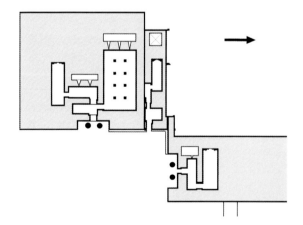

Substructures

In royal tombs, a simple basic design became standardized early in the dynasty, with a descending passage, blocked by one or more portcullises, leading to an antechamber, to the right (west) of which is the burial chamber. The sarcophagus stood at the west end of the latter, with a canopic chest sunk in the floor to the east of the foot from at least the reign of Isesi onwards. The latter king added a store-room, with three niches, to the east of the antechamber. The principal chambers were covered with massive stone gable roofs, frequently composed of multiple layers. The interiors of all these chambers were plain, until the reign of the last king of the dynasty, Unas, whose sepulchre is the first to bear the compilation of religious literature known as the Pyramid Texts.

The arrangements made in Unas' sepulchre became the standard for decorating pyramid burial chambers until the end of the Old Kingdom. Pyramid Texts were not restricted to kings' tombs; queens' pyramids also contained them from the time of Pepy I onwards.[186] These texts, executed in sunk relief and filled with blue paint, adorned and protected the sarcophagus chamber and its antechamber, the spells arranged for the convenience of the king as he made his way heavenward. The ceiling of these subterranean rooms was covered with five-pointed stars, implying that the king lay under the vault of heaven, with the promise of joining with the stars.

The area immediately around Unas' sarcophagus was bare of texts. Instead, it was covered with incised decoration that suggested mats lining the walls of houses, with shelves bearing boxes and jars along the upper reaches. Thus the tradition of mats, or simulacra of mats, in royal burials continued on throughout the Old Kingdom. The implication was that the sarcophagus was equivalent to the king's bed and there he lay in a facsimile of an earthly bed-chamber.

Gabled roofs, protecting shallow-cut burial chambers, are sometimes found in private tombs, a principal example being in the tomb of Ptahshepses at Abu Sir. With its gable roof at ground level, it was clearly closely influenced by contemporary pyramid architecture, perhaps prompted by Ptahshepses being a king's son-in-law. However, the majority of tombs continued to have wholly rock-cut burial chambers. These were approached either by shafts through the body of the mastaba, cut in the floor of one of the rooms

of the chapel, or via a sloping passage. The latter could lie in one of the rooms, a courtyard, or outside the main body of the tomb. Examples of this last option are provided by the Inti family complex at Giza. The superstructures lay on a rock-cut platform, under which sloping passages led westwards to burial chambers containing the stone sarcophagi.

181 (*above*) The pyramid-chambers of the late Old Kingdom were roofed with massive limestone blocks. The activities of stone robbers has here caused one to slip downwards inside the pyramid of Pepy I (Saqqara- South: 6th Dynasty).

182 (*below*) The burial chamber of Ptahshepses at Abu Sir had a burial chamber cut close to the surface and roofed similarly to contemporary royal tombs (L.XIX: mid-5th Dynasty).

Superstructures

There is no cultural break between the 5th and 6th Dynasties, the evolution of the royal funerary complexes continuing with little interruption. Similarly, private funerary monuments of the 6th Dynasty represent, in general, linear developments of those of the 5th Dynasty. Amongst them is one of the most elaborate of all mastabas, that of the Vizier Mereruka, which provides an excellent contrast with the mastabas of the 2nd Dynasty, with their two shallow-niche offering places. While Ruaben's S2302 (see p. 140) had a brick-faced superstructure of 57 x 32 m

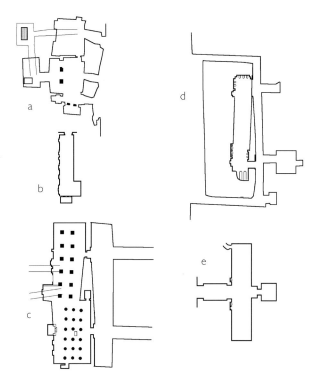

183 (*above*) Rock-cut tomb-chapels of the Old Kingdom:
a. Debhen (Giza LG90: 4th Dynasty), one of the earliest rock-cut tombs; b. Nefer (Saqqara: mid-/late 5th Dynasty); c. Mekhu and Sabni (QH 25 & 26: late 6th Dynasty), this comprises the union of the separate tomb-chapels of a father and son; d. Nikaankh (Tihna 13: early 5th Dynasty), the tomb lies on the east bank, and this rather strange arrangement has been adopted to allow the false-doors to face west; e. Khenuka (Tihna 14: 5th/6th Dynasty), in this case, a conventional tomb is employed, but with the false-doors placed either side of the doorway into the main chamber, to allow them to face the right way.

(190 x 105 ft) filled with nothing but rubble, Mereruka's mastaba of 45 x 35 m (150 x 115 ft) contained nearly 30 rooms, which occupy most of the building's ground area. Access to Mereruka's burial chamber was via a shaft in the floor in front of a false-door.

A feature of Mereruka's chapel is a life-sized statue emerging from one of the false-doors of the tomb (pl. X). Smaller three-dimensional figures are found as parts of a number of false-doors of the 6th Dynasty and the First Intermediate Period. The tomb of Nefershemptah at Saqqara had a false-door flanked by two statues, and a carved bust of the deceased takes the place of the usual offering tablet. A further unusual image was that of Idu (G7102): his bust is set at the bottom of the false-door holding out his arms to form the hieroglyphic symbol for the *ka*.

The decoration of tombs of this period followed the organization and motifs established in the previous dynasties, with new motifs being added to the repertoire. Scenes of outdoor pursuits, crafts, felling trees, wild and domestic animals, visits in carrying chairs, games, including *senet*, agricultural cycles, funerals, force-feeding wild and domestic creatures, the Voyage to Abydos and offering bringers, in the form of estates and bearers, are all found in this period. Unusual scenes of picnics on the river adorn the walls of mastabas, especially at Saqqara, where Mereruka's brother and Ptahhotep ii (tomb D64) are shown on boats, eating and drinking. Divinities were not shown, although invoked in funerary inscriptions, where earlier the king had

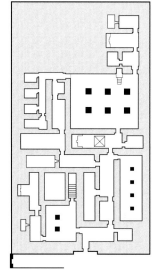

184 (*left*) Mastaba of the Vizier Mereruka at Saqqara (early 6th Dynasty).

185 The false-door of Iteti-Ankheris has a figure of the deceased in the central 'doorway'; from Saqqara D 63 (CM CG 57190: 6th Dynasty).

186 The false-door of Idu at Giza (G7102), showing the unique bust of the deceased holding out his arms in the manner of a *ka*-sign (6th Dynasty).

been the sole focus. An interesting compromise is seen in a block from a 5th Dynasty tomb[187] that shows some sort of ritual or perhaps even dance, being performed, with one of the participants wearing a lion mask. This might be a relatively early depiction of invocations to the household protector-god Bes and the inclusion of the divine in a non-royal tomb. There is also an increase in (auto)biographical texts and scenes during this time, bringing the focus more firmly on the tomb-owner's exploits in life and his expected position in death. Examples of these are found in Harkhuf's tomb at Aswan and Rawer's stela from Giza (CM JE66682).

Private cemeteries accompany most of the royal pyramids, that around Teti's pyramid being particularly extensive. The majority of the kings moved to Saqqara-South and many officials followed; however, the full extent

of these cemeteries remains uncertain, as only that of Pepy II has been properly investigated.[188] Nevertheless, many dignitaries were buried in other parts of the necropoleis, for example in the ancient cemeteries lying north and west of the Step Pyramid. After a reversion to mastabas for the burials of the queens of Unas, small, steeply angled, pyramids are found housing the sepulchres of the wives of Teti (converted from mastabas), Pepy I and Pepy II.

A major motif of the 6th Dynasty is the increase in tomb building outside the area of the principal royal residence. As the Old Kingdom progressed, there was a steady devolution of the authority of the court, in favour of the provinces, or nomes. The Great Chieftains (or nomarchs) of the nomes constructed increasingly imposing tomb-chapels at their local centres.

187 (*above*) The rock-cut chapel of Nefer at Saqqara, with multiple false-doors for members of his family (5th Dynasty).

188 (*below*) The upper part of the false-door of Kaha, the father of Nefer, in his son's tomb.

An important group are those at Aswan, which lie high
above the river on the west bank at Qubbet el-Hawa.
These rock-cut chapels are generally simple, comprising a
columned hall, the number of piers ranging from 2 to 18.
The latter number is found in the tomb (QH25) of Mekhu,
with the contiguous sepulchre of his son Sabni (26) adding
a further 12 pillars. The tombs share an external court,
approached from the riverbank by fine, steeply sloped,
causeways.

Other later Old Kingdom private cemeteries include
Deshasha,[189] where the rock-cut chapels of Inti and Iteti have
main chambers with three rectangular pillars across their
width and a deep niche at the rear. This arrangement is also
found in the tomb of Niankhpepy (14) at Zawiyet Sultan
and in a four-pillared version belonging to Khunes (2) at

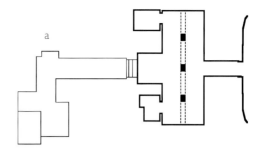

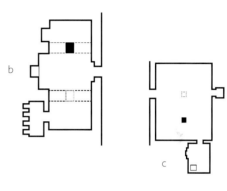

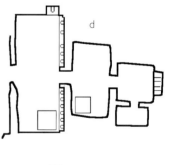

189 (above) The double mastaba of queens Nebet and Khenut, wives
of Unas (Saqqara: late 5th Dynasty).

190 (below) A ruined rock-cut tomb at Zawiyet Sultan, with a
transverse chamber, at the back of which a pair of engaged statues
flank the doorway into the innermost chamber (6th Dynasty).

191 (right) Rock-cut
tomb-chapels of the later Old
Kingdom: a. Inti (Deshasha 1:
5th/6th Dynasty); b. Tjauti (Qasr
w'el-Sayed 2: 6th Dynasty);
c. Pepyankh the Elder (Quseir
el-Amarna 1: mid-6th Dynasty),
in this east bank tomb, the
false-door is in the side room,
oriented towards the west;
d. Meru (Sheikh Said 5: 6th
Dynasty); e. Unknown owner
(Sheikh Said 37: 6th Dynasty).

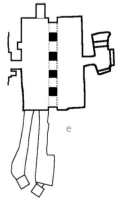

192 The causeways leading up to the tombs of Mekhu and Sabni (QH25 and 26: 6th Dynasty) dominate this view of the Qubbet el-Hawa at Aswan. The tombs to the north are of mixed date, including the 12th Dynasty tombs of Sarenput i (QH36) and ii (QH31 – next to QH26).

the same site. Moving further south, most necropoleis consist mainly of rock-cut sepulchres; contrasting with the usual straightforward set of quarried rooms, at Tihna a series of mastabas are cut from the living rock. These date to the very beginning of the 5th Dynasty (see above, pp. 155–6, 176).

A cemetery of considerable size[190] is located at Sheikh Said.[191] Most of the chapels comprise a transverse chamber and a smaller one beyond. The latter feature is, however, missing from many of the nearby sepulchres at Quseir el-Amarna[192] and Deir el-Gebrawi.[193] Yet more rock-cut tombs of the period are to be found in cemeteries A, D and E at Meir[194] and other such sites as El-Hamamiya,[195] Gebel Sheikh el-Haridi,[196] Naga el-Deir[197] and El-Hagarsa.[198] The area of Abydos contains many sepulchres of the Old Kingdom, many with built superstructures, in particular the Middle Cemetery, which contains burials of high-status individuals, particularly of the 6th Dynasty.

One of the most important examples is the mud-brick mastaba of Weni, Governor of Upper Egypt under Teti, Pepy I and Nemtyemsaf I.[199] It, like other mastabas at

Abydos, was square, with a modest chapel built just north of the centre of the east side, which probably once contained the owner's autobiographical text, now in Cairo. A niche with a false-door lay in the middle of the north face of the mastaba. The 30-m (100-ft) square mastaba comprised a thick outer retaining wall, the interior being filled with sand, save for walls enclosing the upper parts of the three burial shafts and a *serdab* in the south eastern corner.

Dendara's cemeteries contain a range of mastabas from the 6th Dynasty and later.[200] Made of brick with rubble filling, many have panelled eastern façades, generally with very wide, but shallow, chapels directly behind them. In some cases a whole string of rooms lies just inside the eastern margin of the mastaba. One example, that of Meni, has the interesting feature of an open court occupying its northern part, entered through an arched doorway in the western wall and with a bench running along the northern and eastern sides. Similar benches have been found in the 6th Dynasty mastaba of Kagemeni at Saqqara. From this area, a staircase led to the roof of the mastaba; the courtyard was found filled

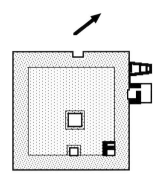

193 (*right*) Plan of the mastaba of Weni at Abydos, comprising a thick outer retaining wall, largely filled with sand (mid-6th Dynasty).

194 (*below*) Plan of the mastaba of Meni at Dendara (6th Dynasty).

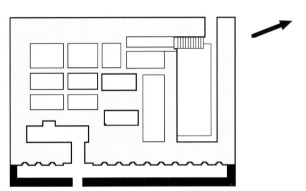

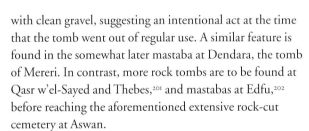

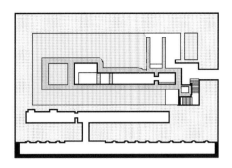

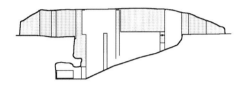

195 Plan and section of the tomb of Mereri at Dendara (early First Intermediate Period).

with clean gravel, suggesting an intentional act at the time that the tomb went out of regular use. A similar feature is found in the somewhat later mastaba at Dendara, the tomb of Mereri. In contrast, more rock tombs are to be found at Qasr w'el-Sayed and Thebes,[201] and mastabas at Edfu,[202] before reaching the aforementioned extensive rock-cut cemetery at Aswan.

Away from the Nile Valley, the latter part of the Old Kingdom saw considerable activity in the Western Desert oases. Amongst the most impressive surviving monuments there are the 6th Dynasty governors' tombs at Balat in the Dakhla Oasis and their associated necropoleis.[203] The latter tombs feature a mud-brick enclosure with a stela at the back, protected within a brick structure, sometimes of mastaba form. A similar arrangement is seen at the governors' tombs, which comprise large panelled mastabas, preceded by a pair of open courts.

Substructures

Burial chambers vary in size throughout the 6th Dynasty, the most impressive being those of Mereruka and Kagemeni in the Teti cemetery at Saqqara. The former also has the

interesting feature of a ramp built against the sarcophagus to facilitate the placement of the lid. Such a feature was doubtless used not infrequently, but it is rare to find it a permanent stone fixture.

Following on from the introduction of decoration into the royal burial chambers at the end of the 5th Dynasty, inscribed and painted burial chambers became not uncommon during the 6th Dynasty. A number of examples are found in the Teti cemetery at Saqqara,[204] in particular the extensive paintings of offerings in the burial chamber of Mereruka. The principal Old Kingdom examples are summarized on pp. 183–5, together with a number of other tombs that may either belong to the 6th Dynasty or the First Intermediate Period.

At first scholars assumed that decorated burial chambers were restricted to certain groups of officials, such as viziers. However, the list of people at Saqqara-South who have such burial chambers includes other ranks of officials, such as Overseers of the Pyramids, Inspectors of Prophets, Overseers of Scribes, Prophetesses of Hathor, Lector Priests and other priestly officials, so the presence of decorated burial chambers cannot be tied to rank, but rather to religious trends of the time, or taste.

On the whole, decoration in these burial chambers tried to avoid depicting people or live animals, as these had the potential magical power to harm the deceased. Instead, the decoration was restricted to offering lists and images of food and drink, including granaries, which signified a plentiful food and commodity supply in the afterlife; examples include the mastabas of Mereruka and Kagemeni (LS10) at Saqqara and Seshemnefer iv at Giza. An unusual example from the same cemetery also contains images of boats and cattle being transported on boats.[205] Further examples of such decorated burial chambers abound in the cemeteries surrounding the pyramid of Pepy II, as well as the walled enclosure of the Teti cemetery.[206]

However, there are exceptions to the avoidance of animate beings, such as the burial chamber in the mastaba of Kaemankh (G4561) at Giza. Surprisingly, this contains the same range of decoration as that found in a chapel. Its paintings include images of offering bearers bringing live produce and livestock, butchers, beer and bread production, food preparation, bed-making, as well as the deceased fowling and fishing in the marshes.[207]

Although tombs outside the Memphite area also had decorated burial chambers, these are a rarity. Bubastis, however, seems to have been an anomaly, as several examples of such tomb-chambers have been found there. A few inscribed chambers have also been recorded at Mendes; perhaps this reflects a Delta tradition. The 6th Dynasty tomb of Meru at Heliopolis/Tell Hisn contains the name and titles of the deceased, but no depictions of offerings, as is the case with the tomb of Hepi-kem (tomb A4) at Meir.[208]

196 Decorated burial chamber of Mereruka, showing the unusual ramp incorporated into the sarcophagus to facilitate the placement of the lid atop the coffer (Saqqara: 6th Dynasty).

The sarcophagus chamber of (another) Meru at Sheikh Said (tomb 5) contained an offering list,[209] while the 6th Dynasty tomb of Inti at Abu Sir South had a false-door, reminiscent of the one found in Meresankh III's earlier tomb at Giza.[210]

Rather surprisingly, highly decorated burial chambers are also found in 6th Dynasty tombs at Balat in the Dakhla Oasis, adorned with scenes of offerings,[211] and in some cases, such as the tomb of Khentika (mastaba III), an image of the deceased himself.[212] The substructures of these large sepulchres took two basic forms.[213] One was based on the construction of the chambers in large open cuttings, the other on building them within galleries accessed by conventional shafts. This technique was predicated on the ground conditions at Balat.

In kings' tombs, the late 5th Dynasty design was perpetuated down to the reign of Pepy II, while the pyramids of queens generally have a simple sloping-passage-and-chamber design. A number of curious burials of members of the royal family seem to date from the end of the 6th Dynasty.[214] One is of a wife of Pepy II, named Ankhenespepy IV, whose tomb was simply a store-room of the mortuary chapel of a fellow spouse of the king, Iput II. A stela had been inscribed on one wall and the sarcophagus improvised out of reused blocks. The other example belonged to a Prince Ptahshepses, who found rest in a fine 4th Dynasty sarcophagus, buried in part of the valley temple of Unas. Clearly, the wherewithal was not available to build proper tombs, nor provide virgin stone for the production of new sarcophagi.

Away from the Memphite necropolis, the shift from approaching the burial chamber via shafts to doing so through sloping passages is also seen at a site such as Dendara. The tomb of Mereri is particularly interesting in preserving a staircase leading up to the roof of the mastaba, from which a well leads to the beginning of a sloping passage, cut as a trench and roofed with brick. The lower part of the passage passes first through an arched doorway, with a series of relieving arches above it, and then into a vestibule, its upper part covered with a dome – one of the oldest of its kind known. The burial chamber beyond was cut in the desert gravel. Sloping passages are also found in most rock-cut tombs, good examples being found in the Qubbet el-Hawa necropolis at Aswan. Of course simple shafts also continue to appear, particularly in less elaborate sepulchres.

197 During the latter part of the Old Kingdom, the distinction between sarcophagi and burial chambers became sometimes somewhat blurred. Small stone-built rooms, only large enough to contain a coffin, were decorated with offering scenes and texts of the same type that were becoming current in some coffins; this example belonged to Deshri, buried near the pyramid of Nemtyemsaf I at Saqqara-South (CM CG1572).

DECORATED PRIVATE SUBSTRUCTURES OF THE OLD KINGDOM				
Site	**Tomb**	**Date**	**Owner**	**Compositions**
Abydos		6th Dyn	Idi	Offerings & list; object frieze & granaries; false-doors
Abydos		5th/6th Dyn	Iuu	Offerings
Abydos		6th Dyn	Weni	Offerings & list; object frieze & granaries; false-doors
Balat	Mastaba III	6th Dyn	Khentika	Offerings
Dendara		6th Dyn	Menankh-Pepy	Painted false-door, offering lists & titles of deceased
Dendara		6th Dyn	Idu	Offerings with texts, titles of deceased
Sheikh Said		Old Kingdom	Meru	Offering list
Giza	G7530+ 7540	4th Dyn	Meresankh III	False-door
Giza	G4561	6th Dyn	Kaemankh	Registers showing offering bringers, offerings, funerary priests, butchers, furniture, servants, dancers, musicians, bakers, farmers, boats, cooks, granaries
Giza		6th Dyn	Seshemnefer	Depictions of offerings on wall with text above; only text legible is 'honoured by Horus'
Giza		6th Dyn?	Rawer	Offerings
Heliopolis		6th Dyn	Meru	Name & titles of deceased
Meir		6th Dyn	Hepi-kem	Name & titles of deceased
Abu Sir-S.		6th Dyn	Inti	False-door
Saqqara		6th Dyn	Raemni	Offerings
Meir	D2	6th Dyn	Pepyankh-heryib	Offering lists, granaries, house-façades and offerings

Site	Tomb	Date	Owner	Compositions
Saqqara		6th Dyn	Idut	Offering list
Saqqara		6th Dyn	Maru Bebi	Walls: offering list, granaries, funerary equipment & texts
Saqqara	LS10	6th Dyn	Kagemeni	Offerings, magazines & offering texts
Saqqara–S.	MVII	6th Dyn	Penu	Doorway: lintel & jambs with offering texts & titles; walls: offering texts, offering list, granaries & offerings
Saqqara–S.	MVII	6th Dyn	Senti	Doorway: lintel & jambs with offering texts & titles; walls: offering texts, offering list & offerings
Saqqara–S.	MVII	6th Dyn	Nekhut	Doorway: titles painted on lintel
Saqqara–S.	MVII	6th Dyn	Nebpupepy Seni	Doorway: jambs with titles & thickness with offerings
Saqqara–S.	MIV	6th Dyn	Washiptah	Lintel: offering list
Saqqara–S.	MIV	6th Dyn	Heneni	Lintel, jamb & walls: offering texts
Saqqara–S.	MIX	6th Dyn	Shey	Doorway: lintel & jambs with offering texts & titles
Saqqara–S.	MX	6th Dyn	Ptahankhu	Walls: offering texts, granaries & offerings
Saqqara–S.	MXI	6th Dyn	Mehi	Doorway: lintel & jambs with offering texts & titles; walls: offering texts, offering list, granaries & offerings
Saqqara–S.	MXI	6th Dyn	Shemait	Doorway: lintel & jambs with offering texts; walls: offering texts, offering lists, granaries & offerings
Saqqara–S.	MXIII	6th Dyn	Imameryre	W. Wall: offering text & offerings; niche with palace façade decoration & titles
Saqqara–S.	MXIII	6th Dyn	Nihebsed	Doorway: lintel with offering texts; walls: offering list, names, offerings & titles
Saqqara–S.	MXIV	6th Dyn	Khabaukhnum Biu	Walls: offering list & offerings
Saqqara–S.	MXV	6th Dyn	Teti	Walls: offering list & offerings
Saqqara–S.	MXVI	6th Dyn	Anu	Doorway: lintel & jambs with offering texts & titles
Saqqara–S.	MXVII	6th Dyn	Sobkhotep	Doorway: remains of text on lintel; walls: offering texts, offering list & offerings
Saqqara–S.	NVII	6th Dyn	Degem Merypepy	Walls: offering texts, offering list, granaries & offerings
Saqqara–S.	NVIII	6th Dyn	Raherka	Lintel: offering text; jamb: titles; walls: offering text, granaries & offerings
Saqqara–S.	NIV	6th Dyn	Biu (usurped from Akhi)	Doorway: offering text on lintel & titles on jambs; walls: offering texts, offering list, granaries & offerings
Saqqara	NV	6th Dyn	Shenay	Fragment of decoration showing offerings
Saqqara–S.	NX	6th Dyn	Ankhnebef	Doorway: offering text; lintel & jamb: titles; walls: offering text, offering list, texts of granaries & names of offerings
Saqqara–S.	O.I	6th Dyn	Nipepy Ni	Doorway: conventional text of building tomb, threat on lintel & jambs; walls & niche: offering texts, offering list, granaries & offerings

Site	Tomb	Date	Owner	Compositions
Saqqara		6th Dyn	Khentika-Ikhekhi	Burial chamber I & II: offerings, offering list & text
Saqqara		6th Dyn	Ankhmahor Sesi	Offering list, offerings & funerary equipment
Saqqara		6th Dyn	Mereruka	Doorway & thickness: 10 lines of text; walls: offerings, offering lists & offering texts
Saqqara		6th Dyn	Ishethi Tjetji	Painted offering list, offerings, granaries & palace façade
Saqqara		6th Dyn	Sesheshet Idut	Offerings, offering lists & chests with feathers on top
Saqqara		6th Dyn	Niankhba	Offerings & funeral equipment painted on walls
Saqqara–S.		6th Dyn	Ihy	Offering texts, offering list & names of offerings
Saqqara–S.		6th Dyn	Neferkhu	Offering texts & names of offerings
Saqqara–S.		6th Dyn	Mereri	E. Wall: 3 registers with offerings, granaries & bound ox; S. wall: 6 chests; N. wall: remains of offering list
Saqqara–S.		6th Dyn	Nebu	Offering text & names of offerings
Saqqara–S.		6th Dyn	Iarti	Offering text & names of offerings
Saqqara–S.		6th Dyn	Iti Khnetkaus	Doorway: offering text & names & titles on lintel & jambs; walls: offerings, texts & names of offerings
Saqqara–S.		6th Dyn	Pepi	Doorway: offering texts on lintel & titles on jambs; walls: offering texts, offering list, granaries & offerings
Saqqara–S.		6th Dyn	Khubawy	Walls: offering texts, granaries & offerings
Saqqara–S.		6th Dyn	Nemtidjeref	Walls: offerings
Saqqara–S.		6th Dyn	Remeni	Walls: offerings
Saqqara–S.	MVI	6th Dyn/FIP	Nesmerut Nesti	Doorway: lintel & jambs with offering texts; walls: offerings
Saqqara–S.	MVII	6th Dyn/FIP	Seni	Doorway: lintel & jambs with offering texts & titles; walls: offering texts, offering list, granaries & offerings
Saqqara–S.	MVIII	6th Dyn/FIP	Setibti Bebi	Doorway: lintel & jambs with offering text
Saqqara–S.	MXII	6th Dyn/FIP	Sebaku (ii)	Doorway: remains of name on jambs & lower part of offering list
Saqqara–S.	MXII	6th Dyn/FIP	Wadjet	Doorway: lintel & jambs with offering texts; walls: texts
Saqqara–S.	MXII	6th Dyn/FIP	Sebaku (i)	Doorway: names on jambs; walls: offering lists & granaries
Saqqara–S.	NXI	6th Dyn/FIP	Neferkarenakhte Khetuihotep	Offering lists, granaries & names of offerings
Saqqara–S.	O.II	6th Dyn/FIP	Khnemu	Walls: fragment of offering list, texts of granaries, names & titles
Saqqara–S.		6th Dyn/FIP	Iri	Doorway: remains of name of deceased; walls: offerings, offering texts and texts of offerings & granaries
Saqqara–S.		FIP	Deshri	Walls & ceiling blocks with offering texts, granaries, offerings & offering list

Chapter 8

The First Intermediate Period, Middle Kingdom and Second Intermediate Period

The end of the Old Kingdom was followed by a rapid collapse of central authority and a corresponding rise in the importance of the provinces. Towards the end of the period, two power centres coalesced around the cities of Herakleopolis and Thebes; in the subsequent civil wars, the Thebans were to be victorious. The ensuing Middle Kingdom saw a number of extremely innovative sepulchres constructed, incorporating an ingenuity not again seen in the archaeological record. The Middle Kingdom was followed by a gradual decline and then by the occupation of the northern part of Egypt by the Palestinian Hyksos: funerary monuments of this latter era are uncommon.

FIRST INTERMEDIATE PERIOD
7th to 11th Dynasties

Superstructures

In the necropoleis around Memphis, only a few small tombs can be dated to the First Intermediate Period; in contrast, sites south of the Fayoum, in Middle and Upper Egypt, contain a considerable number of rock-cut chapels of the period. Most are of simple one-room form, some with pillars, for example that of Tefibi at Asyut (tomb 3). On the other hand, the sepulchre of Ankhtifi at Moalla is a far more impressive monument.[215] The rocky hill into which the chapel is cut is separate from the surrounding cliffs and takes the form of a natural pyramid, and it seems clear that Ankhtifi made this into part of a complex that aped that of

a king. It included a courtyard, a causeway and what seems to be the remains of a valley building, forming the focus of a cemetery of some size.[216]

Chapels of the First Intermediate Period have the same decorative repertoire as tombs of the Old Kingdom, with subtle changes. Many elements of Old Kingdom royal iconography had been taken over by the elite, especially since, in some cases, that elite had set itself up as minor royalty. These usurpations became a part of the stock high-status iconography from this period onwards. They include the wearing of a false beard (starting at the end of the 6th Dynasty), wearing the *shendyt* kilt and using portions of funerary texts. On the other hand, the impoverished state of the country often led to decoration being restricted to stone stelae, frequently of mediocre quality.

This period saw the beginning of the important series of tombs at Beni Hasan, beginning with simple, single-roomed monuments, but later continuing with much more elaborate structures.[217] Towards the end of the period there appeared at Thebes tombs whose offering places are fronted by a wide but shallow fore-hall, the front of which consists of a series of pillars, giving the sepulchres their Arabic name, *saff*, implying a 'line', or 'many doorways' (type IIIb; see ill. 242). The largest examples, which belonged to the Inyotef kings of the early 11th Dynasty, were courtyards sunk into the

198 (*above*) Asiatic traders depicted in the tomb-chapel of Khnumhotep iii at Beni Hasan (BH-III: 12th Dynasty).

desert surface at El-Tarif, with the royal chapel at the rear and the tombs of officials along the sides of the court.[218] At least one of the royal *saffs*, that of Inyotef II, had a chapel at the eastern end of the courtyard, perhaps intended as a kind of valley temple. A Ramesside description of this sepulchre mentions a pyramid as forming part of the tomb; however, no traces have been found. The programme of decoration of the royal *saffs* is unclear, although several stelae are known. These are well carved in relief and show images of the king with offerings, and in the case of the example from Inyotef II's 'valley temple', the king attended by his pet hounds.

At least one of the kings of Herakleopolis seems to have had a pyramid at Saqqara, according to the stelae of its

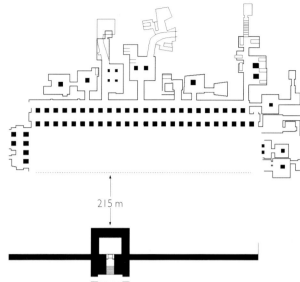

215 m

199 (*above*) Plan of the Saff el-Qisaiyia at El-Tarif, the tomb of Inyotef II. Rooms making up the chapel of the king himself are at the rear of the structure, while the chapels of members of the government and household lie on either side of the courtyard (early 11th Dynasty).

200 (*left*) The rock-tombs of Beni Hasan (11th–12th Dynasties).

201 (*below*) The tomb of Inyotef I at El-Tarif (Saff el-Dawaba), with that of his successor on the left, and smaller *saff*-tombs behind. This area is now almost entirely covered with modern housing.

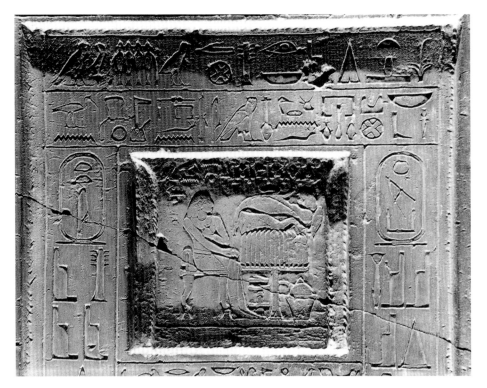

202 The only evidence for the pyramid of King Merykare of the 10th Dynasty are the stelae of some of its priesthood, many of whom also served the 6th Dynasty cult of Teti. This belongs to Gemeni, whose tomb lay near Teti's pyramid (Copenhagen Ny Carlsberg ÆIN 1616).

priests. It would appear to have lain near the pyramid of Teti, but it has never been positively identified.[219] Also apparently belonging to the First Intermediate Period is a huge square brick monument at Dara. This mysterious structure is of considerable size, exceeding the base area of all brick pyramids except for that at Abu Rowash. Its exact form and precise dating are unclear, but it certainly falls during the First Intermediate Period.[220]

Substructures

As with superstructures, the burial arrangements of tombs of the First Intermediate Period largely follow on from late Old Kingdom practice. One change that may be seen is the completion of a shift from square to rectangular shafts that had begun during the Old Kingdom. This was the result of a definitive shift from crouched or flexed burials to fully extended ones, with consequent changes in the proportions of coffins, the principal items to be lowered down shafts. One very interesting monument, however, the 'pyramid' at Dara has unusual substructure arrangements.[221] It was apparently entered via a horizontal vaulted passage in the middle of the north side. Beyond this, a vestibule has a stairway running upwards to the left and a passage to the right; their

destination has been destroyed, along with most of the interior of the superstructure. A passage descends from the end of the vestibule, its roof supported by a series of brick arches, until it ends abruptly in a small stone-lined burial chamber. Strangely, the chamber's floor is at the same angle as the passage, with its ceiling at a slightly shallower angle. This would suggest a hurried change of plan – presumably the intended burial chamber would have been further south.

In the Saqqara necropolis a few tombs dated to the First Intermediate Period carried on the Old Kingdom habit of inscribing the burial chamber with offering lists, offerings and images of granaries. Examples include the tombs of Deshri (ill. 197), Iri, the Sebakus, Wadjet and Neferkare-nakhte. Many of these tombs seem to span the end of the 6th Dynasty and the advent of the First Intermediate Period (cf. pp. 184–5).

MIDDLE KINGDOM
11th Dynasty

Superstructures

Court Burials: During the second half of the 11th Dynasty, the Theban kings obtained the rule of the whole of Egypt. The

203 The mortuary temple of Mentuhotep II at Deir el-Bahari.

king responsible, Mentuhotep II, was nonetheless buried at Thebes, where his funerary installation was clearly based on the models at El-Tarif. However, his tomb was modified to take into account the wholly different topography of Deir el-Bahari: a deep bay in the rock, flanked on the north by high cliffs used for the tomb. The royal temple-tomb itself lay on two levels, both fronted by built colonnades of proto-Doric columns. The upper terrace's central focus was a large square massif, either a mastaba or pyramid, perhaps representing the mound of creation.[222] This was surrounded by a pillared hall, behind which was a colonnaded court and then a hypostyle hall, at the back of which was the main offering place.

From the avenue leading to the monument come a series of statues showing the king standing upright with his arms crossed over his chest and wearing the *heb-sed* jubilee robe. As later depictions of Osiris take this pose,

but with the body wholly shrouded, it was particularly fitted to a king both dead and awaiting rejuvenation, the latter also being the prime objective of the *heb-sed*. Mentuhotep's statues are often termed (misleadingly) as 'Osirid' figures (see p. 17):[223] true 'Osirid' figures, where the king is mummiform, are not found until the reign of Mentuhotep III at Armant.[224]

It is difficult to reconstruct the precise schema of decoration of Mentuhotep's temple, as the remains are very fragmentary, but a sense of the scenes can be made from the fragments that were recovered. The lower colonnade of the temple was decorated with processions of boats and foreign campaigns, showing the king vanquishing the enemy, the royal lion trampling foes, soldiers marching, fighting in siege and battle scenes and foreign prisoners of all ages and both genders. Historical texts detailing battles against the Asiatics are found in this area. The upper colonnade had, on the

southern side, hunting in the desert. Other scenes from this level included images of daily life with herdsmen, boats, the papyrus harvest and scenes of marshlands (presumably from the northern wall). Closer to the central massif, the sacred focus of this monument, images of the king and the gods engage in different activities that ensured the continuation of the cosmic cycle and the eternal life of the pharaoh. Scenes of offering being made, the king being embraced by various divinities, the success of the *heb-sed* race, images of royal ancestors and the king performing the daily ritual for the gods, all work together to ensure the safety of the king and the country.

In addition to the cult for the dead king, Mentuhotep, the temple at Deir el-Bahari also contained chapels for six of his female family members. These shrines are markedly different in their decoration, being more in keeping with private funerary chapels of the period. They show scenes of daily life with, in addition to the usual scenes of butchery and offerings, an emphasis on cows, calves and milking. These are perhaps an allusion to Hathor, goddess of the West in general and of the site of Deir el-Bahari in particular. The motifs are continued on and in the sarcophagi of these women. Another vignette that is typical of these female chapels and sarcophagi is the consumption of liquid offerings. This motif, although seen in a few mastabas at Saqqara, is rare and not repeated in a royal context until the Amarna Period. The ubiquitous presence of lotus flowers underlines the funerary nature of these representations.

Just outside Mentuhotep II's temple was the small, finely decorated rock-cut tomb-chapel of Queen Neferu II (TT319).[225] This had a small façade and a stone-lined passage leading back into a square chapel, with decoration that focused on the usual offering-related scenes, plus others showing the hairdressing of the queen – a motif also found in the tombs of the six royal ladies mentioned just above.

The tombs of the principal officers of state lay along the broad processional way that led from the temple towards the cultivation. Many were built high up in the northern cliffs,

204 (*above left*) Relief of Mentuhotep II embraced by Re, from the rear part of his temple (BM EA1397).

205 (*left*) Reconstruction of the mortuary shrine of Queen Ashayet from within the mortuary temple of Mentuhotep II. Her burial chamber lay at the bottom of a shaft below (11th Dynasty).

with a brick-sheathed flat façade, approached by a steeply sloping rectangular courtyard (Type IIIa). Owing to the poor quality of the rock, the decoration was executed on a limestone lining.

Other tombs of the period continued the *saff* type, a variation using free-standing pillars rather than rock-cut piers being seen in the tomb of Meketre (TT280). With their long, tunnel-like, rear part, these sepulchres provide the prototype for the classic 'T-shaped' Theban tomb-chapel, a form that became particularly common in the New Kingdom. One interesting variation is found in the tomb of Meketre, which had a small chamber cut below the main corridor of the chapel and another below the façade, equivalent to the serdabs of earlier periods. The former contained an exceptional set of tomb models, of a type more usually placed in the burial chamber.[226]

While a number of tombs in the Deir el-Bahari necropolis were used during the latter part of the 11th Dynasty, the funerary arrangements of the last two kings of the dynasty are unclear. It is known that a functioning funerary establishment existed for Mentuhotep III, but it has yet to be firmly identified. One possibility, however, is that it may have been identical with a well-known sanctuary built by the king, atop a rock massif known as 'Thoth Hill'.[227] This temple had, however, been built on the site of an earlier shrine, which might argue against it being a mortuary monument. On the other hand, a ravine on the north side of the hill has revealed, half way up a 35-m (115-ft) cliff, a tomb with a large burial chamber and stone sarcophagus. Turned into a Coptic shrine in the 4th century AD, this could have been Mentuhotep III's burial place.

206 Relief of Queen Ashayet receiving offerings; from her sarcophagus found in her tomb (DBXI.17) in Mentuhotep II's temple (CM JE47267).

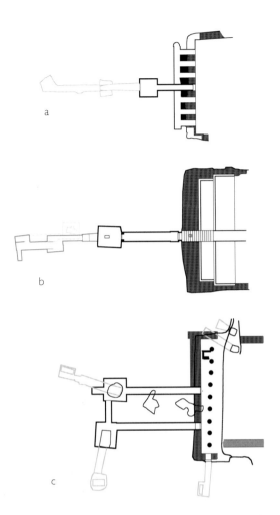

207 Plans of three significant Theban tombs of the latter part of the 11th Dynasty. They all feature mud-brick façades and burial-passages opening from the rear or the floor of the chapel: a. Dagi (TT103: Sheikh Abd el-Qurna); b. Khety (TT311: Deir el-Bahari); c. Meketre (TT280: Wadi S). The small chambers under the façade and main passage contained tomb-models. The southern chapel-complex probably belonged to the tomb-owner's son.

Another candidate is represented by an unfinished mortuary temple in a bay in the cliffs behind Sheikh Abd el-Qurna. Nothing of the building itself remains – indeed, no structure ever seems seems to have been erected – although extensive grading work for the platform and approach are still clearly to be seen and will have formed the basis for a structure much like that at Deir el-Bahari. Moreover, tomb-chapels with steeply sloping courtyard approaches overlook the site. Clearly this bears all the

208 The foundations of a temple similar to that of Mentuhotep II were constructed some way to the south of Deir el-Bahari ('Wadi S'); its founder remains uncertain. The graded platform below the cliffs, with the entrance to the royal tomb (TT281), is at the rear, surrounded by shaft tombs. Grading for the causeway leads into the distance, flattening the southern end of the Sheikh Abd el-Qurna hill before terminating in the vicinity of the Ramesseum (late 11th/early 12th Dynasty).

hallmarks of a royal tomb and thus the temple was long attributed to Mentuhotep III. However, it has now been argued that it may have belonged to the founder of the next, 12th, Dynasty,[228] perhaps following initial work by the ephemeral Mentuhotep IV. Further work on the problem is clearly needed.

The Provinces: The provincial cemeteries that had grown up earlier in the First Intermediate Period continued to flourish. A particularly important site is Beni Hasan, which provides an excellent example of a provincial necropolis of the period. It lies on the east bank of the river and thus reverses the usual orientation of tomb-chapels. The plans of

209 The superstructure of the tomb of Meketre (TT280) incorporated a chamber containing models – a feature more normally found in the substructure. They are of extraordinarily high quality; this one depicts the inspection of cattle by Meketre (CM JE46724: late 11th/early 12th Dynasty).

the earlier tombs are fairly simple, with a single room divided into two by a double row of pillars. The walls opposite their entrances are devoid of a false-door, which had to be located to one side of the doorway in order to face west.

The fully fledged tomb-chapels, such as these, lie on a terrace along the upper part of the cliff. On the slope directly below were cut the simple shaft-tombs of the middle classes, occasionally marked on the surface by a stela. Many were found intact and provide very good examples of the

funerary equipment of the period, including the now-standard placement of wooden models on the lids of the coffins.[229]

At Dendara, in contrast with the mastabas that comprise the vast majority of the necropolis, there is a single tomb-chapel cut in the side of a rising area of desert.[230] Belonging to Inyotefiqer ii, it is very similar to Theban tombs at El-Tarif, with a sunken courtyard fronting a colonnade, in which were found the stelae of the occupants of the tomb. Beyond this, a passage led through a two-pillared room to a small chamber. Shafts opened in the floor of the pillared room, while a sloping passage led down from the innermost chamber of the chapel.

Substructures

The usual mix of simple rock-cut shafts and sloping passages are to be found in the royal and private *saff* tombs of the early 11th Dynasty at El-Tarif. Rather more elaborate designs reappear in the cemeteries of the reign of Mentuhotep II at Deir el-Bahari.

At the rear of the king's own temple, an approximately 150 m (500 ft) long passageway, lined in part with sandstone, descended to a granite-lined, gable-roofed room, containing a calcite shrine in which the king was buried. A similar passageway lay in the northeast corner of the tree-lined courtyard in front of the temple and gave access to a dummy burial that seems to have been linked with the royal jubilee rituals.

A gable-roofed burial chamber was also employed in the tomb of Queen Tem, in the rear courtyard of her husband's temple. In contrast, the substructure of the tomb of Queen Neferu II was concealed behind the south wall of her chapel (p. 190), a sloping passage leading to a stone-lined decorated burial chamber, sealed by a monolithic stone door. The room's walls were covered with offering lists, together with extracts from the Pyramid and Coffin Texts. From the same reign is the chamber of the shaft-tomb of Kemsit (TT308 – belonging to one of the six shrines in Mentuhotep II's temple: see p. 190) depicting offering bringers and the deceased having her hair dressed. Interestingly, these motifs closely match those found on the sarcophagi of Kemsit herself and other royal women buried nearby (cf. ill. 206). As with the earlier case of Kaemankh (pp. 182–3), such 'daily-life' scenes are exceptional as far as a burial chamber is concerned.

In the tombs of the members of the court, the burial chamber was approached from the back of the chapel, either via a vertical shaft or a sloping passageway, hidden behind the false-door. Some of these chambers (e.g. in TT240, 311, 313 and 314) were stone-lined and decorated with depictions of funerary items, false-doors, offering lists and extracts from the Coffin Texts; the sarcophagus in such tombs was often made from separate blocks. An interesting variant is the tomb of Meru (TT240), whose burial chamber is in the form of a sarcophagus, inscribed with a false-door and Coffin Texts.

Built Superstructures and Offering Places

Royal Tombs: The kings of the 12th Dynasty resumed the use of pyramids. That of Amenemhat I at Lisht employed large quantities of re-used stone, much of it clearly from 4th Dynasty pyramid complexes. It has been suggested that some of this re-use had a ritual import, linking Amenemhat with the great kings of the past.[231] On the other hand, if the pyramid were indeed the replacement for an earlier Theban monument, time may have been considered as being of the essence and ready-cut stone used for convenience. Little survives of Amenemhat's mortuary temple, which was built on two levels, perhaps recalling the temple of Mentuhotep II.

Senwosret I's pyramid complex at Lisht was modelled on late Old Kingdom examples and included what may be the last of all subsidiary pyramids. The enclosure also contained nine small pyramids for members of the royal family.[232] Fragments of relief retrieved from the pyramid temple provide a basic idea of mortuary temple decoration at this time.[233] The enclosure wall was decorated with a series of images of the *serekh* (niched palace façade), surmounted by the king's name, with offering bearers marching below. Engaged Osirid and free-standing statues of the king lined the approach to the temple. The ceilings, as always, were engraved or painted with five-pointed stars. Processions of deities adorned the walls, together with scenes of the king offering to the gods and, in turn, being given life, a strong reign and acceptance by them.

210 The pyramid of Senwosret I at Lisht (12th Dynasty).

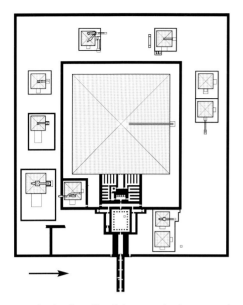

211 (*left*) Plan of the pyramid complex of Senwosret I, showing the large number of small pyramids within its enclosure.

212 (*right*) Plan of the pyramid complex of Senwosret II at Lahun. While the superstructures of the various tombs lay to the north of the pyramid, their substructures were on the opposite side of the pyramid. The exception was tomb 621, almost certainly belonging to the small pyramid, but outside the pyramid enclosure entirely (12th Dynasty).

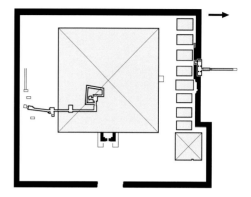

The back walls of the temple that were closest to the pyramid were adorned with stelae, as well as images of the king, accompanied by his *ka*, seated at offering tables. Lists of offerings, and images of priests carrying them, were inscribed on the walls. The decorative themes used are thus essentially those of the Old Kingdom. Also as in the later Old Kingdom, a small chapel lay over the entrance to the pyramid; its decorative programme resembles that found in the mortuary temple.

Amenemhat II's almost entirely destroyed pyramid[234] lay on the very edge of the desert at Dahshur, in contrast with the locations at the site chosen by Seneferu half a millennium earlier. A wholly new site was, however, chosen for the pyramid of Senwosret II, at Lahun in the Fayoum.[235] This monument was also radical in its construction, being the first pyramid since the end of the 3rd Dynasty to be built of brick, albeit with a substantial stone content, beginning with the natural rock knoll that formed the lower part of the pyramid core. Brick was keyed into this, but the stability of the whole structure depended on radial walls of limestone that split the built core into a series of compartments, to be filled with brick. The use of the natural rock was extended to the carving of the mastaba cores for the royal family out of the living rock, to be later sheathed in masonry.

The other major innovation in the layout of the tomb is that substructure entrances are no longer in the expected place. The king's burial galleries were entered from the south

213 Many of the tombs at Lahun utilize the material-saving approach of using natural rock as part of their superstructure, including the king's pyramid (south side shown here).

side of the pyramid, breaking with the 800-year tradition of a northern entrance. In addition, the entrance was further concealed under the floor of what had the appearance of an unused tomb intended for a member of the royal family. Other, real, tombs belonging to the royal family lay alongside, but their solid mastaba superstructures were far away, on the opposite side of the pyramid. All these changes can only be explained by a desire to protect the burials from plunderers.

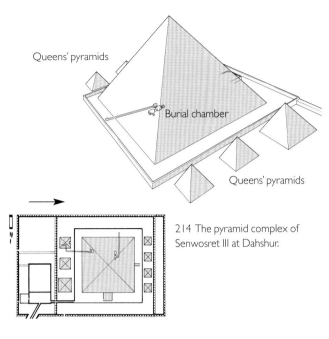

Queens' pyramids

Burial chamber

Queens' pyramids

214 The pyramid complex of Senwosret III at Dahshur.

Wholly brick pyramids were constructed for both Senwosret III[236] and Amenemhat III (pl. XV; ill. 225)[237] at Dahshur. Substructure entrance locations are again apparently random. While the plan of the Dahshur complex of Amenemhat III broadly followed standard practice, that of Senwosret III[238] had a rectangular plan, with its entrance in the southeast corner. In this and other facets it is clearly modelled on the ancient complex of Djoser (cf. ill. 137), although in its details it is wholly a Middle Kingdom confection.[239] The layout ultimately included an exceptional southern temple accessed from the southeast entrance, in addition to the usual eastern mortuary temple. Members of Senwosret III's family owned a series of small pyramids within the enclosure, to the north and south of that of the king.

A second pyramid of Amenemhat III, built after his Dahshur pyramid had suffered structural failure, also had an unusual enclosure design (ill. 226), probably once again inspired by the Step Pyramid.[240] Known to Classical writers as the 'Labyrinth', a large area to the south of the pyramid seems to have contained the principal elements of the mortuary temple.

The devastated state of all these royal monuments makes it difficult to say much about their decoration, but the surviving fragments suggest that most followed the basic approach seen at Senwosret I's complex. In view of its total

destruction, it is a pity that the Classical tourists who left accounts of the 'Labyrinth' of Amenemhat III at Hawara (p. 56) fail to mention anything worthwhile of its decoration.

Private Tombs: The cemeteries around the pyramid of Amenemhat I comprise a mixture of mastabas and simple shaft tombs. Of the latter, perhaps the most significant is that at the southwest corner (tomb 372), apparently belonging to the Chancellor Rehudjersen. Its core was rock-cut, faced with fine-quality limestone, with an offering chamber in the core at the south end. A complex of six subsidiary rooms lay within the enclosure wall on the south, each of vaulted brick construction. The entrance to the substructure was in the roof of the northern end of the mastaba, but the shaft, which slopes down to the south, is now flooded by ground water.[241] Another elaborate mastaba (400), actually within the southeast quadrant of the royal enclosure,[242] belonged to the Inyotefiqer who also constructed a rock-cut tomb at Thebes (TT60).[243]

Most 12th Dynasty mastabas in the Senwosret I cemetery at Lisht were solid, with an adjoining chapel, although one sepulchre, that of Sehetepibre-ankh, had an internal offering chamber which also contained the shaft leading to the substructure.[244] One very large stone mastaba tomb belongs to Senwosret-ankh.[245] It covers some 200 sq. m (2150 sq. ft), but the chapel on its east side covers nearly 500 sq. m (5400 sq. ft). This had been completely destroyed, save a few fragments of sculpture and granite relief. The chapel was almost entirely external, with the exception of a small extension into the mastaba core. The mastaba had a panelled exterior, after the manner of Old Kingdom examples. The entrance to the substructure lay on the north side, under the enclosure wall. Another tomb here that was almost entirely constructed and only partially rock-cut takes the shape of a tripartite shrine with a forecourt. The decorational programme of the courtyard contains the majority of 'daily-life' scenes found in earlier tombs; unfortunately it is impossible to interpret the decoration in the shrine portion of the tomb due to its poor state of preservation.

The rubble-filled mastabas at Lisht (and later at Dahshur) differ from their Old Kingdom predecessors in being surrounded by an enclosure wall, with the substructure approached via a passageway from the north, rather than via a vertical shaft through the body of the superstructures. In some cases, earlier tombs are recalled

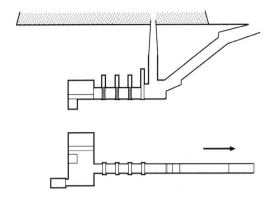

215 Section and plan of the substructure of the tomb of Senwosret-ankh at Lisht. The tomb had a number of ingenious features intended to deter robbers: apart from the shaft which drenched any intruder with sand from above, the first portcullis (now destroyed) had lugs sliding at 45 degrees that locked it down once lowered.

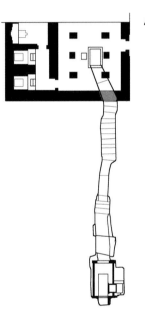

216, 217 A number of built tomb-chapels of the early 12th Dynasty exist at Saqqara. This (above) belongs to Ihi, viewed from its colonnaded court (cf. the plan of the adjoining tomb of Hetep, left), looking west to its two statue chambers and (right) the false door. Behind the tomb are the Old Kingdom monuments of Mereruka and Tjetju.

through a pair of equal-sized niches at either end of the eastern façade.

In the ancient cemetery of Saqqara, activity seems to have been concentrated in the area of the pyramid of Teti. Two good examples of tombs of the time of Amenemhat I are those of Ihy and Hetep, built against the south wall of the Old Kingdom mastaba of Kagemeni.[246] They comprised a peristyle courtyard, in an inner corner of which a doorway led into a vestibule with two statue-rooms and a deeper chamber with the false-door. The entrance to the substructure lay in the centre of the courtyard. The extant decoration of these chapels is principally composed of offering bringers and the receipt of offerings adjacent to the false-door. North of the false-door were a series of rooms holding statues of the deceased.

Such 'temple-tombs' mark a new kind of funerary monument, which is also found at Lisht, for example the tombs of Senwosret and Mentuhotep. These comprise a large enclosure, often incorporating a causeway, with a free-standing offering place, and in some cases priests' houses as well. A halfway house between such tombs and more conventional mastabas is provided by the Lisht tomb of Djehuty, where the mastaba has a four-pillared façade, leading to a symmetrical chapel with a transverse hall and sanctuary.

The private cemetery of Amenemhat II is largely unrecorded, but 800 m (2600 ft) south of the king's pyramid

is the large mastaba of the Vizier Sieset (L.LV), built of brick with a limestone casing. Although elements of the decoration of the chapel survive, nothing is known of the chapel itself, which may have been built into the core of the mastaba.[247]

The cemeteries adjacent to the Lahun pyramid comprised mainly mastabas, often making considerable use of the native rock. Chapels were thus often rock-cut; that of the Chancellor Inpy (tomb 620) comprised a stone-cased brick mastaba, about 21 x 16 m (70 x 50 ft), with a largely rock-cut triple-shrined chapel below on the east side, which incorporated a four-pillared portico and a curious pit in front of the tomb to hinder unauthorized access.[248]

The exterior surface of a number of limestone mastabas dating to the reign of Senwosret III at Dahshur are carved with recessed panelling, recalling the mastabas of the Early Dynastic Period and the enclosure wall of Djoser, albeit with the faces given a distinct batter, with monumental hieroglyphic texts often running along the top of the mastaba, as well as vertically around and between areas of panelling. Examples include the monuments of Khnumhotep, Sieset and Nebyot, with the panelling clearly linked to the various aspects of archaism to be seen in Senwosret III's funerary complex.[249]

The area north of the Hawara pyramid of Amenemhat III contained many mastabas, reused in Graeco-Roman times for sacred crocodile interments. These mastabas comprised very thick brick retaining walls enclosing limestone chip from the cutting of the substructure, the whole cased with fine limestone. Recorded sizes of the mastabas vary from 6 to 18 m (20 to 60 ft) long, while only a few scraps of decorated limestone survive from their chapels.

In provincial cemeteries such as Abydos, wide varieties of sizes and shapes of brick chapels are to be found, but the general approach at the site is sloping-sided plastered brick structures – in some cases pyramids – housing a vaulted chapel containing the offering stela. The Abydene examples could have been actual tomb-chapels, or may have acted as cenotaphs to permit the deceased to take part posthumously in the festivals of Osiris.[250]

While the Theban necropolis was generally characterized by rock-cut chapels, Cemetery 200 at Deir el-Bahari has a number of tombs with largely built superstructures.[251] Dating towards the end of the 12th Dynasty, one of them, that of one Senwosret-ankh (tomb MMA211) comprised a brick structure with a forehall supported by painted wooden columns. Another, of a certain Amenemhat (MMA202), had a similar structure with a series of limestone shrines set into the walls, containing statues of the deceased and his wife, as well as reliefs of him and his family.

Rock-cut Superstructures and Offering Places

In contrast with the 11th Dynasty, few 12th Dynasty major private tombs are known at Thebes. The best-known example is TT60, generally attributed to Senet and/or her son, Inyotefiqer,[252] the owner of a mastaba at Lisht (see p. 196). TT60 comprises a long corridor and a simple chapel. The apparent lack of large tombs at Thebes may be explained in part by the move of the court to the north, although the vagaries of preservation may also be to blame – including the possible usurpation of a number of 12th Dynasty sepulchres during the early 18th Dynasty. A number of tomb-chapels of this date have features that suggest that they may be adaptations of Middle Kingdom monuments.

In the north, the majority of tomb-chapels were built structures, although there are rock-cut examples and some built structures with rock-cut elements, for example the aforementioned tomb of Inpy at Lahun. However, as previously, most rock-cut sepulchres lay in Middle and Upper Egypt, due to the terrain, with Beni Hasan remaining one of the key sites. The 12th Dynasty tombs there differ in

218 Painting in TT60 (Senet/Inyotefiqer), one of the few surviving decorated 12th Dynasty tombs at Thebes.

design from those of the previous dynasty: a two-columned portico and four-pillared main hall, with a sanctuary at the very back being features of the tombs of Ameny and Khnumhotep iii (BH-II and III). The sanctuary incorporated a rock-cut statue of the tomb-owner.

Deir el-Bersha was also an important provincial cemetery during the First Intermediate Period and early Middle Kingdom. As at Beni Hasan, a simple doorway giving access to a rectangular chamber is replaced by a columned portico and more elaborate interior. Elaboration is also a feature of 12th Dynasty tombs at Qubbet el-Hawa (Aswan), those of Sirenput i (QH36) and ii (QH31: pl. XVII) having pillared fore-halls and then a long passage leading to a columned offering place. Tomb 31 is particularly interesting in that its passage has a series of niches, each holding a rock-cut mummiform figure.

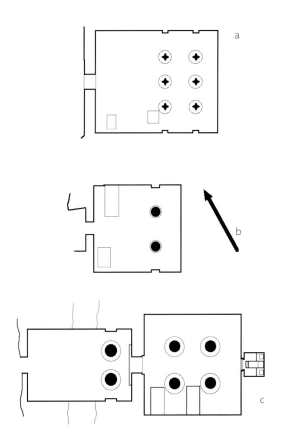

219 (*right*) Tomb-chapels at Beni Hasan, showing the appearance and growth of the forecourt: a. Khety i (BH-XVII: 11th Dynasty); b. Khnumhotep i (BH-XIV: Amenemhat I); c. Ameny (BH-II: Senwosret I).

220 (*below*) Reconstruction of the tomb of Khnumhotep (tomb 2) at Dahshur, showing the elaborate panelled design, reminiscent of Early Dynastic practice, but using different patterns (12th Dynasty, reign of Senwosret III).

The most dramatic 12th Dynasty private tombs are those of the nomarchs of Qau el-Kebir, where a core rock-cut element was supplemented by brick structures and walled causeways leading down towards the edge of the desert. They are amongst the latest of the great provincial tombs of the Middle Kingdom, as a series of governmental reforms carried out by Senwosret III concentrated far more power – and hence high-status individuals – at the national capital. This resulted in a major reduction in the number of large private tombs built away from the royal necropoleis after his reign, although this was certainly a gradual process, with some prominent provincial burials taking place under Amenemhat III.

Although the themes represented in the decoration of these tombs are the same as those of previous dynasties,

221 Amongst the tombs of the later 12th Dynasty at Qau el-Kebir are the gigantic monuments of three of the local governors, incorporating causeways and chapels of almost royal dimensions. This view looks up the causeway of the tomb of Wahka i (7).

variations and new details appear within scenes. A variant of the hunt scene shows the activity as being carried out in an enclosure, a detail that carries into the 18th Dynasty hunt scenes (e.g. TT100). Some of the animals shown in these scenes (e.g. Beni Hasan BH-III, XV, XVII; Bersha 4, 5) are also quite exotic, while others are mythical: a rhinoceros-type animal, a griffin, a serpopard (a leopard or panther with a serpent's neck) and the Set animal. Other unusual creatures that rarely feature in two-dimensional formal art also appear in these tombs: a herd of pigs emerging from a papyrus thicket (BH-XVII), bats and several different bird species (BH-XV), monkeys, ichneumon (BH-XV) and a mixture of a dog and a bird. The hunt scenes at Meir and Thebes also contain exotic animals, such as deer and a giraffe (B2; TT60). Innovative details within the fowl-catching scenes include bird traps of different varieties (BH-XV, XVII) that are still in use today.

In addition to the usual crafts, new scenes are added to the decorative repertoire: arrow- and knife-making, spinning, weaving and laundering. New details appear in cooking scenes, such as roasting a whole ox (e.g. in Meir B4). A group of tombs at Beni Hasan also show several registers of wrestlers on the back wall, with smaller vignettes of a fortress being stormed (BH-II, XIV, XV and part of XXIX). Wrestling men are also shown in the tombs at Meir (B1, B2) and El-Bersha (tomb 4).

Depictions of foreigners, other than nomads, are also found in the tombs at Beni Hasan. Enigmatic representations of families carrying their worldly possessions coming from the Near East (BH-III), as well as what are presumably prisoners from Libya (BH-XIV), are found here. Perhaps this relates to actual emigrations and battles that occurred during the tomb-owners' lifetimes.

Several intriguing scenes grace the pilasters of BH-XVII at Beni Hasan. These depict medical endeavours, including cupping, removing thorns and carrying people, as well as games like hockey and one of the rare depictions showing human sexual intercourse. The object friezes known from coffins of the Middle Kingdom are also transposed into tombs in registers that are separate from the conventional offering scenes (e.g. tomb B1 at Meir).

Engaged statuary continues to be a feature of tombs of the Middle Kingdom. In Sirenput ii's tomb we have seen the passageway leading to the shrine lined with rock-cut Osirid statues of the deceased. Increasing elaboration is also seen in

222 (*above*) The end wall of the tomb-chapel of Khety at Beni Hasan, with a set of scenes of wrestling (top) and warfare (bottom). Such depictions are only found in a handful of tombs at this site (BH-XVII: late 11th Dynasty).

223 (*left*) A curious series of vignettes found on a pilaster in BH-XVII show a man standing on his head, another one being carried by his comrades, cupping(?), and hockey playing. These are all unique to this tomb (11th Dynasty).

the design of false-doors as the dynasty progresses, with some acquiring a pair of eyes on the lower lintel. The eyes have a dual function: they are a vehicle that permits the deceased to look out, and they serve an apotropaic function, by protecting the deceased and his body.

Substructures

The earliest pyramids of the 12th Dynasty broadly followed Old Kingdom practice in having entrances on the north side. In Amenemhat I's tomb, the corridor led down to a chamber under the centre of the pyramid, from which a shaft led downward; unfortunately a rise in the level of the local groundwater has prevented further exploration. For similar reasons it has been impossible to penetrate even this far in Senwosret I's pyramid; however, Amenemhat II's monument at Dahshur lies well clear of the water table, revealing a single chamber under the pyramid's centre. Apart from an elaborate roof, designed to reduce crushing forces from above, the main innovation was that the sarcophagus had been hidden under the floor, with the canopic chest some distance away, under the floor of a passage directly below the doorway of the burial chamber. These were clearly intended to enhance the security of the tomb and foreshadowed major changes in subsequent reigns.

The tombs of the royal family at Lisht also display odd arrangements of substructures. Tomb 493, perhaps that of Amenemhat I's wife, was entered by a shaft, which gave access to a sloping passage, its end lost under the ground water; however, half way along, a passage runs to the right, ending in a chamber. At the junction of the two passages, another shaft ascends to emerge directly under the tomb's chapel. This may have been a 'construction shaft' intended for heavy items and covered over in favour of a smaller definitive entrance.[253] Another interesting arrangement is seen in tomb 378, whose entrance is in the roof of the mastaba, but rather than a perpendicular shaft we find one sloping at about 40 degrees from vertical, which plummets down for some 25 m (80 ft) before hitting the water table.

To the north of the king's pyramid is the 'Mastaba du Nord'.[254] The two elements of its substructure were constructed in fairly shallow cuttings in the bedrock. That below the mastaba itself is interesting in that the burial chamber was of the same width as the approach corridor and also had a floor sloping at the same angle as that of the passage. The latter may have been to aid the placement of the sarcophagus in the limited space available.

At Saqqara, the tombs of Ihy and Hetep have extensive substructures.[255] In both cases, a main entrance shaft

224 Plan of the 'Mastaba du Nord' at Lisht. The substructure below the mastaba itself had its approach corridor entirely filled with blocks of stone (early 12th Dynasty).

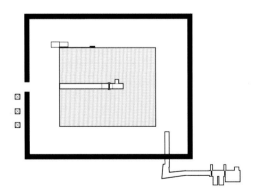

descended from the outer courtyards of their chapels, leading to a slightly descending passage, which after some 20 m (70 ft) terminated in a burial chamber. Just before the burial chamber, a second shaft penetrated from above, a remnant from a pre-existing tomb. The corridors were lined with limestone, with the paving derived from reused blocks of Old Kingdom date. The burial chambers were also limestone-lined, with painted decoration comprising texts, supplemented by images of a house façade, offerings and the 'object frieze' that is regularly found in sarcophagi and coffins of this period. This frieze is composed of objects that were used in daily life and that might be needed in the hereafter; these objects are additionally charged with religious power and significance, such as bags of natron that were used in mummification as well as personal hygiene, or oils that have sacred significance as well as practical use. Its origins might lie as far back as the 3rd Dynasty (cf. S2405). A decorated sarcophagus was sunk in the floor, with a canopic niche to the south east.

In the complex of Senwosret I, the pyramids of the king's womenfolk display a variety of innovative substructure designs.[256] In pyramid 3, there was both an entrance shaft and a 'construction' shaft for the introduction of building material. From the former, a corridor ran towards the sepulchral room, two sets of sliding stone doors being incorporated to block access.

A security imperative is also to be seen in high-status private tombs. At the mastaba of Senwosret-ankh at Lisht, the substructure was approached from the north, but the actual entrance lay under an enclosure wall.[257] A sloping passage then led down to a horizontal gallery and then to the burial chamber (ill. 215). However, not only was the horizontal passage equipped with four vertical portcullises, but directly before them a unique 'chimney' had been constructed, leading up into the superstructure. This had been filled with sand, so that any intruders would find a constant stream of sand from above hindering any attempt at forcing the first portcullis and blocking any retreat. However, robbers had never faced the problem, as they had tunnelled into the burial chamber directly from the south end of the tomb, bypassing the entrance passage entirely! The chamber contained a sunken sarcophagus and canopic chest and is decorated with Pyramid Texts.[258] Indeed the substructure is reminiscent of late Old Kingdom royal tombs and may be a conscious imitation of them.

A noble of Amenemhat II's reign also had a Pyramid Text-decorated burial chamber: the Vizier Sieset, who had a large mastaba at Dahshur (L.LV).[259] The substructure was entered from a shaft on the north side, leading to a brick-vaulted sloping passage and a limestone burial chamber, with two annexes, one for the canopic containers.

The tombs of the women of Amenemhat II's family lay to the west of the main pyramid, where the main enclosure wall annexed an area of some size.[260] The three tombs there are of a type apparently new. Each is a built structure of masonry sunk in a pit, covered by a brick relieving arch. A passage runs the entire length of the tomb, off which open two niches, each containing a sarcophagus, its lid just below the level of the floor of the passage. From the west side of each sarcophagus-cut, three low openings give access to an offering/canopic chamber, below the paving of the passage above. At the time of the burial, the niche was filled with stone slabs, locked in place by a vertical key-stone. With their passages filled with plug blocks, the tombs effectively became solid masses of stone; doubtless this explains the fact that two of the tombs remained intact.

The tombs of Senwosret II and his family at Lahun also include major innovations. Not least of them was, as we have already seen, the divorce, in whole or part, of their substructures from their time-hallowed relationship with the superstructures. The entrance to the king's tomb was for the first time on the south side of the pyramid, where a shaft led a dozen metres (40 ft) below the surface, joining a spacious passageway that led via a limestone antechamber to the very fine granite-lined burial chamber under the pyramid. The entrances to most of the tombs of the royal family lay adjacent to that of the king, the sepulchres themselves being of simple form. An entrance shaft led to an antechamber, its floor sunk to a lower level, at the end of which was the burial chamber. Virtually all of the area of this was occupied by the sarcophagus, a niche in the right-hand wall containing the canopic equipment, a further opening at the far end of the same wall giving access to the offering chamber.

The pyramid of Senwosret III at Dahshur[261] has a substructure reminiscent of the 5th/6th Dynasties.[262] However, the tombs of his womenfolk were mainly placed in a catacomb of unique design at the north end of the enclosure. A long east–west gallery linked the substructures of four small pyramids, which also joined them with a lower level in which seven sarcophagi and canopic chests were

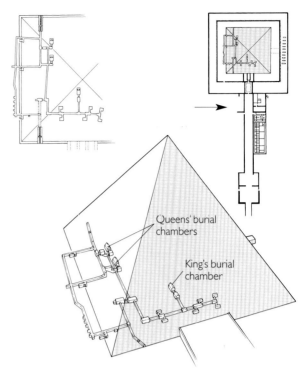

225 (*above*) The first pyramid-complex of Amenemhat III, the 'Black Pyramid' at Dahshur (12th Dynasty).

226 (*below*) The second pyramid-complex of Amenemhat III, at Hawara.

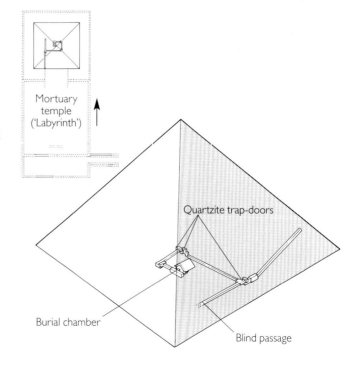

placed in niches in a single room. The rooms under the four pyramids included so-called 'ka-chambers', seemingly an equivalent to a king's subsidiary pyramid.

South of the king's pyramid were three more small pyramids, one of which (number IX), belonging to Queen Weret II, had its entrance some distance to the northeast of its superstructure, the shaft joining a north–south passage half way along its 60-m (200-ft) length. To the north, it gave access to an antechamber, a canopic room and a burial chamber, which all lay under the body of the king's pyramid, some 50 m (165 ft) away from the queen's own monument. Under the latter, the southern part of the passage led to the 'ka-chamber'.

More unusual forms are found under the pyramids of Amenemhat III at Dahshur and Hawara. The former had an elaborate arrangement of passages and chambers, including 'ka-chambers' under the southern edge of the pyramid. Some of these ka-chambers belonged to royal wives who, like Weret, lay below the king's pyramid. However, their interments were accessible both from their own entrance on the opposite side of the pyramid and from the king's apartments. This arrangement seems to be unique. Amenemhat's second pyramid introduced sliding trap-doors in roofs to conceal the route to the burial chamber and also the concept of having a burial chamber carved from a single block of quartzite. The entrance was by means of a raised

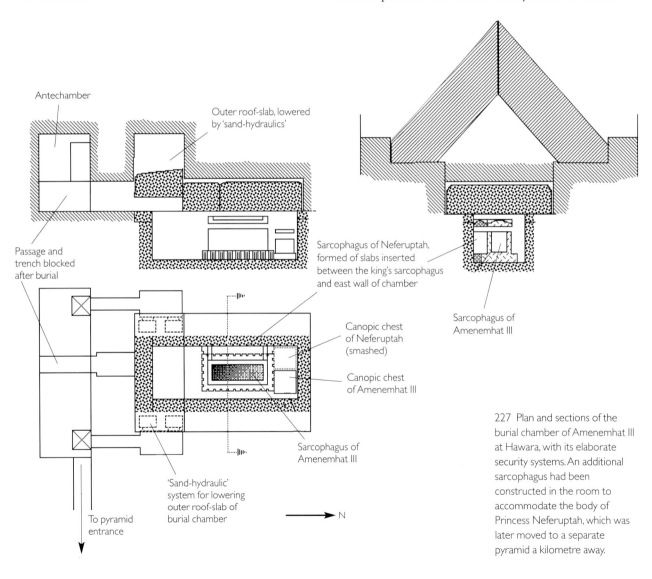

Antechamber

Outer roof-slab, lowered by 'sand-hydraulics'

Passage and trench blocked after burial

Sarcophagus of Neferuptah, formed of slabs inserted between the king's sarcophagus and east wall of chamber

Canopic chest of Neferuptah (smashed)

Canopic chest of Amenemhat III

Sarcophagus of Amenemhat III

To pyramid entrance

'Sand-hydraulic' system for lowering outer roof-slab of burial chamber

N

Sarcophagus of Amenemhat III

227 Plan and sections of the burial chamber of Amenemhat III at Hawara, with its elaborate security systems. An additional sarcophagus had been constructed in the room to accommodate the body of Princess Neferuptah, which was later moved to a separate pyramid a kilometre away.

roof block, lowered after the burial by a 'hydraulic' device using sand: by breaking seals, sand flowed out of shafts, thus causing props to descend and place the roofing block atop the chamber. This system was also used in a number of 13th Dynasty pyramids and would be revived a thousand years later for some private tombs of the 26th Dynasty.

The substructures of the mastabas of the officials that accompanied the pyramids of the kings of the late 12th Dynasty vary considerably in form. That of Inpy at Lahun (620) was entered via a steep corridor from just beyond the north end of the mastaba leading to a flat-roofed chamber, built at the bottom of a construction shaft; a gable-roofed relieving cavity lay directly above the room, to protect

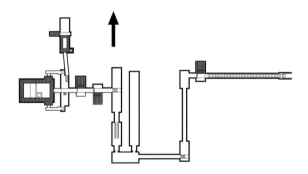

against the supercumbent weight of the rubble in the shaft. Beyond this lay an apparent burial chamber, complete with a canopic niche. However, this was a dummy, a room under the floor giving access to the real sepulchral chamber, directly below the gable-roofed room. The ingenuity displayed in the royal tombs was thus now being employed in private burials as well.

Under Senwosret III, the tomb entrance was generally well beyond the perimeter of the mastaba and usually took the form of a shaft.[263] A variety of designs exist at Dahshur, tombs 17 (Sobkemhat) and 20 having a simple passage leading to a gable-roofed chamber. However, in both cases, the sarcophagus and canopic chest lay deeply buried below the chamber floor. On the other hand, the sepulchre of the Vizier Khnumhotep (2) differed entirely. Here, the shaft led to a vestibule, a right-hand turn giving access to a further vestibule. The sarcophagus lay in a stone-lined, gable-roofed, niche beyond, while the canopic chest was at the end of a passage that ran parallel with the niche, from the end of a corridor at the east end of the vestibule.

Little is known of private tombs around Amenemhat III's pyramid at Dahshur, but a series of simple shaft-tombs

228, 229 The 13th Dynasty Unfinished Pyramid at Saqqara-South has the most elaborate substructure of any known pyramid (*above*). Its canopic chest was carved as one with the sarcophagus and surrounding burial chamber from a single block of quartzite (*below*).

230 (*below*) Private substructures of the 12th Dynasty: (left) section of the tomb of Inpy, including dummy chambers above the real burial chamber; plans of tombs 2 (Khnumhotep: centre) and 19 (unknown: right) in the Senwosret III cemetery at Dahshur. In tomb 2, the sarcophagus and canopic chest lay in separate deep niches, accessed from a vestibule. In tomb 19, these two items lay close together, but deeply buried under the floor of the burial chamber.

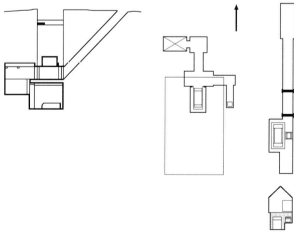

DECORATED SUBSTRUCTURES OF THE MIDDLE KINGDOM

Site	Tomb	Date	Owner	Scene
Thebes	TT319	11th Dyn	Neferu	Offering lists, Coffin Texts, Pyramid Texts and funeral outfit
El-Qatta		Middle Kingdom	Neha	Texts
Saqqara		Middle Kingdom	Haishetef	Offering list
Saqqara	SQ75	Middle Kingdom	Ipi	Painted decoration, offering texts and probably Coffin Texts
Saqqara	Shaft 276	Middle Kingdom	Tja	Painted decoration
Saqqara		Middle Kingdom	Sihathor-Ipi	Pyramid Texts; Coffin Texts
Abu Sir el-Meleq		Before 12th Dyn	Heryshefnakhte & Ukh(et)hotep	Ritual scenes; offerings and religious texts
Saqqara		12th Dyn	Hetep	Funerary and offering text
Saqqara		12th Dyn	Ihy	Painted decoration; texts and friezes of objects
Riqqa	191	12th Dyn	Senmeri	Offerings and offering scenes
Saqqara		12th Dyn	Sekawesket	Pyramid Texts; Coffin Texts
Dahshur		12th Dyn	Sieset	Pyramid Texts
Lisht		12th Dyn	Senwosret-ankh	Pyramid Texts
Meir		12th Dyn	Ukhhotep-son-of-Iam	Wooden door of tomb with names and titles of the deceased
Qau el-Kebir	18	12th Dyn	Wahka ii	Walls with cursive texts (fragmentary)

existed along its north side. At Hawara,[264] most mastabas placed their substructure entrances on the north side, one group of tombs (1–10) having particularly deep shafts, some plumbing over 13 m (40 ft); other sepulchres were of more modest depth. In a number of examples, at the bottom of the shaft an inclined plane led down to the burial chamber.

Away from the royal cemeteries, elaborate substructures are also to be seen at Riqqa cemetery A. Here, amongst a considerable number of large, but generally simple, shaft tombs with one or two quarried chambers, were two big sepulchres with stone-built rooms.[265] Tomb 306, the better preserved, was approached by a sloping cutting, 20 m (65 ft) long, leading to a limestone chamber, with a pointed roof and containing a granite sarcophagus, whose design allows the tomb to be dated to the reign of Senwosret III or Amenemhat III. A niche in the left wall of the burial chamber had contained the canopic equipment, while a

brick arch above the chamber had been intended to relieve the weight above, a feature reminiscent of the Hawara pyramid.

In contrast to such elaborate arrangements, the vast majority of Middle Kingdom substructures consist of simple vertical shafts, leading directly to one or more burial chambers. At Abydos, there are many examples of family tombs comprising a number of parallel shafts, with chambers one above the other in each shaft. All had their upper parts enclosed in a common sleeve of brickwork, linked to a single chapel.[266]

Also at Riqqa is a rare decorated burial chamber, that of Senmeri (191). A 7-m (25-ft) shaft led to this vaulted room, with a niche in the east wall for the canopic chest and also a bench along the same wall. The walls of the room were whitewashed, with paintings providing a dado around three sides of the chamber. The west wall showed the tomb-owner in front of a pair of heavily laden offering tables, with wine and beer below them, beyond which his sons knelt with yet more offerings of food and drink. His wife and daughters also offer food on the south wall, the nutrition-related theme being completed by a procession of offering bearers on the east wall. The ceiling was adorned with a 'woven' pattern of red and blue crosses.

Other less regular examples of decoration include the double tomb of Heryshefnakhte and Ukhhotep at Abu Sir el-Meleq/el-Haraga,[267] with ritual scenes in addition to the more standard texts, and the tomb-chamber in Ukhhotep's tomb at Meir (A3), whose wooden door is inscribed with the names and titles of the deceased.

As can be seen, although the few decorated substructures from this period show a preference for funerary inscriptions such as extracts from the Pyramid and Coffin Texts and offering lists, other images are also found.

231 All that survives of the pyramid of Aya is its pyramidion, apparently carried off to the northeast Delta by Hyksos looters (CM JE43267: 13th Dynasty).

THE 13TH DYNASTY AND THE SECOND INTERMEDIATE PERIOD

Very little is known of tombs of the end of the Middle Kingdom and the Second Intermediate Period. Pyramids were begun for a number of the earlier kings of the 13th Dynasty, but none seem to have been completed and very little can be divined about the layout of their chapels, other than that they remained on the east side. One curious aspect of some of these complexes is the wavy form of their enclosure walls; other monarchs seem to have done without superstructures altogether.[268] After the middle of the dynasty, no royal tombs are known at all until the 17th Dynasty.

Private tombs with any kind of superstructure are even more elusive, although at Thebes some modest built chapels seem to have existed in Cemetery 200 at Deir el-Bahari. One of the few datable groups of substantial tombs is at El-Kab. Here, the essentially single-chambered tomb-chapels of Renseneb (EK9) and Sobknakhte (EK10)[269] span the 13th to 16th/17th Dynasties.

Up in the Hyksos realm of Avaris (Tell el-Daba), few superstructures have been found. One example, however, was F/1-p/19:1, which had a superstructure of approximately square plan, fronted by a chapel containing a statue of an Asiatic dignitary.[270] Unfortunately, its building date is uncertain, being possibly as early as the end of the 12th Dynasty, to which time also date two mortuary chapels associated with cemetery area A/II.

During the 15th Dynasty itself, the Levantine practice of building mud-brick tombs within urban houses or courtyards begins to be found, a special room sometimes being added against the outside wall of the bedroom. Archaeological remains suggest that the mortuary practices also followed foreign approaches. Some examples conform to Levantine norms by employing domed mud-brick buildings, combined with the Egyptian features of tree-pits at the entrance, an allusion to the burial rites associated with the Delta sites of Buto and Sais.

As far as substructures are concerned, below the aforementioned F/I-p/19:1 lay a rectangular brick structure in a cutting in the soil, conforming to normal Delta practice, in this case the chamber being roofed with a brick dome, other sepulchres at the site having vaults. A number of tombs had a grave for a donkey in front of the entrance: this is certainly a manifestation of Palestinian culture.

The Levantine cultural background becomes even more pronounced as the Second Intermediate Period progresses, when Avaris became the capital of the 14th/15th Dynasty Palestinian kings. Some single-chamber tombs can hold multiple burials. These later tombs are still vaulted, but the constructional technique used is more usually found in Mesopotamia.

The principal necropolis of the native 16th and 17th Dynasties at Thebes lay on Dra Abu'l-Naga. Substructures were generally simple and only one private substructure is known. Dating to the time of Inyotef VI, this chapel, of one

Teti, comprised a small brick structure, with a painted decoration including the deceased receiving offerings.[271]

The kings of the period were interred in the same location, equipped with brick pyramids.[272] The only excavated example, that of Inyotef VI,[273] was less than 10 m (30 ft) square, faced with white plaster and built on the slope of the hill, its sides rising at an angle of around 65/68 degrees; it had a decorated cap-stone, while a pair of obelisks stood in front. The capstone bore the king's names, titles and pedigree, as did that of the adjacent pyramid of Inyotef V.[274]

Nothing is yet definitely known of the substructure of Inyotef VI's pyramid, none of the adjacent shafts being demonstrably part of it. The burial chambers of both Inyotef V and VI both were discovered by plunderers during the early 19th century, the latter being reported as being approached by a brick-lined shaft and corridor and lying at Dra Abu'l-Naga 'halfway up the hill'.[275] However, neither has yet been rediscovered and precisely localized.

232 Aerial view of the remains of the pyramid of Inyotef VI at Dra Abu'l-Naga. The shaft in the middle is from an earlier, over-built, tomb.

233 Fragments of the capstone of the pyramid of Inyotef VI's predecessor, Inyotef V, have been found close to the pyramid of the former. This one is now in the British Museum, London (BM EA478: 17th Dynasty).

Chapter 9

The New Kingdom: the Early Years

With the reunification of Egypt following the expulsion of the Hyksos, the principal cemetery of Egypt settled at Western Thebes for much of the 18th Dynasty. Here, a major revision of royal funerary provision was implemented, while an extensive series of private rock-cut tombs were built, a number of which are classic examples of the Egyptian mortuary chapel.

THE 18TH DYNASTY: FROM AHMOSE I TO AMENHOTEP III

Superstructures

Royal Tombs: At the very beginning of the new dynasty, Ahmose I built a very unusual mortuary complex at Abydos, comprising a pyramid, a cenotaph for his grandmother, two temples and a pyramid – plus a substructure – spread out along an 1.25-km (¾-mile) axis across the desert.[276] One temple was a terraced structure against the cliff, the other built in front of the pyramid, the last example known to have been built in Egypt for a king. It remains unclear whether the complex was the king's actual tomb or a cenotaph.[277]

During the early years of the 18th Dynasty, the old 17th Dynasty necropolis at Dra Abu'l-Naga continued to host most known interments, apparently including several members of the royal family. One of a pair of rock-cut chapels has been proposed as that of Amenhotep I (K93.11). It comprises a short passage with a four-pillared hall, with a

shaft leading down to the burial chamber.[278] No contemporary decoration has survived, but K93.11 was extended during the 20th Dynasty by the High Priest of Amun, Ramessenakhte, apparently converting it into a shrine. The surviving texts clearly link this pious task with the cult of Amenhotep I.[279] If this attribution is correct, the adjoining K93.10 could be a chapel of Ahmose I, Amenhotep I's mother, Ahmes-Nefertiry, or his wife, Meryetamun. Two potential free-standing mortuary chapels of Amenhotep I have also been identified. One lies in front of Dra Abu'l-Naga, below K93.11,[280] the other at Deir el-Bahari. The latter stood for only 40 years before being demolished when the mortuary temple of Hatshepsut was extended to cover its site.

The uncertainties surrounding the funerary monuments of Ahmose I and Amenhotep I obscure who exactly was responsible for one of the most momentous developments in royal burial practice – the separation of the offering place from the burial chamber. However, the presence of kingly tombs in the Valley of the Kings from the time of Thutmose I onwards clearly shows that the change had taken place by that king's death.

The separation of the royal mummy from its offerings and the solar link provided by the pyramid can only have been due to some major imperative, presumably that of

234 (*above*) The Mayor Sennefer and his wife receiving offerings in a boat in their burial chamber (TT96A: mid-18th Dynasty).

235 (*above*) The pyramid of Ahmose I at Abydos (early 18th Dynasty).

236 (*below*) Plan of the Abydene funerary complex of Ahmose I; 'T' indicates the cenotaph-pyramid of Tetisherit.

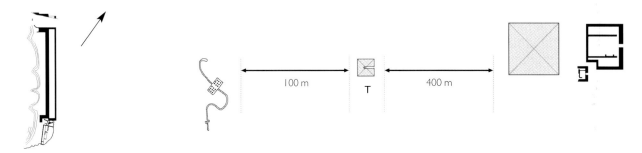

security. The significance of the pyramid may still have weighed heavily, however, if the oft-remarked resemblance of the peak of El-Qurn to a pyramid, looming above the Valley of the Kings, was indeed a factor in the ancient choice of this wadi.

While no mortuary temple is known for Thutmose I, chapels for his prematurely deceased son, Wadjmose, and his successor, Thutmose II, lie at the southern end of the necropolis, near Medinet Habu. Both were of simple design, later modestly extended.

The reigns of Thutmose III, Amenhotep II and Thutmose IV saw the creation of the first large-scale free-standing royal offering places. It is now being increasingly realized that the meaning of the New Kingdom mortuary temple was much more complex than that of its Old Kingdom predecessors. Indeed, it has been suggested that the difference was so great that a different term is required for the New Kingdom monuments, perhaps 'memorial temple', or the contemporary Egyptian term, 'Mansion of Millions of Years'. In contrast to earlier royal funerary sanctuaries, the focus widens from the king himself to the gods in general. The New Kingdom royal mortuary temples thus celebrate not only the royal cult, but also the Theban triad: the god Amun, his wife Mut and their son, Khonsu, as well as other divinities[281] and royal ancestors.

The first great temples of the dynasty are characterized by their construction on sloping sites that resulted in a terraced design. The best-preserved and most striking is that of Hatshepsut, built of limestone at Deir el-Bahari.[282] The complex began in the plain, near the edge of the cultivation, in a valley building with two levels and a colonnade of square pillars. A causeway, lined with sphinxes, led for over 1 km (⅔ mile) up to the main temple.

A decorated colonnade, the second also having subsidiary chapels of the deities Hathor and Anubis, fronted each terrace. The ramp that led up from the second court gave access to the inner part of the temple, fronted once more by a pair of colonnades, the pillars embellished with

237 Hatshepsut's mortuary temple at Deir el-Bahari is the best preserved of the earlier 18th Dynasty structures. Its design was almost certainly influenced by that of the adjacent 11th Dynasty monument of Mentuhotep II, seen at left (and ill. 203).

Osirid figures of the queen. Beyond the colonnades was the peristyle court, at the back of which lay the main sanctuary of the temple, dedicated to the local version of Amun – 'Amun of Djeser-djeseru'; Djeser-djeseru was the name of Hatshepsut's temple.

The Deir el-Bahari temple and subsequent structures of the same kind, had four specific cult-foci. The central one was dedicated to Amun – or rather a special form of the Theban god, unique to the specific locale. The kings' specific divine essence was now relegated to a secondary position, their own cult chambers lying away to the left of the principal god's, although linked to it as the king was fused with Amun after death; a solar court containing an altar, situated to the north of the Amun sanctuary is found in all Theban mortuary temples and links the solar element of the more ancient royal burials with the more recent ones; the final element was the veneration of the ruler's father, a chapel of Thutmose I lying directly adjacent to Hatshepsut's.

The arrangement of the decoration moves from the profane to the sacred, with the lower terraces showing military and naval motifs, as are often found on the exterior of cult temples, or perhaps inspired by the adjacent temple of Mentuhotep II. The southern colonnade shows the transport of a pair of obelisks from the granite quarries at Aswan to the great temple of Karnak. Its badly mutilated northern counterpart had reliefs of Hatshepsut fowling and fishing – just as one would find in a private mortuary chapel – as well as offering to her fellow gods.

The middle terrace has exquisitely carved and detailed images of the famous voyage to Punt that Hatshepsut commissioned to bring back incense, incense trees and other goods from Africa. North of the ramp is the Birth Colonnade, with scenes concerning the impregnation of Hatshepsut's mother by Amun-Re while incarnated in her earthly father, Thutmose I. This idea of the supernatural paternity of the pharaoh is an ancient concept in Egyptian kingship, but explicit depictions have only survived in a few

238 The mortuary temples of the New Kingdom included 'historical' scenes, a good example being a series in the temple of Hatshepsut depicting her trading expedition to the east African territory of Punt. These incorporate this image of the obese queen of Punt (CM JE14276).

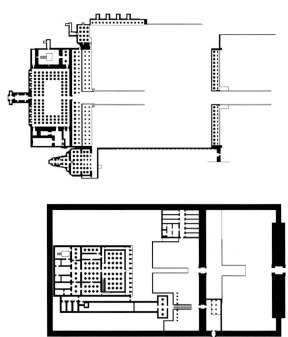

239 (*above*) Plans of the mortuary temples of Hatshepsut (top) and Thutmose III, both built in a terraced arrangement; the latter, however, includes more conventional pylon gateways (18th Dynasty).

240 (*opposite*) All that survives of the façade of the mortuary temple of Amenhotep III: the famous quartzite statues now known as the Colossi of Memnon.

places; these formed the basis of a standardized composition found in (at least) one cult temple (Amenhotep III at Luxor) and one other mortuary temple (Ramesses II).[283] The topmost terrace, the holiest area in the temple, contains a large-scale continuous scene of the progress of Amun's barque during the Festival of the Valley (see pp. 220-1) and images of royalty.

The remaining 18th Dynasty mortuary temples are largely destroyed, but one might assume that they followed a similar pattern of topics, mixing standardized elements (hunting, divine birth and ritual scenes) with 'historical' ones. The inclusion of the latter in the pyramid-temple of Ahmose I at Abydos would support such an assumption.

Thutmose III's mortuary temple lay on the edge of the desert and is in very poor condition, due to its position and also because many parts were built in mud-brick. Its basic layout, which is visible, was similar to Hatshepsut's monument, with the exception that brick pylons fronted the first courtyards. Subsequent kings followed this scheme, the best-preserved temple being that of Thutmose IV.

Far larger, but now almost entirely destroyed was the temple of Amenhotep III. Originally of dimensions broadly in keeping with those of the temples of his predecessors, for

his Jubilee in his 30th year the building was enlarged to breathtaking size, filled with hundreds, if not thousands, of superbly carved statues in soft and hard stones. By far the largest of its genre ever built, the temple's entrance was flanked by a pair of huge quartzite colossi, dubbed in Classical times the 'Colossi of Memnon'. Three successive pylons were followed by an avenue lined with great recumbent jackals and crocodile-bodied sphinxes, beyond which lay a great peristyle court and the inner temple.

Unusually for a New Kingdom temple of this kind, the focus is not Amun, but rather the king and manifestations of the sun god. Much of this enormous temple was formed by open courts that were decorated with scenes of the king celebrating his jubilee. As far as can be determined, a major part of the temple's decoration was in the form of statuary that was laid out in a specific pattern, perhaps in a celestial or other plan. The court of the temple was apparently

constructed so that it would flood during the annual Nile inundation, with the temple re-emerging after the waters subsided. This mirrored the story of the creation of the world, when the first land emerged from the chaos of the primeval waters of Nun.

Private Tombs: The rock-cut tomb-chapels of the first part of the 18th Dynasty were of simple design. Both at Dra Abu'l-Naga and some 80 km (50 miles) further south at El-Kab, one finds chapels of single-room types (ill. 242, Types I–II[284]). However, as the dynasty progressed, 'T'-shaped (Type V) tombs, reminiscent of those found at Thebes in the Middle Kingdom (Type III) appeared. Indeed, some examples of such sepulchres may actually have been re-used older monuments, particularly on the Sheikh Abd el-Qurna hill, which was to become the principal noble necropolis of the middle of the 18th Dynasty. One particular example is

241 The tomb of Re on Sheikh Abd el-Qurna (TT72). The tomb is reminiscent of the Deir el-Bahari temple of Hatshepsut, built on two levels, with a colonnaded lower level (18th Dynasty: reign of Amenhotep II).

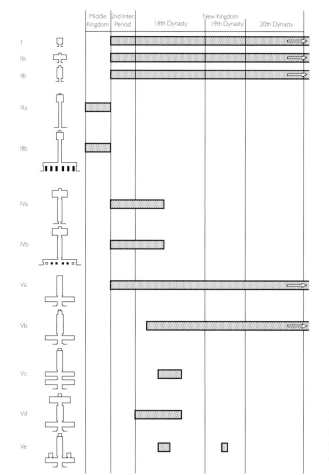

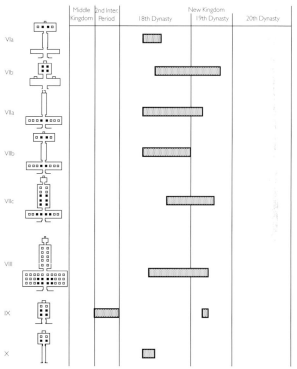

242 Time-spans of the various forms of Theban tomb-chapels, classified according to the scheme of Friederike Kampp-Seyfried. Broken lines and un-filled columns indicate possible ranges of variation.

243 (*above*) and 244 (*right*). One of the classic tombs of the 18th Dynasty is that of Rekhmire. Above, the plain forecourt and façade are to be seen on the Sheikh Abd el-Qurna hill. To the *right* is its long hall, unique in having a ceiling level that rises greatly from east to west. This allowed a multi-level offering place, with a niche for a statue at the top, a small false-door stela below it (see ill. 246) and the main false-door at the bottom (18th Dynasty, reigns of Thutmose III and Amenhotep II).

the tomb of Ineni (TT81), which seems to have been converted from a *saff* tomb with a pillared façade into a 'T-shaped tomb' with a flat façade by filling the gaps between the pillars with brick walls.

Such 'T'-shaped chapels are typical of the period and vary considerably in elaboration. The simplest have a wide, shallow, hall, with a doorway at the rear leading to the offering place. Variations on this theme include the piercing of the rock wall between the façade and the transverse chamber, creating pillars or windows and the addition of one or more rows of pillars across the outer chamber. Similarly, the approach to the offering place may be enlarged and equipped with pillars, or extra rooms.

Examples of the simple form are common, but the tomb of Rekhmire, Vizier of Thutmose III (TT100), provides an interesting variation.[285] In this case, the corridor that leads from the rear of the transverse hall has a ceiling that rises steadily to place the bottom of the statue-niche some 6 m (20 ft) above floor level. That of Senenmut (TT71) has a set of pillars across its transverse hall, dividing it into aisles, each of which has a different kind of ceiling (Type VIIa); yet another fairly early variation places a room at the very end of the tomb (Types Vd, VIa and VIIb). TT71 and TT100 are interesting in that neither has a substructure immediately adjoining (cf. pp. 225–6).

A feature particularly associated with Theban tombs of the 18th Dynasty (although found from the 11th to the 26th Dynasties) is the employment of funerary cones, tapered pottery items of circular section impressed on their flat end with the name and titles of a tomb-owner. They were apparently placed in lines above the tomb entrance, with the

245 (*left*) A unique feature of TT71 was a series of carved panels with the title, name and pedigree of its owner, Hatshepsut's favourite, Senenmut. It is unclear how they related to the main body of the decoration, which was painted on plaster adhering to the rough parts of the walls (18th Dynasty).

246 (*bottom left*) Detail of Rekhmire's upper false-door showing the deceased and his wife before an offering table (from TT100: now Louvre C74).

247 (*below*) The tomb of Qenamun (TT93), one of the earliest Theban private tombs to have an elaborate substructure, approached by a stairway and sloping passage (18th Dynasty: reign of Amenhotep II).

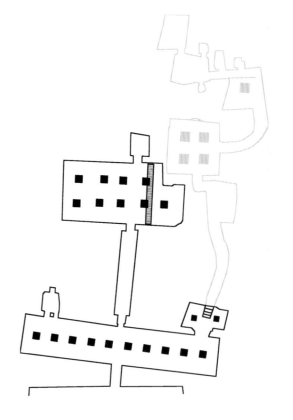

embossed flat side facing out, although only one set has been observed in situ.[286] The visible area was usually inscribed with the name and titles of the tomb-owner, sometimes his wife, as well as prayers and vignettes showing the sun god. They have variously been interpreted as dummy roofing poles, mummy labels, boundary stones, dummy offering loaves or pieces of meat, 'visitors' cards', representations of sun disks and an allusion to the solar cycle, or merely a decorative element.[287] Possibly their meaning and use changed over time.

The reign of Amenhotep II witnessed a considerable increase in the proportion of the more elaborate chapel types built at Thebes. While the very simple T-shaped tombs remained current throughout the dynasty, ever more vast

248 (*above*) During the reign of Amenhotep III the cross-halls of the highest status Theban tombs became hypostyle halls, as seen here in the Vizier Ramose's TT55.

249 (*right*) Plan of one of the grandest examples of the large sepulchres of the reign of Amenhotep III: the tomb of Kheruef, Steward of Queen Tiye, at Thebes (TT192: 18th Dynasty).

structures were excavated during Amenhotep III's reign. The 'simpler' examples (e.g. TT55 and TT192[288]) converted the shallow transverse hall into a space akin to a temple's hypostyle hall. Similarly, the inner chamber was broadened and equipped with two rows of pillars (Type VIII). Some other tombs went even further, the largest of them all, Amenhotep-Surero's TT48, having four chambers, respectively with 20, 20, 24 and 6 columns – a total of 70. Substructures now tended to open from the southwest corner of the first hall, rather than from shafts in the forecourt, as had earlier been the case.

Such tombs of Amenhotep III's reign, and other contemporary but simpler examples, were often cut much lower down the Theban hills than hitherto. This may have had two motivations. First, the quality of the rock at this level is finer, allowing more carved decoration. Secondly, by this time the upper levels of Sheikh Abd el-Qurna were becoming extremely congested (cf. Map 5C), making the construction of tombs there very difficult. Accordingly, tomb-owners had to either move elsewhere (Qurnet Murai received its first major tombs under Amenhotep III), or use the lower slopes of the hill of the Sheikh. The latter solution led to the enhanced role of the outer courtyard, now sunk into the rock and sometimes with a monumental approach, the most impressive being that of TT192, with a stairway enclosed in a decorated vestibule. Protection in such a closed courtyard encouraged the decoration of the tomb façade, the finest example also being that of TT192. The latter tomb is, however, also an exemplar of another characteristic of such low-lying tombs: the relatively thin rock above the great columned hall has given way, leaving the sepulchre an utter ruin, a fate shared by TT55 (albeit now restored) and others.

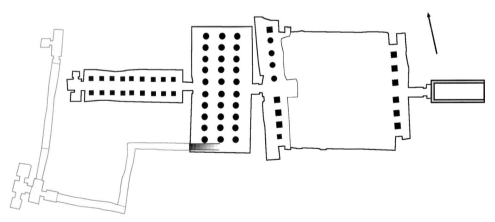

250 (*above*) The tomb of Ramose contains raised relief decoration of almost unsurpassed quality, albeit never finished and still unpainted. This is part of a banquet-scene (TT55: 18th Dynasty, reign of Amenhotep III).

251 (*left*) The end-wall of the much smaller chapel of Kha (TT8). This lay within the core of a brick pyramid at Deir el-Medina (mid-18th Dynasty).

At the opposite extreme of elaboration are the tombs in the workmen's community at Deir el-Medina, where single-room chapels began to be surmounted by small pyramids. One of the most important of this period is TT8, built for the head of the community during the middle of the dynasty.[289] This form of superstructure remained current at Deir el-Medina down to the end of the Ramesside Period.

The 18th Dynasty saw a variety of decorative motifs employed in private tomb-chapels, with certain themes distinctive of a particular group of reigns. For example, desert hunting scenes are to be found in tombs dating from the reign of Thutmose I (TT21) until the time of Amenhotep II (or perhaps Thutmose IV – TT276). The

252 Cretans, Nubians and Syrians bringing tribute to King Thutmose III. They are depicted in the tomb of Rekhmire as part of an enumeration of the owner's vizierial duties (TT100).

largest number come from the reigns of Thutmose III and Amenhotep II, perhaps reflecting those two kings' public fondness for the sport. During the reign of Thutmose III, the tomb-owner was also shown hunting hippopotami (TT39, TT53, TT81, TT82, TT85, TT123, TT125, TT155, TT164, TT342), a scene that became obsolete shortly thereafter.

During this time fresh details enliven the venerable scenes of the agricultural cycle. Gleaners can be found in the wake of harvesters (TT69), as can girls squabbling over the fruits of the gleaning. Pulling thorns from feet, sleeping under trees, measuring the fields for taxation (TT69) and the presence of a 'corn-doll' to ensure a fruitful harvest (TT38, TT52, TT57) are other new features.[290] Offering scenes continue to be shown, but there are fewer rows of offering bearers depicted; offerings being brought to the deceased now include fish (e.g. TT52, TT69 and TT192). Images of the tomb-owner before his house are also found

on tomb walls (e.g. TT254), perhaps related to Book of the Dead spell 132, which permits the deceased to see his house on earth.[291] The house is inscribed with an offering formula, which has been found in actual houses.[292]

Although tomb walls of the New Kingdom continue to depict images of the funeral, changes occur within the cycle. Those dating to the first half of the 18th Dynasty show an assortment of traditional representations of the burial, including rituals that were probably archaic by the 18th Dynasty. After the reign of Thutmose IV obsolete rituals were omitted and a single sequential representation of the actual funeral employed. Such scenes form the basis for a series of Book of the Dead vignettes.[293] Images of the tomb-chapel itself, capped by a pyramid, seem to have become more popular after the reign of Amenhotep III, perhaps due to the increased focus on solar worship.

Foreigners begin to appear far more commonly in Egyptian tombs of the mid-18th Dynasty, probably

253 While tomb-owners were always shown formally, minor characters could be seen in a variety of poses. This rare image in the tomb of Rekhmire (TT100) depicts a servant girl from the rear.

reflecting Egypt's increasing contacts abroad. Most foreigners appear in tombs of viziers who had to deal with them. In addition to Nubians, other Africans, Libyans, Syro-Palestinians and many Aegeans feature in Theban tombs, appearing in some 40 chapels dating to the New Kingdom, as well as the much later TT36, dating to the reign of Psametik I. The earliest tomb to feature these people was that of Senenmut (TT71). Clearly, interaction with the denizens of the Mediterranean Sea had increased dramatically by this time.[294]

Banquet scenes are particularly prominent during the earlier 18th Dynasty, becoming increasingly elaborate and extensive. The details show people turning around and interacting with one another (starting in the reign of Amenhotep II), drinking and even vomiting. Figures of lesser importance may be shown in unusual poses: in the tomb of Rekhmire (TT100) a young serving girl is shown in a three-quarters view from the back. The imagery of food,

drink and fertility remains inherent in these scenes. Dancers and musicians continue to feature as part of the entertainment. An interesting light is thrown on changing attitudes by the fact that many of the dancers and serving-girls in 18th Dynasty tombs are shown effectively nude. However, when one such tomb (TT52) was usurped in Ramesside times the dancers were provided with clothes.

An innovative scene found primarily in Theban tombs of the 18th Dynasty shows the celebration of the '(Beautiful) Festival of the Valley'. The festival itself, according to textual evidence, was probably celebrated from the Middle Kingdom onwards, although it only seems to be prominent in 18th Dynasty tomb art. The festival occurred on an annual basis in the second month of the season of *Shemu* (nominally Summer) and was related to Amun, as well as Hathor as the goddess of Deir el-Bahari and associated with the west. The image of Amun of Karnak crossed the Nile and processed through the west bank, stopping at all the royal mortuary temples along the way. Images of deceased and divine kings were also carried as part of the procession and the whole event was a time of renaissance for the cemeteries of the west bank of Thebes. After the tour Amun returned by boat to the east bank. This festival, more than any other, was an occasion for the rejuvenation of the cemeteries and a time for the meeting of the living and the dead. People would visit tombs and make offerings to their ancestors, as well as the king and the gods and generally commemorate and celebrate the beyond. This might be likened to the Mexican Day of the Dead celebrations.

Tomb scenes show elements of the festival, such as the procession, visiting tombs, revering the ancestors, the king, etc. Images of the king are also frequently shown in tombs of this period, starting in the reign of Hatshepsut. For the most part, these show the relationship between the deceased and the pharaoh, thus underlining the tomb-owner's position in society. Most commonly, a large-scale image of the king

flanks the doorway that leads from the transverse hall to the rest of the tomb. The king is shown seated on a throne in a kiosk, to whom the tomb-owner brings offerings and pays his respects. In certain instances, most commonly from late in the reign of Amenhotep III through the Amarna period (see below) until the reign of Ay, the king is shown rewarding the deceased. Less frequently the king is shown in relation to the gods, thereby ensuring the upholding and continuation of *maat*. Images of the ruling king in conjunction with former rulers are almost always a part of the Festival of the Valley. A few less-regular royal representations include the king hunting (TT72, TT143); worshipping divinities (TT192); being suckled by his wet nurse (e.g. TT85, TT92, TT350); on the lap of his tutor or nurse (TT63, TT64, TT78, TT85, TT93, TT109, TT226); and being suckled by divinities (TT57). Aside from such images were those of certain ancient kings who were especially revered as patrons of the Theban necropolis.

254 Vizier Rekhmire had many responsibilities, including the overseeing of King Thutmose III's sculpture, and the execution of these duties is thus shown in Rekhmire's tomb. What is particularly delightful is that some of the statues survive to this day (TT100).

255 Part of the cross-hall of the tomb of Menena (TT69: 18th Dynasty, reign of Thutmose IV).

Most prominent was Amenhotep I, who apparently appears for the first time under Amenhotep III (TT161) and is then a frequent feature of Ramesside tombs, as was his mother Ahmes-Nefertiry, his fellow patron of Deir el-Medina's workmen.

Although stelae appeared outside tomb-chapels or above shaft tombs throughout Egyptian history, a variation on the theme occurs in the New Kingdom. Carved and/or painted inscriptions that mimic stelae appear on the end walls of the transverse corridor in Theban 'T'-shaped tombs. The lunette of some of these show the tomb-owner praying to a divinity or divinities, or an image of a solar disk – more common from the reign of Amenhotep III – which indicates the worship of a solar divinity. Sometimes Opening-of-the-Mouth rituals are also depicted in the lunette. The decoration on the opposite wall often shows a false-door as a counterpoint to this motif, which balances the composition of the schema of decoration.

Certain individuals living in the 18th Dynasty (generally only dating from the reign of Hatshepsut/Thutmose III to Amenhotep II) each have two tombs cut into the Theban hills. It has been hypothesized that they are indicative of an elevation in status (see p. 26). TT131, the second tomb of User (his first being TT61), may be the first private tomb at Thebes to have been surmounted by a pyramid, a feature that until a few years previously had been the attribute of royalty. By the end of the dynasty, its use by private

individuals had become common. Interestingly, User's burial chamber, in TT61, also had royal affiliations, in being decorated with the Book of Amduat (see p. 130).

The reign of Amenhotep III also saw a major upsurge in the usage of the ancient necropolis of Saqqara for high-status burials, perhaps as the result of the establishment of a separate northern Vizierate in the latter part of the dynasty. Few tombs dating to the earlier part of the 18th Dynasty are known, but whether this reflects a lack of burials there, or is an accident of discovery remains uncertain. Nevertheless, the fact remains that from this point onwards a number of high-status burials are known at Saqqara.

Amongst the most important is that of the Vizier Aperel (I.2), datable to the early years of Amenhotep IV and comprising a four-pillared hall with three niches at the back; the entrance to the substructure lay in the left-rear corner of the chapel.[295] The tomb lies on the escarpment that fronts the northern part of the Saqqara necropolis, just south of the southern end of the Early Dynastic Period cemetery, southeast of the pyramid of Teti. It is now becoming clear that the whole hillside here resembled the cliffs at Thebes, with tier upon tier of rock-cut tombs, some with built external elements. However, re-use as a cat-cemetery (the Bubasteion) in Late/Roman times and the accumulation of thousands of tons of debris have long hidden this fact.

Although the vast majority of private mortuary chapels at Thebes were rock-cut, at least one individual had a free-standing structure, closely following the design of that of a contemporary cult-temple. This belonged to Amenhotep-

256 The New Kingdom cliff-cemetery at Saqqara.

son-of-Hapu, who enjoyed a very high-status at Amenhotep III's court and was later deified. He may have also owned a rock-cut chapel at Qurnet Murai (TTFK396), due west of the free-standing example, although its identification is highly tentative. His exceptional status is signalled by his possession of a stone sarcophagus – a very rare item for a private person of the New Kingdom, although anthropoid coffins in the material are not uncommon.[296]

Substructures

Royal Tombs:[297] In the expanse of desert between his pyramid and temple at Abydos, Ahmose I constructed a subterranean tomb of unusual form. Mostly cut only a few metres below the surface, a pit entrance gives access to a twisting passageway that eventually opens into a great hall, its roof formerly supported by 18 columns. Below the hall, a further passage, seemingly unfinished, leads deeper into the matrix.

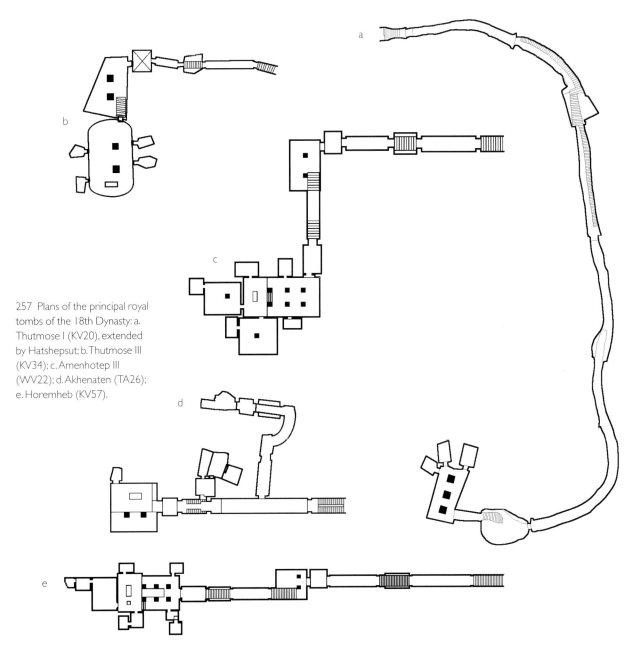

257 Plans of the principal royal tombs of the 18th Dynasty: a. Thutmose I (KV20), extended by Hatshepsut; b. Thutmose III (KV34); c. Amenhotep III (WV22); d. Akhenaten (TA26); e. Horemheb (KV57).

This pattern was followed by the earliest certain New Kingdom royal tomb at Thebes, KV20, in a wadi now known as the Valley of the Kings. Ultimately, it was completed for Hatshepsut, but it is also possible that all but the deepest chamber had been excavated by her father Thutmose I. Five successive galleries descend at a steep angle into the mountainside, turning gradually to the south, evidently in a search for better rock. This remained poor, however, and when a final chamber was added by Hatshepsut, it had to be lined with blocks of limestone to provide a surface that could be decorated.

This 'long-and-deep' plan was abandoned by subsequent rulers in favour of a pair of stairways, joined by a fairly short corridor, giving access to an antechamber and finally a pillared burial hall. In the first three such tombs, KV34, 38 and 42, the burial chamber had the oval shape of the cartouche, the frame used for the principal royal names and symbolic of eternity. KV34 had been built by Thutmose III and it appears that KV38 had also been built by him for a reburial of Thutmose I. KV42 was later appropriated for the planned interment of Thutmose III's wife, Meryetre, but seems to have been intended originally for Thutmose II – although whether built by him or by his son is unclear.

The burial chambers of KV20 and KV34 both preserved the first decoration to be seen in a royal burial chamber since the end of the Old Kingdom. In KV20 it had been drawn on a limestone lining of the burial chamber, in KV34 upon the plastered rock walls of the burial and antechambers. The principal material used for this decoration was taken from the Book of Amduat (see p. 130) and down to the reign of

Amenhotep III was drawn with a pen and ink on a plain buff ground, using stick figures and cursive hieroglyphs. In KV34's case, the background was painted the colour of papyrus, with the apparent intention of giving the impression of a giant ancient scroll unrolled around the curving walls.

After Thutmose III's reign, the pillars of the burial chamber and the outer rooms of the tomb received full-scale images of divinities and the pharaoh, in polychrome after the reign of Thutmose IV. The pharaoh praises the gods and, in return, the gods welcome him and offer him eternal life within the context of solar resurrection. This all links into a conception of the royal tomb as a gateway to the underworld. The architecture of the tomb leading to the burial chamber thus emulated the topography of the Duat,[298] and different portions of the perilous journey, entailing passage through a series of gates after routing foes and passing tests, that had to be made before finally arriving at the court of Osiris.[299] This paralleled the journey of the sun god Re, who traversed the underworld during the 12 hours of the night, vanquishing his enemies, to be triumphantly reborn the following day.

The tomb and its decoration thus had an implicit, though not always geographical, east–west axis mimicking the path of the sun, with the idea that the burial chamber was located in the most western part, the part associated with death. Thus the king, having successfully triumphed

259 On the left, Thutmose III is shown in his burial chamber with his wife, Meryetre; on the right, he is depicted being suckled by a sycamore tree, labelled as being Isis – probably with the double-meaning of the goddess and the king's earthly mother of the same name.

258 Sectional view of the tomb of Thutmose III (KV34: 18th Dynasty).

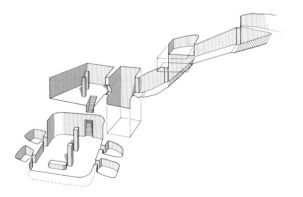

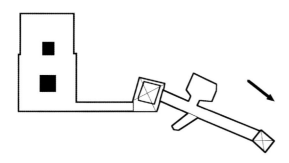

260 Plan of the probable tomb of Queen Ahmes-Nefertiry (and perhaps later also Ahmose I) at Dra Abu'l-Naga (early 18th Dynasty).

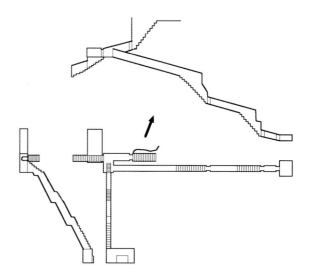

261 Plan of KV39, possibly completed as a communal tomb for the family of Amenhotep II.

over his enemies and passed through a series of challenges, was united with Osiris and could be reborn together with the sun god the next day. This royal resurrection in a divine state was crucial to the stability of the nation and the cosmos and was an expression of the triumph of *maat* over chaos. Thus the royal tombs of the New Kingdom were carved and painted with a series of funerary texts that would facilitate and ensure a successful voyage.

The basic plan of these kingly sepulchres had previously been used in the reign of Amenhotep I for the burial places of two queens, Meryetamun (TT358 at Deir el-Bahari and Ahmes-Nefertiry at Dra Abu'l-Naga), both including a 'well' at the end of the approach passage. This feature became permanently incorporated into kings' tombs from Thutmose III onwards and is generally believed to have served both the practical purpose of protecting the tomb from storm-water and providing the dead king with an easy access to the underworld, also perhaps signifying the tomb of the death-god Sokar. Like most other non-kingly tombs, those of the royal family were undecorated.

Burial arrangements for members of the royal family vary greatly during the 18th Dynasty.[300] Early queens, such as Ahmes-Nefertiry and Meryetamun, had independent tombs of some size. Hatshepsut, as Regent, had a similar tomb in the Wadi Sikkat Taqa el-Zeide. However, during the second part of the dynasty royal family tombs seem to be restricted to modest shafts in the Valley of the Queens and interments in side-chambers of kings' tombs. A possible exception is KV39, an elaborate tomb that seems to have been intended for a multiple occupancy, perhaps by members of the family of Amenhotep II, to judge by its foundation deposits.

Private Tombs: During the first half of the 18th Dynasty, substructures were generally approached via a shaft, normally in the forecourt of the chapel, but sometimes within the chapel itself. It should be noted that in addition to the principal burial place, other complexes might be dug contemporaneously, or later, in and around the tomb, to house the bodies of other members of the family.[301] The forms of the burial chambers vary considerably, but are generally fairly simple, the main additional feature being niches to contain the protective magic bricks. These were inscribed with a protective spell from the Book of the Dead (Chapter 151) and equipped with an amulet, to ward off danger coming from each of the cardinal points. A handful of tombs have decorated burial chambers (see below).

While most substructures lie within the immediate vicinity of the main tomb-chapel, in some cases they lay up to 1 km (⅔ mile) or so away. At least four high officials had modest burial chambers in the Valley of the Kings (KV36, 45, 46 and 48), with other unattributed tombs likely to have belonged to such individuals as Thutmose III's vizier, Rekhmire, whose chapel (TT100) has no tomb-shafts. The designs of these tombs are generally simple, with either a shallow shaft or a stairway and descending passage. A single room is the most common arrangement, but the tomb of Yuya and Tjuiu (KV46) had a second staircase before the chamber and KV21 a column and store-room added to the burial chamber. A similar tomb (KV62) was modestly extended at the end of the dynasty for the burial of King Tutankhamun.

Another example of a 'remote' substructure is that of Senenmut, whose chapel (TT71) is on Sheikh Abd el-Qurna, but whose burial chambers are at Deir el-Bahari (TT353).[302] This is a particularly elaborate example, with a series of three stairways and passages leading to the intended burial chamber. The antechamber provides perhaps the earliest New Kingdom example of decoration in a private substructure, with texts from the Book of the Dead supplemented by an astronomical ceiling, the prototype of most other subsequent ceilings of this type.[303] Other images included Senenmut praising Hatshepsut's cartouches, images of Anubis and the Bull and Seven Cows motif from the Book of the Dead that ensured nourishment in the hereafter.

TT353 is one of the earliest examples of the new practice of having substructures approached by sloping passages, rather than shafts. Clearly, they made access to the burial chamber easier, but may have reflected a conscious imitation of kingly practice, since the design of the funerary chambers also became more elaborate, sometimes including pillared halls. Such substructures were provided for the Mayor Sennefer under Thutmose III (TT96 – the burial chamber is designated TT96A) and for the Steward Qenamun in the reign of Amenhotep II (TT93). In the former case, the entrance lay in the forecourt of the chapel, in the latter, within the columned fore-hall. The latter became by far the most common location.[304] Some tombs combine both shaft and sloping-passage approaches; for example, in Puiemre's sepulchre (TT39), a shaft at the northern end of the transverse hall descends 3 m (10 ft) to the beginning of a series of rough descending galleries, ending in a sandstone-lined burial chamber.

Only eight Theban private tombs-chapels of the 18th Dynasty are presently known to have had associated decorated substructures (TT71/ TT353, TT61, TT82, TT87,

263 A column in the burial chamber of Sennefer showing the deceased being offered a drink by his wife (TT96A: mid-18th Dynasty).

262 The substructure of the tomb of Senenmut (TT353). Unlike most private tombs of the period, this lay a considerable distance from its chapel. While the latter (TT71) was high on the Sheikh Abd el-Qurna hill, the burial passages lay at Deir el-Bahari, close to Hatshepsut's temple.

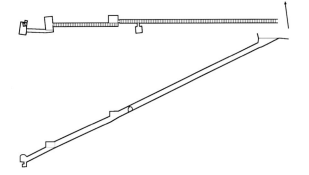

264 The decoration of the burial chamber of Sennefer (TT96A) differs considerably from that of other private examples in its richness and variety. Here we have the Voyage to Abydos; the rough ceiling has been painted as though it were a grape-arbour.

TT96, TT201, and TT383: see summary on next page), although the poor recording of the subterranean portions of such monuments clearly distorts the picture. In the case of the Vizier User (TT61), the adornment of his burial apartments uniquely borrows from contemporary royal practice in employing the Amduat, otherwise exclusively a royal prerogative until the 21st Dynasty.[305] Amenemhat (TT82), in contrast, covered the walls of his burial chamber with extracts from the Book of the Dead and the ancient Pyramid Texts, along with images of the deceased receiving offerings from his children.[306] The Book of the Dead also provided the basis for the decoration of the burial chamber of Minnakhte (TT87), which may also have been present in TT383 (Merymose), although only fragments of columns of text remain there.

In contrast, an almost entirely figurative approach was adopted by Sennefer in TT96 (pl. VIII): the deceased and his wife before tables of different offerings, offering bearers, different funerary divinities, including Osiris, Hathor and Anubis, the funeral procession, selections of the Book of the Dead and the Abydos pilgrimage. The most remarkable feature of this tomb is the ceiling, which is painted. The naturally poor rock made it very difficult for the tomb builders to smooth out the rock; instead they plastered it over and painted it to resemble the undulating curves of a grape arbour. A winged vulture, rare in a non-royal context, spreads protective wings over the tomb from its lofty perch.

A thus-far unique burial chamber belongs to Re (TT201).[307] It is painted in yellow paint on a black background, apparently intended to imitate the schema of decoration of 18th Dynasty 'black' coffins.[308] The painted decoration gives the burial chamber its orientation, with the image of Isis on the south (the feet) and Nephthys on the north (the head). In addition, the walls of the burial chamber of TT39 (Puiemre) were faced with thin sandstone slabs that were smeared with a plaster wash, as if in preparation for painting that was never executed.

At Deir el-Medina, the substructure of the tomb of Kha (TT8 – died reign of Amenhotep III) lies in the rock face opposite his pyramid and is approached by a steep stairway, at the bottom of which a horizontal corridor leads to the burial chamber. The corridor was used to store some funerary equipment, while the burial chamber was secured by a wooden door with a mechanical lock.

In the main body of the Theban tombs, shaft-approaches steadily decrease in number as the dynasty progresses, with a corresponding increase in the occurrence of sloping passages, until the latter is the dominant design by the beginning of the Amarna Period. Elaborate substructures survive from the reign of Amenhotep III; a good example is that of Ramose (TT55) which, as is fairly standard at the time, begins with a ramp in the far left-hand corner of the first hall of the chapel. Descending steeply, stairs flank a central ramp that describes a 135 degree turn before turning left into a four-pillared hall, presumably the burial chamber, equipped with a series of subsidiary rooms. However, designs vary considerably between tombs, TT192 having four long passages that led ultimately to a chamber that lay just behind and below the innermost niche of the chapel.

DECORATED PRIVATE SUBSTRUCTURES OF THE EARLIER NEW KINGDOM				
Site	Tomb	Date	Owner	Scene
Thebes	TT39	18th Dyn (Thutmose III)	Puiemre	No decoration, but faced with thin sandstone slabs that were smeared with a plaster wash
Thebes	TT61	18th Dyn (Thutmose III)	User	Book of Amduat
Thebes	TT82	18th Dyn (Thutmose III)	Amenemhet	BoD; Pyramid Texts; deceased kneeling with ointment and taper below a niche. Son (sem-priest) and other children offer to deceased and wife. Deceased and mother. Bull and sacred cows
Thebes	TT87	18th Dyn (Thutmose III)	Minnakht	BoD
Thebes	TT96	18th Dyn (Amenhotep II)	Sennefer	Priests with offerings, deceased, deceased with daughter, men with funeral equipment, priest libating, deceased with wife, Anubis-jackals, offering texts, deceased going to 'see the sun-disk' with wife, Osiris-Wennefer with Western Hathor, dancers, ceremonies, shrines, son libating and censing, deceased and wife being purified by sem-priest, BoD, mummy on a couch with Anubis and ba, deceased and wife before Isis and Osiris
Thebes	TT201	18th Dyn (Thutmose IV/ Amenhotep III)	Re	Scheme imitates that of a sarcophagus
Thebes	TT353	18th Dyn (Hatshepsut)	Senenmut	Texts, sketch of deceased, BoD, deceased with Horus, purification, Fields of Iaru, false-door, deceased with parents, deceased with offerings, Anubis, mummified god, bull with seven cows, and gods of sacred oars. Ceiling: astronomical
Thebes	TT383	18th Dyn (Amenhotep III)	Merymose	Uncertain: traces of inscriptions and titles

Chapter 10

The New Kingdom:
the Amarna Years

The accession of Amenhotep IV, soon to change his name to Akhenaten, marked a major upheaval in Egypt's ritual life. The king effectively abolished the majority of traditional public cults in favour of a single sun god, the Aten. He also moved the royal residence to Amarna, a virgin site in Middle Egypt. The brand-new city, called Akhet-Aten, was constructed in a great bay in the cliffs, at the back of which a large wadi led out towards the high desert and the royal necropolis – a new Valley of the Kings (Map 3).[309] This was flanked by hills into which were carved the tomb-chapels of the royal officials.

Superstructures

No trace of any royal mortuary temple has come to light at Amarna. It is not unlikely that Akhenaten's close link with his god meant that his worship fused with that of the Aten, obviating the need for any separate mortuary temple. On the other hand, private tomb-chapels were constructed in the cliffs to the north and south of the Royal Wadi (Wadi Abu Hisah el-Bahari). The southern group appear to have been founded three or four years later than the northern and,

265 (*above*) Image of Ay and Tey receiving gifts from the king, from the scene in ill. 268 (CMTR 10/11/26/1).

266 (*right*) The southern section of the Northern Tombs at Amarna, comprising tombs TA3 (Ahmose), 3A–3F (unknown), 4 (Meryre i), 5 (Pentju), 6 (Panehsy) and 6A–6D (unknown). Tombs TA1 (Huya) and 2 (Meryre ii) lie just beyond the wadi at the top of the photograph (cf. Map 3).

rather than lying high up the cliff face, are much lower down and are consequently submerged by sand. The construction of the new capital clearly required large amounts of labour, as did the foundation of tombs for many of the worthies, and a shortage of labour was clearly one reason why all the Amarna tombs are unfinished to some degree.

Interestingly, only one of the men to be buried at Amarna certainly gave up a Theban tomb in favour of one at the new city. This was Parennefer, whose TT188 is one of the few there to contain clear examples of Amarna art.[310] On relocating to Amarna he founded TA7.[311]

Some Amarna tomb-chapels were built along Theban lines, albeit with entirely novel decorative schemes. Such tombs ranged from large sepulchres of type VIII (e.g. Ay's TA25 and May's TA14) to a number of examples of type IVa – something that had essentially gone out of use at Thebes in Thutmose III's day – with a very wide hall. However, the basic Theban 'T'-shaped tomb is rare, while there was also a considerable number of tombs of a basic pattern not generally found at Thebes. This featured square,

267 View of the interior of the first hall of the tomb of Meryre ii at Amarna (TA2).

round-pillared, fore-halls and sometimes a pillared inner hall as well. The innermost part of Amarna chapels generally included a rock-cut statue of the deceased – although the unfinished state of many of the tombs obscures the true extent of this fashion. The locations of substructure entrances vary, some following Theban fashion in being in the left-hand end of the forehall, while in others it is at the opposite end. Some are stairways, while others, especially in the Type IVa tombs, are shafts.

Tomb decoration in Amarna Period tombs is markedly different from that of any other era of Egyptian history. Due to the change in the nature of the religious ritual of the time, the schema of decoration of these tombs has a great deal in common with contemporary temples. Both depict the king and his family in various poses, whether praying to the Aten, or going about their daily life in the palace, the temple, or around the city, surrounded by adoring courtiers and dignitaries. Scenes of the city of Akhetaten occur frequently in these tombs. The tomb-owner features rarely in these tombs, except in specific situations: being rewarded by the king and on the jambs at the tomb entrance. In the Memphite tombs of this time the owner is more commonly featured than in the contemporary tombs at Akhetaten itself.

The façade of TT188 well illustrates the differences between the decoration of Amarna Period tombs and others of the New Kingdom and, for that matter, most other periods as well. Leaving aside the style itself, with its distortions of bodily proportions, the most striking feature is the complete dominance of the king and queen and the almost complete absence of the tomb-owner. While the monarch is depicted in many New Kingdom tombs, it is in a limited, defined context. In TT192, the royal family are prominent in the surviving decoration, but this may be a function of the tomb-owner's intimate relationship with them as the queen's Steward.

This situation is clearly rooted in the Aten theology, which placed the royal family in the position of sole intermediaries between humanity and the god. Thus, coupled with the new cult's abandonment of the traditional funerary values manifested in earliers tombs through scenes of 'daily life', the Amarna tombs show the royal family's journey from palace to the central city; the royal family dining; the royal family visiting the temple; the royal family worshipping; and the royal family receiving gifts.

268 (above) The largest figures in an Amarna tomb tend to be the royal couple. Here they are shown at the window-of-appearances rewarding the tomb owner and greeting the populace in the tomb of Ay (TA25).

269 (left) The most prominent place for the tomb owner in an Amarna tomb was on the doorjambs of the tomb's entry. This couple, Ay and Tey, later King and Queen, are shown raising their arms in praise to the sun with the text of a hymn carved above them (TA25).

Another departure from previous practice is the fact that Amarna compositions take up the whole available height of the wall, rather than dividing it into a series of registers. A wall surface thus received a complete composition, usually dominated by the king and queen at the centre. Registers are only employed within the basic composition to accommodate lesser figures and features.

As regards their overall arrangement, tombs at Amarna had antechambers that contained hymns of praise to the king at the door jamb; the tomb proper was inscribed with images of the activities of the royal family, including rewarding the deceased, as well as scenes of the city. Unusual scenes show the king not only in intimate family scenes, but also indulging in very secular activities, such as eating and drinking (TA1); perhaps the earliest representation of a kebab is shown on the wall of a tomb at Amarna (TA1). The only truly large-scale image of the deceased took the form of engaged statues at the rear of the tomb-chapel. It has been suggested that at Amarna it was believed that the dead slept during the night in their tombs and arose to greet the sun, as depicted on the door-jambs, after which they accompanied the king to the temple.[312] An unexpected and much more traditional scene shows offering being made before a mummy (TA1), but such an image is rare at Amarna.

Although the majority of tombs attributable to Akhenaten's reign have been found in the southern part of Egypt, other sepulchres have been identified at Saqqara. The tomb of Aperel (p. 222) certainly overlapped the period, while the first of a long series of tomb-chapels with built superstructures was erected in a long-abandoned area south of the causeway of Unas. Such monuments followed the basic form of a contemporary god's temple, with an entrance pylon, peristyle court(s) and sanctuary – just as had the aforementioned Theban sanctuary of Amenhotep-son-of-Hapu. The earliest thus-far identifiable example at Saqqara (H9) belonged to a High Priest of the Aten. Its owner had started work under the name Meryneith, changing it to Meryre and then back to Meryneith,[313] indicating that his career must thus have spanned the period, probably late in Akhenaten's reign, when the king had execrated all gods save his own Aten. Other tombs of this general date in the area include those of Paatenemheb (now Leiden AMT. 1–35) and Huy (S2735); the area would become a major necropolis in the years immediately following the end of the Amarna Period.

Substructures

Royal Tombs:[314] The basic 'bent' substructure design introduced for royal tombs earlier in the dynasty continued in use up to the time of Amenhotep III, albeit with slight expansion, including the addition of a further antechamber. An innovation fairly late in Amenhotep III's reign was the construction of new chambers, specifically for members of the royal family. Such individuals had certainly been interred with the king in the Valley of the Kings sepulchres of Amenhotep II and Thutmose IV (KV35 and 43), albeit without special architectural provision. In Amenhotep III's WV22, however, store-rooms were greatly enlarged into a pair of single-pillared burial chambers, each with their own subsidiary room. These are likely to have been intended for the king's two queens, Tiye and Sitamun.

This provision for royal family members was further expanded under Akhenaten. His tomb was built far down the wadi that lies behind the city of Tell el-Amarna (Map 3). Some 5 km (3 miles) down the wadi and 10 km (6 miles) from the heart of the city, a high and broad corridor, 3.2 m (10 ½ ft) square, was cut into the cliffs. Its stairways are interesting in being the earliest to have a ramp down the centre, to aid the introduction of a sarcophagus. The tomb was never finished, the burial chamber being improvised out of what had been intended as a pillared antechamber. In addition to Akhenaten's mummy, the room seems to have contained the burial of his mother, Tiye.

270 Axonometric view of the royal tomb at Amarna (TA26).

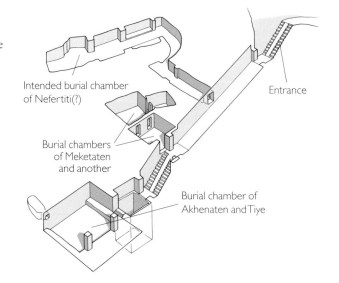

Intended burial chamber of Nefertiti(?)

Entrance

Burial chambers of Meketaten and another

Burial chamber of Akhenaten and Tiye

XIX (*previous page*) The conventional style of bas-relief as found in the tomb of Ramose at Thebes. It is beautifully carved and modelled, and reflects the best of the style in the time of Amenhotep III (TT55: 18th Dynasty).

XX (*above*) Upper part of the south wall of the crypt of the burial chamber of Sety I in the Valley of the Kings, showing a winged figure of the goddess Isis and texts from the Book of Amduat. Also visible is part of the vaulted astronomical ceiling that covers the crypt, in which lay the mummy of the king (KV17: 19th Dynasty).

XXI (*opposite*) The burial chamber of Pashedu x at Deir el-Medina. Figures of Anubis guard the entrance, while texts from the Book of the Dead adorn the walls and ceiling. On the end wall is an image of the Western Mountain, in front of which Osiris sits enthroned; the area below this tableau was formerly occupied by a stone sarcophagus, destroyed during the 19th century (TT3: 19th Dynasty).

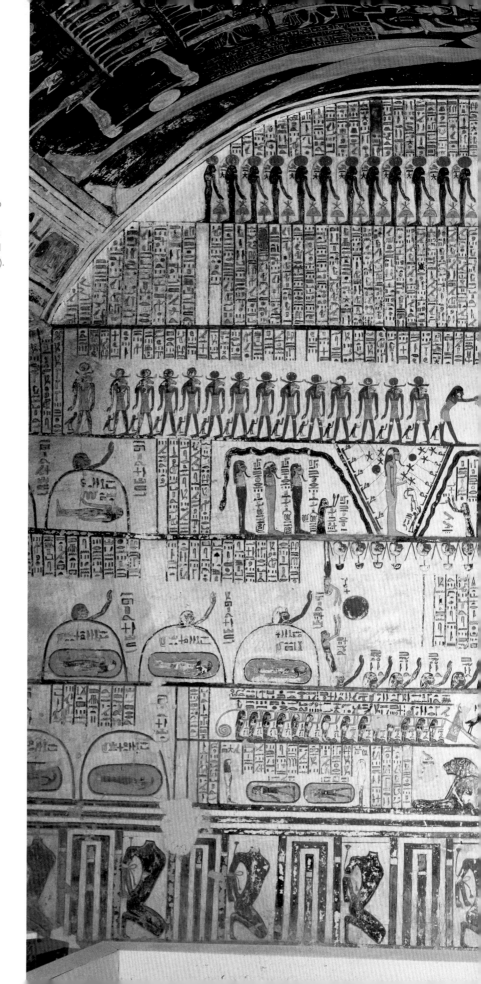

XXII (*right*) North wall of the burial chamber of Ramesses VI in the Valley of the Kings, with Part A of the Book of the Earth (KV9: 20th Dynasty).

XXIII (*overleaf*) The burial chamber of Nefertiry, wife of Ramesses II, in the Valley of the Queens. The column in the foreground depicts the Iunmutef priest who performed the Opening-of-the-Mouth ceremony for the mummy. The sarcophagus formerly lay across the centre of the central crypt of the chamber (QV66: 19th Dynasty).

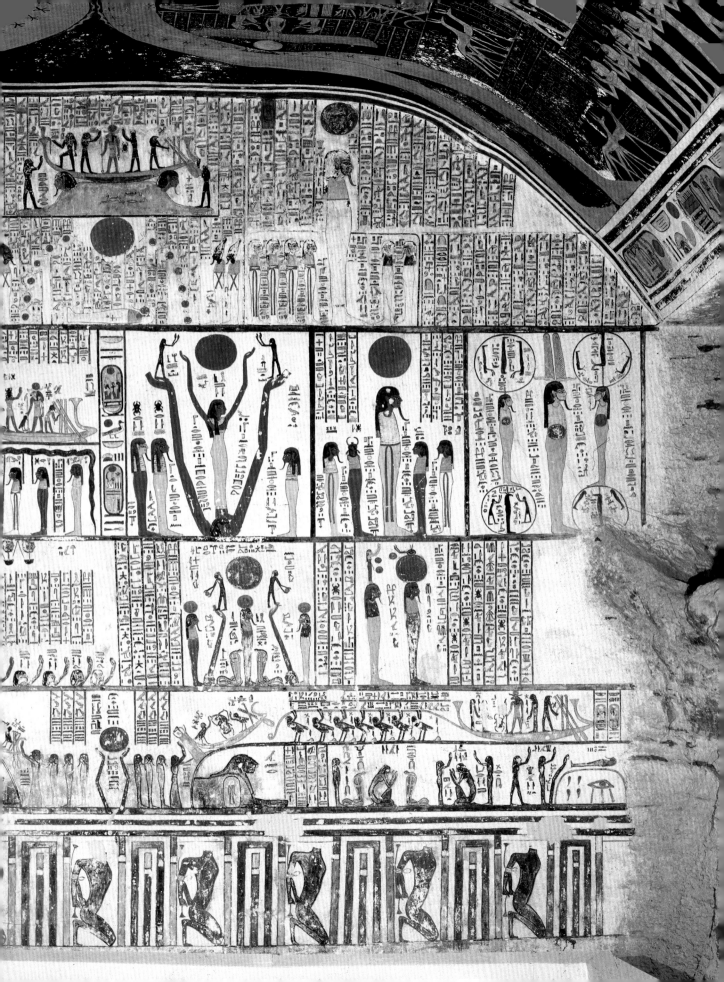

XXIV The north wall of the original burial chamber of Tawosret in the Valley of the Kings showing the final scene from the Book of Caverns, with the sun god emerging at the top as a scarab and as a child (KV14: 19th Dynasty).

Other members of the Amarna royal family were also provided with burial places within the king's tomb, suites of rooms being cut to the right of the main corridor, one for the burials of at least two female members of the family, another perhaps for Queen Nefertiti.

As might be expected given its owner's change in belief system, the Amarna royal tomb was decorated in a completely different way from its predecessors. The Amarna royal reliefs, like those in the contemporary tombs and temples, focus on scenes of royal daily activities in conjunction with the worship of the Aten. The sunk relief shows scenes of the king and his family praising the Aten in temples, going about their daily cultic business and most poignantly, scenes of the deathbeds of female members of the royal family.[315]

Private Tombs: The same kinds of substructures found at Thebes are to be found at Amarna, although examples are generally unfinished, thus making detailed comparisons

difficult. At Saqqara, in the tomb of Aperel, a flight of steps gives access to a passage, from the floor of which a shaft leads down to a vaulted chamber. Beyond this yet another shaft leads down to a shallow staircase, under which was the burial chamber. This proved to be largely intact, although the contents had been quite badly damaged by humidity and still held the coffins of the vizier, his wife, son and daughter-in-law, together with their canopic equipment and other material.

18TH DYNASTY – FROM TUTANKHAMUN TO HOREMHEB

Superstructures

Royal Tombs: The Atenist 'heresy', as it has been dubbed, was ended with Akhenaten's death, the state necropoleis shifting back to their traditional locations. No mortuary temple has yet been identified for Tutankhamun, although one was begun by Ay at Medinet Habu and finished by Horemheb.[316]

271 A major concentration of New Kingdom burials at Saqqara was adjacent to Teti's pyramid. These included that of Ipuia (S2730), whose hall is seen here; the blocks from the tomb are now in the Cairo Museum (JE44755, JE44924, TR21/6/24/16, TR27/3/25/17: late 18th Dynasty).

In its final form, the temple was fronted by three pylons, a massive gateway giving access to the great court. A palace was constructed between the third pylon and the gateway, a feature that became standard in Ramesside temples. Behind the court was a broad hypostyle hall, two columns deep and ten wide, giving access to further, smaller, pillared courts and the three-fold cult complexes beyond. The temple was razed to the ground in antiquity, but recovered fragments show a return to conventional decorative themes.

Private Tombs: A bare half-dozen private tombs of the late 18th Dynasty are known at Thebes, with a major upsurge in the numbers constructed at Saqqara.[317] At Saqqara, they centred on the area around the pyramid of Teti and south of Unas' monument. It is possible that these locations were chosen owing to the easy access up the steep escarpment afforded by the remains of these ancient monuments' causeways.

The rock-cut cemetery in the cliff east of Teti's pyramid (p. 222) continued in use, including the tomb of the Lady Maya (I.20), wet-nurse of Tutankhamun, while free-standing tombs began to be placed near the pyramid itself. Their structures comprised mud-brick walls faced with stone and generally consisted of small single-roomed chapels, perhaps fronted by a pair of columns (ill. 271). Similar monuments were also built in the cemetery south of the pyramid of Unas, but part of its major expansion involved the erection of huge temple-tombs for key officials on sites apparently made available by the demolition of a number of Old Kingdom (and earlier) mastabas.

The shafts of the latter formed the basis for a number of New Kingdom substructures, while their masonry was also re-used, along with blocks from nearby pyramids. At least one other cemetery of such tombs lay in the Memphite necropolis, in the area between Saqqara-South and Dahshur, where was found the tomb of the Royal Butler, Ipay.[318]

Of the same mud-brick construction as the smaller tombs, that of the general, later pharaoh, Horemheb[319] underwent a gradual evolution, beginning as three chapels opening from the rear of a peristyle court, with a plain forecourt. The latter was then converted into a vestibule, flanked by statue rooms and a new forecourt added, which still later had colonnades added around it and a large pylon in front of it.

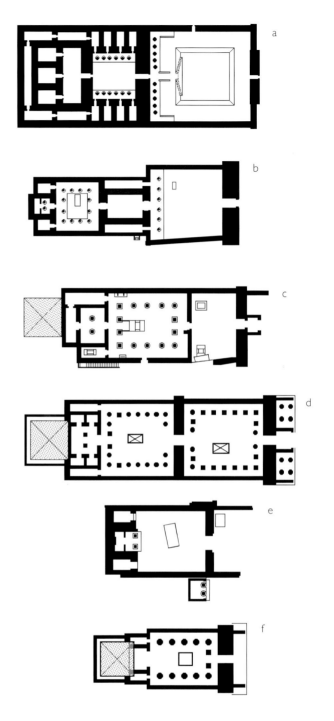

272 'Temple-tombs' of the late 18th/early 19th Dynasties: a. Amenhotep-son-of-Hapu (Thebes: reign of Amenhotep III); b. Maya (Saqqara LS27: Horemheb); c. Tjia and Tia (Saqqara: Ramesses II); d. Neferrenpet (Saqqara ST0: Ramesses II); e. Tasihuy (Saqqara ST5: Ramesses II); f. Paser (Saqqara: Ramesses II).

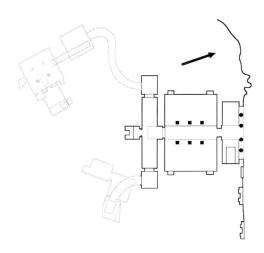

273 Plan of the tomb of the Overseer of Nurses, Sennedjem, at Awlad Azzaz, near Sohag (18th Dynasty: reign of Tutankhamun).

274 Another provincial tomb of the post-Amarna period is that of Nefersekheru at Zawiyet Sultan. This view shows the principal chamber, with statue niches at the rear (late 18th/early 19th Dynasty).

Of very similar design was the contemporary tomb (LS27) of the Treasurer Maya (Maya was a common name, used by both men and women). The inner chapels of these tombs were surmounted by brick pyramids and in some cases the chapels lay in the actual pyramid core.

Aside from these monuments at the capitals, a number of other sepulchres are known from other parts of the country during the post-Amarna Period. A significant example is that of the Overseer of Nurses, Sennedjem, at Awlad Azzaz, near Sohag in Middle Egypt.[320] It is rock-cut, with a particularly impressive façade, flanked by large stelae, but otherwise similar to Theban tombs in its overall layout.

Tomb decoration of this period shows the transition from the Amarna style of art to a naturalistic yet less exaggerated style. Scene types that were common prior to the Amarna Period are reinstated and images of the king decrease dramatically.

275 In the post-Amarna period some scenes that had appeared previously, such as funerary rituals, regained popularity. However, new variations, such as the smashing of the pots, were introduced into the mourning sequence (Saqqara, tomb of Horemheb: 18th Dynasty, reign of Tutankhamun).

276 Although Horemheb's Saqqara tomb was left for the burial of his female relations, the previously carved images of Horemheb had the royal *uraei* added to the new king's brow to emphasize his now-royalty (RMO H.III.CCCC).

Substructures

Royal Tombs: A tomb (TA29) may have been begun for Tutankhamun (or perhaps Neferneferuaten) at Amarna, comprising a 45-m (148-ft) corridor at the time of its abandonment and showing a clear resemblance to that of Akhenaten. However, the remaining royal tombs of the 18th Dynasty were built at Thebes and were far closer in conception to those of the earlier part of the dynasty, albeit with the bend removed. Only that of Horemheb (KV57: ill 257e) was ever (nearly) completed, as Tutankhamun was buried in an enlarged private tomb (KV62) and Ay was interred in WV23. This last was probably begun for

Tutankhamun and continued by Ay, but hurriedly finished off to an abbreviated plan due to Ay's untimely demise.

Exceptional scenes occur in the tombs of both Tutankhamun (KV62) and Ay (WV23). The Amduat is no longer pictured in full in the diminutive tomb of the boy king. Instead, only abbreviated extracts of it are shown in large-scale polychrome in the burial chamber, the only room in the tomb to be decorated. Perhaps due to the space

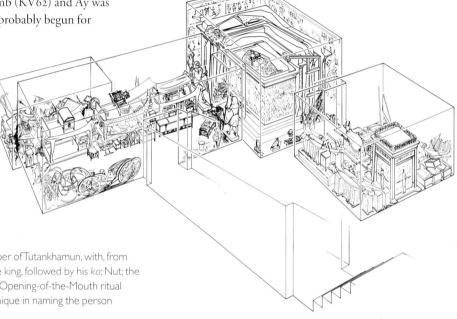

277 (*right*) Sketch of Tutankhamun's tomb as discovered. It had been constructed as a private tomb – perhaps for Ay? – but had been pressed into service as a royal sepulchre – hence the gross over-crowding of the tomb. The objects will have been designed to fit into a far larger monument (KV62: late 18th Dynasty).

278 (*below*) Wall of the burial chamber of Tutankhamun, with, from the left: Osiris being embraced by the king, followed by his *ka*; Nut; the king; the king's mummy, receiving the Opening-of-the-Mouth ritual from his successor, Ay. The scene is unique in naming the person carrying out the ritual.

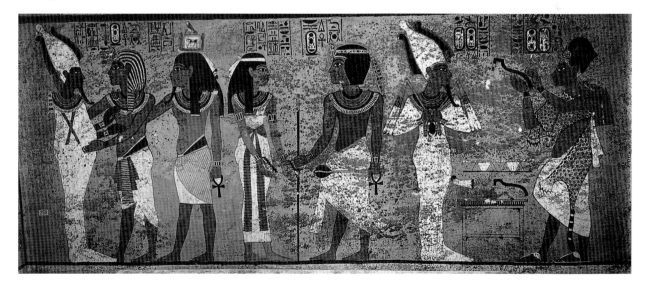

constraints, further funerary texts taken from the Amduat, the Litany of Re and the Book of the Dead, together with unidentified texts written in cryptographic hieroglyphs, were placed on the shrines that were placed around Tutankhamun's sarcophagus.[321]

The sepulchre also includes a scene that was hitherto only found in superstructures: his heir (Ay) officiating as the *sem* or funerary priest at the funeral. Since conducting these rites conferred legitimacy to the heir, their presence here may reflect Ay's desire to present himself to the gods as Tutankhamun's true heir. Thus, political expediency rather than any religious intent may provide the reason for including this scene that is unique in such a context.

Ay's tomb is also unusual decoratively as, in addition to further large-format selections from the Amduat and scenes of the king in the presence of the gods, he chose to include a double-scene showing himself, with his wife, spearing hippopotami on a canoe and fowling from a canoe. These latter scenes are normally specific to the decoration of the private tomb-chapel or royal mortuary temple[322] and are unique in the context of (royal or private) burial chamber decoration at any time. Are these a vestige of Atenist usage or due to some ambivalence on Ay's part as to his posthumous destiny?

279 (*below*) The burial chamber of King Ay is unusual in his inclusion of the fishing and fowling scene that is normally only found in private tomb-chapels and some royal mortuary temples – never in a substructure (WV23: late 18th Dynasty).

In Horemheb's tomb (KV57), the now-traditional Amduat texts were supplanted by the Book of Gates (p. 130). This tomb is also noteworthy as it contains the first example of a burial chamber carved in raised relief. The decoration was not complete at the time of the king's death, thus allowing us to study the technology that was used in its fabrication.

Private Tombs: Shaft approaches are standard in the 'temple-tombs' at Saqqara. Substructure layouts are to some degree influenced by their re-use of the shafts from over-built Old Kingdom tombs and are often of very considerable depth. The principal shaft of Horemheb's tomb ultimately descends to a four-pillared chamber, a final, much smaller, burial room being approached via a shaft at its far end.[323]

The substructure of the tomb of his contemporary, the Treasurer Maya (LS27), is interesting (and unique for its location and period) in that its principal chambers were lined with limestone blocks, to allow the addition of relief-decoration, impossible in the poor native rock of this part of Saqqara. The scheme employed showed the deceased and his wife, Meryet, worshipping various deities. The background was painted a golden yellow, both the schema of decoration and the colours used being reminiscent of royal burial chambers.[324] These rooms were approached via a shaft in the inner courtyard of the chapel, leading to a series of chambers, from which a further shaft led to the lowest level, where a decorated room led to a passageway, giving access to the final pair of stone-lined burial chambers.[325]

Moving to more provincial cemeteries, the tomb of Sennedjem near Sohag (p. 235) has two sets of substructures, entered from the left and right rear corners of the chapel. The latter has a complex set of chambers, including one with four pillars connected to the previous room by a stairway that descends and then rises again to emerge at its original level.

At Riqqa cemetery F, only substructures survive, although fragments of offering places were identifiable. That of Ipiy (F201) was approached by a 6-m (20-ft) shaft giving access to a chamber to the east and another to the west.[326] The latter had a southern extension, from which a further 4-m (12-ft) shaft led to the burial chamber. The neighbouring tomb 202 was generally similar, but the upper chamber featured a pair of pillars.

Chapter 11 The New Kingdom: the Ramesside Years

Following the end of the 18th Dynasty, the country's centre of gravity gradually moved northwards, with the Memphite necropolis increasingly supplementing the Theban as the cemetery of the elite. Civil disorder and economic decline led to a gradual fall-off in the construction of monumental tombs as the period progressed.

19TH AND 20TH DYNASTIES

Superstructures

Royal Mortuary Temples:[127] Ramesses I appears to have been unable to complete a mortuary temple for himself and provision for his cult seems to have been restricted to the 'paternal' section of the temple of his son. Sety I's mortuary temple was built in front of Dra Abu'l-Naga, at Qurna, at the opposite end of the necropolis from those of his late-18th Dynasty predecessors. The building was incomplete at its founder's death and was ultimately finished by his son, Ramesses II. The decoration applied by the latter, in sunk relief, is far inferior to Sety's own work, in raised-relief of the very highest quality. The temple was fronted by two courts and pylons, now almost totally destroyed, but much of the main temple remains intact. The ten-columned portico gives access to the usual three parallel sets of rooms.

The temple of Ramesses II, known today as the Ramesseum, is considerably larger and more elaborate. Its great enclosure contains, besides the temple itself, a chapel possibly dedicated to his mother, Tuy and wife, Nefertiry, and a large number of brick-vaulted store-houses – some of which were used for burials in the Third Intermediate

280 (*above*) The sun god in his bark as he crosses the underworld at night in the tomb of Sety I (KV17· 19th Dynasty).

281 (*below*) The façade of the inner part of the mortuary temple of Sety I at Qurna (19th Dynasty).

282 (*above*) The Ramesseum, the mortuary temple of Ramesses II on the west bank at Thebes (19th Dynasty). The remains in the foreground are of brick store-rooms, some of which were re-used as burial places during the 22nd Dynasty (see. pp. 273–4).

283 (*right*) Plan of the Ramesseum.

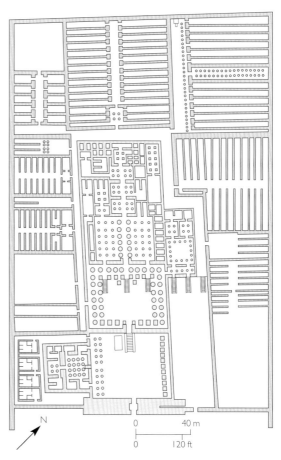

Period. The temple itself is built of stone throughout, in contrast to the extensive use of brick for the outer elements of temples down to that of Sety I. However, the basic layout of three cult complexes, of the king/his father, Amun and Re, is retained from earlier monuments. Beyond the pylon lay the ruined First Court, flanked by colonnades. That on the right was supported by Osirid columns; that on the left fronted a small palace.

The Second Court was surrounded on three sides by colonnades and beyond lay the main Hypostyle Hall, its roof held up by 48 columns. Those flanking the aisle were rather more massive than the rest, supporting a clerestory, which was the sole light-source. The standard set of three complexes lead from the hall. The central suite, of Amun, featured a series of small hypostyle halls.

The basic plan of Merenptah's mortuary temple reverted to the more modest dimensions of the monument of Sety I. Of the remaining Ramesside mortuary temples, most are

almost entirely destroyed, or unidentified, the exception being that of Ramesses III at Medinet Habu, whose temple is the best preserved of all such buildings.[328] It is in essence an enlarged copy of the Ramesseum, this lead being followed by Ramesses IV who began a similar temple, albeit half as large again, on the Asasif. He never finished it and neither did Ramesses V and VI who followed him; this last of the known New Kingdom royal mortuary temples was abandoned years from completion.[329]

During the Ramesside Period, something of a standardized decorative arrangement was established in royal mortuary temples. Scenes dealing with battles and the triumph over the enemies of Egypt were placed on the exterior of pylons and walls, as well as on the walls of open courtyards. Sometimes these are generic scenes of victory, but they are also frequently a record of actual historic events, such as the battle of Qadesh against the Hittites featured in the Ramesseum and the struggles with the invading Sea Peoples from the Aegean, found on the walls of Ramesses III's mortuary temple. Scenes of hunting become, for the most part, obsolete, with a notable exception being a bull hunt found on the exterior of the Medinet Habu temple.

Osirid pillars are still found, but their location is generally restricted to the piers in the open courtyard of the

284 (*above*) The mortuary temple of Ramesses III at Medinet Habu. It basically follows the design of a contemporary cult-temple, one exception being the presence of a royal palace, the remains of which can be seen in the foreground.

285 (*below*) Reconstruction of Medinet Habu in the Ptolemaic Period. Originally centred on an 18th Dynasty temple, the mortuary temple of Ramesses III was added to the complex in the 20th Dynasty. During the 23rd Dynasty a royal necropolis was established there, with new pylons and courtyards added to the 18th Dynasty temple in Late and Ptolemaic periods.

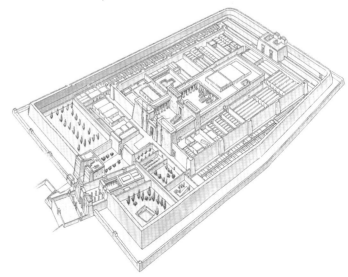

temples. At Medinet Habu the reliefs of the second courtyard were concerned with divine festivals, in particular those of Min and Ptah-Sokar-Osiris. The ceiling decorations of temples of the 19th Dynasty mark a change from earlier 18th Dynasty practice, in that the ceiling of the hypostyle hall of the Ramesseum is adorned with an entire astronomical ceiling. A lunar calendar with Ramesses II offering to the different divinities of the months is also shown.

Most of the wall and pillar scenes in the interiors of Ramesside temples beyond the open courts show the king interacting with gods, with Amun being the main recipient of his devotions. The cult of Re is relegated to his special sanctuary in the northwest corner of the temples; certainly the Old Kingdom scenes evocative of the sun's goodness are nowhere to be found in the decoration of these mortuary temples. Recurring themes in the inner part of the temple show the king's name being written on the *ished*-tree, inscriptions that ensure his eternal life and rule; the offerings of incense, bouquets, oils, images of *maat* and food and drink to the gods; offering lists; offerings; a false-door or offering area for the king; prayers to various gods; and the giving of life to the king. The *heb-sed* scenes that dominated older temples are reduced in scope, with the idea of eternity for such celebrations frequently being provided by scenes of the gods offering the deceased pharaoh multiple hieroglyphic images of the words '*heb-sed*'. The increase of the scenes showing different divinities, especially the Theban triad, is also linked to the Festival of the Valley (see pp. 220–1). An interesting set of scenes are those found in the complex of rooms associated with Osiris at Medinet Habu, which have vignettes from the Book of the Dead, in particular Chapter 110, most unusually featuring the king in the Fields of Iaru.

Private Tombs: The Saqqara cemeteries continued to grow during the 19th Dynasty. A notable change was a move towards the use of stone, rather than brick, for the structure of the tombs, although solid stone was reserved for the decorated facings, wall-cores being of rubble or mud-brick. An important example is the tomb of Tia, sister of Ramesses II and her husband Tjia (ill. 272c).[330] Although this follows the same basic patterns as the earlier tombs, there are a number of changes, also found in the other tombs of the period at Saqqara. In particular, the statue rooms between the courtyards disappear and the pyramid is made a free-standing element directly behind the tomb (cf. ill. 272d–f).

286 (*above*) Typical scenes of the king smiting his enemies adorned the pylons of both cult and mortuary temples. Whether or not the ruler had fought a battle (as had Ramesses III, shown here at Medinet Habu), this scene was necessary as it epitomized the ruler's role and was crucial to the continuation of *maat*.

287 (*opposite*) At his mortuary temple, Ramesses II sits within an *ished*-tree, and has his name inscribed on the leaves for longevity and a continuous rulership.

The 'temple-tomb' approach was also found at Thebes. The High Priest Nebwenenef had a free-standing structure in front of Dra Abu'l-Naga, including granite colossi of his master, Ramesses II. The ruinous state of the structure makes its details difficult to discern, but it seems to have resembled the Saqqara structure of Tjia and Tia, with a peristyle courtyard fronting a number of smaller rooms, at least one with two columns supporting the ceiling. This was in addition to his normal tomb-chapel, TT157, nearly 1 km (⅔ mile) to the north, a vast structure with a cross-hall supported by twelve Osirid pillars and an inner hall with a dozen square piers. A mud-brick pyramid above the chapel completed Nebwenenef's public mortuary installation.

Other structures – at both Thebes and Saqqara – combined both rock-cut and built elements. For example,

Djhutymose's TT32 had two brick pylons and a colonnaded court, the latter backed with statue niches and a false-door. The rock-cut chapel, in contrast, had a simple cross-hall with four pillars, behind which lay a passage and the offering place. Similarly, the very basic 'T'-shaped tomb of the High Priest Bakenkhonsu (TT35) was fronted by an extensive set of pylons and courtyards and topped by a pyramid.

Such tombs had a far more 'monumental' form than sepulchres of the previous dynasty, with an apparent conceptual change as well,[331] the pyramid and the small brick-vaulted chapel housed within it adding for example a specifically solar element to the monument.[332] In TT288/9 the pyramid-chapel was arranged so as to lie directly above the statue niche of the rock-cut chapel.

288 The development of the Ramesside tomb-chapel: a. TT106 (Paser); b. TT288/9 (Setau); c. TT283 (Roma-Roy); d. TT222 (Heqamaatre-nakhte). The latter two tombs have extensive built elements in front of the rock-cut chapel, while the first three all had associated pyramids, TT106's being some distance away.

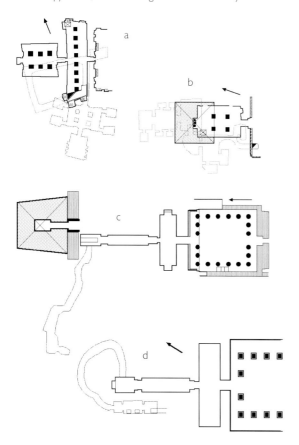

As the Ramesside Period proceeded, the number of known Theban tomb-chapels decreased; apart from the tombs of the Deir el-Medina community, few are precisely datable, with an increasing number of instances of usurpation of older chapels. Designs generally reverted to the simple 'T'-shaped Types Va and b, sometimes with statues cut into the ends of the cross-hall and a pyramid on the hillside above. One of the more elaborate examples was Roma-Roy's TT283, fronted by a peristyle court and pylon.

The return to orthodoxy was accompanied by changes in both artistic styles and the choice of scenes. As consolidated during the Ramesside Period, this change shifted focus from the deceased or the king to the gods.[333] Scenes relating to the individual's career became fairly rare, although examples continued to exist, for example a 20th Dynasty reward scene in TT148. Agricultural scenes decreased dramatically in number, although several late 18th/early 19th Dynasty tombs (e.g. TT16, TT255 and TT324) contained vignettes showing agricultural activities. Instead, scenes of funerary ritual abounded, plus extracts from the funerary 'books' that were previously appropriate only to burial chambers (cf. pp. 129–31).

Initially some Amarna themes are found at both Saqqara and Thebes: tombs dating from the reign of Tutankhamun/Ay and later show images of the king bestowing the gold of honour upon the deceased, as well as depictions of towns (e.g. TT49, showing Thebes). Somewhat later, TT409 has a rare image of Ramesses II engaged in worship.

However, the switch to the realm of the divine asserted itself as the Ramesside Period began. In addition to the usual funerary divinities, Ptah-Sokar-Osiris gained prominence, perhaps due to the post-Amarna shift of the political gravity to Memphis where this god was prominent and where many of the elite were now being buried.[334]

By the 19th Dynasty, images of the funerary cortege with the grave goods, *muu* dancers, *tekenu*, journey to Abydos, shrines of Buto and Sais, butchery and the elaborate Opening-of-the-Mouth ritual had been abandoned in favour of an image of the tomb-chapel with the Theban hills in the background, fronted by images of the deceased and the performance of the Opening-of-the-Mouth ceremony. Sometimes the image of a calf with a bleeding leg, the accompanying vignette to Chapter 1 in the Book of the Dead, was placed near or within the funeral scene (TT19, TT23, TT45, TT135, TT277). The appearance of royalty in Ramesside tombs is less frequent than in tombs of the 18th

289 Scenes which are predominantly religious are typical of chapels of the Ramesside Period. Here, men adore a *djed* pillar that supports a sun-disk, embraced by the arms of Nut, which emerge from the Western Mountain; tomb of Neferrenpet-Kenro (TT178: 19th Dynasty, reign of Ramesses II).

Dynasty (e.g. TT10, TT50, TT51, TT65, TT106, TT217 and TT255), perhaps a reaction against the excess of kingly depictions found in chapels of the Amarna Period.[335]

By the reign of Sety I the basic format for tomb decoration of the 19th Dynasty was in place, as can be seen in the tomb-chapel of Roy (TT225), with variations being visible in other tombs of a similar date, such as those of Userhat (TT51) and Hatiay (TT324). Scenes in Ramesside tombs contain many more funerary prayers and texts and divinities worshipped by the deceased. These appear on upper registers, while lower registers show the provisioning of the deceased, an earthly activity. Images showing Hathor, the Lady of the Sycamore, dispensing nourishment to the deceased and his *ba* (e.g. TT158) and vignettes showing the

the two of them on occasion drinking water from T-shaped pools that are very reminiscent of the shape of the tomb itself, proliferate. These more explicitly religious scenes make the chapel increasingly similar to a mortuary temple, with the transition to the next world being stressed, rather than the fine life that would be had there.[336] The inscriptions in tombs of this period are painted on a special separately coloured background, while those of the 18th Dynasty are painted on the same background as the scene, or on a blue-grey ground.[337] The dominant background colour for tombs of this period is yellow, suggesting the golden light of the sun, as well as alluding to the metamorphosis of the flesh into gold that was believed to take place after death and the attainment of eternal life and divinity by the deceased. Engaged statuary

290 Musicians in the tomb of Nakht at Thebes. Originally naked, they were given clothes during a Ramesside usurpation, the paint of which has now largely fallen away (TT52: 18th Dynasty).

remains a part of the adornment, as can be seen in the tombs of Khaemopet and Paser (TT105, TT106). The former shows statues of the husband and wife carved into a niche above the entrance to the substructure, while the courtyard of the latter's tomb contains nine statues of the deceased, three of which are Osirid.

It was during the 20th Dynasty that portions of books of the underworld began to be inscribed in the chapels of private individuals. This move was accompanied by a shift in the balance between text and image in a tomb in favour of the former.

The patterns described above are best seen at Thebes, although they broadly hold good throughout Egypt. There are, of course, local variations and it may be observed that 'Theban' motifs are not always found in the Memphite area, while tombs at El-Kab and Thebes often have common themes and even identical scenes. The Voyage to Abydos is rare, but not unknown at Saqqara (e.g. Tjia and Tia and Pabes), as are images of the king, while the Saqqara scene of ritual pot-breaking is not found in Thebes. However, it is interesting to note that a tomb dating to Tutankhamun's reign at Sohag (p. 235) has more in common with the decoration of contemporary Memphite tombs than with those of the much nearer Theban area.[338]

The Memphite tombs, mainly of a Ramesside date, continue to show residual stylistic influences of the Amarna Period, coupled with the iconographic shift that is seen at Thebes. Images of Osiris and other deities enthroned and adored by the tomb-owner abound.

Substructures

Royal Tombs:[339] The initial tombs of the 19th Dynasty followed the architectural pattern of that of Horemheb. However, with Ramesses II (KV7) a number of changes occurred. First, the simple stairway previously seen in the Valley of the Kings was replaced by a ramp, flanked by stairs, as seen a little earlier in the royal tombs at Amarna. Second, the axis of the burial chamber shifted through 90 degrees, with the result that the crypt now ran across the chamber, with four pillars in front of it and another set of four behind.

This arrangement remained constant in all completed royal tombs into the 20th Dynasty, although a number were finished off to abbreviated plans. Another change seen towards the end of the 19th Dynasty was a reduction in the angle of descent of the tombs, together with a considerable enlargement in the height and width of the passages. Roughly in parallel with this, the entrances of the tombs became larger and were placed in prominent places in the Valley, contrasting with the inconspicuous, easily obliterated, locations seen earlier. Indeed, it seems that the 20th Dynasty royal tombs were never intended to be hidden. Instead, it is possible that 'pylons' of rubble were arranged to flank decorated gateway-entrances that lay several metres above the contemporary ground level. The tombs seem to have been closed by simple wooden doors; no evidence of the sealed blockings found in earlier tombs was present in those of Ramesses II and his successors. Indeed, it has been suggested that the doors of royal tombs may have been on occasion opened ceremonially subsequent to the burial.[340] In this situation, the security of the tombs will have relied paradoxically on their visibility and the reliability of the necropolis police – the latter perhaps an unwise approach in the troubled times of the late 20th Dynasty.

From this period we also have information on the names anciently given to the various parts of the royal tomb, derived from a number of ancient documents.[341] From the entrance, they are as follows:

MODERN AND ANCIENT TERMS FOR THE PARTS OF A KING'S TOMB	
Corridor 1	*setja-netjer en wat shu* First God's Passage [of Re] of the Sun's Path
Corridor 2	*setja-netjer sen-nu* Second God's Passage
Corridor 3 right niche left niche	*setja-netjer khemet-nu* Third God's Passage *khemyu enty hetepu na netjeru iabtet im* Sanctuaries in which the gods of the east rest *khemyu enty hetepu na netjeru imentet im* Sanctuaries in which the gods of the west rest
Corridor 4 niches	*setja-netjer fed-nu* Fourth God's Passage *at iry-aa sen* 2 door-keepers' rooms
Well-room	*weskhet iseq* Hall of waiting
Pillared hall	*weskhet merkbet* Chariot Hall
Burial chamber	*per n nub (enty hetep tu im-ef)* House of Gold (in which One rests)

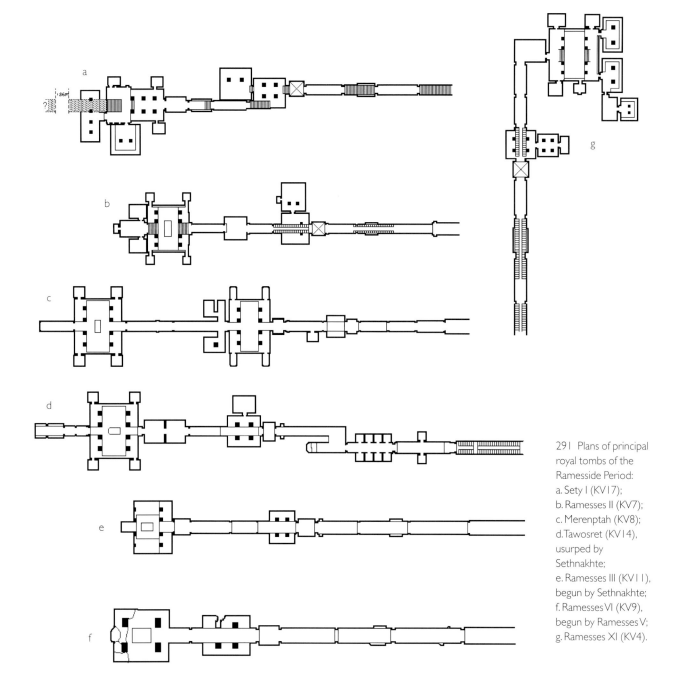

291 Plans of principal royal tombs of the Ramesside Period:
a. Sety I (KV17);
b. Ramesses II (KV7);
c. Merenptah (KV8);
d. Tawosret (KV14), usurped by Sethnakhte;
e. Ramesses III (KV11), begun by Sethnakhte;
f. Ramesses VI (KV9), begun by Ramesses V;
g. Ramesses XI (KV4).

It is uncertain how far these designations applied to tombs before the 20th Dynasty.

To be considered in conjunction with the Valley of the Kings tombs is the so-called Osirion of Sety I at Abydos.[342] This cenotaph 'tomb' lay behind his finely decorated temple, dedicated to seven of the gods of Egypt, including his deified self. A series of passages and rooms lead to the great hall of the Osirion, its roof supported by granite pillars and formerly covered by an earthen mound surrounded by trees. The central part of the hall is encircled by a channel, intended to be filled by subsoil water to make an island, upon which cavities suggestive of a sarcophagus and canopic chest are cut. This was intended for a symbolic interment linking the king with Osiris, whose tomb was believed to lie a few kilometres away at Umm el-Qaab.

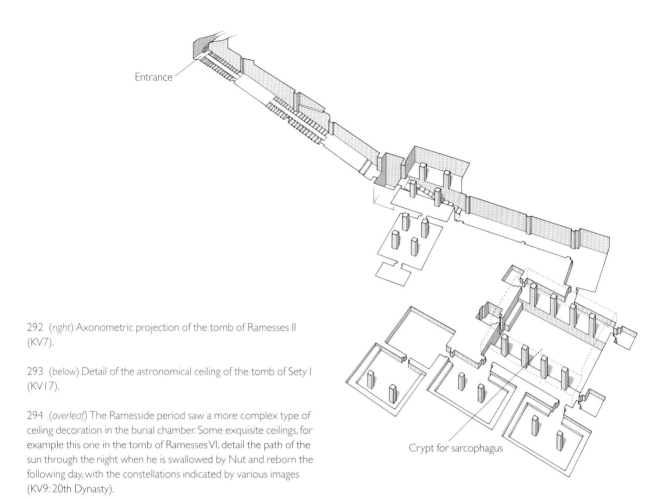

Entrance

292 (*right*) Axonometric projection of the tomb of Ramesses II (KV7).

293 (*below*) Detail of the astronomical ceiling of the tomb of Sety I (KV17).

294 (*overleaf*) The Ramesside period saw a more complex type of ceiling decoration in the burial chamber. Some exquisite ceilings, for example this one in the tomb of Ramesses VI, detail the path of the sun through the night when he is swallowed by Nut and reborn the following day, with the constellations indicated by various images (KV9: 20th Dynasty).

Crypt for sarcophagus

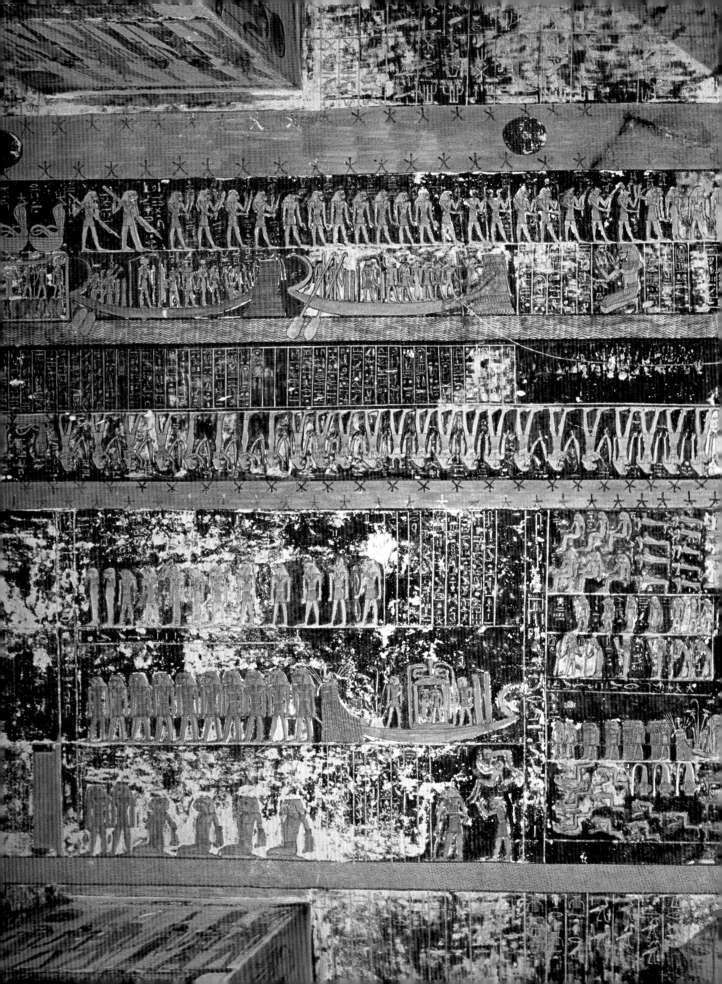

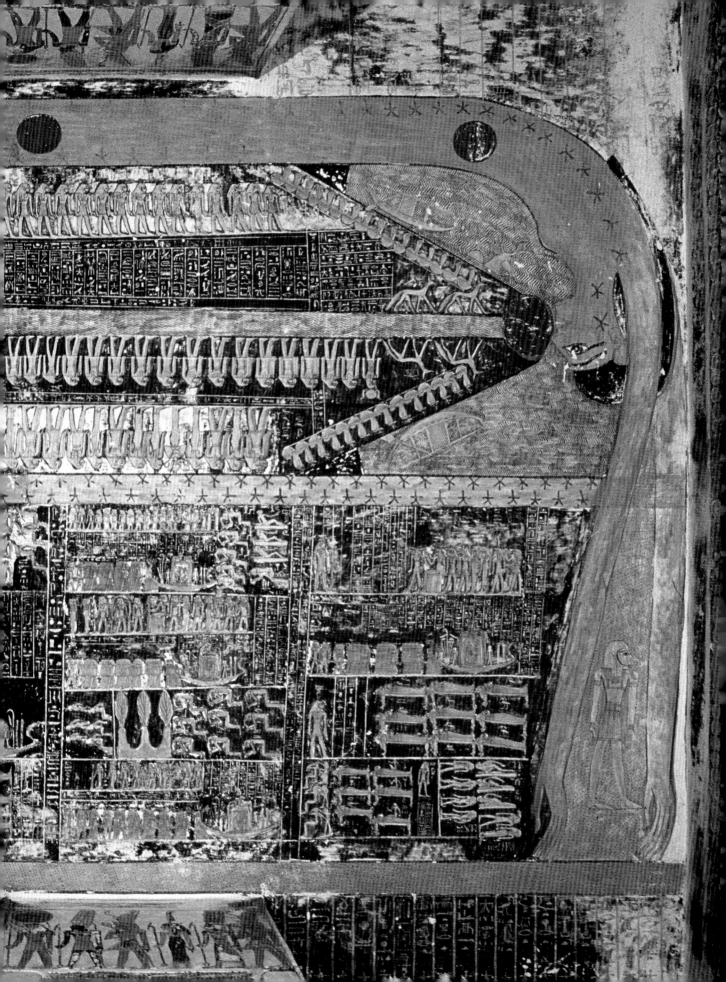

The decoration of Ramesside royal tombs further emphasized the journey of the king's soul through their decoration. The front portion, which was regarded as nominally 'east', closest to daylight, is dedicated to Re, while the back portion, the 'west' and dark portion, is dedicated to Osiris, Lord of the West. The division is frequently marked by two images of Osiris enshrined that are located on the far wall of the first pillared hall of the tomb.

The tomb of Sety I in the Valley of the Kings (KV17) is innovative in its inclusion of the first astronomical ceiling after that of Senenmut (TT353: see above, p. 226). Sety's ceiling, adopted with enthusiasm by later Ramesside kings (e.g. Merenptah (KV8), Ramesses VI (KV9), Ramesses VII (KV1) and Ramesses IX (KV6)) is an artistic tour de force and one of the most elegant and evocative images from the royal necropolis. The ceiling, hovering above the place where the mummy lay, illustrates the passage of the sun through the body of the sky goddess Nut at night and its rebirth the following day, thus promising the king a role in the eternal cycle of the cosmos. Sety's tomb is also the first to include an early version of the Book of the Divine Cow (see p. 131). This book had only been used once before: on the shrines that enclosed the sarcophagus of Tutankhamun. At this point, or shortly thereafter, the arrangement of divinities within the sepulchre was regularized, with female divinities associated with the sun and sky dominating the first or upper part of the tomb and male, chthonic deities dominating the second or lower part of the tomb.[343]

Sety I's Osirion at Abydos also contains celestial images: the eastern chamber's ceiling is decorated with an image of Nut stretched over Geb, the earth god, with Shu, god of air, separating them. This is the first such depiction and one that becomes a stock image subsequently. When the Osirion was completed by Sety's grandson, Merenptah, the Book of Caverns, another 19th Dynasty funerary text, was added to the entrance passage to the structure. This book was regularly featured in the royal tombs of the 20th Dynasty and is most strikingly featured in the tomb of Ramesses VI (KV9).

Ramesses II's KV7 adds a variation to the exterior of the tomb: instead of a blank sealed doorway, the lintel above the entrance to the tomb bears a panel depicting the solar disk of the sun god, Re, flanked by images of the king and Isis and Nephthys. The disk on KV7's lintel contains images of the sun in its three guises at different times of the day and is painted yellow, the colour of the sun during the day. Inside the tomb the sun is painted red, indicating that it is later in the day and corresponds to the sun's passage through the sky. This device is adopted by subsequent rulers. Images of the goddess Maat flanked the tomb's doorway, each kneeling on a basket that was balanced on lotus/lily (the symbol of the south) or papyrus (the symbol of the north) plants, the heraldic plants of Egypt. This further emphasized the nominal orientation of the tomb east–west.[344]

Ramesses II's KV7 and his sons' KV5 (see below, pp. 262–4) include a rock-cut full-frontal image of Osiris, apparently to emphasize that the deep and dark parts of the

295 The lintel of the tomb of Ramesses X in the Valley of the Kings, with the disk of the sun in the centre flanked by two figures of the king, behind whom stand Isis and Nephthys (KV18: 20th Dynasty).

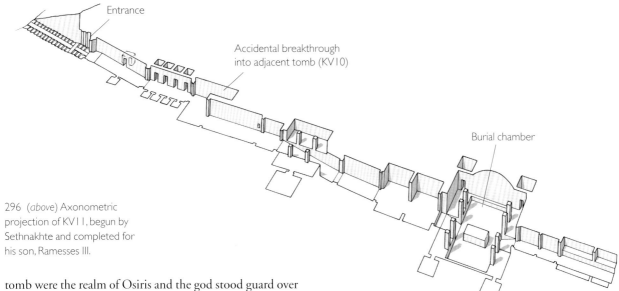

296 (*above*) Axonometric projection of KVII, begun by Sethnakhte and completed for his son, Ramesses III.

Entrance

Accidental breakthrough into adjacent tomb (KV10)

Burial chamber

tomb were the realm of Osiris and the god stood guard over them. Although a motif found in a number of private tomb-chapels (e.g. that of Aperel (Saqqara I.2)) and revived in the much later tomb of Mentuemhat (TT34), it is not otherwise found in royal substructures.

Interestingly, burial chambers were called the 'House of Gold' by the ancient Egyptians (see p. 255). This might have been due to the treasures placed within, the golden colour of the walls,[345] or the fact that the king's flesh, like that of a god, was supposed to be made of gold. Certainly the gold/yellow used in decorating these burial chambers, especially in the Ramesside Period, was indicative of divinity.[346]

Later Ramesside kings of the 20th Dynasty maintained the solar focus in their tombs through texts known as the 'Book of Night' and 'Book of Day', as well as the other, older texts. These emphasize the royal responsibility of maintaining the course of the sun through the sky. Another composition used in late New Kingdom royal tombs is the 'Book of the Earth' and deals with different earth gods and their relationship to the sun god.[347] The positioning of texts varies through the Ramesside Period, as shown in the table on the next page, the principal fixed point being the concentration of the Litany of Re near the entrance.[348] By using different texts placed in specific areas the tomb allowed the recreation of the cosmos. Thus, in the sarcophagus chamber the books of the heavens were placed on the ceiling and the books of the underworld and the earth were inscribed on the walls, creating the world by word and by situation.

297 (*below*) Early copy of one of the figures of harpers that are, uniquely, to be found in a side chamber in the entrance-way of the tomb of Ramesses III (KVII: 20th Dynasty).

The tomb of Ramesses III (KV11) is extremely unusual as, in addition to being inscribed with standard funerary texts, it contains scenes in the corridor, as well as in a side chamber (side-chamber C) that are more commonly associated with 18th Dynasty elite tomb-chapels. A remarkable image of a harper found in the corridor earned this tomb the sobriquet 'the Harper's tomb'. Side-chamber C is enlivened with images of bakers, brewers, butchers, cooks and leather-workers, all standard scenes in 18th Dynasty tomb-chapels, but extremely unusual in tomb-chapels of the later New Kingdom – let alone a royal substructure. Side-room K is also unusual in depicting ploughing, sowing and reaping in the Fields of Iaru, something also seen in Ramesses III's Medinet Habu temple. Otherwise it, like other 20th Dynasty royal tombs, continues to emphasize the rebirth of the king in the guise of the sun god. This unification is stressed by writing the royal name in a disk formed by the bodies of two entwined serpents or along the centre of an astronomical ceiling.

A new series of royal family tombs also began during the Ramesside Period in the Valley of the Queens (Map 5F).[349]

Those of the earlier royal wives are in many ways miniature versions of kingly tombs, generally with a descending corridor, an antechamber and a burial hall, sometimes pillared and sometimes with a sunken crypt. The most elaborate tombs of this kind are those of Tuy and Nefertiry (QV80 and 66), mother and wife of Ramesses II.

However, far surpassing them is the stupendous catacomb built for a number of the same king's sons in the Valley of the Kings. KV5 seems to have been an enlargement of a much smaller tomb of the 18th Dynasty, the rear part of which was extended into a 16-pillared hall, work perhaps begun in Year 19 of Ramesses II, on the basis of a graffito on the roof. Two smaller pillared annexes may also have been intended as burial chambers, while a 'T'-shaped set of corridors at the back of the main pillared hall gave access to no fewer than 56 small rooms of unknown purpose. On the opposite wall from the entrance to the 'T'-shaped corridors, two further passages plunged into the bedrock, lined with yet more small chambers and at least one of them leading to another pillared room and a further descending passage: the total number of passages and chambers known at the time of

DECORATIVE SCHEMES OF ROYAL TOMBS OF THE NEW KINGDOM						
Element of tomb	**Thutmose III (KV34)**	**Amenhotep III (WV22)**	**Horemheb (KV57)**	**Sety I (KV17)**	**Ramesses III (KV11)**	**Ramesses VI (KV9)**
Burial chamber	Book of Amduat; Litany of Re	Book of Amduat; the king and the gods	Book of Gates;	Book of Gates; Book of Amduat; astronomical ceiling; the king and the gods	Book of Gates; the king and the gods	Book of Earth
Antechamber	List of divinities	The king and the gods	The king and the gods	The king and the gods	Book of the Dead; the king and the gods	Book of the Dead; the king and the gods
4th and 5th corridors				Opening-of-the-Mouth	Opening-of-the-Mouth	Book of Amduat
Mid-length pillared hall			The king and the gods	Book of Gates	Book of Gates	Book of Gates; Book of Caverns
Well-room				The king and the gods	The king and the gods	Book of Gates; Book of Caverns
3rd corridor				Book of Amduat	Litany of Re; Book of Amduat	Book of Gates; Book of Caverns
2nd corridor				Litany of Re	Litany of Re	Book of Gates; Book of Caverns
1st corridor				Litany of Re	Litany of Re	Book of Gates; Books of Caverns

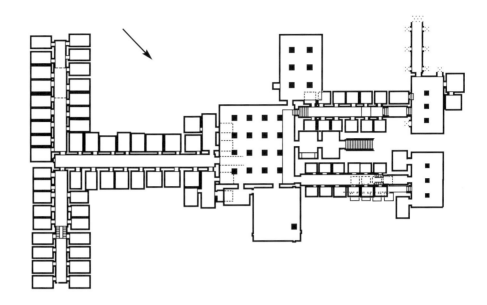

298 (*right*) Plan of the tomb of the sons of Ramesses II in the Valley of the Kings (KV5: 19th Dynasty).

299 (*below*) Lintel of the burial chamber of Amenhirkopshef in the Valley of the Queens, showing at the top a winged sun-disk, and below the cartouches of Ramesses III protected by winged cobras; the sarcophagus is visible beyond (QV55: 20th Dynasty).

writing exceeds 130. Nevertheless, it remains unclear exactly how many burials were made in this huge tomb: only five names have come to light, but excavation of the many parts of the tomb which remain choked with debris will doubtless help resolve this issue.

Later in the dynasty, a somewhat reduced king's-style tomb was built for the Queen-Regent Tawosret in the Valley of the Kings (KV14), a location also used for a tomb intended for a son of Ramesses III (KV3). The dadoes in the lower chambers of her tomb, like those in other later Ramesside royal sepulchres, are decorated with images of funerary goods and religious emblems reminiscent of the object frieze found in Middle Kingdom sarcophagi and coffins. A series of further tombs was also built for sons of Ramesses III in the Valley of the Queens; these are generally of much shallower descent than earlier examples – mirroring contemporary kingly trends – and fairly long and narrow, with one or two subsidiary rooms. The same basic scheme

300 Scene from the tomb of Amenhirkopshef B: the prince with his father, Ramesses III (QV55: 20th Dynasty).

also applies to the handful of queens' tombs of the 20th Dynasty that also lie in the same wadi.

In these sepulchres of the royal family, decoration was usually straightforward, with the tomb-owner shown in the company of various deities and selections from the Book of Gates. One notable feature in the tombs of the sons of Ramesses III was that their father was the most prominent protagonist, while in the case of the sepulchres of royal ladies their husband or father is wholly missing.

Private Tombs – Rock-cut: Radical changes appear in the form of the substructures of private tombs at Thebes during the Ramesside Period. The shift to the use of sloping-passage approaches is completed, the change being neatly illustrated in the tomb of the Viceroy of Nubia, Setau, of Ramesses II's reign (TT288/9: ill. 288b). The simple four-pillared chapel originally had a shaft sunk in its northwest corner, but this was replaced by a sloping passage to the right of the forecourt, that led to a complex of no fewer than 12 chambers. Their plan is reminiscent of that of the innermost rooms of contemporary royal tombs; the majority of the rooms are also remarkable in being decorated (see below).

In contrast to the essentially straight axis seen in this tomb, a major development during early Ramesside times is the appearance of substructure access-passages that describe a descending spiral course. The most extreme example appears in TT32 (Djehutymose), where the gallery turns 360 degrees through a single turn before heading a further 30 m (100 ft) down to a decorated burial chamber. Similarly, TT106 (Paser, ill. 288a) has a stairway that descends the four sides of a rectangle before exiting into a columned antechamber with four store-chambers – highly reminiscent of royal burial halls – and an innermost burial chamber, with four niches in each side-wall. TT157 is yet more elaborate, with an eight-pillared hall preceding the burial apartment.

Apart from a few tombs such as TT106, which retain the late-18th Dynasty placement of the substructure-entrance in the floor of the left-side of the first hall, most Ramesside examples have instead an opening in the side-wall of the rear part of the chapel, apparently closed only with a wooden door. This also echoes royal practice, since the later tombs in the Valley of the Kings were similarly sealed.

The 'spiral' descent, which may have attempted to symbolize elements of the netherworld[350] seems to have died out in the later part of the 19th Dynasty, the tomb of

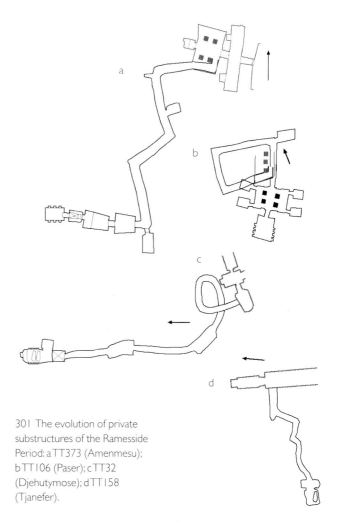

301 The evolution of private substructures of the Ramesside Period: a TT373 (Amenmesu); b TT106 (Paser); c TT32 (Djehutymose); d TT158 (Tjanefer).

Tjanefer (TT158) having a sinuous, but broadly straight passage leading from an inner left wall of the chapel. This led to a rough, shallow, but wide, antechamber and a square burial chamber. A rather different 'straight' substructure is found in the tomb of the late 19th Dynasty Chancellor Bay, whose sepulchre was built in the Valley of the Kings on a royal scale (KV13).

Most of these substructures were simply rock-hewn, in some cases fairly roughly finished, the principal exceptions being KV13 and TT289 and the burial apartments of TT32 and TT156. The tomb-chamber of TT32 has painted scenes of the deceased adoring deities; similar motifs are found in TT156 (Pennesuttawi), possibly painted rather later than the decoration of the tomb's chapel. In the substructure of Setau (TT289), ten rooms contain extensive decoration on a scale exceeding that of any private tomb-chambers prior to the end of the Third Intermediate Period. They largely comprise standard scenes of the deceased before the gods, but there are depictions of the funerary procession and extracts from the Book of Gates. Bay's KV13 also had a decoration that recalled royal practice, perhaps in keeping with his pretensions to power, with images of Isis and Nephthys over the main entrance and the first corridor beginning with figures of kneeling goddesses spreading their wings, followed by a series of images of Bay before various gods and the king. The second and third passageways were largely taken up with sections from the Book of the Dead. Any decoration that might originally have been applied to the following chambers has long since vanished.

In contrast to the sparse adornment of the substructures of most of the elite tombs, at Deir el-Medina, many tomb-chambers were given brick vaults, upon which were applied plaster and painted decoration. This circumstance is certainly the direct result of the tombs' owners being the artisans responsible for decorating the royal tombs in the Valley of the Kings. In both conception and execution the decorative approach is often very similar – not surprisingly, of course, as the same artists were responsible for both! Amongst the results were the some of the jewels of Ramesside art.

The majority of the decorated substructures at Deir el-Medina date to the 19th Dynasty, although a handful also come from the 20th Dynasty. The well-known TT1 (Sennedjem)[351] is oriented so that the west wall of the burial chamber is indeed in the west and is therefore covered with scenes related to the netherworld. The east wall shows the sunrise and a paradisiacal world for farmers in the Fields of Iaru from Chapter 110 of the Book of the Dead. The remaining scenes show mummification by Anubis (a popular scene repeated in several other tombs at the site, with some variations, including TT219, TT220, TT290, TT323 and TT360), Osiris and other divinities of the underworld. The majority of these images are attached to Spell 17 of Book of the Dead.

The majority of the other decorated burial chambers in the Deir el-Medina cemetery contain large-scale illustrations from different spells of the Book of the Dead as well as images of funerary divinities, demons and manifestations of the deceased's *ba* (TT290, 292). Other images found in these tombs include traditional views of family members engaged in different activities and poses (TT3 even shows a manifestation of old age in the form of grey hair!), offerings, the Voyage to Abydos and the Opening-of-the-Mouth scene. One other motif (found in TT2, 284, 306 and 359) is

302 (*left*) Inherkhau shown with Thoth before Osiris in the burial chamber of TT359 at Deir el-Medina (20th Dynasty, reigns of Ramesses III and IV).

303 (*opposite*) A hare slaying a serpent: allusions to the triumph of the sun god over Apophis are implicit in this scene (TT359).

the adoration by the deceased of the 'Lords of the West', a group of ancient kings, queens, princes and princesses, headed by Amenhotep I and Ahmes-Nefertiry, who were patrons of the Theban necropolis. The 'Lords' range back to Mentuhotep II of the 11th Dynasty, but mainly belong to the late 17th/early 18th Dynasty and provide a useful catalogue of royalties of the period.[352]

A somewhat unusual scene found in these tombs is one of Anubis leaning over a fish mummy (TT2) as a variant of the more common image where the mummy of the tomb-owner is featured. Tree-goddess scenes, found in the chapels of contemporary tombs, are quite common (e.g. TT211, 212, 292). Delightful vignettes showing a cat, a symbol of Re, slaying a serpent, the representation of Apophis, with a sharp knife are also found in these tombs (e.g. TT216, 335) and are related to several of the spells found in the various funerary books. A particularly lovely and unique scene shows one tomb-owner kneeling before a palm tree and drinking from a pool of fresh water (TT290).

A handful of Ramesside private tombs away from Thebes have decorated substructures, including that of Amenhotep at Deir Durunka in Middle Egypt.[353] There, decoration is preserved on three walls of the chamber, showing the judgment scene, scenes of offerings and the deceased being conducted to the hereafter by Hathor and Anubis. At Abydos lies the vaulted burial chamber of Deduhorankh (v40),[354] with decoration in red and black ink. The end wall showed the deceased before Osiris, with

the usual kinds of funerary vignettes on the side walls, together with text of the Negative Confession. The entrance was flanked by knife-wielding demons, the whole room being reminiscent of Deir el-Medina burial chambers. Yet another tomb is that of Sobkmose from Rizeiqat, whose stone-built chamber has images of the deceased and the gods.[355]

Private Tombs – Built: In other areas of Egypt, in particular the Delta, where rock-cut structures were impossible, the old approach of building the substructure in a cutting was continued. Important examples belonging to Viceroys of Kush are known at Bubastis, where the tomb of Hori iii comprised a corridor of baked brick – a fairly uncommon material in pharaonic Egypt – flanked on each side by three vaulted chambers. Their walls were also of baked brick, as was the pavement of the tomb, presumably to guard against damp, but the upper walls and roofs were of mud-brick. Four of the rooms held stone sarcophagi. Other tombs of similar type had been built nearby, including that of Hori's like-named father, also a Viceroy.[356] Other examples of such vaulted tombs are well known at Abydos, where the earliest specimens appear to date to the first part of the 18th Dynasty and can be seen to have been surmounted by mastabas. An interesting tomb at Abydos is G100, which is approached both via a shaft, giving access to antechambers, a right-angled turn into a passage and the sepulchral chambers and a sloping passage that opens directly into the main burial chamber.[357]

DECORATED SUBSTRUCTURES IN THEBAN TOMBS OF THE RAMESSIDE PERIOD			
Tomb	Date	Owner	Scene
TT6	18th–19th Dyn	Neferhotep & Nebnefer	Shrine and divinities, extracts from Book of the Dead (BoD), Fields of Iaru, Book of Gates, deceased and wife
TT156	18th–19th Dyn	Pennesuttawi	Deceased adoring Western hawk, Hathor cow and Sobek; Weighing of the Heart; image of deceased and wife
TT1	19th Dyn (Sethy I/Ramesses II)	Sennedjem i	Netherworld scenes; mummy, banquet; extracts from BoD; Osiris; deceased in front of gods of the underworld
TT298	19th Dyn (Ramesses II)	Baki i & Wennefer i	Anubis and mummy with Isis and Nephthys; text with list of relatives
TT323	19th Dyn (Sety I)	Pashedu vii	Hawk; *Benu* bird; family before gods; Anubis and mummy
TT2	19th Dyn (Ramesses II)	Khabekhnet i	Re, Osiris, Hathor and king; Hapi and offerings; winged Isis; Anubis and fish mummy; various divinities with and without deceased

Tomb	Date	Owner	Scene
TT10	19th Dyn (Ramesses II)	Penbuy i & Kasa i	Vaulted ceiling with Anubis, Thoth and Four Sons of Horus
TT32	19th Dyn (Ramesses II)	Djehutymose	Ceiling decorated with text
TT212	19th Dyn (Ramesses II)	Ramose i	Offering texts and tree-goddess
TT292	19th Dyn (Ramesses II)	Pashedu ii	Anubis, mummy and other gods being adored by deceased and wife; tree-goddess and *bas* drinking; Osiris; vaulted ceiling: Anubis-jackals, demons and other funerary divinities
TT335	19th Dyn (Ramesses II)	Nakhtamun ii	Nut in mountain; Osiris; deceased and wife adoring gods and emblems of gods; family member offering to deceased; Opening-of-the-Mouth; mummies before tomb; guests at a banquet; vaulted ceiling: offering texts, cat slaying Apophis as serpent, and funerary gods
TT336	19th Dyn (Ramesses II)	Neferrenpet ii	Coffins; banquet; divinities; deceased and wife; Weighing of the Heart; Anubis and mummy; vaulted ceiling: horizon and scarab, Western Mountain, the sun god
TT339	19th Dyn (Ramesses II)	Huy iv & Pashedu xv	Texts
TT356	19th Dyn (Ramesses II)	Amenemwia i	Offering texts; tree goddess; family members; divinities, deceased and wife
TT360	19th Dyn (Ramesses II)	Qaha i	Anubis-jackal; mummy and Anubis; deceased; vaulted ceiling: deceased
TT3	19th Dyn (Ramesses II)	Pashedu x	Deceased and divinities; Abydos pilgrimage; deceased and other family members (pl. XXI)
TT5	19th Dyn (Ramesses II)	Neferabet i	Gods and deceased; family members and deceased adoring divinities
TT214	19th Dyn (Ramesses II)	Khawy ii	Guardians and personification of the West; deceased and Renutet and Harsiesi, Maat, Thoth & Hathor; son mourns mummy; vaulted ceiling: divinities and the Gate of the West
TT219	19th Dyn (Ramesses II)	Nebenmaat ii	Anubis jackal; son as priest censing and libating to parents; deceased and wife with gods and family member; Anubis and mummy on couch; offerings by deceased to divinities, offerings made by wife and son to gods; funeral procession to tomb; vaulted ceiling: gods and deceased
TT220	19th Dyn (Ramesses II)	Khaemteri i	Anubis-jackals; divinities; mummy on couch; funeral banquet
TT290	19th Dyn (Ramesses II)	Irynefer i	Inscription with titles, family members, Anubis-jackals, BoD, divinities, offering to divinities, Anubis tending mummy; vaulted ceiling: deceased kneels before a palm tree and drinks from pool, divinities, *ba* and shadow
TT216	19th Dyn (Sety II)	Neferhotep ii	Nephthys; Anubis-jackals; deceased and wife; adoration of Western emblems; cat slaying a serpent; gates and guardians with knives; vaulted ceiling: divinities
TT211	19th Dyn (Siptah)	Paneb i	Sokar's bark; deceased and family; mummy on couch; parents, wife and gods; vaulted ceiling: tree-goddess, divinities
TT359	20th Dyn (Ramesses IV)	Inherkhau ii	Deceased and wife; Book of Gates; gods
TT267	20th Dyn (Ramesses V)	Hay vii	Names and titles; deceased with family members; *sem*-priest and divinities
TT355	20th Dyn	Amenpahapi i	Deceased and wife adoring

Chapter 12 The Third Intermediate and Saite Periods

The decline in the monumentality of tombs after the New Kingdom was dramatic, reflecting the lack of central control that was a feature of much of the Third Intermediate Period. However, after four centuries of universally modest sepulchres, a revival saw the construction of some of the largest and most elaborate tombs ever built in Egypt, as well as others that marked the high-point in the long battle between tomb-builders and tomb-robbers.

21ST DYNASTY

Superstructures

A major motif of the new regime is the almost complete disappearance of monumental, decorated tomb-chapels from the archaeological record. A few Middle or New Kingdom chapels at Thebes received summary additions (e.g. TT68, 70, 117, 337 and 348), but no new chapels are certainly identifiable. Indeed, all of the identifiable high-status burials of the dynasty at Thebes (TT320; MMA60) were clearly designed without a superstructure. The reason for this is unclear, but at the same time funerary deposits were being reduced to simply the mummy and its coffins and suggest a major re-think, perhaps in part motivated by security considerations.

There are a handful of examples in other cemeteries, in particular in Cemetery D at Abydos, where a group of New Kingdom sepulchres was joined by the tomb of Pasebkhanut A, son of the High Priest of Amun, Menkheperre (D22).[358] It

was a mastaba, the chapel consisting of a main chamber, at the back of which is a small offering place, which once contained a fine stela showing the tomb-owner before Osiris, Isis and Horus. A number of contemporary tombs in the same area had similar plans.

Elsewhere, virtually nothing has been identified from the dynasty. It is assumed that the royal tombs at Tanis, located within the city temple precinct, had been surmounted by brick chapels, but any possible traces were swept away during excavation. Nevertheless, it is conjectured that they may have resembled those later built above the substructures of the tombs of the God's Wives of Amun at Medinet Habu (pp. 227–8), taking the form of miniature temples.[359]

Substructures

Royal Tombs: The tombs constructed for the kings of the 21st Dynasty at Tanis were wholly unlike those of their immediate predecessors in the Valley of the Kings in design. As had long been the case in the Delta, the tombs were built structures, sunk a few metres into the ground, not far above the water table.[360] The first examples (NRT-I and III) possessed granite burial chambers within a limestone structure that also contained an antechamber, approached

304 (*above*) Outer lintel from the 26th Dynasty Theban tomb of Pabasa (TT279), showing the elevation of the bark of the sun god, flanked by the God's Wives of Amun Nitokris I (left) and Shepenwepet II (right) and the deceased (twice).

by a shaft in a further room. Later examples were plainer, consisting only of limestone rooms.

The dominant decorative themes in these tombs are largely consistent with those of the Ramesside Period. The antechamber of NRT-III, built by Pasebkhanut (Psusennes) I, has, on the north and west walls, processions of genii, surmounting scenes of the king offering to Osiris and Isis. On the east, Pasebkhanut offers to Re-Harakhty, above which scene are to be found a series of demons. The tomb had separate granite burial chambers for the king and the queen (who was later evicted to make way for the (re?)burial of King Amenemopet), each having a mummiform figure of the deceased on their rear walls. A further room, which held the burial of the General Wendjebaendjed, has scenes of this favoured courtier doing homage to Osiris, Harakhty and Apis.

Private Tombs: No private tomb has been found in situ at Tanis, although re-used blocks discovered there attest to their adornment with the usual kinds of Ramesside mortuary scenes. Of the small number of monumental tombs of the dynasty that are known in Upper Egypt, one of the most important is the aforementioned tomb of Pasebkhanut A at Abydos (D22). Access to its substructure was via a brick-lined shaft, 6 m (20 ft) deep. Five chambers lay at the

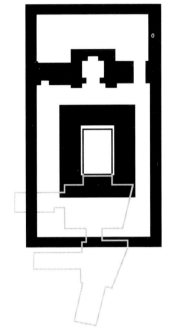

305 (*left*) Plan of the mastaba of Pasebkhanut A, son of the High Priest of Amun Menkheperre (Abydos D22: late 21st Dynasty).

306 (*below*) The main group of 21st/22nd Dynasty royal tombs at Tanis: from the left that of Amenemopet (NRT-IV); Pasebkhanut I (NRT-III); Osorkon II (NRT-I – probably built for Nesibanebdjedet I); unknown king (NRT-VI); Pimay (NRT-II). That of Shoshenq III (NRT-V) lies at a higher level a short distance to the left of the photograph: see ill. 307.

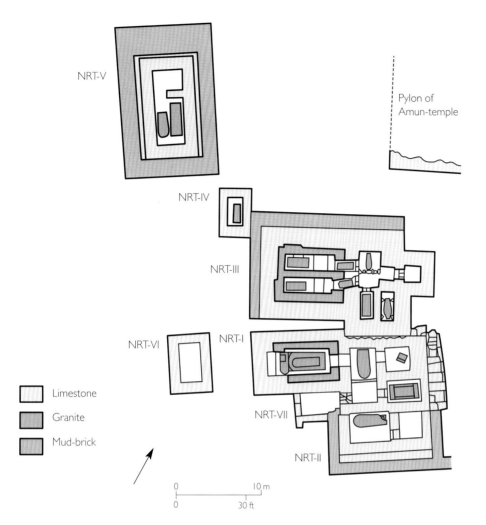

NRT-V

NRT-IV

NRT-III

NRT-VI   NRT-I

NRT-VII

NRT-II

Pylon of
Amun-temple

Limestone

Granite

Mud-brick

0   10 m

0   30 ft

307 (*left*) Plan of the royal
necropolis at Tanis:
NRT-I: Nesibanebjedet(? – 21st
Dynasty); usurped by Osorkon II
for himself, Prince Harnakhte C
and Takelot I; also used for burial
of Shoshenq V (? – all 22nd
Dynasty);
NRT-II: Pimay (22nd Dynasty);
NRT-III: Pasebkhanut I, Queen
Mutnodjmet B, Prince
Ankhefenmut C and General
Wendjebaendjed (21st
Dynasty); later also used for
Amenemopet, Siamun,
Pasebkhanut II (21st Dynasty)
and Shoshenq II (22nd Dynasty);
NRT-IV: Amenemopet; later
used for Siamun(?);
NRT-V: Shoshenq III and IV
(22nd Dynasty);
NRT-VI: Unknown;
NRT-VII: Extension to NRT-I,
mid-22nd Dynasty.

308 (*below*) Upper register
of the west wall of the
antechamber of the tomb of
Pasebkhanut I, with processions
of funerary deities (Tanis NRT-III:
21st Dynasty).

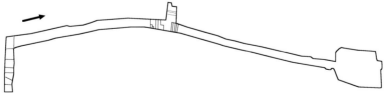

309 (*left*) Plan of the tomb of
Pinudjem II, south of Deir
el-Bahari, and later used as the
Royal Cache (TT320: 21st
Dynasty).

bottom, two of them stone-lined, but the tomb proved to be entirely robbed, save a few shabtis of the tomb-owner.[361]

At Thebes, the known 21st Dynasty burial places are generally usurped from earlier owners and equipped with little more than a nest of coffins.[362] The burial places involved include both the superstructures and substructures of these earlier sepulchres. This is common to all levels of society, including members of the quasi-royal high priestly family. One of the latter, Nauny, daughter of Pinudjem I, had her coffins and mummy placed in the outer corridors of the tomb of the 18th Dynasty queen, Meryetamun (TT358) at Deir el-Bahari, some years after the restoration of the latter's tomb during the reign of Nesibanebdjedet I (Smendes). Another three ladies, a sister and two nieces of Nauny, were placed in a tomb (MMA60) nearby, in which they were later joined by a number of other mummies. As the tomb filled up, previous occupants were removed to make room for new arrivals. The tomb, for once apparently purpose-built, took the form of a sloping passage, leading to a large shaft, with a stairway at the side, leading down to the burial chamber.[363]

The area of Deir el-Bahari seems to have been particularly popular during the 21st Dynasty, containing the two largest sepulchres of the dynasty. The earlier one is the only tomb of a High Priest to have been identified, belonging to Pinudjem II (TT320).[364] Lying 100 m (330 ft) south west of the temples of Deir el-Bahari, it seems likely that the sepulchre had been constructed on a much smaller scale during the early New Kingdom and then substantially extended for the interment of the high priest and his immediate family. The burial chamber seems initially to have held just the bodies of Pinudjem and his wives; they were later joined by his daughter and son-in-law and then (during the 22nd Dynasty reign of Shoshenq I) by some 40 royal or distinguished individuals of the New Kingdom. They were transferred there for security purposes from their own tombs via a number of other provisional resting places, making up the famous 'Royal Cache'.

Another communal burial seems to date to the very end of the dynasty, under the High Priest Pasebkhanut II. This is the Bab el-Gasus, close to the temple of Hatshepsut and adjacent to MMA60 and another near-contemporary tomb, MMA59. It contained 153 coffins or nests of coffins, together with various other items, such as shabti-boxes and wooden stelae. The burials range across much of the last half of the dynasty and seem to have been moved to the tomb

simultaneously, being placed close together in the chambers of the tomb and along its corridors.

Apart from the principal cluster of interments at Deir el-Bahari, smaller groups of 21st Dynasty burials are known from other parts of the Theban necropolis, generally intrusive within earlier tomb-complexes. Given the evidence of the Bab el-Gasus, it is possible that a number of other such deposits may have been cleared to be replaced by mass reinterments, in parallel with the reburials of the New Kingdom royal mummies which took place at roughly the same time.

22ND AND 23RD DYNASTIES

Superstructures

Early in the new dynasty, the lack of superstructures seen with Theban private tombs during the 21st Dynasty apparently continued. However, under Osorkon I, although burials continued to be made further west, such as in the New Kingdom tombs of Sheikh Abd el-Qurna,[365] the favoured centre of burial moved down from Deir el-Bahari to the locale of the Ramesseum. Small brick chapels, sometimes lined with sandstone slabs with painted decoration of a very similar type to that found in Ramesside tombs,[366] were built within the vaulted brick store-rooms of the temple (ills 273–4).[367] Similar mud-brick chapels were also built slightly further afield down into the 25th Dynasty. Of a fairly standardized form with a small pylon and a triple sanctuary arrangement, they lay along the edge of the desert, behind the New Kingdom royal mortuary temples.[368]

Elsewhere in Egypt, few tomb superstructures survive; those that do show that decoration was minimal, being generally restricted to a stela. One place which does provide some data is Abydos, where some tombs seem to have had mastabas – or even pyramids – above their tomb-shafts, forming the centre of a walled complex fronted by one or more pylons.

Substructures

Royal Tombs: There is a hiatus in the sequence of tombs known at Tanis during the early part of the 22nd Dynasty and there are indications that the royal necropolis may have shifted elsewhere (perhaps to Bubastis), but was abandoned in the face of flooding.[369] Osorkon II returned to Tanis, usurping what seems to have been the sepulchre of the 21st

310 (*above*) A number of 22nd Dynasty tombs were built within the brick store-chambers of the 19th Dynasty Ramesseum.

311 (*left*) Reliefs from the mortuary chapel of Nakhtefmut (Ram88) at the Ramesseum, including his daughter, Djedmutiusankh (Philadelphia E1824-6: 22nd Dynasty, reign of Osorkon I).

Dynasty founder, Nesibanebdjedet I (NRT-I: ill. 307). Partly rebuilt and decorated anew, it also held the body of Osorkon's father Takelot I.

The decoration of the tomb continued to employ the kind of motifs and compositions that had been found in royal tombs since the 18th Dynasty. The ceiling of the antechamber bore the celestial decans, its west wall showing the sun's journey across the sky, bracketed by a figure of the goddess Nut. On the south wall the dead king prepares to approach Osiris, while the remaining wall surfaces are occupied by episodes from the Book of the Dead, including the weighing of the heart: no longer is the king a god on earth gone to join his brothers in heaven, but one who must now submit to judgment like a mere mortal. Scenes showing the king in the Fields of Iaru underline the intruding mortal aspects of the king. Elsewhere in the tomb are more traditional royal scenes, including extracts from the Amduat, while in the burial chamber are scenes of the regeneration of the sun.

The Tanite tombs of Shoshenq III and Pimay (NRT-V and II) were new constructions of very simple form, reminiscent of late Predynastic tombs: a rectangular cavity, divided in two by a stub-wall. NRT-II is undecorated, but NRT-V was adorned with elements largely derived from the Amduat, supplemented by various less-usual scenes and vignettes from the Book of the Dead.

During the reign of Osorkon II, a separate royal line established itself at Thebes, beginning with the former High Priest of Amun, Harsiese. His tomb lies within the temple enclosure at Medinet Habu, a sandstone structure probably once surmounted by a chapel (MH1).[370] A stairway led down to a burial chamber, in the centre of which the priest-king had been laid to rest in the trough of the granite coffin made for Ramesses II's younger sister, Henutmire, but equipped with a new lid. Two niches in the wall on each side of the coffin held canopic jars. No other tomb of a Theban 23rd Dynasty king has been identified, but that of Osorkon III may be mentioned in 26th and 27th Dynasty papyri, whose implication is that it may also have lain at Medinet Habu.[371]

In the latter part of the Third Intermediate Period, a number of petty kingdoms arose to join those already in place at Tanis and Thebes. One was at Leontopolis (Tell Moqdam), where a queen named Kama(ma) was buried in a stone-built tomb, intact in 1921, but with its contents largely destroyed by water.[372]

Private Tombs: The most impressive private tombs of the 22nd Dynasty are those of the High Priests of Ptah at Memphis, in form much like the royal tombs of Tanis, being stone structures sunk in the temple court.[373] That of Shoshenq D (son of Osorkon II) comprised a single room, built of re-used blocks and decorated both on its façade and on its interior. The west wall was taken up by extracts from the Book of the Dead, the others by various deities and more parts of the Book of the Dead.

Another High Priest, this time of Amun at Thebes, had a tomb at Abydos, in cemetery G. Here, Iuput (Shoshenq I's son) had a granite burial chamber, decorated with scenes from the Book of Amduat, approached by a long corridor.[374] The whole structure had been built in a long narrow pit.

At Thebes, burials of officials continued to be made in older tombs throughout the period. In many cases this happened repeatedly, with one generation cleared out to make way for a new one.[375]

312 (*above*) The burial chamber of Shoshenq III at Tanis (NRT-V) was decorated with extracts from the books of the underworld (22nd Dynasty).

313 (*below*) The tomb of the priest-king Harsiese at Medinet Habu, built within the temple-enclosure there. The niches in the lateral walls were intended for the canopic jars. A chapel was presumably built above along the line of the later ones of the God's Wives of Amun (see below, ills 317–18).

A popular priestly venue for burial during the latter part of the Third Intermediate Period was the mortuary temple of Hatshepsut at Deir el-Bahari.[376] One of the few such burials to be properly recorded comprised a pit 4 m (12 feet) deep cut in the floor of the Hathor shrine of the temple, which led to a chamber; the room was no more than 4 m (12 feet) or so square, but contained three wooden sarcophagi, which had clearly been assembled in situ.[377]

25TH AND 26TH DYNASTIES

Superstructures

Royal Tombs:[378] The increasing fragmentation of the country culminated in the invasion of the King of Kush (Nubia), Piye, founder of the 25th Dynasty. Fully Egyptianized, the Kushite ruling family had formerly been buried under tumuli and mastabas, but had now adopted the pyramid shape for their tombs, built in their homeland, at El-Kurru

314 (*above*) Burial chamber of the High Priest of Ptah, Shoshenq D, from Memphis (CM JE88131: 22nd Dynasty, reign of Osorkon II).

315 (*left*) The granite coffin-lid of Harsiese, from his tomb at Medinet Habu (CM JE59896). Although the lid had been made for him, the trough was usurped from Ramesses II's sister, Henutmire (19th/23rd Dynasty).

and Nuri. These pyramids were small and very steeply angled, with a chapel on the east side, atop the stairway leading to the substructure. The largest of these was that of Taharqa, the penultimate Nubian ruler of Egypt, constructed at Nuri, a little way downstream from El-Kurru (Nu1). It was some 52 m (170 ft) square, as compared to the 7.6 m (25 ft) of Piye's monument.

The last Kushite to rule Egypt was Tanutamun, whose rule in Egypt was ended by an Assyrian invasion. However, his successors continued to rule in what is the modern Sudan for centuries more. Pyramids also continued in use, although their contents and ornamentation show a steady shift towards a distinctly Kushite interpretation of the ancient motifs. It was in the Sudan, at Meroë, that the last Nilotic pyramid was built, around AD 350, 3,000 years and 1,600 km (1,000 miles) from the first such monument at Saqqara.

By the 25th Dynasty, the premier role at Thebes had been assumed by the God's Wife of Amun, usually the eldest daughter of the king. Their tombs were built at Medinet Habu, within the old temenos of Ramesses III, which had become an important place of burial during the 23rd Dynasty (ills 317–18). The best-preserved example, built by Shepenwepet II for Amenirdis I, is a stone-built structure fronted by a pylon. This gives access to a four-pillared hall and then to a sanctuary, surrounded by a corridor. Its decoration featured Pyramid Texts, the Opening-of-the-Mouth texts and ceremony, as well as images of the tomb-owner offering to different gods, purifying temples, making offerings and being granted life by the various divinities. As in the Old Kingdom, the texts are situated for the convenience of the deceased, rather than in a sequence that makes sense to the visitor.

The royal cemetery of the 26th Dynasty lay at its city of origin, Sais. Following the practice of the Tanites, these kings' tombs lay within the enclosure of the local temple of the goddess Neith, their probable site now marked by a huge water-filled pit.[379] The only record of them survives in the writings of Herodotus, who visited Sais *c.* 450 BC; he writes that Wahibre, fourth king of this dynasty was:

> buried in the family tomb in the temple of Athena [Neith], nearest to the shrine, on the left-hand as one goes in. The people of Sais buried all the kings who came from the province inside this area. The tomb of Amasis [Ahmose II] is also in the temple court, although further from the shrine than that of Apries [Wahibre] and his ancestors. It is a great cloistered building of stone, decorated with pillars carved in the imitation of palm trees and other costly adornments. Within the cloister is a chamber with double doors and behind the doors stands the sepulchre.
>
> HERODOTUS, *HISTORIES*, BOOK II: §169.

316 The pyramid of Taharqa at Nuri (Nu I: 25th Dynasty).

317 (above) The tombs of the God's Wives of Amun at Medinet Habu were surmounted by small chapels of a kind that may have been also found at sites such as Tanis (25th–26th Dynasty).

318 (below) Plans of the mortuary chapels of the God's Wives of Amun at Medinet Habu. From left to right: Shepenwepet I (with section of burial chamber: MH17); Amenirdis I; Shepenwepet II (central shrine, flanked by Nitokris I and Mehytenweskhet C).

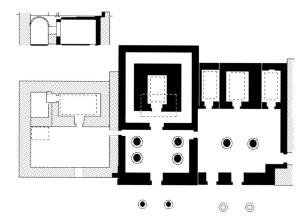

This implies that the earliest Saite kings were buried in a single tomb – or perhaps that each had a separate tomb below a single superstructure. The description of Ahmose II's monument seems to conjure up a standard Egyptian peripteral shrine, with a central cult-room surrounded by a colonnade. Presumably, the burial chamber was sunk in the ground beneath – suggesting an affinity with the tombs of the God's Wives of Amun at Medinet Habu.

Private Tombs:[380] The latter part of the 25th Dynasty saw a sudden revival in monumental tombs. The most outstanding of these lie on the Asasif at Thebes, the majority belonging to officials connected with the God's Wife of Amun, the key figure at Thebes during the 25th and 26th Dynasties.[381] The tombs combine both brick-built and rock-cut elements, the former comprising principally a massive niched enclosure wall and pylons fronting both the main axis and the stairways that usually led down at right angles. It has been suggested that their location, close to the ancient tombs and temples at Deir el-Bahari, was chosen to link the sepulchres explicitly

319 View of the Asasif, showing the location of the principal tombs.

with the remote past, further reinforced by the decoration that in some cases directly copied ancient prototypes.

The designs of the rock-cut chapels that form the kernel of these tombs seem to owe something to the royal mortuary temples of the New Kingdom, as well as the 'temple-tombs' of the nobility at Saqqara and the small brick chapels of the middle part of the Third Intermediate Period. While their plans all differ in detail, they generally centre on an open courtyard, frequently surrounded by a colonnade. Beyond this are one or two hypostyle halls, with subsidiary chambers, giving access to the offering place and the entrance to the substructure. The innermost sanctuary varies in form, with either a false-door or statues of the deceased. In the earliest tombs of the type, dating to the latter part of the 25th Dynasty (e.g. TT223 and 391), the arrangement of the chambers along a single axis is fairly rigorously maintained; later, more changes of direction are to be seen.

The decoration of these monuments employed scenes and texts from the entire span of Egyptian history. This very much ties in with the archaism which is the hallmark of the art and to some extent, the culture, of the 26th Dynasty. The rise of archaism in art, harking back to the golden ages of Egyptian culture, was linked with an increase in tomb decoration. Artists relied heavily for their inspiration on scenes from Old and New Kingdom tombs that were slightly altered in their new format.

Motifs that included scenes of fishing and fowling, butchery, apiculture, offering and sculpting are arranged side by side with funerary texts of every type. Even the textile designs found on the ceilings of earlier sepulchres are reproduced in the Theban tombs of this era. In a delightful adaptation of the scene showing the overseeing of royal statuary, a striding statue of the God's Wife of Amun, whom many of the Asasif tomb-owners served, is substituted for

320 (*above*) The pylon of the tomb of Mentuemhat at Thebes (TT34: 25th Dynasty).

321 (*below*) The tomb of Shoshenq on the Asasif (TT27), dating to the end of the 26th Dynasty; its exterior walls are panelled, recalling structures of the Early Dynastic Period.

322 (*opposite*) TT34, showing the West Portico, leading into the second courtyard and the inner part of the tomb (25th Dynasty).

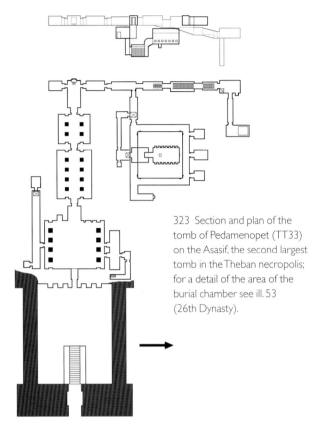

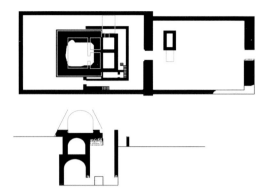

323 Section and plan of the tomb of Pedamenopet (TT33) on the Asasif, the second largest tomb in the Theban necropolis; for a detail of the area of the burial chamber see ill. 53 (26th Dynasty).

324 Plan and section of the tomb-chapel of the Vizier Nespamedu at Abydos (D57: 25th Dynasty, reign of Taharqa).

that of the king. This is appropriate enough as hers was the royal presence reigning over Thebes at the time.

Although not on the same scale as the sepulchres on the Asasif, the resumption of the construction of large tomb-chapels is to be found elsewhere. In cemetery D at Abydos are the tombs of two Viziers.[382] That of Nespamedu, datable to the reign of Taharqa, comprised two large brick-built courts, each fronted by a pylon, the whole structure standing some 3 m (10 ft) high and measuring 36 m (118 ft) from east to west (D57). The chapel formerly had a domed roof (a fairly common arrangement at the site) and, to judge by the angled exterior wall, may once have been enclosed inside a pyramid. Nakht's D15 was of very similar size and layout, albeit shifted around so that its main axis ran from north to south.

At Saqqara, another Vizier, Bakenrenef (who served Psametik I), built a sepulchre that rivalled the size and elaboration of those on the Asasif. The tomb (LS24)[383] lies on the escarpment at the very eastern edge of the Saqqara plateau and has a built outer portion giving access to a rock-cut inner element. The initial vestibule of the latter leads to a four-pillared hall, followed by one with six pillars. Beyond the latter are two main rooms, surrounded by a corridor and culminating in a false-door.

Tombs combining rock-cut and built elements are also to be found at Giza, behind the Great Sphinx. Their brick outer parts are badly destroyed, as are the inner elements, although reliefs and columns were seen in 1820/1, allowing two to be attributed to General Pedubast and one Ptahirdis.[384] A wholly built tomb of the same period at Giza is that of Tjeri, with a massive stone superstructure containing a longitudinal hall leading to a cruciform arrangement of rooms, all extensively decorated.[385] The same kind of decorative approach used at Thebes is seen in such tombs as those of Bakenrenef and that of Tjeri, with daily life scenes appearing in the courtyard and religious texts within the chapel proper.

Concentrated around and near a number of Old Kingdom pyramid complexes are a series of great shaft tombs with sand-based protective devices (pp. 286–9). In contrast to the tombs just discussed, they seem generally to have had very simple superstructures. At the tomb of Iufaa, this comprised a wall around the perimeter of the shaft. A huge stela had been embedded in a deep and wide niche in the centre of the eastern façade of its brick enclosure. Fragments of limestone in front of the niches in the other three sides suggest that these too had stelae. However, Iufaa's tomb also had a set of rooms on the surface directly to the east of the shaft, which exhibit a plan highly reminiscent of the tombs at Thebes and the tomb of Bakenrenef.[386] The

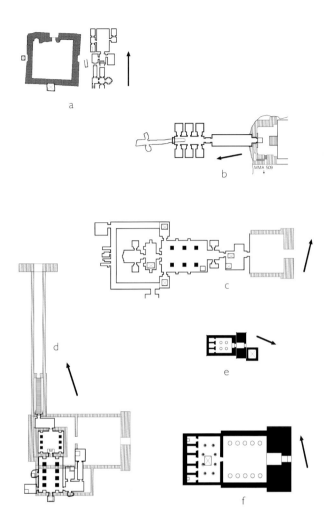

a

b

MMA 509

c

d

e

f

325 (*above*) View of the surviving portion of the superstructure of the tomb of Iufaa at Abu Sir (early 27th Dynasty).

326 (*left*) Plans of tomb superstructures of the Saite and Late Periods: a. Iufaa (Abu Sir: 27th Dynasty); b. Nespaqashuti (TT312: early 26th Dynasty); c. Bakenrenef (Saqqara LS24: early 26th Dynasty); d. Pabasa (TT279: early 26th Dynasty); e. Wennefer (Saqqara: late 30th Dynasty); f. Nesidjehuty (Saqqara QS412: early 26th Dynasty).

327 (*below*) View of the rock-cut tomb-chapel LG81 at Giza; the name of the owner is now lost.

328 The tomb of Udjahorresnet at Abu Sir, showing the simple stone wall that surrounded the mouth of his shaft (early 27th Dynasty).

steps at the far end of the sepulchral chamber, or a pair of stairways just outside the doorway of the antechamber. The usual bed-bench lay in the centre of the burial chamber.

Later Kushite monarchs, beginning with Tanutamun, standardized on the simpler plan introduced by Shabaka, with a burial chamber adorned with paintings.[388] The vignettes and texts essentially follow the age-old association of royal burials with solar matters, the entrance doorway being surmounted by painted apes adoring the sun god in his bark, a similar motif also appearing on the rear wall.

Private Tombs: While a number of the great tombs of the Asasif have simple shaft-substructures (e.g. TT196 and TT279), the substructure often begins with a corridor leading from the right-hand side of the main offering place to a series of descending corridors and stairways. A notable point is the way in which the substructure is 'layered', with an interest in the relative vertical placement of elements one above the other. In Pedamenopet's TT33, the burial chamber is approached from below, its floor lying some distance above the base of the access shaft – clearly a security feature (ills 53, 323).

These elaborate substructures have equally elaborate decorations.[389] In the tomb of Mentuemhat (TT34), the descending passages and vestibules were fairly simply decorated, mainly with texts, including a stela at the foot of one stairway, plus a figure of the deceased with Anubis and Maat. They also included a full-face engaged statue of Osiris overlooking the shaft that led from the antechamber to the burial chamber, the latter adorned with an astronomical ceiling reminiscent of those found in royal contexts of the Ramesside Period.

Far more elaborate, however, is the decoration of the substructure of TT33.[390] Here, the adornment of the long series of descending galleries starts with offerings, offering-bringers and butchers, before moving on to divinities and extracts from the Book of the Dead. Above the burial chamber, the Amduat features heavily, while the rock lying above the roof of the burial chamber, isolated like an ambulatory, has protective goddesses at its corners like a late-18th Dynasty royal sarcophagus (see pp. 56–7). The immediate approach to the burial chamber bears sections from the Book of Caverns, while the sepulchral chamber itself has the Amduat on its walls and an astronomical ceiling. Altogether the tomb is a wonderful pastiche of the

lower parts of the rooms were cut out of the bedrock, some at least being equipped with vaulted roofs; the upper parts of the walls were free-standing. These appear to have been undecorated. Although Iufaa's tomb seems to be one of the latest of its kind, it is possible that others may have had similar superstructures which are now wholly lost. A fragment of an offering scene was found at the tomb of Udjahorresnet, suggesting that it might have come from some form of superstructure.

Substructures

Royal Tombs:[387] The pyramids of the 25th Dynasty surmounted relatively simple substructures, that of Piye (Ku17) being a corbel-roofed room, approached by a stairway. Instead of a sarcophagus, a rock-cut bench lay in the middle of the burial chamber, with a socket in each corner, to receive the legs of a bed. Interment on a bier has been characterized as a typical feature of Nubian burials since Kerman (Second Intermediate Period) times.

Shabaka's tomb displays a fully rock-cut substructure, with a few traces of paintings in its burial chamber, but his successor Shabataka's reverts to corbelled roofing. However, Taharqa's pyramid has the most elaborate substructure of any Kushite royal tomb. A conventional stairway, over which a mortuary chapel may have been built, led into a small antechamber, which in turn gave access to a six-pillared burial chamber, the aisles of which were vaulted. A curious corridor completely surrounded the subterranean rooms, at a slightly higher level, accessible via a flight of

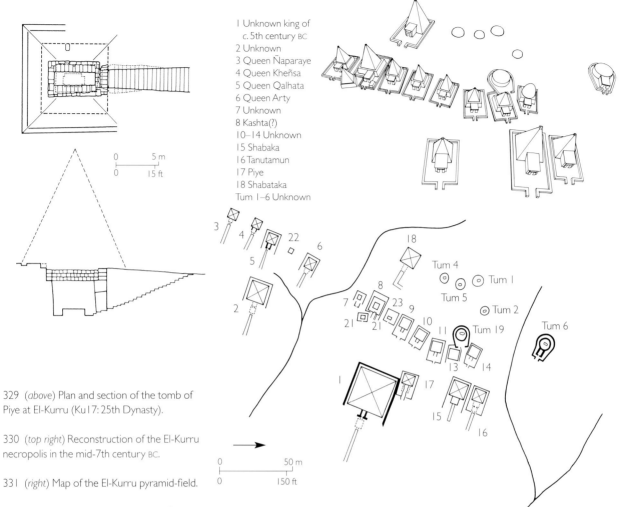

1 Unknown king of
  c. 5th century BC
2 Unknown
3 Queen Ñaparaye
4 Queen Kheñsa
5 Queen Qalhata
6 Queen Arty
7 Unknown
8 Kashta(?)
10–14 Unknown
15 Shabaka
16 Tanutamun
17 Piye
18 Shabataka
Tum 1–6 Unknown

0   5 m
0   15 ft

0   50 m
0   150 ft

329 (above) Plan and section of the tomb of
Piye at El-Kurru (Ku17: 25th Dynasty).

330 (top right) Reconstruction of the El-Kurru
necropolis in the mid-7th century BC.

331 (right) Map of the El-Kurru pyramid-field.

332 (below) Plan of the substructure of
Mentuemhat's tomb, culminating in a niched
burial chamber (TT34: 25th Dynasty).

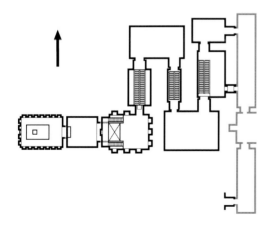

imagery of a New Kingdom royal tomb's decoration, which
is consistent with its vast scale.

Directly under the mortuary chapels of the God's Wives
of Amun at Medinet Habu lay the chambers that held the
ladies' sarcophagi, in all cases but that of Amenirdis I
equipped with a vaulted roof. Shepenwepet I's tomb (MH17:
ill. 318) may have had an entrance passage from the north
(destroyed by a later tomb), but the others seem to have
been accessed directly from above. The chambers were only
large enough to hold a sarcophagus; a few traces of text
could be seen in that of Mehytenweskhet C, wife of
Psametik I and mother of Nitokris I, under the chapel she
shared with her daughter.[391]

At Abydos, the underground apartments of the tomb
of Nespamedu (D57: ill. 324)[392] comprised a main shaft,
containing two arched, built, chambers, one above the other

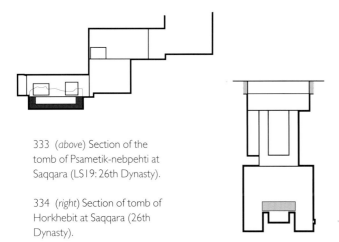

333 (above) Section of the tomb of Psametik-nebpehti at Saqqara (LS19: 26th Dynasty).

334 (right) Section of tomb of Horkhebit at Saqqara (26th Dynasty).

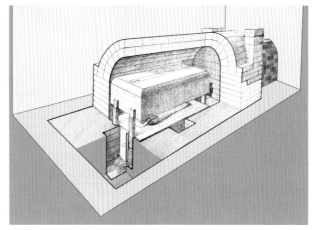

335 Isometric section of the burial chamber of an example of the most developed form of a 26th Dynasty shaft tomb at Saqqara, showing the 'sandraulic' sarcophagus-closing mechanism.

and a smaller one alongside, with a rock-cut room. Access to the chambers seems to have been via an adjacent stairway.

Moving to the north, a number of different forms of substructure are to be found at Saqqara, all generally approached by shafts. A simple set of rooms formed the burial chambers of Bakenrenef's LS24, contrasting with its elaborate superstructure (pp. 283–4). Slightly more elaborate are the burial apartments of Psametik-nebpehti (LS19) and Irahor (LS23); although comprising only an antechamber and a burial chamber, the latter had a pair of niches in the end wall and also two niches on each side-wall. These four locations were intended for canopic jars; this shift of canopics from the foot of the body to its flanks is to be seen in other tombs of the Saite Period, although often with only a single, wide, niche on each side, designed to hold a half-size canopic box with two jars.

A very distinctive kind of tomb-substructure appears in the Memphite necropolis during this era. The earliest known example lies half-way between the edge of the escarpment and the Step Pyramid enclosure and belonged to Horkhebit.[393] Any superstructure that might have existed is lost, but the substructure comprised a very large chamber (8.1 x 9.55 x 8.6 m or 27 x 31 x 28 ft) at the bottom of a deep shaft, with approximately half the area of the chamber, but concentric with it. After the body had been placed in the sarcophagus in the centre of the chamber, the whole tomb was filled with sand, the labour of removing which led to its surviving intact until 1902.

Such use of sand led to the development of a more elaborate version of the design that represents perhaps the most sophisticated of all Egyptian attempts to safeguard a

high-status body from robbers. The kernel of such a tomb was an arched-roofed stone-built burial chamber, built at the bottom of a deep, wide shaft. This contained a simple rectangular stone sarcophagus, flanked by niches intended for canopic jars.

These shaft tombs were designed to be entirely filled with sand after the burial. Temporarily closed holes in the chamber roof were opened after the funeral to allow sand in from the main shaft to engulf the sarcophagus. The burial party retreated through an arched brick passage that joined the burial chamber to a rock-cut access tunnel and shaft beyond the wall of the main shaft. This arch was pulled down during the exit, sand pouring into the passage.

The net result was that access to the burial was impossible, unless almost every grain of sand had been removed from the tomb first – running into hundreds of cubic metres. In the most elaborate examples the sarcophagus lid was lowered into place by props resting on sand-filled cavities. When released from below, the escaping sand allowed the lid to come down on the trough. This contained an anthropoid cavity, in which lay a large stone anthropoid coffin, which in turn held the mummy, with or without an inner wooden case.

The best-known examples of such tombs are found in two clusters at Saqqara, one close to the pyramid of Unas, the other in the ruins of the mortuary temple of the 5th Dynasty king Userkaf. The choice of sites directly adjacent

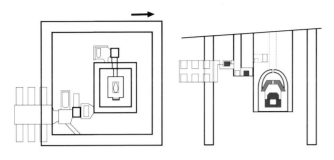

336 & 337 LG 84, the tomb of Pakap at Giza, employed the same sand protection as the tombs at Saqqara, plus a sand-filled protective trench around the perimeter (the latter also found at the tomb of Udjahorrsnet at Abu Sir). Generally known as 'Campbell's Tomb', an additional burial chamber was cut in the side of the entrance shaft under Darius I for the Overseer of the Treasury Ptahhotep. A new, secondary, entrance shaft was cut at around the same time, and gave access to a group of chambers occupied by at least three further burials, including that of the Priest Nesisut. Still later, in Graeco-Roman times, a large chamber with twelve loculi was added to this complex (originally late 26th Dynasty).

338 This view of LG 84 shows the main shaft, the secondary entrance shaft, and one part of the surrounding trench.

to Old Kingdom monuments can hardly have been fortuitous and may be linked with the investigations and copying of ancient monuments well attested during the Saite Period (see p. 56). Another group lie to the southwest of the 5th Dynasty pyramids at Abu Sir, that of Iufaa proving to be both the largest of the type thus far known and to be intact.[394]

While the sand-filled shafts greatly enhanced security, certain tombs added to the effect by arranging a set of concentric sand-filled trenches around their perimeter, penetrating to a level below the bottom of the main shaft. These made it much more difficult to bypass the sand filling of the shaft by tunnelling down outside the perimeter and coming up inside the burial chamber. At least one such tomb lies at Abu Sir and belongs to Udjahorresnet, who held high office under the last kings of the 26th Dynasty and the Persian invaders of the 27th Dynasty.[395]

At Giza is another example with just this kind of additional protection, the so-called 'Campbell's Tomb' (LG84).[396] On the other hand, a simpler shaft tomb of the period there had a shaft only 3 m (10 ft) square.[397] The deepest of the series of chambers of this tomb, G7757A, at 12.5 m (40 ft) depth, was that of the General Kheperre. It was lined with cemented blocks, with the sarcophagus trough sunk in the floor.

A major cemetery lay in the area around the temple of Re at Heliopolis.[398] The tombs here were primarily vaulted stone structures, sunk in the ground surface. These could include multiple chambers, often each containing an interment. Like the other decorated tombs in the Memphite necropolis, they drew their decorative inspiration from the Old Kingdom, being inscribed primarily with the Pyramid Texts, plus additional verses taken from the other Books of the Underworld. The same approach is seen in the shaft tombs, their burial chambers being dominated by the Pyramid Texts, together with extensive offering lists.[399] The Book of the Dead is also prominent in other such contemporary tombs as LS23.

A wholly different decorative approach is to be seen in the oases, especially in Bahariya (Sheikh Sobi). Here, a series of tombs have pillared chambers approached by shafts, their rooms extensively painted with scenes of the gods, the funerary procession, mummification, the judgment of the dead and other suitable underworld scenes.[400] Amongst the most impressive are those of Djedamuniufankh (reign of Ahmose II), his son Baennentiu (pl. XXVII) and his contemporary, the Governor Djedkhonsufankh. The latter had painted reliefs cut into the plaster of walls of the vaulted antechamber while the burial chamber, approached by a shaft from the antechamber, was adorned with divine figures in yellow.

Chapter 13   The Late and Graeco-Roman Periods

THE LATE PERIOD

The early years of the Late Period were occupied by the 27th
Dynasty, during which Egypt was but a province of the
Persian empire. A few of the shaft tombs at Saqqara and Abu
Sir date to the first part of the dynasty, but all seem to have
been begun in 26th Dynasty times and there are effectively
no tombs which have been unequivocally dated to the years
of Persian rule. The same is true of the following native 28th
and 29th Dynasties, although a large amount of material has
been attributed to the 30th Dynasty.[401] This 'gap' is certainly
illusory, the problem being the lack of clear criteria to
distinguish between tombs constructed in the late 26th and
early 30th Dynasties and those constructed during the
intervening decades.

Superstructures

The only unequivocal trace of a 27th Dynasty funerary
chapel is a stela from Saqqara showing the owner in Persian

339 (*above*) A scene in Greek style in the tomb of Petosiris at Tuna
el-Gebel (early Dynasty of Macedon).

340 (*right*) Stela from a tomb of a certain Djedherbes, son of Artam,
with an interesting compound of Egyptian and Persian styles. The
name of the owner's father is clearly Persian. This piece is one of the
few unequivocal funerary monuments of the Persian domination of
the 27th Dynasty; it was found in a secondary deposit in the area of
the Gisr el-Mudir at Saqqara (CM JE98807).

341 Relief from the tomb of Neferseshempsamtik at Memphis/Kom el-Fakhry (CM JE10978: 30th Dynasty).

dress; unfortunately it was found in a re-used context.[402] However, a major group of later Late Period tombs is in Cemetery G at Abydos-Central.[403] One of the earliest of the group had a large brick courtyard, one part of which was columned and roofed (G57).[404] Another type of tomb here has its mastaba built integrally with the brick-built substructure (see below).[405]

In the Memphite necropolis, tombs of the 29th/30th Dynasties are to be found in a number of locations at Saqqara,[406] in particular along the avenue to the Serapeum, a major focus for local activity in Late times and on into the Ptolemaic Period. Superstructures of brick and stone faced the Serapeum Way, a stone example being that of Wennefer, which consisted of a pyloned vestibule with a four-pillared hall, at the back of which were three niches (ill. 326e). The entrance to the substructure lay in front of the pylon, just to the left.

Another burial of the 30th Dynasty provides interesting light on the widespread re-use of tombs during the Third Intermediate and Late Periods. Tjaisetenimu, Secretary of Nakhtnebef (Nectanebo I), took over the Memphite sepulchre of Ahmose-sineith, who had served under Ahmose II. The doorjambs of the tomb preserve a text in which the usurper claims his action to have been a favour to the former owner and that the latter would act as an intermediary in transferring divine goodwill to Tjaisetenimu.[407]

Only one Late Period royal tomb has been found, that of Naefarud I at Mendes in the Delta. The whole tomb had been devastated (see below), but there is a suggestion that it might have been topped by a mastaba. On the other hand, the superstructure may have resembled those reported by Herodotus to have stood above the earlier royal tombs at Sais, or else those over the sepulchres of the God's Wives at Medinet Habu.

342 (*above*) Mendes/Tell el-Ruba, showing the position of the tomb of Nefarud I, just inside the enclosure wall of the temple of Banebdjedet, with the giant granite naos of the temple sanctuary in the distance (29th Dynasty).

343 (*below*) The sarcophagus of the pharaoh Nakhthorheb (Nectanebo II), the only trace of his tomb (from Alexandria; BM EA10: 30th Dynasty).

Substructures

Royal Tombs:[408] Following the departure of the Persians in 404 BC, three native dynasties ruled in succession, from Sais, Mendes and Sebennytos, which cities thus became royal necropoleis in the time-honoured manner. The only excavated example comprised a large limestone sarcophagus, together with fragments of the walls of the chamber that had once surrounded it; these bore funerary texts for Naefarud I, founder of the 29th Dynasty.

Only the sarcophagi (and a few shabtis) survive from two 30th Dynasty royal tombs, wholly divorced from their original locations. Belonging to Nakhtnebef and Nakhthorheb (Nectanebo I and II), first and last kings of the 30th Dynasty, the sarcophagi found their ways to Cairo and Alexandria respectively – both sites devoid of contemporary pharaonic remains. That of Nakhtnebef was recovered in fragments from various modern buildings, while the other sarcophagus came from Alexandria's Attarin Mosque, where it had been used as a ritual bath. It was never occupied by its royal owner, who fled to Kush before another Persian invasion. It has been generally assumed that the kings' tombs had been built at their natal town, Sebennytos (Sammanud), although it is not impossible that they might have lain elsewhere, for example Saqqara, where Nakhtnebef, in particular, built extensively.[409]

Private Tombs: During the Late Period there was a move towards tombs designed for multiple burials, with large chambers flanked with deep niches intended to hold stone sarcophagi. In addition to new-builds, Saite tombs were extended along such lines in later times. LG84 (ills 336–8) is a good example, where a chamber was cut high up in the entrance shaft in early Persian times, while still later, in Graeco-Roman times, this secondary complex was extended by the addition of a large room with two levels of loculi, to accommodate 12 interments. In G7757A (cf. above, p. 287), later burials were placed in chambers further up the tomb's shaft, the latest being of Roman date;[410] in Bakenrenef's LS24, two large hypogaea were cut underneath for Pedineith, Vizier early in the 30th Dynasty.[411]

A fascinating tomb in this genre is the so-called 'Osiris Shaft', near the causeway of Khafre at Giza.[412] Two successive shafts lead down to a chamber with six niches, two of which held a sarcophagus. One of the empty niches contains a shaft in its floor that descends to a level about 25 m (80 ft)

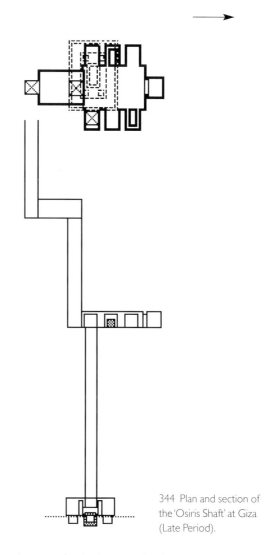

344 Plan and section of the 'Osiris Shaft' at Giza (Late Period).

underground, which is completely flooded by infiltrating water. Drained and cleared in 1998, the chamber at the bottom revealed a trench and four pillars, surrounding a large granite sarcophagus with the lid thrown off. This appears to have been arranged so that it was surrounded by water infiltrating from the ground, reminiscent of the Osirion of Sety I. Indeed, Zahi Hawass suggests that this curious chamber was a symbolic tomb for the god Osiris. The tomb is datable to Saite/Late Period times and it was at this very time that Herodotus reported that Khufu was buried under the Great Pyramid on an island surrounded by water: could this tomb be what Herodotus' informant had in mind?

The predilection for multiple family interments is also seen in Abydos G57.[413] A shaft behind the superstructure led to a chamber with no fewer than five sarcophagi, belonging to one Irtuharerau and his family. Another type of tomb in Cemetery G is one with one or more vaulted brick chambers, built integrally with the mastaba superstructure.[414] These sepulchres were intended to be family burial places, with individual chambers often having multiple interments. G50, found intact, had seven occupants, distributed over two chambers, the family of one Djeho.

More limited numbers of burials are also to be found in tombs of the 29th/30th Dynasties at Saqqara.[415] That of Wereshnefer had a simple substructure, with the burial chamber lying directly south of the 2-m (6-ft) square shaft, containing three sarcophagi.

In contrast, other Saqqara tombs had more extensive substructures housing a whole series of burials. One that lay somewhere on the Serapeum Way and at least part of whose contents dated to the reign of Nakhthorheb, held the sarcophagi of no fewer than 16 people, including Tjaiharpata, Djehor (a dwarf), Peftjaukhonsu and Isetirdis. Another, near the pyramid of Unas, belonged to the family of one Kanefer, with three chambers and seven interments; three more lay in the adjoining sepulchre of Inemhes. Both tombs were reached by shafts, the latter taking the form of a large chamber with four loculi.

As at other periods, the preservation of tombs in the Delta is generally poor and in most cases substructures continue to be brick, or sometimes stone, compartments sunk just below the surface. An extremely elaborate example

at Athribis comprises a complex of multiple compartments, apparently constructed in more than one phase.[416] The tomb was built some way above the modern ground level, a number of the rooms containing stone sarcophagi, as well as simpler interments.

THE GRAECO-ROMAN PERIOD

The independent Egyptian monarchy was brought to an end with renewed Persian occupation in 342 BC. The country was then absorbed into the empire of Alexander (III) the Great ten years later, ultimately becoming the kingdom of the Macedonian general, Ptolemy (I) in 310, after the murder of Alexander IV. Finally, the Ptolemaic state collapsed before the power of Rome, Egypt becoming a Roman province after Cleopatra VII's death in 30 BC. This foreign rulership had little immediate effect on Egyptian funerary practices, although as time went by alien elements began to be absorbed. However, in parallel, the arriving Hellenic settlers brought with them their own traditions of funerary monuments and traditions, which bore little or no relation

346 Alexandrine cinerary urn (GRM 16152).

345 This tomb at Saqqara contained the burials of two men named Psametik and, probably intrusively, the 30th Dynasty Queen Khedebneithirbinet II.

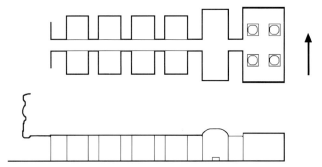

to time-hallowed pharaonic concepts. It is worth remembering that for many Hellenes and Romans the principal funerary rites involved cremation or urn burials. In Rome, laws forbade cemeteries within a city's walls and often burials were to be found lining approach-roads – one of the most famous of such necropoleis being the Appian Way. Walled cemetery enclosures are also to be seen throughout the northern provinces including Britain. Large cemeteries of cremations in urns emerged during the 1st century BC, beginning in northern Spain and spreading to Gaul and then towards Britain and the Danube provinces. In the 2nd century cremation was appearing in North Africa as well, including Alexandria, where a cinerary urn might be placed in a loculus, rather than the corpse. This rite was clearly not adopted by those who favoured 'Egyptian'-style interment, burning of the corpse being anathema to Egyptian mortuary belief. From about AD 60 inhumation was restricted to the Aegean and Near East.

The new Graeco-Roman cities in Egypt, however, often developed funerary beliefs that merged the different traditions. Thus, the tombs from this era show an interesting fusion of both Classical and Egyptian architectural and decorative elements. The style of monuments, with their decorative motifs derived from Egyptian practices and beliefs, were ultimately exported to other parts of the empire, with cemeteries aping those of Alexandria spreading to Britain and Gaul.[417]

TOMBS IN THE EGYPTIAN TRADITION.

Superstructures

It is often difficult to distinguish early Ptolemaic monuments from those of the 30th Dynasty. However, one tomb that can certainly be dated to the very dawn of Greek rule is that of Petosiris at Tuna el-Gebel.[418] The tomb follows the New Kingdom practice of making the chapel a

347 Part of the Tuna el-Gebel necropolis, with tombs ranging in date from Petosiris (right: Dynasty of Macedon) to the Roman Period.

348 The tomb of Petosiris at Tuna el-Gebel has the exterior appearance of a miniature version of a contemporary temple (Dynasty of Macedon).

miniature version of a contemporary temple, but differs from New Kingdom examples in lacking a pylon, its façade being a 'pronaos' – a forehall with pillars joined by half-height (screen) walls. The decoration of this monument is interesting from a number of points of view. First, while the outer pronaos is decorated with agricultural scenes, scenes of *senet* and technology, the inner chapel has mythological carvings clearly derived from Ramesside royal tomb prototypes, in addition to the standard offering bearers and offerings. Second, while the reliefs of this inner room are in a purely Egyptian style typical of the Late Period, the reliefs in the pronaos are in a hybrid Greek/Egyptian style. However, this was not to be a new start, as no further tombs with this particular style of work seem to exist and with the establishment of the Ptolemaic regime, monumental superstructures in Egyptian style largely disappear from the record.

Other tombs at Tuna el-Gebel have superstructures more akin to houses, with doors, trellis windows and drain-spouts carved onto the exterior.[419] In Roman times, the superstructures of such tombs became the actual places of interment, with the body laid out in the principal room of the building, thus moving far more towards Classical conceptions of the tomb. The interior dadoes and walls of these tombs are often painted to resemble inset panels of stone, such as marble and granite, also a Classical conceit.

Some rock-cut tomb-chapels of classic Egyptian type are known at Thebes,[420] particularly at the north end of Deir el-Medina, where a series of large tombs were cut in early Ptolemaic times,[421] two (DM2003 and 2005) being furnished with sarcophagi taken from the sepulchres of the God's Wives of Amun at Medinet Habu. They consisted of a passage that sloped down to a square underground room in which a vertical shaft led down to the substructure.

349 In content, the decoration of the pronaos of Petosiris' chapel very closely followed that of New Kingdom and earlier tombs, with scenes of 'daily-life' forming the majority of the decoration. However, the scenes were executed in a particular style that combined the Greek with the Egyptian, as can be seen in this scene of threshing grain.

Away from the Nile Valley, the oases of the Western Desert attained a considerable level of prosperity in the Graeco-Roman Period, with a number of major cemeteries established. Particularly good examples are to be found at Bahariya,[422] Dakhla and Siwa,[423] with fine painted decoration. Some contain interesting decorative features. Apart from the usual images of divinities, some have curious motifs showing foxes eating grapes, reminiscent of the fox in Aesop's fable. The tomb of Mesuiset at Siwa has a cornice decorated with a uraeus surmounted by a sun disk and images of Osiris and Isis, as well as hieroglyphic texts.

The adornment of the Siwan tomb of Siamun, dating to either the end of the 30th Dynasty or early Ptolemaic times, is somewhat reminiscent of Ramesside tomb decoration. It shows the embalming scene, Opening-of-the-Mouth ritual, the weighing of the heart and an image of the mummy being taken on a wheeled cart to the cemetery. The ceilings in some of the tombs are particularly spectacular. Some sections are painted to resemble wood, while others show the starry night sky, texts and protective images of vultures and falcons with outstretched wings that are traditionally associated with temples and royal tombs.[424] Simpler rock-cut tombs have been found in Kharga Oasis. They retain fragments of plaster, thus suggesting some form of painted decoration, as can be seen in the rock-cut and brick-constructed chapel at Ain Lebekha.[425]

Pyramids were reintroduced during this period. At Amheida and Bir Shaghala in Dakhâla Oasis, pyramidal mud-brick superstructures surmounted a complex series of long vaulted rooms that were probably plastered and painted.

350 Pyramids were reintroduced during Graeco-Roman times in remote areas. Here at Amheida in Dakhla Oasis, pyramidal mud-brick superstructures surmounted a complex series of long vaulted rooms.

Substructures

In the early Ptolemaic tomb of Petosiris at Tuna el-Gebel, the substructure was approached from a shaft in the middle of the rear part of the chapel, which gave access to chambers on both the east and west. These held the burials of Petosiris, his wife and son, the first two in stone sarcophagi.

Such a basic kind of shaft-superstructure remains typical, as do vaulted or domed brick tombs, sunk into the desert gravel. Also common is the re-use of earlier sepulchres,

frequently for collective burials. Often little or no architectural change is made, but fresh chambers with loculi were added to a number of Late Period tombs, for example, LG84 and G7757 at Giza.[426] These new rooms were cut in the sides of the tombs' shafts. A considerable number of cases of re-use are known at Thebes, where the chapels and substructures of New Kingdom tomb-chapels were occupied by Ptolemaic and Roman interments.[427]

One of the best known examples was a Theban sepulchre taken over by the family of one Mentuemsaf around the transition from Ptolemaic to Roman rule.[428] The funerary equipment of the new occupants was spread between the old chapel and the substructure area, which seems to have been extended to receive a stone sarcophagus. Another tomb taken over was TT32, which held the remains of the family of Soter, of the reign of Hadrian.[429] There are also a number of examples of re-use of tombs at Deir el-Medina;[430] indeed, not only sepulchres became the homes of mummies: the cellar of house C3 contained a number of bodies, including that of one Pebos.

Other sorts of communal tombs are to be found in later Roman times. In some regions, rather than being immediately buried, mummies apparently remained for considerable periods among the living, at home and/or in a public repository, in which homage could be offered to them, perhaps housed in some kind of wooden shrine.[431]

It would appear that groups of bodies would periodically be removed from homes or repositories to the cemetery, where they would be placed in mass brick-lined burial pits, the mummies being piled one on top of the other. This presumably reflected the need to make way for more recent dead amongst the living. The best-excavated such cemetery lies at Hawara, the tombs varying in their precise form.[432] The earlier burial groups were in large brick structures, divided into four chambers by crossing walls and originally cased by limestone blocks. Each of the chambers was filled with an evenly laid brick filling. Only in one case did a stone chamber survive, within which lay a pit containing mummies. Another large grave group was housed in a long, narrow, chamber with an arched roof. There were also some more elaborate structures.

Such interments in brick structures are particularly known from the Fayoum. Another approach is seen at Bahariya Oasis in the Roman Period, where broad loculi open off wide rock-cut corridors.[433] Half a dozen or more mummies were here laid out in each loculus, their heads facing towards the central corridor. Tomb 54, for example, had six of these large loculi, together with two smaller ones at the end of the tomb. Other sepulchres in the area were shafts, with multiple chambers and niches opening from the bottom.

The cemetery associated with the city of Karanis (Kom Ushim) contained late Ptolemaic tombs with short shafts or

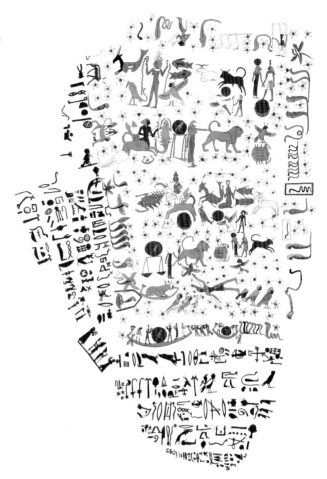

351 Ceiling of the 'Zodiac Tomb' at Wannina, a single-chambered monument apparently owned by one Meryhor. The two zodiacs have been assessed as giving dates in the years AD 52 and AD 59, one presumably the birthday of the tomb's owner and the other perhaps of his wife.

inclined passages. The dead were found in radiating loculi or in a bed scraped out of the ground of the rocky passage floor.[434] In one tomb were crude representations of the husband-and-wife occupants, but generally these sites were lacking in decoration.

A traditional type of tomb continuing into the Ptolemaic Period is the brick-vaulted burial chamber, of which some 40 examples lie at the eastern extremity of the Asasif at Thebes.[435] The structures showed signs of plastered paint decoration on some exteriors; it is thus possible that they at one time stood proud of the ground surface. Constructed of mud-brick, of an elongated rectangular form, the side walls were between 6 and 10 courses high and one-and-a-half thick. Inside, the longer wall has a ledge to take the weight of the roof and outside the narrower walls continue up to meet the apex of the 'Flown Vaulting'. Access is often by a doorway in the end wall and a majority have small brick shrines in front of the entrance. If this was not present, then entry was through a chimney-like hole in one of the vaulted ends.

TOMBS IN THE CLASSICAL TRADITION[436]

For the majority of the Graeco-Roman Period a variety of tomb types appear. In many of these the super- and substructures are merged, or so little of the former remains that one cannot sensibly comment on them. Many tombs, following the Classical models, become communal tombs, especially in Roman times. Furthermore, besides these Egyptian-derived tombs, purely Classical sepulchres were constructed in some areas, in particular at Alexandria and other newly founded cities. The very earliest tombs follow the Macedonian concept of built chambers under a tumulus. Only one example survives, the Alabaster Tomb in the Latin cemetery at Alexandria, of which only the outer part of the underground chambers is preserved. It has been suggested that this might have been a royal tomb, Alexander and all the Ptolemies having been interred at Alexandria. However, the evidence for the form and even precise location of these tombs is equivocal at best, and secure conclusions remain elusive.[437]

Some of the earliest Classical tombs in Egypt are to be found at Shatby in Alexandria and seem to have consisted of a simple stairway leading down to a room whose walls were filled with loculi. Early examples of more monumental sepulchres lie at Hadra as well as at Shatby, where are to be found the remains of Hypogeum A. A stairway led down into the rock to a vestibule and then an anteroom. Beyond this was an open court, to the left of which was a room which accommodated the loculi. It was later extended with additional loculus-rooms.

During the Ptolemaic Period, a uniquely Alexandrine type of tomb emerges, combining super- and substructures and their functions. This abandons the old Hellenic tumulus in favour of an open courtyard sunk in the rock, approached by a stairway, which gives access to the other parts of the tomb. Although there are many variations, the courtyard usually had an altar and a well that provided water

352 Many Roman Period tombs had no superstructure save for a vertical marker with an elaborate finial, and sometimes a niche; Marina el-Alamein.

for ceremonial purposes. Off the courtyard lay burial complexes, generally with a couch placed in the outer part, presumably for laying out the body and beyond this, rooms of loculi for the final interment. The entrance façades to these chambers were decorated in plaster and paint. For the most part the decoration of such tombs, where it survived, followed the Hellenistic tradition, but with Egyptian overtones in terms of iconography, often combining the

Egyptian Osirian tradition with the Greek cycle of Persephone in the Underworld. Egyptian underworld deities, dressed in Greek garb, jostled with cherubs and more conventional Hellenistic and Roman geometric and vegetal motifs. In some instances the loculi were fronted by stelae that bore the name and titles of the deceased; otherwise the blocking stones remained plain, or were carved or painted to resemble doors or windows.

In Roman times, the room with the couch disappeared along with the well, but dining rooms for memorial feasts were added. Such a hall, or triclinium, with rock-cut benches for reclining diners is to be found in the great Roman Period hypogeum at Kom el-Shugafa at Alexandria.[438] The entrance to the hypogeum is via a spiral staircase, giving access to a vestibule or rotunda built around a well, the domed roof supported by eight pillars. To the left is the triclinium.

From the rotunda a stairway leads down to the second level, which is elaborately decorated (see ills 358–59). Beyond is a 'burial chamber', with three dummy sarcophagi carved from the natural rock; the actual burial passages, with loculi, lay behind and below. The majority of the decoration of the catacomb is carved from the living rock and was probably once painted. The decoration in the main tomb, fashioned like a diminutive temple, shows a delightful mix of the two dominant cultures. The approach is marked by a portico with composite columns supporting a curved pediment, adorned with a winged sun disk with uraei, a pair of hawks and another sun disk. Immediately beyond, a pair of niches, one on each wall, guard the approach to the sarcophagus chamber; carved in the classic Egyptian style, complete with torus mouldings and cavetto cornices, they contain a male (right) and a female statue respectively. These figures are clearly Roman in inspiration and are dated on the

353 (*right*) The main room of Anfushi tomb 2 at Alexandria is almost entirely decorated in Classical style. However, the stairway leading into the sepulchre has purely Egyptian-type scenes.

354 (*below*) Plan of Hypogeum A at Shatby, Alexandria; the solid lines represent the original, early Ptolemaic, parts of the complex. Additional loculus chambers were added later.

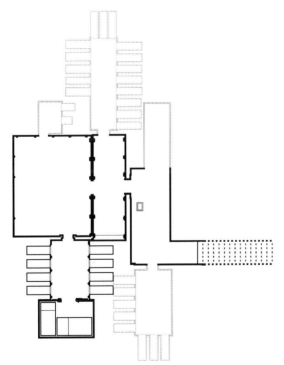

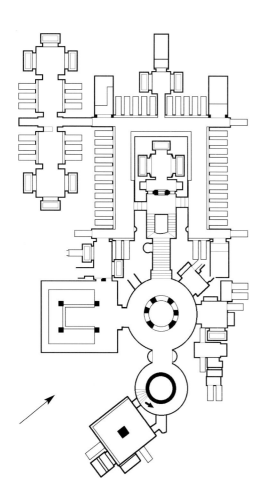

355 Plan of Hypogeum I at Kom el-Shugafa at Alexandria.

356 Closure of a loculus (cavity for the body) incorporating the image of a temple, from Alexandria (GRM).

basis of style to between AD 81 and AD 138, thus providing a date for the main tomb.

Beyond, two bearded snakes (agathodaemon), each with a caduceus (the symbol of Hermes, equivalent to Anubis, who guided the dead between the two worlds), a thyrsus (symbol of Dionysus who became associated with Osiris) and an Egyptian double crown, guard the doorway to the burial chamber or underworld. Above each of them is carved a shield, each with a Medusa, to act as traditional Hellenistic protective devices, guarding the dead against demons as well as thieves.

The chamber is further protected by a winged sun disk and a row of uraei, guaranteeing a solar rebirth. The snake was a chthonic deity (i.e. associated with the underworld and resurrection) in the Graeco-Roman world and thus fitted well with the many serpents shown in Egyptian tombs that were associated with resurrection.

The interior of the burial chamber with its three rock-cut sarcophagi is carved in high relief with Egyptian funerary scenes interspersed with Graeco-Roman funerary motifs, such as Medusa heads, images of Silenus (the companion of Dionysus), ox-heads and funerary wreaths. The Egyptian scenes include images of the deceased as Osiris lying on a funerary bed, with Anubis, Thoth and Horus attending him. Canopic jars are placed below the bed. Other walls show priests censing female divinities, with pseudo-hieroglyphs carved on one side, Apis being offered to by a pharaoh and images of Isis, Osiris and the Four Sons of Horus.

The doorway leading back out to the portico is adorned with the most extraordinary of images: a pair of Anubis figures that truly show the fusion of the Hellenistic and Egyptian traditions. On one side of the doorway Anubis,

357 Loculi within the lowest levels of Hypogeum I at Kom el-Shugafa.

crowned with a sun disk, is shown dressed as a Roman legionary, in a typically Classical twisting (contraposto) pose. The opposite image is the same, save for the fact that a serpent's tail has been substituted for Anubis' legs. He is crowned with Osiris' *atef* crown. Clearly the Roman tomb-owner had adopted Egyptian funerary beliefs, or at least a version of them.

In the nearby, but later, tomb known as the Hall of Caracalla, decoration is entirely painted, with scenes associated with Osiris and his resurrection, mummification, as well as what appears to be the Judgment of Paris, a typically Hellenistic scene, but odd in these surroundings. It is quite probable that similar painted scenes appeared elsewhere in these catacombs, but the paint has long since disappeared.

Other Alexandrian catacombs with painted decoration include the Tigran Tomb with images of a mummy on a funerary bed, flanked by Isis and Nephthys, images of Osiris, Anubis and Horus. The ceiling is painted in a typically Roman way with geometrical and vegetal motifs. These tombs are also frequently painted to resemble marble, other stones and tiles. In some instances very Classical motifs, such as a four-horse chariot, are painted on the pediments.

Elsewhere in Alexandria, there are examples of the tomb paintings apparently imitating what one might expect in a wealthy house: geometric patterns, vegetal motifs and the occasional scene painted on a wall within a border. The scenes are, however, unlike those found in houses as they naturally pertain to the afterlife. At the site of Wardian,

358 (*opposite*) The main chamber of Hypogeum 1 at Kom el-Shugafa.

359 (*right*) The left-hand niche of the main chamber of Hypogeum 1 at Kom el-Shugafa, showing a pharaoh offering to the Apis bull and a winged Isis.

false-doors were executed in paint and at Gabbari, tomb B23's painted roof, imitating a deeply panelled ceiling and the fragments of painted cherubs and vines on walls, hint at the glories it once contained. The grand tomb B26 has a carved façade, as well as elaborately garlanded Ionic columns and was painted very much in the style of a house. Serpents, conforming to both Graeco-Roman and Egyptian funerary iconography, together with Egyptian funerary deities, often garbed in togas or tunics, form the focus of the decoration of the sarcophagus chamber and funerary bed.

A good range of specimens of Graeco-Roman Classical tombs has been excavated at Marina el-Alamein, along the coast to the west of Alexandria.[439] Some had pyramidal superstructures, stepped rather than smooth-sided, up to 2 m (6 ft) in height and 'crowned' by some form of funerary sculpture – a type well-known from Asia Minor. Another superstructure form was a square base consisting of three steps, supporting a square-capitalled pillar; the shaft of the latter sometimes bore carvings of the deceased reclining on a couch. The bases of some of these tombs contained the loculus-chamber; in others, it lay below ground. These column/pillar tombs could be as high as 7 m (25 ft) or more.

Other kinds of tombs had a superstructure that held the triclinium and a central room, at the back of which was a corridor, leading to a staircase, which gave access to a peristyle hall or court some distance below. This then gave access to the burial chambers, generally equipped with loculi.

Several cemeteries of Roman date have also been found in the oases. For the most part only the basic structures remain, with little indication of their decoration, if they had any. The majority of elite Roman tombs in Kharga Oasis are cut into the desert *tafla* and then built up in mud brick. They are intended for multiple burials in chambers that are generally rectangular with vaulted ceilings. At the site of Umm el-Dabadib fragments of plaster were found within the ruined tombs and in some cases, especially at Qasr Sumayra and Sumayra South, plaster still adhered to the walls, confirming that they were originally plastered and possibly painted as well. The bodies were placed in the main chamber, though in rare instances, as at Douch, they were sometimes placed in additional smaller chambers cut further back into the *gebel*.[440]

Shaft tombs from this period also exist here. None of these tombs that have thus far been explored shows evidence of decoration. The few rock-cut tombs examined, probably dating to the Ptolemaic Period, retain fragments of plaster, thus suggesting some form of painted decoration, as can be seen in the rock-cut and brick constructed chapel at Ain Lebekha.

These Graeco-Roman Period tombs mark the end of the line of monuments that stretch back to beyond the dawn of history, in which the continued interaction between the

dead and the living was a key driver in the design of superstructures. Some vestiges of this tradition remain in the early Christian tombs of Egypt, especially the beautifully painted tombs of Bagawat in Kharga Oasis and the diverse funerary stelae that adorned many Coptic burials.[441] Ultimately, however, the monotheistic faiths of Christianity and Islam wholly changed the conception of the relationship between the fate of the physical body and the afterlife. Although the austere idea of 'ashes to ashes, dust to dust' was soon subverted by human pride into the continued building of monumental sepulchres, the magical machinery to ensure rebirth was no more required: salvation lay elsewhere than in the Judgment Hall of Osiris.

360 (*above*) The rear wall of the Tigran Tomb at Alexandria, showing a heavily debased version of the classic scene of Isis and Nephthys standing at the head and foot of the mummy. The latter is shown with wrappings of the lozenge design popular in Roman times.

361 (*below*) Plan of Tomb 54 in Bahariya Oasis' so-called 'Valley of the Golden Mummies'.

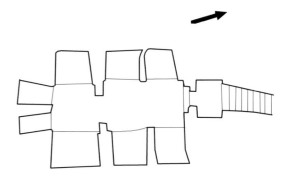

XXV View into the first open court of the tomb-chapel of Mentuemhat on the Asasif at Thebes (TT34), showing the West Portico, leading into the second courtyard and the inner part of the tomb (see also ill. 322); late 25th/early 26th Dynasty.

XXVI Detail of a relief in the pronaos of the tomb of Petosiris at Tuna el-Gebel, showing the tomb's unique Graeco-Egyptian decorative style, dating to soon after Alexander the Great's incorporation of Egypt into his empire.

XXVII (*above*) View from the pillared hall of the substructure of the tomb of Baennentiu at Qaret Qasr Selim, Bawiti, Bahariya Oasis, looking into the inner chamber beyond. The tomb dates from the end of the 26th Dynasty, its decoration resembling that of a New Kingdom royal sepulchre.

XXVIII (*overleaf*) Tomb B1 at Gabbari in the western part of Alexandria, looking south towards chamber B1.5, and showing the vast number of loculi (cavities for the body) in these monuments. B1 had no fewer than 220, some of which held up to ten burials, including both cremations and inhumations, some of the latter with mummified bodies. The tomb was begun in the 3rd century BC and was extended and re-modelled through the 4th century AD. The necropolis was revealed by clearances for a new road – visible in the background – and this particular tomb has now been buried under the completed road, largely destroyed by its foundation piling.

Part IV

NOTES

CHRONOLOGY

GLOSSARY

THE PRINCIPAL CEMETERIES

MAPS

ABBREVIATIONS AND BIBLIOGRAPHY

SOURCES OF ILLUSTRATIONS

INDEX

Notes

1. Dziobek 1998: 78–80.
2. Lichtheim 1973: 58.
3. Named after the low benches found outside village houses in Egypt – known in Arabic as *mastabas*.
4. See Ikram and Dodson 1998: 109–112; 155–6.
5. After Davies and Gardiner 1915: 56.
6. Gardiner 1955: 9–17 dissects an ancient Egyptian funeral.
7. Although the names of many cemeteries are lost to us, a few remain. In the Old and Middle Kingdoms these took their names from the royal pyramids erected at the site. The New Kingdom royal necropolis of Thebes was the Place of Truth (cf. Ventura 1986).
8. Otto 1960.
9. Roth 1992.
10. Extensive studies of such letters can be found in Gardiner and Sethe 1928 and Ritner 1993.
11. Borghouts 1998: 23.
12. Studies using grave goods include Richards 2004.
13. One must be conscious of making a series of assumptions about the relative value of objects, labour and skills in antiquity and also to realize that cemeteries might not exactly reflect social organization.
14. Harpur 1987: 20–31.
15. See Smith 1992 for a study of intact tombs from the 17th and 18th Dynasties.
16. An Egyptian month consisted of 30 days broken into 3 ten-days. Textual information from the New Kingdom workers' village of Deir el-Medina indicates that the average working week was 8 days long, festivals and other holidays were days off and that every day the workers worked for two shifts of 4 hours each, with a break in between.
17. Krauss 1996.
18. Ventura 1988: 43.
19. Brand 2000: 258.
20. Manniche 1987: 11.
21. Ibid.
22. Robins and Shute 1987.
23. See Rossi 2004: 96–147.
24. CM unnumbered, published in Arnold 1987: 86-88, and Hawass 2002: 34.
25. Manniche 1987: 11.
26. Owen and Kemp 1994: 121–29.
27. Such potential 'dual use' of a feature is not uncommon in Egyptian practices.

28. The basic work on the subject is Spencer 1979.
29. The standard work on the subject is Arnold 1991, although the older Clarke and Engelbach 1930 is also of use.
30. Wood 1987.
31. Aston, Harrell and Shaw 2000.
32. Harrell and Baun 1995.
33. For the most recent discussion of the subject, see Chapter 2 of Nicholson and Shaw 2000.
34. Morschauser 1991.
35. Although a great deal has been published on the technical aspects of tomb decoration, Chapter 1 of Manniche 1987 remains a useful summary.
36. Gay Robins has expressed some reservations about the use of grids in 19th Dynasty private tombs, although royal tombs, such as that of Ramesses XI (KV4) do show that grids were initially used and then erased prior to the work of the relief sculptor to avoid confusion.
37. According to Robins (1994: 64–9), the grid in the Old Kingdom was less formal and consisted more of a series of guidelines than an actual grid.
38. See Robins 1994 for a thorough discussion of the canon of proportions in Egyptian art.
39. Manniche 1988b: 31.
40. Several scholars are currently analyzing the paint used in tombs. The two most comprehensive sources on the subject are Chapter 14 of Lucas and Harris 1989 and Chapter 4 of Nicholson and Shaw 2000.
41. Mackay 1920: 35–6.
42. Wachsmann 1987: 11.
43. For a more thorough discussion of pattern books, see Wachsmann 1987: 12–26.
44. Manuelian 1994a: 1–59.
45. Sist 1993b.
46. Manniche 1988b: 18.
47. See Keller 1991: 62–3.
48. Currently being excavated by Mark Lehner: see Lehner 2002.
49. David 1986.
50. There is a considerable body of literature pertaining to the village and its inhabitants. These include Černý 1973a, Romer 1984, Bierbrier 1982, Valbelle 1985, Ventura 1986, Lesko 1994, Janssen 1997, Davies 1999, McDowell 1999 and most recently Meskell 2002.

51. Strudwick 1995: 101; Romer 1994: 211–32.
52. E.g. the tomb of Nefermaat at Meidum (Harpur 2001).
53. Peet 1930.
54. See El-Daly 2005.
55. Firth and Quibell 1935: 5–6.
56. See Vyse 1840, II, for descriptions of the pyramids by Arab writers.
57. For many of the early travellers see Greener 1966.
58. Dodson 2000d.
59. Manniche 1987; 1988a.
60. Rhind 1862; Dodson and Janssen 1989.
61. Dodson and Janssen 1989.
62. One of the most notorious being the destruction of the private tombs at Meidum: see Harpur 2001.
63. Dodson 1997/8.
64. Long feared lost, Loret's detailed records of his work were finally published in Piacentini and Orsenigo 2005.
65. James (ed.) 1982: 141–60.
66. Gardiner and Weigall 1913.
67. Davies 2003.
68. See James 1997 for a discussion on Howard Carter's epigraphic techniques.
69. Jéquier 1940.
70. Brunton 1937, 1948
71. Habachi 1957.
72. Goyon 1987.
73. Dodson 1992b.
74. Dodson 1999.
75. Nicholson 1996, 1999.
76. Martin 1991.
77. Verner 1994.
78. Labrousse 1999.
79. Swelim and Dodson 1998.
80. Alexanian 1999.
81. Arnold and Oppenheim 1995; Oppenheim 1995.
81a Schaden 2007.
81b cf. Ryan 1992.
82. Hawass 2000a, 2000b.
83. Hawass 2000b.
84. Manniche 1988a.
85. For a good overall discussion of this problem, see Van Walsem 1998: 1205–13.
86. An icon in this context is defined as a symbol (or symbolic language) in which iconographic features or attributes form a visual vocabulary that can be 'read' and understood by an illiterate audience with a common cultural background.

87. Hodel-Hoenes 2000: 136.

88. Derchain 1975.

89. Peters-Altrock in Derchain 1975: 69.

90. This has been especially noted and commented upon by Teodozja Rzeuska, who first noted this whilst working at Saqqara with Karel Myśliwiec.

91. Types of scene described in more detail in this chapter are printed in bold.

92. This is especially true in the Old and Middle Kingdoms, with greater variation occurring in the New Kingdom.

93. There appear to be no fixed rules concerning scene location and the preferences that exist do change over time, as well as from cemetery to cemetery. This chapter merely explains general trends in scene location.

94. The following volumes are of particular use in the study of scene types in private tombs: Harpur 1987, Manniche 1988a, b and Vandier 1964 and 1969.

95. Gardiner 1957: 170–3; Davies and Gardiner 1915: 73–93.

96. Müller 1975.

97. Vanek 1989: 311–22.

98. Säve-Söderbergh 1953.

99. Robins 1993: 188.

100. Brewer and Friedman 1989: 77; Sandon 1950.

101. Robins 1993: 188.

102. For lists of tombs containing images of butchery and fish and poultry processing see Tables I–IV in Ikram 1995: 297–305.

103. Aufrère 1999.

104. Harer 1985: 49–54.

105. Lists of meat, fish and poultry preparation scenes can be found in Ikram 1995.

106. Hodel-Hoenes 2000: 41.

107. See Ikram 1995: table 4 for a brief list of scenes in which pigs appear.

108. Kanawati 1993–95;

109. Kanawatai 1980–92.

110. For practical information regarding these activities, see Shaw and Nicholson 2000 and Lucas and Harris 1962.

111. See Decker 1992 for a full discussion of the different games played by the ancient Egyptians.

112. Milde 1988: 89.

113. Roth 1994.

114. Harpur 1987: 81.

115. Harpur 1987: 57.

116. See Eaton-Krauss 1984 for a full discussion of this topic.

117. Wild 1961: 177–97.

118. Aufrère 1991: 581–86.

119. Manniche 1997.

120. Manniche 1988: 45.

121. Cherpion 1994: 86ff; Manniche 1988: 229, Müller 1984: 366–67.

122. Manniche 1988c: 240.

123. Lichtheim 1976: 115–18.

124. See Hassan Hassan 1932–60: VI/2 and Barta 1963 for detailed discussions of offering lists.

125. Vandier 1964: 135.

126. Altenmüller 1975, Junker 1940: 1–39.

127. Manniche 1987: 41.

128. Junker 1953: figs. 87, 96, 97a, 98.

129. Kendall 1981: 105.

130. Now CM CG1447. Thanks are due to Petra Vlckova for discussing these images with Ikram.

131. El-Khouli and Kanawati 1990.

132. Hornung 1999.

133. Allen 1994.

134. Quibell and Green 1898: 20ff; Payne 1973 and Kemp 1973.

135. Adams 2004.

136. Dreyer 1998.

137. Allen 1988.

138. Kemp 1966; O'Connor 1989.

139. Ward 2000: 39–43.

140. Emery 1949–58.

141. Kemp 1967.

142. Dreyer 1993 and 1996.

143. Emery 1949–58: III, 60.

144. Montet 1938.

145. Wood 1987.

146. Leclant and Clerc 1993: 206–7; Munro 1993b.

147. Dodson 1996a.

148. Mathieson and Tavares 1993; Mathieson et al. 1997.

149. This change of interpretation, the result of further excavation, was announced by David O'Connor at the American Research Center in Egypt meeting in Baltimore in April 2002. The alleged 'mound' had previously been canvassed as the prototype for the pyramid in a number of recent works.

150. Quibell 1923.

151. Saad 1947, 1957, 1969.

152. Reisner 1936: 138.

153. Munro 1983; Dreyer 2006.

154. Raven 2006: 64–66.

155. Saad 1957.

156. Firth and Quibell 1935.

157. Although no tell-tale post-holes have been identified within the Shunet or the adjacent enclosures at Abydos.

158. Dodson 1998.

159. Swelim 1987.

160. Ibid.

161. Garstang 1903.

162. Seal-impressions naming Djoser's mother, Nymaathap, were found inside K1.

163. Quibell 1913.

164. Garstang 1904.

165. Reisner 1936: 267–9.

166. The other has never been explored, owing to its dangerous condition, the result of it having been cut into by a later animal catacomb.

167. Maragioglio and Rinaldi 1964–77: III.

168. Although the mid-Third Dynasty Layer Pyramid at Zawiyet el-Aryan has never been properly excavated, the topography of the area makes it unlikely that it ever had a 'classic' rectangular enclosure, while potential remains of a valley temple may exist (cf. Dodson 2000c).

169. The latter six have also been attributed to Huni; they are summarized in Dodson 2003c: 54–6.

170. Maragioglio and Rinaldi 1964–77: IV.

171. Ward 2000: 45–82.

172. Harpur 2001.

173. Bárta 1998. Earlier, Djoser had had a *serdab* in his Step Pyramid mortuary temple.

174. A masterful analysis of the decoration of Old Kingdom private tombs can be found in Harpur 1987.

175. Alexanian 1999.

176. Reisner 1942.

177. Maragioglio and Rinaldi 1964–77: V.

178. Arnold 1979.

179. Quibell 1898b.

180. Fraser 1902; Brunner 1936: 14–20.

181. Kamal 1903; Brunner 1936: 22–3.

182. The small pyramids noted above have no substructures.

183. See Reisner 1942: 85–129.

184. Dunham and Simpson 1974.

185. Maragioglio and Rinaldi 1964–77: VI–VIII.

186. Labrousse 1999.

187. Smith 1949: 211.

188. Jéquier 1929.

189. Petrie 1898; Kanawati and McFarlane 1993.

190. Davies 1901a.

191. Davies 1901a.

192. El-Khouly and Kanawati 1989.

193. Davies 1902.

194. Blackman 1914–53.

195. Mackay, Harding and Petrie 1929; El-Khouly and Kanawati 1990.

196. Publication of the site for the EES is in preparation.

197. Reisner 1932.

198. Petrie 1908; Kanawati 1993–1995.

199. Richards 2001, 2002, 2003, 2004.

200. Petrie 1900.
201. Saleh 1977.
202. Alliot 1933–5.
203. Minault-Gout and Deleuze 1992;
Valloggia 1986; 1998.
204. Firth and Gunn 1926.
205. Naguib Kanawati, personal
communication.
206. Jéquier 1929.
207. Junker 1929–55: IV.
208. Daressy and Barsanti 1917; Blackman and
Apted 1914–53: I, 10–11.
209. Davies 1904a: 30–1.
210. Personal communication, Miroslav Bartá.
211. Castel et al. 2001, Valloggia 1986, 1998,
Minault-Goult and Deleuze 1992.
212. Minault-Gout and Deleuze 1992;
Valloggia 1986; 1998.
213. Minault-Gout and Deleuze 1992;
Valloggia 1986; 1998.
214. Dodson 1992b.
215. At the time of writing being investigated
by a Liverpool University expedition, to which
we are indebted for information.
216. Personal communications, Mark Collier
and Bill Manley.
217. Newberry and Griffith 1893–4; see
further, below.
218. Arnold 1976.
219. Malek 1994; however, excavations by Zahi
Hawass have now confirmed that his
candidate is actually a pyramid of the 5th
Dynasty, attributable to Menkauhor (cf.
Berlandini 1979).
220. Weill, Tony-Revillon and Pillet 1958.
221. Weill 1958.
222. Arnold 1974.
223. Naville 1896: 26, pl. 13.
224. Mond and Myers 1940: 188, pl. 16–18.
225. Winlock 1942: 87, 101–4. 130.
226. Winlock 1955.
227. Vörös 1998.
228. Arnold 1991.
229. Garstang 1903; Tooley 1995.
230. Petrie 1900: 21.
231. Goedicke 1971.
232. Arnold 1988; 1992.
233. Arnold 1988: 78ff.
234. De Morgan 1903: 29–39.
235. Brunton 1920; Petrie 1891; Petrie et al.
1923.
236. Arnold 2002.
237. Arnold 1987.
238. Arnold 2002.
239. Arnold 1979b.
240. The material for this is summarized by
Uphill 2000, albeit with a probably erroneous
reconstruction.

241. Mace 1921: 14–15.
242. Gautier and Jéquier 1902: 98–100.
243. Davies 1920.
244. Lansing 1924: 41.
245. Lansing 1933: 9–15.
246. Silverman 2000.
247. Simpson 1988.
248. Petrie et al. 1923: 26–7.
249. See also Ikram and Dodson 1998: 252;
Dodson 1988c.
250. Simpson 1974.
251. Winlock 1942: 52.
252. Davies 1920.
253. Mace 1914: 214–17.
254. Gautier and Jéquier 1902: 66–9.
255. Silverman 2000.
256. Arnold 1992.
257. Lansing 1933: 15–26.
258. Hayes 1937.
259. Simpson 1988.
260. It has been suggested that the tombs in
this area were built much later in the Middle
Kingdom; however, this extension of the
temenos seems designed to enclose them,
suggesting that they were indeed part if
Amenemhat II's original plan. The contrary
arguments, based on pottery types, probably
over-states the refinement of pottery
typologies for the middle of the 12th Dynasty.
261. Arnold 2002.
262. As does the probable tomb of the wife of
Senwosret II at Lahun (621).
263. De Morgan 1895.
264. Uphill 2000: 75–9.
265. Engelbach 1915.
266. Peet et al. 1913–14: II, 35–41.
267. Engelbach 1923: 14, 20–23.
268. Dodson 2000b.
269. Tylor 1896.
270. Bietak 1996: 20–1.
271. Polz 2003: 13.
272. Winlock 1924.
273. Polz 2003; Polz and Seiler 2003.
274. Polz 2007: 120–22, 133–7.
275. Dewachter 1985; Dodson 1994: 42.
276. Harvey 1994; O'Connor 2003.
277. Dodson forthcoming.
278. Dodson 2003e.
279. Polz 1995a, b.
280. Van Siclen 1980.
281. Frequently the term 'Mansion of millions
of years' is applied to this group of temples
(Haring 1997: 23–4).
282. Naville 1896–1900; Winlock 1942.
283. Blocks found at Medinet Habu, but
clearly originally from the Ramesseum
(Habachi 1969).

284. Using the typology devised and published
by Frederike Kampp (1996); see also
Kampp-Sifried 2003.
285. Architectural detail and bibliography of
all New Kingdom Theban tombs is provided
in Kampp 1996.
286. Rhind 1862: 136–7.
287. Manniche 1987: 16.
288. The Epigraphic Survey 1980.
289. Vandier and Jourdain 1939.
290. Blackman 1922: 235–40.
291. Strudwick 1994, 37–47.
292. Strudwick 1994, 37–47.
293. Milde 1994: 17.
294. Wachsmann 1987: 126.
295. Zivie 1990; 2000.
296. Ikram and Dodson 1998: 258.
297. Dodson 2000b; Reeves and Wilkinson
1996.
298. Hornung 1990: 74–6.
299. The best explanation of the imagery in
the Valley of the Kings can be found in
Hornung 1982.
300. Dodson 2003a.
301. Cf. Dorman 2003.
302. Dorman 1988, 1991.
303. Neugebauer and Parker 1969.
304. Cf. Kampp 1996: 93–4.
305. Mond 1905: pl.III.
306. Davies and Gardiner 1915.
307. Redford 1994: pls XXVIII–XXXII.
308. Ikram and Dodson 1998: 210–12.
309. Martin 1974, 1989; El-Khouly and Martin
1987.
310. Davies 1923b: 135–45; the other significant
example is of course that of Ramose.
311. Davies 1903–8: VI, 1–6.
312. Hornung 1992b: 48–9; 1992c: 125–7.
313. Raven 2002; 2006; van Walsem 2003.
314. Dodson 2000b; Martin 1974, 1989; Reeves
and Wilkinson 1996.
315. Martin 1974, 1989.
316. Hölscher 1939.
317. Cf. Tawfik 2003.
318. Hasegawa 2003.
319. Martin 1991.
320. Ockinga 1997.
321. Piankoff 1955.
322. E.g. in that of Hatshepsut (p. 211).
323. Martin 1989.
324. Martin 1991: 179–85.
325. Martin 1991: 177–85.
326. Engelbach 1915.
327. Dodson 2000b: 87–128.
328. Murnane 1990.
329. Winlock 1942: 9–13.
330. Martin 1997b.
331. Assmann 2003a.

332. Seyfried 1987: 219–22.

333. Assman 1984: 282–4.

334. Van Dijk 1988: 42.

335. Strudwick 1994: 322.

336. Although some tombs from the 18th Dynasty do have scenes of a religious nature, such as the Judgment of Osiris (TT69).

337. Strudwick 1994: 326.

338. Ockinga 1997.

339. Dodson 2000b; Reeves and Wilkinson 1996.

340. Roehrig 1995.

341. Černý 1973b: 23–34.

342. Frankfort, De Buck and Gunn, 1933.

343. Hornung 1995: 70–3.

344. Wilkinson 1994.

345. Carter and Gardiner 1917: 139.

346. Keller 1991: 61.

347. Forman and Quirke 1996: 128, Ikram 2003: Chapter 2, Hornung 1999.

348. Reeves and Wilkinson 1996: 36–7.

349. Leblanc 1989; Weeks 1998; 2000.

350. Seyfried 1998.

351. Shedid 1994b.

352. Winlock 1924.

353. Kamal 1916: 90–93 [89°].

354. Ayrton, Currelly and Weigall 1904: 9.

355. Hayes 1959: 269–71.

356. Habachi 1957: 97–102.

357. Garstang 1901: 21, pl. XXXIII.

358. Randall-MacIver 1902: 65, 77–8, 94.

359. Lull 2002: 51–9.

360. Dodson 2000b: 140-6; Montet 1951.

361. Randall-MacIver 1902: 65, 77–8, 94.

362. Niwinski 1988: 21–8; 205.

363. Winlock 1942: 94–7.

364. Graefe 2003.

365. Strudwick 2001: 7.

366. Quibell 1898a.

367. Quibell 1898: 9–12.

368. Nelson 2003; Aston 2003: 138–42.

369. Dodson 2003d.

370. Hölscher 1954: 8–10.

371. Leahy 1990: 186.

372. Gauthier 1921.

373. Badawi 1957.

374. Amélineau 1899b: 16–28; Vernus 1976: 67–72.

375. See Strudwick 2001 for a case-study in the form of the tomb of Sennefri of the 18th Dynasty (TT99), used on repeated occasions from the 21st through the 26th Dynasty, a pattern that was certainly not uncommon.

376. Barwik 2003; Sheikholslami 2003.

377. Naville 1894–5; the contents of the tomb are now in Oxford, Boston and New York.

378. Dunham 1950; 1955; 1958; 1963; Dunham and Chapman 1952.

379. Personal communication Penny Wilson, September 2003; a possible fragment of the sarcophagus of Psametik II is in the Louvre Museum.

380. Aston 2003.

381. For all these tombs, see Eigner 1984.

382. Randall-MacIver 1902: 80.

383. Bresciani 1988.

384. Porter and Moss 1974: 291.

385. El-Sadeek 1984.

386. Bareš 2003.

387. See n. 372, above.

388. Gasm El Seed 1985.

389. Eigner 1984.

390. Dümichen 1884–1894.

391. Hölscher 1954: 27.

392. Randall-MacIver 1902: 80.

393. Arnold 1997: 31–3.

394. Verner 2002.

395. Verner 1994: 195–208.

396. Vyse 1840: I, 216–18, 232–3; II, 131–44.

397. D'Auria et al. 1988: 176–80.

398. Bickel and Tallet 1997; Hawass 2003: 174–79.

399. Drioton 1954.

400. Hawass 2000: 185–92; 2003: 214.

401. Aston 1999.

402. Mathieson et al. 1995; 1997: 31; pl. VI.

403. Petrie 1902: 34–40.

404. Petrie 1902: 34.

405. Petrie 1902: 36–7; these tombs were mis-reconstructed by Mariette as pyramids.

406. Arnold 1997.

407. Jansen-Winkeln 1997.

408. Dodson 2000b: 162–3.

409. In particular major work in the necropoleis of the sacred animals.

410. D'Auria et al. 1988: 17, 25, called in error 'Saite'.

411. Bresciani 1983.

412. Hawass 2007.

413. Petrie 1902: 34.

414. Petrie 1902: 36–7; these tombs were mis-reconstructed by Mariette as pyramids.

415. Arnold 1997.

416. Gomaà and Hegazy 2001.

417. Morris 1992.

418. Lefebvre 1923–4; the owner's brother, Djedthutefankh had served under Nakhthorheb, but had collaborated with the Persians and had therefore been executed under Alexander.

419. Gabra 1932.

420. Riggs 2006; Strudwick 2003.

421. Nagel 1929: 1–5.

422. Fakhry 1973–4: II; Hawass 2000a.

423. Fakhry 1973–4: I.

424. Fakhry 1973: 183ff.

425. Rossi and Ikram 2004.

426. See above, p. 214.

427. Strudwick 2003.

428. Rhind 1862.

429. Kákosy 1995.

430. Montserrat and Meskell 1997.

431. Ikram and Dodson 1998: 275.

432. Petrie 1911; Bierbrier (ed.) 1997.

433. Hawass 2000a.

434. Grenfell and Hogarth 1900: 41.

435. Carnarvon and Carter 1912: 5.

436. Fedak 1990: 129–33; the definitive work on the subject is Venit 2002.

437. For a recent survey of the evidence, see Chugg 2004/2005.

438. Empereur 1995.

439. Daszewski 1997.

440. Dunand et al. 1992; Ikram and Rossi 2003, Rossi and Ikram 2004.

441. Exploring Christian funerary tradition is beyond the scope of the present work; however, see Thomas 2000 for a discussion of funerary sculpture as well as an extensive bibliography on Christian funerary traditions in Egypt.

Chronology

A Note on Egyptian Chronology

The scheme used by modern scholars for structuring the chronology of historical ancient Egypt is based upon one drawn up by the Egyptian priest, Manetho, around 300 BC. He divided the succession of kings into a series of numbered 'dynasties', corresponding to our idea of royal 'houses' (e.g. Plantagenet, Windsor, Bourbon, Hapsburg, Hohenzollern). These broadly fit in with our knowledge of changes in the ruling family, but in some cases the reason for a shift is unclear.

Historians of ancient Egypt refined this structure by grouping dynasties into 'Kingdoms' and 'Periods', during which constant socio-political themes can be identified; these are broadly the basis for the chronological section of this book.

Ancient dating was by means of regnal years, rather than the kind of 'era' dating used today (eg BC, AD and AH). No comprehensive lists of royal reign-lengths survive today, and thus in most cases the generally accepted lengths of rule for Egyptian monarchs is only an estimate based on often-scanty evidence. In addition, absolute dates, in terms of years BC, have to be established through various indirect methods. Some reigns can be fixed by relation to events linked to better-dated cultures, while others can be placed by reference to mentions of various astronomical phenomena. These allow other reigns' extent to be calculated by dead-reckoning. Nevertheless, there remain many areas of uncertainty and, while dating is solid back to 663 BC, margins of error before then may run in excess of a century. Accordingly, the dates given here should be regarded prior to the 7th century as merely indicative, and liable to comprehensive revision as more data become available.

Rulers shown in parentheses ruled in parallel with others, either as a formal co-regent, or as a rival during a period of strife.

PREDYNASTIC PERIOD

Badarian Culture 5000–4000 BC
Naqada I (Amratian) Culture 4000–3500 BC
Naqada II (Gerzian) Culture 3500–3150 BC
Naqada III Culture 3150–3000 BC

EARLY DYNASTIC PERIOD

1st Dynasty 3050–2820
Narmer
Aha
Djer
Djet
Den
Anedjib
Semerkhet
Qaa

2nd Dynasty 2820–2660
Hotepsekhemwy
Nebre
Ninetjer
Weneg
Sened
Sekhemib/Peribsen
Neferkare
Neferkasokar
Khasekhem/Khasekhemwy

OLD KINGDOM

3rd Dynasty 2660–2600
Djoser
Sanakhte
Sekhemkhet
Khaba
Nebkare
Huni

4th Dynasty 2600–2470
Seneferu
Khufu
Djedefre
Setka
Khafre
Menkaure
Shepseskaf

5th Dynasty 2470–2355
Userkaf
Sahure
Neferirkare

Shepseskare
Neferefre
Niuserre
Menkauhor
Isesi
Unas

6th Dynasty 2355–2190
Teti
Pepy I
Nemtyemsaf I (Merenre)
Pepy II
Nemtyemsaf II

FIRST INTERMEDIATE PERIOD

7th/8th Dynasties 2190–2160

9th/10th Dynasties (Herakonpolis) 2160–2040

11th Dynasty (Thebes)
Mentuhotep I 2160–
Inyotef I   –2123
Inyotef II 2123–2074
Inyotef III 2074–2066

MIDDLE KINGDOM

11th Dynasty
Mentuhotep II 2066–2014
Mentuhotep III 2014–2001
Mentuhotep IV 2001–1994

12th Dynasty
Amenemhat I 1994–1964
Senwosret I 1974–1929
Amenemhat II 1932–1896
Senwosret II 1900–1880
Senwosret III 1881–1840
Amenemhat III 1842–1794
Amenemhat IV 1798–1785
Sobkneferu 1785–1780

13th Dynasty 1780–1650
Sobkhotep I
Sonbef
Nerikare
Amenemhat V
Ameny-Qemau
Amenemhat VI
Nebnuni
Iufeni
Sihornedjhiryotef
Swadjkare
Nedjemibre
Sobkhotep II
Rensonbe
Hor

Amenemhat VII
Wegaf
Khnedjer
Imyromesha
Inyotef IV
Set(y)
Sobkhotep III
Neferhotep I
Sihathor
Sobkhotep IV
Sobkhotep V
Sobkhotep VI
Iaib
Aya
Ini I
Sewadjtu
Ined
Hori
Sobkhotep VII
Ini II
Neferhotep II
[9 obscure kings]
Mentuhotep V
…
Ibi II
Hor[…]
Se[…]kare
Sankhptahi
[…]s
Senebmiu

SECOND INTERMEDIATE PERIOD

14th Dynasty (N. E. Egypt)
15th Dynasty (Hyksos: N. Egypt) 1650–1535
Semqen
Aper-anati
Sakirhar
Khyan
Apepi 1585–1545
Khamudy 1545–1535

16th Dynasty (Thebes) 1650–1590
Djehuty
Sobkhotep VIII
Neferhotep III
Mentuhotepi
Nebiriau I
Nebiriau II
Semenre
Bebiankh
Sekhemre-shedwaset
Dedumose I
Dedumose II
Mentuemsaf
Mentuhotep VI
Senwosret IV

17th Dynasty (Thebes) 1585–1549
Rehotep
Sobkemsaf I
Inyotef V
Inyotef VI
Inyotef VII
Sobkemsaf II
Taa I
Taa II 1558–1553
Kamose 1553–1549

NEW KINGDOM

18th Dynasty
Ahmose I 1549–1524
Amenhotep I 1524–1503
Thutmose I 1503–1491
Thutmose II 1491–1479
Thutmose III 1479–1424
(Hatshepsut 1472–1457)
Amenhotep II 1424–1398
Thutmose IV 1398–1389
Amenhotep III 1389–1352
Amenhotep IV/Akhenaten 1352–1335
(Smenkhkare 1339)
Neferneferuaten 1388–1332)
Tutankhaten/amun 1335–1325
Ay 1335–1321
Horemheb 1321–1291

19th Dynasty
Ramesses I 1291–1290
Sety I 1290–1279
Ramesses II 1279–1203
Merenptah 1203–1193
Sety II 1193–1187
(Amenmesse 1192–1188)
Siptah 1187–1181
Tawosret 1181–1179

20th Dynasty
Setnakhte 1179–1177
Ramesses III 1177–1145
Ramesses IV 1145–1139
Ramesses V Amenhirkopshef I 1139–1135
Ramesses VI Amenhirkopshef II 1135–1127
Ramesses VII Itamun 1127–1119
Ramesses VIII Sethirkopshef 1119–1118
Ramesses IX Khaemwaset I 1118–1099
Ramesses X Amenhirkopshef III 1099–1096
Ramesses XI Khaemwaset II 1096–1069

THIRD INTERMEDIATE PERIOD

21st Dynasty
Nesibanebdjedet 1069–1043
Amenemnesu 1043–1039
(Pinudjem I 1054–1032)
Pasebkhanut I 1039–990
Amenemopet 990–980
Osorkon the Elder 980–974
Siamun 974–955
Pasebkhanut II 955–941

22nd Dynasty
Shoshenq I 943–922
Osorkon I 922–886
(Shoshenq II 890)
Takelot I 886–870
Osorkon II 870–832
Shoshenq III 832–792
Shoshenq IV 792–782
Pimay 782–776
Shoshenq V 776–739

23rd Dynasty (Thebes)
Harsiese 860–850
Takelot II 835–810
Pedubast I 824–801
Iuput I 809–793
Osorkon III 793–765
Takelot III 770–760
Rudamun 760–740
Iny 740–735
Peftjauawybast 735–725

23rd Dynasty (Tanis)
Pedubast II 739–737
Osorkon IV 737–720

24th Dynasty (Sais)
Tefnakhte 732–724
Bakenrenef 724–718

25th Dynasty
Piye 753–722
Shabaka 722–707
Shabataka 707–690
Taharqa 690–664
Tanutamun 664–656

SAITE PERIOD

26th Dynasty
Psametik I 664–610
Nekau II 610–595
Psametik II 595–589
Wahibre (Apries) 589–570
Ahmose II (Amasis) 570–526
Psametik III 526–525

LATE PERIOD

27th Dynasty (Persians)
Cambyses 525–522
Darius I 521–486
Xerxes I 486–465
Artaxerxes I 465–424

28th Dynasty
Amenirdis (Amyrtaios) 404–399

29th Dynasty
Naeferud I 399–393
Pasherenmut 393
Hagar 393–380
Naeferud II 380

30th Dynasty
Nakhtnebef (Nectanebo I) 380–362
Djehor 362–360
Nakhthorheb (Nectanebo II) 360–342

31st Dynasty (Persians)
Artaxerxes III Ochus 342–338
Arses 338–336
Darius III 335–332

HELLENISTIC PERIOD

Dynasty of Macedon
Alexander III 332–323
Philip III Arrhidaeus 323–317
Alexander IV 317–310

Dynasty of Ptolemy
Ptolemy I Soter 310–282
Ptolemy II Philadelphos 285–246
Ptolemy III Euergetes I 246–222
Ptolemy IV Philopator 222–205
Ptolemy V Epiphanes 205–180
Ptolemy VI Philometor 180–164
Ptolemy VIII Euergetes II 170–163
Ptolemy VI (again) 163–145
Ptolemy VIII (again) 145–116
Ptolemy IX Soter II 116–110
Ptolemy X Alexander I 110–109
Ptolemy IX (again) 109–107
Ptolemy X (again) 107–88
Ptolemy IX (again) 88–80
(Ptolemy XI 80)
Ptolemy XII Neos Dionysos 80–58
Berenice IV 56
Ptolemy XII (again) 55–51
Cleopatra VII Philopator 51–30
(Ptolemy XIII 51–47)
(Ptolemy XIV 47–44)
(Ptolemy XV Caesar 41–30)

ROMAN PERIOD

30 BC–AD 395

BYZANTINE PERIOD

395–640

ARAB PERIOD

640–1517

OTTOMAN PERIOD

1517–1805

KHEDEVAL PERIOD

1805–1914

BRITISH PROTECTORATE (SULTANATE)

1914–1922

MONARCHY

1922–1953

REPUBLIC

1953–

Glossary

Agathodaemon benevolent divinity in the form of a serpent, common in the Graeco-Roman Period.

Amentet 'The West', the dwelling place of the Dead.

Ammit 'The Devourer'. The composite crocodile-lioness-hippopotamus monster that ate up the parts of the accursed dead in the Judgement Hall of Osiris.

Amun(-Re) chief god of Thebes and paramount god of Egypt from the New Kingdom onward.

Anubis god of embalming, represented with a jackal's head.

Apis sacred bull of Memphis, a form of Ptah.

Apophis snake-enemy of the Sun-god.

Aten the physical sun, worshipped during the late 18th Dynasty.

Atum human form of Sun-god, Re.

barrel vault semi-circular vaulting found throughout Egyptian history.

ben-ben sacred stone of Heliopolis, perhaps a meteorite, believed to take a roughly pyramidal shape.

block statue stone statue showing a squatting individual, with knees drawn up to the chin, and frequently inscribed with texts.

Book of the Dead 'Book of Coming Forth By Day': one of the many funerary books containing spells that would help transport the deceased safely to Amentet. Common from the New Kingdom onward.

caduceus the wand of Hermes, a staff with two interlaced serpents, topped by small wings,.

canopic of or pertaining to the preservation of the viscera removed from the body in the course of embalming.

cartonnage: a. material made from mixture of linen/papyrus, glue and plaster; b. painted whole-body casing made from cartonnage.

cavetto cornice concave moulding on top of walls and stele.

cenotaph grave marker or tomb, not containing a corpse.

Coffin Texts texts inscribed on the interior of the coffin during the Middle Kingdom to aid the deceased in reaching *Amentet*.

colonnade a row of columns, supporting a roof.

corbel-roofing arrangement for spanning a space by setting each successive course of the walls slightly further out than the one below until they meet at the apex.

dentil toothlike cubes found in Classical cornices.

Duamutef mortuary genius and Son of Horus, usually represented with a jackal head, and associated with the stomach. Under the tutelage of Neith.

false door a stone doorway in a tomb inscribed with offerings and the name and titles of the deceased; a focus for the mortuary cult.

funerary cone flat pottery cone, generally 10–15 cm long, with the flat end often inscribed with the names and titles of the deceased, or prayers. Used to adorn tomb façades.

Geb Earth-god; husband of Nut.

gesso mixture of glue and gypsum plaster used to cover coffins, statues, etc.

Hapy mortuary genius and Son of Horus, usually represented with an ape head, and associated with the lungs. Under the tutelage of Nephthys.

Hathor goddess, represented in either human or cow form.

Heb-sed the jubilee festival celebrated by the Egyptian king, usually after thirty years on the throne, and then repeated every three years.

Hermes Greek messenger of gods, who guided the dead between the two worlds; equated with Anubis.

hypostyle hall chamber with its room supported by a number of columns.

hetep-di-nesu funerary formula for the provision of offerings to the deceased.

hypogeum an underground chamber.

Iaru, Fields of the idyllic land of the hereafter.

Imseti mortuary genius and Son of Horus, represented with a human head, and associated with the liver. Under the tutelage of Isis.

Isis goddess; sister-wife of Osiris, mother of Horus and protector of Imseti. Usually found on the foot of a coffin.

lintel an horizontal architectural element, generally over a doorway or window.

loculus deep niche to receive a body lying lengthwise.

Maat Goddess of cosmic order.

mastaba a tomb-type, common from the Early Dynastic Period onward. The name, *mastaba*, derives from the Arabic word for mudbrick bench, which they resemble.

Medusa mythological female being with serpents for hair whose gaze could turn one to stone, and having an apotropaic function.

Meretseger snake-goddess of Western Theban necropolis.

mortuary temple temple designed to house the cult of the deceased and sometimes other divinities.

mummy artificially preserved human or animal corpse. The word is derived from the Persian, *mum*, meaning wax or bitumen.

Neith one of the four tutelary goddesses of the dead; a goddess of warfare and hunting.

Nephthys sister of Osiris, Isis, and Seth, and wife of the latter. One of the four tutelary goddesses of the dead, always shown at the head of the corpse.

Nut sky Goddess often pictured on tomb-ceilings and lids of coffin and sarcophogi. Wife of Geb.

Opening-of-the-Mouth ceremony which served to reanimate the corpse.

Osiris god of the dead and resurrection, brother-husband of Isis, murdered by his brother Seth and who consequently became the first mummy.

Osirid columns a pillar fronted by a figure shown with its feet together, and frequently sheathed like Osiris.

papyrus column column with papyrus capitals, and often having triangular sections similar to those found in real papyrus stems.

peristyle court courtyard with a row of columns around its edges.

pillar a rectangular column.

pilaster an engaged pillar.

portico a covered entrance, supported by pillars or columns, in front of a window.

pit tomb a shallow tomb cut into the desert gravel or scooped out of the sand.

Proto-Doric column faceted columns resembling the Greek Doric order, but antedating them by some 1800 years.

pylon massive ceremonial gateway, comprised of two tapering massifs joined by a gateway, and thought to symbolise the horizon (*akhet*).

pyramidion cap-stone of a pyramid, often made of hardstone and bearing inscriptions; some examples may have been gilded.

Pyramid Texts magical texts inscribed in the burial chambers of pyramids from the end of the 5th Dynasty onward.

Qebehsenuef mortuary genius and Son of Horus, usually represented with a hawk head, and associated with the intestines. Under the tutelage of Selqet.

Re the sun god.

relief: a. sunk two-dimensional design carved into a surface;
b. raised/raised two-dimensional design where the background is carved away, leaving the standing image.

rock-cut tomb a sepulchre whose chapel is carved out of the living rock, with minimal, if any, built structure.

sarcophagus rectangular/quasi-rectangular outermost container, intended to hold coffins of a different form or material. It may be composed of stone or wood.

Selqet one of the four tutuleray goddesses; sacred creature is the scorpion.

Sem **Priest** priest who performs funerary rights clad in leopard skin, notably the Opening-of-the-Mouth. Often the deceased's eldest son.

serdab closed room in a tomb, containing statue(s) of the deceased; from the Arabic for 'cellar'.

serekh rectangular frame, with panelled lower section, used to enclose the Horus name of a king.

Seth brother and murderer of Osiris.

shabti/ushabti magical servant figure found in tombs mid-Middle Kingdom onward. From the middle of the 18th Dynasty large numbers are to be found in a single burial, ultimately exceeding four hundred in certain interments.

shaft tomb a rock-cut tomb that goes straight down into the bedrock and opens into a room or series of room.

skeuomorph item imitating the form of another.

slab stela a rectangular stone slab bearing depictions of tomb owner seated before table of offerings. Found from Early Dynastic Period to Old Kingdom. Also known as offering slab, when it is incorporated into the false door.

step pyramid pyramid rising in a series of deep steps to the summit, perhaps symbolic of a stairway to heaven.

temenos sacred enclosure.

triclinium a dining room with couches on three sides, often made of stone and found in Graeco-Roman contexts.

true pyramid pyramid intended to have a uniform, smooth, slope to the summit. Perhaps representative of the sun's descending rays and a ramp to aid the kings ascension.

'T'-shaped tomb a tomb, primarily dating to New Kingdom Thebes, the ground-plan of which resembles the letter 'T'.

Thoth ibis-headed secretary of the gods.

thrysus insignia of Dionysus: a staff crowned with ivy, vine leaves or a pine cone.

tomb models wooden models showing daily life activities, generally found in Middle Kingdom tombs, especially in burial chambers.

torus moulding semi-circular moulding found below cavetto cornice and thought to simulate bound reeds. Found in buildings and on false doors.

valley temple cultic building on the edge of the desert, giving access to the causeway that leads to the mortuary temple.

The Principal Cemeteries

SITE NAME	NUMBER ON MAP 1	DATES OF PRINCIPAL BURIALS AT SITE									
		PD	EDP	OK	FIP	MK	SIP	NK	TIP	LP	GR
Abu Ghaleb	21			•		•					
Abu Qir	10										•
Abu Rowash	28		•	•R		•					
Abu Sir	34	•	•	•	•	•				•	
Abu Sir el-Meleq	51		•					•			
Abydos	105	•	•R	•	•	•	•	•	•	•	•
Akhmim	95					•				•	•
Alexandria	11										•R
Amada	131										
Amara	139										
Aniba	132							•			
Arab el-Miteir	83			•							
Armant	115		•	•		•					
Asasif (Thebes-West)	114							•		•	
Asyut	85			•	•	•		•		•	
Awlad el-Sheikh	62		•	•							
Bahariya Oasis	148							•		•	•
Balabish	106							•			
Balansura	68							•			
Baqlia/Tell el-Zereiki	7									•	
Barnugi	13					•					
Batn el-Baqara (Fustat)	26									•	
Beit Khallaf	103			•							
Beni Hasan	69			•	•	•		•	•	•	
Biban/Wadi el-Harim (Valley of the Queens) (Thebes-West)	114							•			
Biban/Wadi el-Moluk (Valley of the Kings) (Thebes-West)	114							•R			
Buhen	136										
Dahshur	39			•R		•R		•		•	•
Dahshur-South	40					•R					
Dakhla Oasis	149			•		•			•		•
Dara	81		•	•	•R	•					
Debeira East	135										
Dehmit (Betekon)	128										
Deir el-Bahari (Thebes-West)	114					•R		•	•	•	•
Deir el-Ballas	110		•	•	•	•					
Deir el-Bersha	73			•	•	•					
Deir el-Gebrawi	80			•	•						
Deir el-Medina (Thebes-West)	114							•		•	
Deir Rifeh	87			•	•	•	•	•			

PD Predynastic Period
EDP Early Dynastic Period
OK Old Kingdom
FIP First Intermediate Period
MK Middle Kingdom
SIP Second Intermediate Period
NK New Kingdom
TIP Third Intermediate Period
LP Late Period
GR Graeco-Roman Period

'R' = Royal tombs

SITE NAME	NUMBER ON MAP I	DATES OF PRINCIPAL BURIALS AT SITE									
		PD	EDP	OK	FIP	MK	SIP	NK	TIP	LP	GR
Deir Tasa	89			•						•	
Dendara	109		•	•	•	•				•	
Deshasha	59			•							
Dra Abu'l-Naga (Thebes-West)	114						•R	•		•	
Edfu	124			•	•	•	•				
Ehnasiya el-Medina (Herakleopolis)	58				•				•	•	•
El-Atamna	82			•							
El-Atawla	84					•					
El-Badari	91	•	•			•	•				
El-Bahnasa (Oxyrhynchus)	64									•	•
El-Deir	120		•	•	•	•					
El-Hagarsa	98			•	•						
El-Hamamiya	92		•	•							
El-Hawawish	96			•	•	•					
El-Hiba	60									•	
El-Itmania			•	•							
El-Kab	122	•	•	•	•	•	•	•			
El-Khawalid			•	•						•	
El-Kurru	144									•R	
El-Maabda	79			•							
El-Mahasna	104	•		•	•	•					
El-Masara	33	•	•								
El-Qantara	3									•	
El-Qatta	22		•	•				•		•	
El-Rizeiqat	117		•	•	•	•		•			
El-Saff	42	•	•								
El-Salamuni				•	•	•					
El-Sawamia							•	•			
El-Tarif (Thebes-West)	114		•	•	•	•R					
El-Tod	116							•			
El-Zawiya				•							
Esna	121		•		•	•					
Gebel Barkal (Napata)	143									•	
Gebel el-Teir el-Bahari	65			•							
Gebel Sheikh el-Haridi	94			•							•
Gebelein	119		•	•	•	•					
Gerzeh	45	•		•	•	•		•	•		
Giza	29	•	•	•R	•			•		•	•
Gurob	55		•	•	•			•			
Harageh	54		•	•	•	•					
Hawara	50					•R			•	•	•
Helwan	36		•	•		•					
Hierakonpolis	123		•	•		•	•	•			
Hu-Abadiya	108			•	•	•	•	•			
Imbaba	27									•	

SITE NAME	NUMBER ON MAP I	DATES OF PRINCIPAL BURIALS AT SITE									
		PD	EDP	OK	FIP	MK	SIP	NK	TIP	LP	GR
Istabl Antar	70			•						•	•
Kafr Ammar	44			•	•				•		
Kerma	142									•	
Kharga Oasis	97	•		•?			•	•?			•
Khokha (Thebes-West)	114			•	•			•		•	
Kom Abu Billo	20			•		•		•		•	
Kom Aushim (Karanis)	48										•
Kom Ausim (Letopolis)	24			•							
Kom el-Ahmar Sawaris	63			•							
Kom el-Hisn	15		•	•		•					
Kom Firin	14					•		•		•	
Kom el-Kharaba el-Kebir (Philadelphia)	49										•
Kom Ombo	126					•					•
Koshtemna	129										
Lahun	52			•	•	•R		•	•		•
Lisht	43			•	•	•R					•
Maadi	30	•	•								
Marina el-Alamein	12										•
Matariya (Heliopolis)	25			•				•		•	•
Matmar	86			•	•	•		•	•		
Mazghuna	41			•	•	•R		•			
Medinet Habu	114								•R	•	
Meidum	47			•R		•			•	•	•
Meir	77			•	•	•					
Meroë	146								•R		•
Mersa Matruh	14		•							•	
Minshat Abu Omar	5		•	•							
Mirgissa	137										
Mit Rahina	35					•		•	•		
Moalla	118				•	•		•	•		
Mostagedda	88		•	•	•	•	•	•		•	
Nabesha	4									•	
Nag el-Hisaia	125									•	
Naga el-Deir	99		•	•	•	•		•			
Naga el-Meshayikh	101										
Naga el-Wissa				•							
Naqada	113	•	•	•	•	•					
Nuri	145								•R		
Qasr el-Sagha	57			•		•				•	
Qasr w'el-Sayed	107			•	•						
Qau el-Kebir	93			•	•	•	•	•		•	•
Qift (Koptos)	112			•						•	
Qubbet el-Hawa (Aswan)	127			•	•	•				•	
Qurnet Murai (Thebes-West)	114							•			
Quseir el-Amarna	78			•		•		•			•

SITE NAME	NUMBER ON MAP I	DATES OF PRINCIPAL BURIALS AT SITE									
		PD	EDP	OK	FIP	MK	SIP	NK	TIP	LP	GR
Ramesseum (Thebes-West)	114								●	●	
Raqaqna	102			●							
Sa el-Hagar (Sais)	9									●R	
Saft el-Henna	18							●	●	●	
San el-Hagar (Tanis)	2								●R		
Saqqara-North	37		●	●R	●	●	●	●	●	●	●
Saqqara-South	38			●R		●R				●	●
Sayala	130										
Sedment el-Gebel	56		●	●	●		●				
Semna West	138										
Serra East	134										
Sesebi	141										
Sheikh Abada	72		●	●		●		●			
Sheikh Abd el-Qurna (Thebes-West)	114							●		●	
Sheikh Atia	76			●							
Sheikh Farag	100				●	●					
Sheikh Said	74			●							
Siwa Oasis	147									●	●
Soleb	140										
Tarkhan	46	●	●								
Tell Atrib	19									●	●
Tell Basta (Bubastis)	17			●		●		●	●	●	
Tell el-Amarna	75							●R			
Tell el-Daba (Avaris)	1						●	●			
Tell el-Farain (Buto)	8									●	●
Tell el-Ruba (Mendes)	6		●	●		●				●R	
Tell el-Yuhudiya	23		●	●		●		●	●	●	
Tell Moqdam (Leontopolis)	16									●	
Tell Umm el-Briegat (Tebtunis)	53										●
Thebes-West	114										
Tihna el-Gebel	66			●	●				●		
Toshka East	133							●			
Tuna el-Gebel	71							●		●	●
Tura	32			●		●					
Wanina (Athribis)	97										●
Zarabi	90			●							
Zaweida	111			●				●			
Zawiyet Barmasha	61									●	●
Zawiyet Sultan/el- Amwat/el- Maitin)	67			●	●			●		●	
Zawiyet el-Aryan	31	●	●	●R				●			

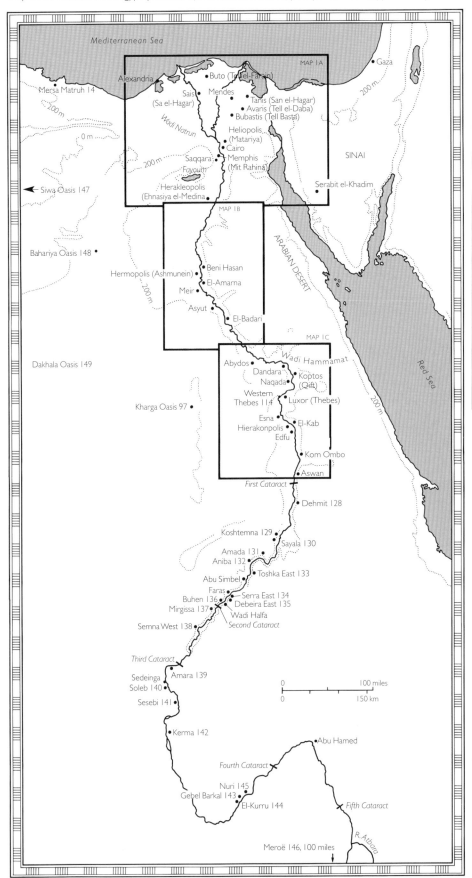

Map 1 The Cemeteries of Egypt (*numbers refer to those in the list of principal cemeteries, pp. 320–23*).

Mediterranean Sea

MAP 1A

Gaza

Alexandria
Buto (Tell el-Farain)
Mersa Matruh 14
Sais
(Sa el-Hagar)
Mendes
Tanis (San el-Hagar)
Avaris (Tell el-Daba)
Bubastis (Tell Basta)

Wadi Natrun

Heliopolis
(Matariya)
Cairo
Memphis
(Mit Rahina)
Saqqara
Fayoum

SINAI

Serabit el-Khadim

Siwa Oasis 147

Herakleopolis
(Ehnasiya el-Medina)

MAP 1B

Bahariya Oasis 148

ARABIAN DESERT

Hermopolis (Ashmunein)
Beni Hasan
El-Amarna
Meir
Asyut
El-Badari

MAP 1C

Wadi Hammamat

Dakhala Oasis 149

Abydos
Dandara
Naqada
Koptos
(Qift)
Western
Thebes 114
Luxor (Thebes)
Esna
Kharga Oasis 97
El-Kab
Hierakonpolis
Edfu

Red Sea

Kom Ombo

Aswan
First Cataract

Dehmit 128

Koshtemna 129
Sayala 130
Amada 131
Aniba 132
Toshka East 133
Abu Simbel
Faras
Serra East 134
Buhen 136
Debeira East 135
Mirgissa 137
Wadi Halfa
Second Cataract
Semna West 138

Third Cataract

Sedeinga
Amara 139
Soleb 140
Sesebi 141

0   100 miles
0   150 km

Kerma 142

Abu Hamed

Fourth Cataract

Nuri 145
Gebel Barkal 143
El-Kurru 144
Fifth Cataract

R. Atbara

Meroë 146, 100 miles

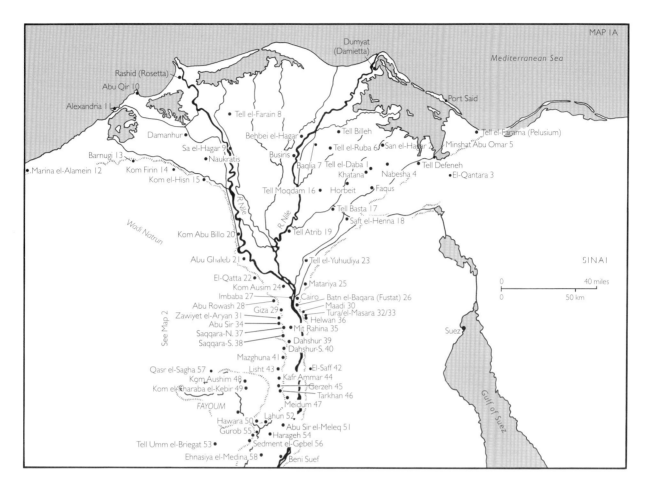

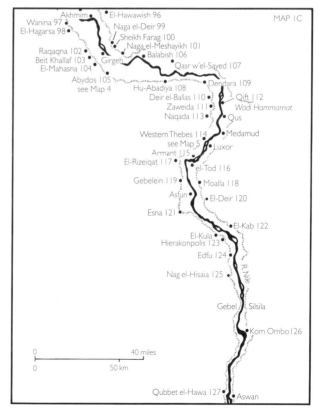

Map 2 The Memphite Necropolis (*for key to numbered tombs, see appropriate cemeteries' entries in the index*).

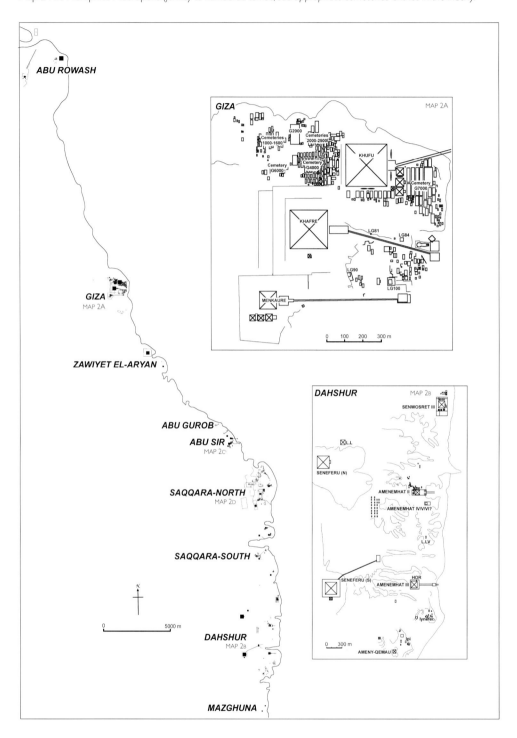

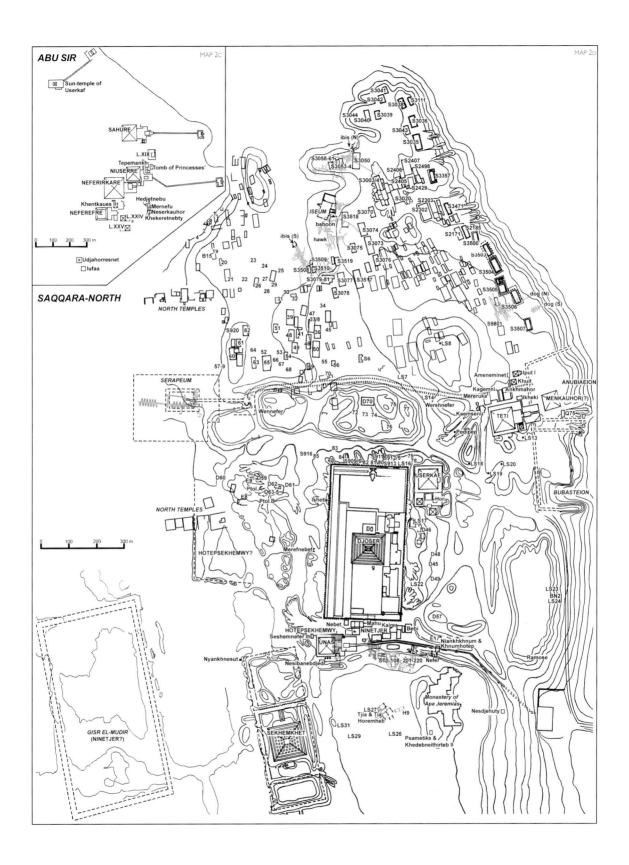

ABU SIR

Sun-temple of
Userkaf

SAHURE

L.XIX

Tepemankh
NIUSERRE · 'Tomb of Princesses'

NEFERIRKARE

Khentkaues II
Mernefu
NEFEREFRE · Neserkauhor
L.XXIV · Khekeretnebty
L.XXV

0   100   200   300 m

Udjahorresnet
Iufaa

SAQQARA-NORTH

B15

20
21   22   23   24
26   27   29   25
28

NORTH TEMPLES

S920   62
61
60   64   52   53   54
63   65   66   67
57-9   68

SERAPEUM

Wennefer

NORTH TEMPLES

0   100   200   300 m

HOTEPSEKHEMWY?

Merefnebef

Nyankhnesut

Nesibanebdjed

GISR EL-MUDIR
(NINETJER?)

SEKHEMKHET

S3041
S3042   S3111
S3038
S3044   S3039   S3036
S3040   S3043
S3035
ibis (N)
S3058-61   S3050   S2407
S3053-4   S2498
S2406   S3357
S3003/4   S2405
S2429
ISEUM   S3020
S3518   S3070   S2303
baboon   S3074   S2202   S3471
hawk   S3073   S2171
ibis (S)   S3075   S2185
S3076   S3500
S3509   S3519   S3503
S3508   S3510
S3079-81   S3077   S3517   S3504
S3078   S3505
dog (N)
S3506   dog (S)
34   S9801   S3507
47
39   37/8
48   41   36   LS8
49   45
42   50
55   56   S6
69
S7   LS7
70   Ameneminet   Iput I
Kagemni   Khuit
Mereruka   Ankhmahor
D70   75   Ikheki
72   73   74   77   Wershnefer   MENKAUHOR(?)
76   Kaemsenu   TETI   Q75
Pedipep   ANUBIAEION
LS14
83   LS18   LS13
S916   85   84   S911 S912/5   79   LS20
S909/6/82   81/80 S913   LS16/78   LS19
D60   USERKAF   BUBASTEION
E9   D59   Ishetih   Hor
Ptol.A   D62   D61
E8   D63-5
Ptol.B   LS17
D46
D48
DJOSER   D45
D49
LS22
LS23
BN2
LS24
D57
Nebet   Mahu Kaires
HOTEPSEKHEMWY,   NINETJER   Bebi
Seshemnefer III   E1   Niankhkhnum &
UNAS   Khnumhotep
ST0-108, 201-220   Nefer   Ramose
Monastery of
Apa Jeremias
LS27   Nesdjehuty
Tjia & Tia   H9
Horemheb
LS31
LS26
LS29   Psametiks &
Khedebneithirteb II

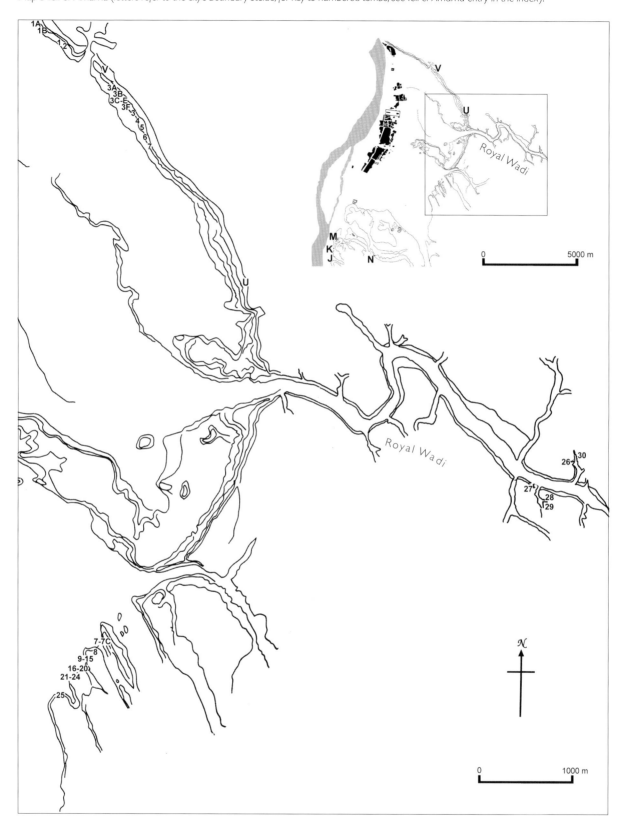

Map 4 Abydos (*letters denote specific cemeteries; for individual tombs within them, see Abydos entry in the index*).

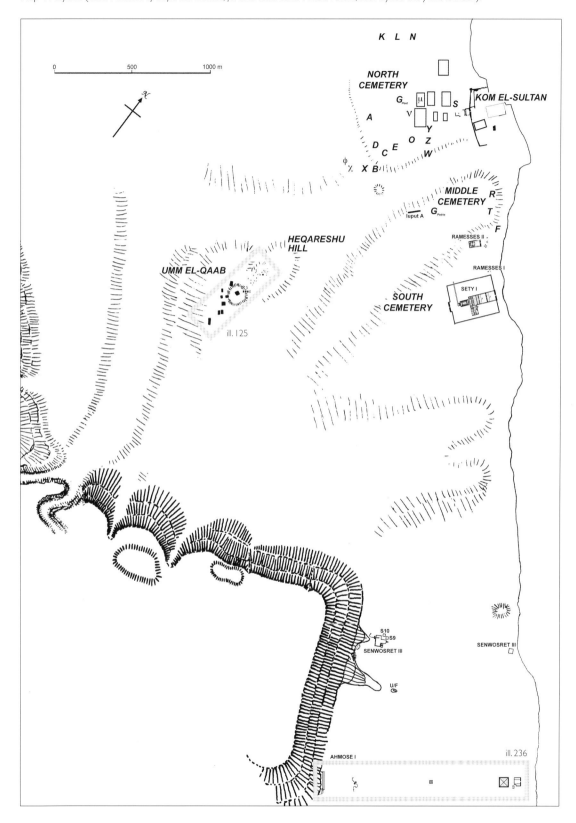

K L N

NORTH
CEMETERY

G_Peet

μ

A

V

S

KOM EL-SULTAN

Y

O Z

D
C E

W

φ
χ   X B

MIDDLE
CEMETERY

R

T

F

Iuput A   G_Petrie

RAMESSES II

RAMESSES I

HEQARESHU
HILL

UMM EL-QAAB

SOUTH
CEMETERY

SETY I

ill. 125

0   500   1000 m

S10
S9
SENWOSRET III

SENWOSRET III

U/F

ill. 236

AHMOSE I

Map 5 The Theban Necropolis

EL-TARIF

INYOTEF III

INYOTEF II

INYOTEF I

QURNA

SETY I

MAP 5A

Nebwenenef

AMENHOTEP I &
AHMES-NEFERTIRY

DRA
ABU'L
NAGA

BIRABI

RAMESSES IV/VI

MAP 5C

MAP 5B

THUTMOSE III

SIPTAH
AMENHOTEP II

ASASIF

RAMESSES II

THUTMOSE IV

DEIR EL-
BAHARI

SHEIKH
ABD EL
QURNA

TAWOSRET

SOUTH
ASASIF

AMENHOTEP III

MERENPTAH

MAP 5D

QURNET
MURAI

RAMESSES IV
Amenhotep s. Hapu
THUTMOSE II

VALLEY
OF THE
KINGS

MAP 5E

DEIR EL-
MEDINA

RAMESSES III

AY &
HOREMHEB

WEST
VALLEY
OF THE
KINGS

MEDINET HABU

MAP 5F

VALLEY
OF THE
QUEENS

Map 5A (*for key to numbered tombs, see the Theban Tombs entry in the index*). Inset Map 5B.

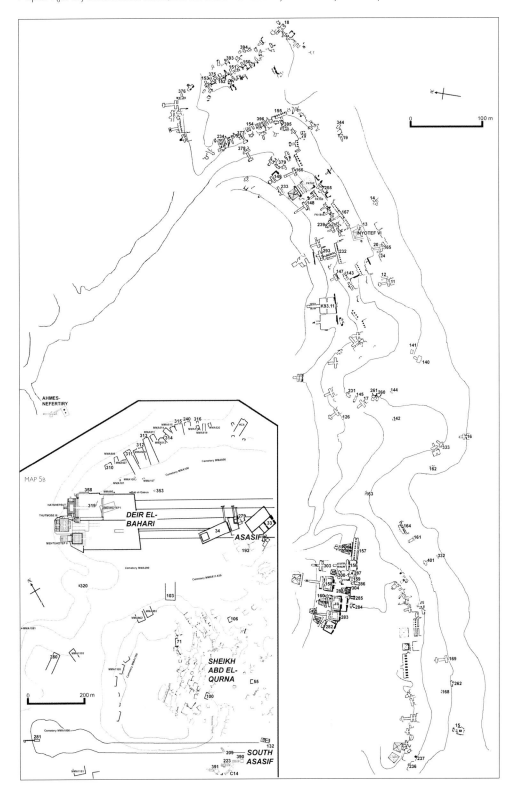

HATSHEPSUT
(Valley Temple)

KAMOSE?

Cemetery MMA 700

RAMESSES IV/VI

Cemetery
MMA 300

0   100   200 m

THUTMOSE III

SIPTHAH

AMENHOTEP II

RAMESSES II

Map 5D The Theban Necropolis: The Valley of the Kings (*for key to numbered tombs, see the Valley of the Kings entry in the index*).

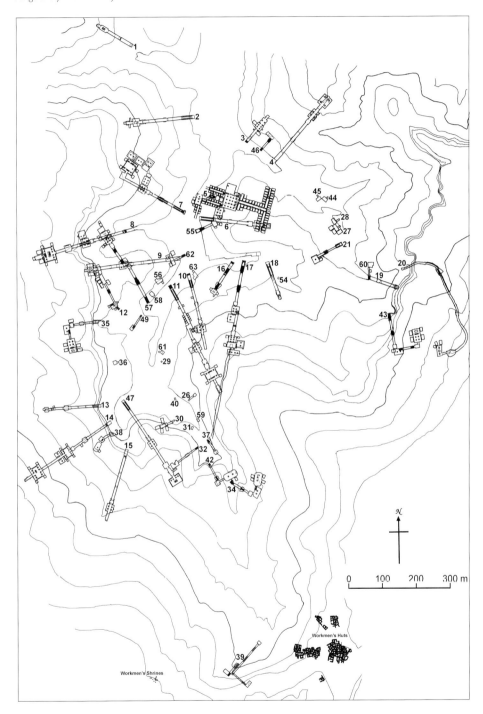

DM1447

DM 2005

DM2002

DM2003 DM2004 DM2001

HATHOR
TEMPLE

0   50 m

5

357

DM1407

290-1

330
323
321 8A 8
322 211

10 339
321
292

265

217

216 266 6 267

328 327

326
338
325 DM
1138 356
DM1069 268
250
DM1159
329 DM
1108
354 290
3 218-20 1 359 361 360
340
DM1099 335
210 2
213 9
299 214

Map 5F The Theban Necropolis: the Valley of the Queens (*for key to numbered tombs, see the Valley of the Queens entry in the index*).

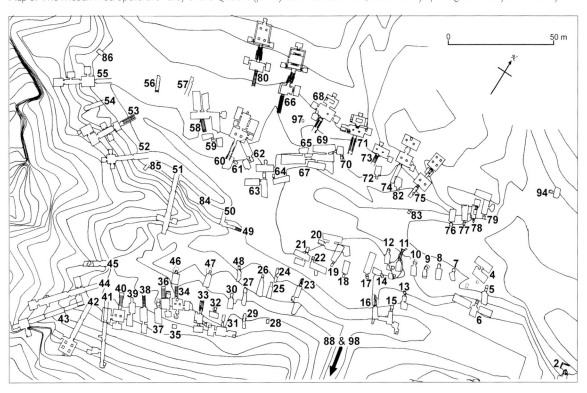

Abbreviations and Bibliography

LIST OF ABBREVIATIONS

A1ICE W.F. Reineke, *Acts. First International Congress of Egyptologists* (Berlin: Akademie Verlag).

A6CIE *Atti del VI Congresso Internazionale di Egittologia*, 2vv. (Turin: Comitato Organizzativo del Congresso)

AbSaq2000 M. Barta and J. Krejčí, *Abusir and Saqqara in the Year 2000* (Prague: Academy of Sciences of the Czech Republic).

AJAH *American Journal of Ancient History*

AL *Amarna Letters* (San Francisco).

AR *Amarna Reports* (London).

ArchOr *Archiv orientální* (Prague)

ASAE *Annales du Service des Antiquités de l'Égypte* (Cairo).

ATut C.N.Reeves (ed.), *After Tut'ankhamun* (London: Kegan Paul International, 1992).

Beamtennekropolen J. Assmann, E. Dziobek, H. Guksch, and F. Kampp (eds.), *Thebanische Beamtennekropolen* (Heidelberg: Heidelberger Orientverlag, 1995).

BES *Bulletin of the Egyptological Seminar* (New York).

BIFAO *Bulletin de l'Institut Français d'Archéologie Orientale du Caire* (Cairo).

BioAnth W.V. Davies and R. Walker (eds.) *Biological Anthropology and the Study of Ancient Egypt* (London: BMP, 1993).

BiOr *Bibliotheca Orientalis* (Leiden).

BM British Museum, London.

BMP British Museum Press/Publications.

BMFA *Bulletin of the Museum of Fine Arts* (Boston).

BMMA *Bulletin of the Metropolitan Museum of Art* (New York).

BoD Book of the Dead

BSAA *Bulletin Societé archéologique d'Alexandrie* (Alexandrie).

BSFE *Bulletin de la Societé Français d'Egyptologie* (Paris).

CAH *Cambridge Ancient History* (Cambridge).

CAJ *Cambridge Archaeological Journal* (Cambridge).

CdE *Chronique d'Egypte* (Brussels).

CG Catalogue Général des Antiquités Egyptiennes du Musée du Caire.

ChSeers E. Goring, N. Reeves and J. Ruffle (eds.), *Chief of Seers: Egyptian Studies in Memory of Cyril Aldred* (London & New York: Kegan Paul International/ Edinburgh: National Museums of Scotland, 1997).

CM Egyptian Museum, Cairo.

CT Coffin Texts

DE *Discussions in Egyptology* (Oxford).

D&T S.E. Orel (ed.), *Death and Taxes in the Ancient Near East* (Lewiston/ Queenston/Lampeter: E. Mellen Press, 1996).

EArch *Egyptian Archaeology: the Bulletin of the Egypt Exploration Society* (London)

EEFAR *Egypt Exploration Fund Archaeological Report*

L'Ég 1979 *L'Egyptologie en 1979, Axes prioritaires de recherches*, 2vv. (Paris: Centre National de la Recherche Scientifique, 1982).

Essays Goedicke B.M. Bryan and D. Lorton (eds.), *Essays in Egyptology in honor of Hans Goedicke* (San Antonio: Van Siclen Books, 1995).

Études Lauer C. Berger and B. Mathieu (eds.), *Études sur l'Ancien Empire et la nécropole de Saqqâra dédiées à Jean-Phillipe Lauer* (Montpellier, 1997).

FS Altenmüller N. Kloth, K. Martin and E. Pardey (eds.), *Es werde niedergelegt als Schriftsück: Festschrift für Hartwig Altenmüller zum 65. Geburtstag* (Hamburg: Helmut Buske Verlag).

FS Edel M. Görg, K.-J. Seyfried and E. Pusch (eds.), *Festschrift Elmar Edel* (Bamberg, 1979).

FHK D. Silverman (ed.), *For His Ka: Essays Offered in Memory of Klaus Baer* (Chicago: University of Chicago, 1994).

FSR Kamstra, H. M. and K. Wagendonk (eds.), *Funerary Symbols and Religion* (Kampen: J. H. Kok, 1988).

GM *Göttinger Miszellen* (Göttingen).

GRM Graeco-Roman Museum, Alexandria.

Homm. Leclant C. Berger, G. Clerc and N. Grimal (eds.), *Hommages à Jean Leclant* (Cairo: IFAO).

Homm. Haikal N. Grimal, A. Kamel, and C. May-Sheikholeslami (eds.), *Hommages Fayza Haikal* (Cairo: IFAO).

HPA High Priest of Amun at Thebes

IFAO Institut Français d'Archéologie Orientale.

IHE U. Luft (ed.), *The Intellectual Heritage of Egypt. Studies presented to László Kákosy by Friends and Colleagues on the Occasion of his 60th Birthday* (Budapest).

JARCE *Journal of the American Research Center in Egypt* (New York, &c).

JE Journal d'Entree (CM).

JEA *Journal of Egyptian Archaeology* (London).

JMFA *Journal of the Museum of Fine Arts, Boston* (Boston).

JNES *Journal of Near Eastern Studies* (Chicago).

JSSEA *Journal of the Society for the Study of Egyptian Antiquities* (Toronto).

LÄ *Lexikon der Ägyptologie* (Weisbaden).

MDAIK *Mitteilungen des Deutschen Archäologischen Instituts, Kairo* (Mainz).

MelMasp *Mélanges Maspero* (Cairo 1935–53)

MelMokh *Mélanges Gamal Eddin Mokhtar* (Cairo: IFAO, 1985).

MIFAO *Memoirs de l'institut Français d'Archéologie Orientale* (Cairo).

MFA Museum of Fine Arts, Boston.

MKS S.Quirke (ed.),*Middle Kingdom Studies* (New Malden, 1991).

MMA Metropolitan Museum of Art, New York.

MMJ *Metropolitan Museum Journal* (New York).

NARCE *Newsletter of the American Research Center in Egypt* (New York).

Obj. no. Excavators' object number.

OMRO *Oudheidkundige Mededelingen uit het Rijksmuseum van Oudheden te Leiden* (Leiden).

P7ICE C.J. Eyre (ed.), *Proceedings of the Seventh International Congress of Egyptologists* (Leuven, 1997).

P8ICE Z. Hawass & L.P. Brock (eds.), *Egyptology at the Dawn of the Twenty-First Century: Proceedings of the Eighth International Congress of Egyptologists, Cairo, 2000* (Cairo: American University in Cairo Press, 2003).

P&P J. Assmann, G. Burkard, and V. Davies (eds.), *Problems and Priorities in Egyptian Archaeology.* (London: KPI, 1987).

PSBA *Proceedings of the Society for Biblical Archaeology* (London).

PT Pyramid Texts

Pyr. Stud. J. Baines, T.G.H. James, A. Leahy and A.F. Shore (eds.), *Pyramid Studies and other essays presented to I.E.S. Edwards* (London: EES).

RecChamp *Recueil d'Etudes Egyptologiques Dédiée à la Mémoire de Jean-François Champollion* (Paris: Honoré Champion/Edouard Champion).

RdE *Revue d'Egyptologie* (Leuven).

RMO Rijksmuseum van Oudheden, Leiden.

SAK *Studien zur altägyptschen Kultur* (Hamburg).

SJH *Smithsonian Journal of History* (Washington).

Stat. H. Guksch and D. Polz (eds.), *Stationen. Beiträge zur Kulturgeschichte*

Ägyptens. Rainer Stadelmann gewidmet (Mainz: Philipp von Zabern, 1998).

StudSimp P. der Manuelian (ed.), *Studies in Honor of William Kelly Simpson*, 2vv. (Boston: Museum of Fine Arts, 1996).

StudSmith A. Leahy and J. Tait (eds.), *Studies on Ancient Egypt in Honour of H.S. Smith* (London: EES, 1999).

SR Special Register (CM).

TAE B.E. Schafer (ed.), *Temples in Ancient Egypt* (London: I.B. Tauris, 1998).

ThNec N. Strudwick and J.H. Taylor (eds.), *The Theban Necropolis: Past, Present and Future* (London: BMP, 2003).

TR Temporary Register (CM).

UC Petrie Museum, University College London.

UReed C. Eyre, A. Leahy and L.M. Leahy (eds.), *The Unbroken Reed: Studies in the Culture and Heritage of Ancient Egypt In Honour of A.F. Shore* (London: Egypt Exploration Society, 1994).

VA *Varia Aegyptiaca* (San Antonio, TX).

VSK R.H. Wilkinson (ed.), *Valley of the Sun Kings: New Explorations in the Tombs of the Pharaohs* (Tucson, AZ, 1995).

ZÄS *Zeitschrift für Ägyptische Sprache und Altertumskunde* (Leipzig, Berlin).

70GMAE B. Manley (ed.), *Seventy Great Mysteries of Ancient Egypt* (London and New York: Thames & Hudson).

BIBLIOGRAPHY

ABD EL-WAHAB, F. 1959. *La Tombe no 1 de Sen–Nedjem à Deir El–Médineh* (Cairo: IFAO).

ABDALLA, A. 1992. *Graeco–Roman Funerary Stelae from Upper Egypt* (Liverpool: University Press).

ABITZ, F. 1989. *Baugeschichte und Dekoration des Grabes Ramesses' VI* (Freiburg: Universitätsverlag/Göttingen: Vandenhoeck und Ruprecht).

— 1994. 'The Structure of the Decoration in the Tomb of Ramesses IX', *ATut*, 165–85.

ABOU EL-ATTA, H. 1992. 'The Relation between the Egyptian Tombs and the Alexandrian Hypogea', *Études et Travaux* 16: 11–19.

ABOU-GHAZI, D. (ed.) 1984. *Sami Gabra From Tasa to Touna* (Cairo: Dar el-Maaref).

ABU-BAKR, A.-M. 1953. *Excavations at Giza 1949–1950* (Cairo: Government Press).

ADAM, S. 1958. 'Recent Discoveries in the Eastern Delta (Dec. 1950–May 1955)', *ASAE* 55: 301–24.

ADAMS, B. 1987. *The Fort Cemetery at Hierakonpolis* (London: Kegan Paul International).

— 1995. *Ancient Nekhen* (New Malden: Sia).

— 2004. 'Excavations in the Elite Preynastic Cemetery at Hierakonpolis Locality HK6: 1999–2000', *ASAE* 78:35–52.

ADRIANI, A. 1940. 'Tombeau en alabatre du cimetière Latin', *Annuaire du Musée Gréco-Romain* (1935–1939), 15–23.

ALDRED, C. 1949. *Old Kingdom Art in Egypt* (London: Tirani).

— 1979. 'More light on the Ramesside Tomb Robberies', in J. Ruffle, G.A. Gaballa and K.A. Kitchen (eds.), *Glimpses of Ancient Egypt: Studies on Honour of H.W. Fairman* (Warminster: Aris and Phillips): 92–9.

ALEXANIAN, N. 1999. *Dahschur II: Das Grab des Prinzen Netjer–aperef. Die Mastaba II/1 in Dahschur* (Mainz: Philipp von Zabern).

ALEXANIAN, N. and S.J. SEIDLMAYER 2000. 'Die Nekropole von Dahshur. Forschungsgeschichet und Perspektiven', *AbSaq2000*: 283–304.

ALLEN, J.P. 1988. *Genesis in Egypt: The Philosophy of Ancient Egyptian Creation Accounts* (New Haven: Yale University Press).

— 1989. *Religion and Philosophy in Ancient Egypt* (New Haven: Yale University Press).

— 1994. 'Reading a Pyramid', in *Homm. Leclant*: 5–28.

— 2003. 'The high officials of the early Middle Kingdom', *ThNec*: 14–29.

ALLEN, T.G. 1974. *The Book of the Dead, or Going Forth by Day* (Chicago: University of Chicago).

ALLIOT, M. 1933–5. *Rapport sur les fouilles de Tell Edfou* (Cairo: IFAO).

ALTENMÜLLER, H. 1975. 'Butisches Begräbnis', *LÄ* I: 887.

— 1983a. 'Das Grab des Königin Tausret im Tal des Könige von Thebes', *SAK* 10: 1–24.

— 1983b. 'Bemerken zu den Königsgraben des Neuen Reiches', *SAK* 10: 25–62.

— 1983c. 'Lebenszeit und Unsterblichkeit in den Darstellungen der Gräber des Alten Reiches', in J. Assmann and G. Burkard (eds.), *5000 Jahre Ägypten: Genese und Permanenz Pharaonischer Kunst* (n.p.: IS Edition): 75–88.

— 1992. 'Zweiter Vorbericht in die Arbeiten des Archäologischen Instituts der Universität Hamburg am Grab des Bay (KV13) im Tal der Könige von Theben', *SAK* 19: 15–36.

— 1994. 'Dritter Vorbericht über die Arbeiten des Archäologischen Instituts Hamburg am Grab des Bay (KV13) im Tal der Könige von Theben', *SAK* 21:1–18.

— 1997. 'Der Grabherr des Alten Reiches in seinem Palast des Jenseits. Bemerkungen zur sog. Prunkscheintür des Alten Reiches' *Études Lauer.* 11–19.

— 1998. *Die Wanddarstellungen im Grab des Mehu in Saqqara* (Mainz: Philipp von Zabern).

AMÉLINEAU, E. 1899a. *Le tombeau d'Osiris: monographie de la découverte faite en 1897–1898* (Paris: E. Leroux).

— 1899b. *Mission Amélineau: Les nouvelles fouilles d'Abydos 1895–1896 Compte rendu in extenso des fouilles, description des monuments et objets découverts* (Paris: E. Leroux).

ANDERSON, W. 1992. 'Badarian burials: evidence of social inequality in Middle Egypt during the early Predynastic era', *JARCE* 29: 51–66.

ARNOLD, Di. 1962. *Wandrelief und Raumfunktion in ägyptischen Tempeln des neuen Reiches* (Berlin: Bruno Hessling).

— 1974–1981. *Der Tempel des Königs Mentuhotep von Deir el-Bahari*, 3vv. (Mainz: Philipp von Zabern).

— 1976. *Gräber des Alten und Mittleren Reiches in El-Tarif* (Mainz: Philipp von Zabern).

— 1979a. *The Temple of Mentuhotep at Deir el-Bahri* (New York: MMA).

— 1979b. 'Das Labyrinth und seine Vorbilder'. *MDAIK* 35: 1–9.

— 1987. *Der Pyramidbezirk des Königs Amenemhet III in Dahschur I: Die Pyramide* (Mainz: Philipp von Zabern).

— 1988. *The Pyramid of Senwosret I* (New York: Metropolitan Museum of Art).

— 1991. *Building in Egypt: Pharaonic Stone Masonry* (New York: Oxford University Press).

— 1992. *The Pyramid Complex of Senwosret I* (New York: MMA).

— 1997. 'The Late Period Tombs of Hor-Khebit, Wennefer and Wereshnefer at Saqqâra', in *Études Lauer*: 31–54.

— 1998. 'Royal Cult Complexes of the Old and Middle Kingdoms', *TAE*: 86–126.

— 2002. *The Pyramid Complex of Senwosret III at Dahshur: Architectural Studies* (New York: MMA).

— 2003. *The Encyclopaedia of Ancient Egyptian Architecture* (London: I. B. Tauris).

ARNOLD, Di. and A. OPPENHEIM 1995. 'Reexcavating the Senwosret III Pyramid Complex at Dahshur', *Kmt* 6/2: 44–56.

ARNOLD, Do. 1991. 'Amenemhat I and the early Twelfth Dynasty at Thebes', *MMJ* 26: 5–48.

ARNOLD, F. et al. 1990. *The Control Notes and Team Marks* (New York: Metropolitan Museum of Art).

ASSMANN, J. 1974. *Der Grab des Basa (Nr. 389) in der thenbanischen Nekropole* (Mainz: Phillip von Zabern).

— 1977. *Das Grab der Mutirdis* (Mainz: Phillip von Zabern).

— 1978. 'Eine Traumoffenbarung der Göttin Hathor Zeugnisse «Persönlicher Frömmigkeit» in thebanischen Privatgräbern der Ramessidenzeit', *RdE* 30: 22–50.

— 1983. *Sonnenhymnen in thebanischen Gräbern* (Mainz: Phillip von Zabern).

— 1984a. 'Das Grab mit gewundenem Abstieg. Zum Typenwandel des Privat-Felsgrabes im Neuen Reich', *MDAIK* 40: 277–90, 282.

— 1984b. 'Totenkult, Totenglauben', *LÄ* VI: 670.

— 1987. 'Priorität und Interesse: Das Problem der Ramessidischen Beamtengräber', *P&P*: 31–42.

— 1989. 'Death and Inititation in the Funerary Religion of Ancient Egypt', *Religion and Philosophy in Ancient Egypt* (New Haven: Yale University) 135–59.

— 1991. *Das Grab des Amenemope (TT41)* (Mainz: Phillip von Zabern).

— 2003a. 'The Ramesside Tomb and the construction of sacred space', *ThNec*: 46–52.

— 2003b. 'The Ramesside tomb of Nebsumenu (TT183) and the ritual of Opening the Mouth', *ThNec*: 53–60.

ASSMANN, J., E. DZIOBEK, H. GUKSCH, and F. KAMPP 1995. *Thebanische: neue Perspektiven archäologischer Forschung* (Heidelberg: Heidelberger Orient).

ASSOCIATION FRANÇAISE D'ACTION ARTISTIQUE 1987. *Tanis: L'or des pharaons* (Paris: Association française d'action artistique).

ASTON, D.A. 1999. 'Dynasty 26, Dynasty 30, or Dynasty 27? In Search of the Funerary Archaeology of the Persian Period', *StudSmith*: 17–22.

— 2003. 'The Theban West Bank from the Twenty-fifth Dynasty to thePtolemaic Period', *ThNec*: 138–66.

ASTON, D.A. and B. BADER 1998. 'Einige Bermerkungen zur späten Neuen Reich in Matmar', *MDAIK* 54: 19–48.

ASTON, B., J. HARRELL, and I. SHAW 2000. 'Stone', *Ancient Egyptian Materials and Technology*, P. Nicholson and I. Shaw, eds (Cambridge: Cambridge University Press) 5–77.

AUFRÈRE, S. 1991. *L'Univers Minéral dans la Pensée Égyptienne*, 2vv. (Cairo: IFAO).

— (ed.) 1999. *Encyclopédie religieuse de l'Univers végétal* (Montpellier: Université Paul Valéry-Montpellier III).

AUFRÈRE, S. and J.-Cl. GOLVIN 1997. *Sites, temples et pyramides de Moyenne et Basse Égypte. De la naissance de la civilisation pharaonique à l'époque gréco-romaine* (Paris: Errance).

AUGENOT, V. 2000. 'La vectorialité de la scène de travaux de champs chez Méréruka', *GM* 176: 5–24.

AYRTON, E., C.T. CURRELLY and A.E.P. WEIGALL 1904. *Abydos* III (London: EEF).

BÁCS, T.A. 1998. 'First Preliminary Report in the Work of the Hungarian Mission in Thebes in Theban Tomb No 65 (Nebamun/Imiseba)', *MDAIK* 54: 49–64.

BADAWI, A. 1957. 'Das Grab des Kronprinzen Scheschonk, sohnes Osorkon's II und Hohenpristers von Memphis', *ASAE* 54: 153–77.

BADAWY, A. 1948. *Le Dessin Architectural Chez les Anciens Egyptiens* (Cairo: IFAO).

— 1954–68. *A History of Egyptian Architecture*, 3vv. (Cairo; Berkeley: University of California Press).

— 1956. 'The Ideology of the Superstructure of the Mastaba-Tomb in Egypt', *JNES* 15: 180–83.

— 1976. *The Tombs of Iteti, Sekhem'ankh-Ptah, and Kaemnofert at Giza* (Los Angeles: University of California Press).

— 1978. *The Tomb of Nyhetep-Ptah at Giza and the Tomb of 'Ankhm'ahor at Saqqara* (Berkeley and Los Angeles: University of California Press).

— 1986. 'Ancient Constructional diagrams in Egyptian architecture', *Gazette des Beaux-Arts* 107: 51–6.

BAGNALL, R.S. and D.W. RATHBONE 2004. *Egypt From Alexander to the Copts: an archaeological and historical guide* (London: British Museum Press).

BAINES, J. 1985. 'Color Terminology and Color Classification: Ancient Egyptian Color Terminology and Polychromy', *American Anthropologist* 87: 282–97.

— 1987. 'Practical Religion and Piety', *JEA* 73: 79–98.

— 1989. 'Communication and display: the integration of early Egyptian art and writing,' *Antiquity* 63: 471–82.

— 1994. 'On the Status and Purposes of Ancient Egyptian Art', *CAJ* 4.1: 67–94.

BAINES, J. and J. MÁLEK 1980. *Atlas of Ancient Egypt* (New York and Oxford: Facts on File).

BAKR, M.I. 1992. *Tombs and Burial Customs at Bubastis* (Cairo: University of Zagazig).

BALCZ, H. 1939. 'Zu den Szenen der Jagdfahrten im Papyrosdickicht', *ZÄS* 75: 32–8.

BANKES, T. 1788. *New System of Geography* (London: C. Cooke).

BARD, K. 1994. *From Farmers to Pharaohs: Mortuary Evidence for the Rise of Complex Society in Egypt* (Sheffield: Sheffield Academic Press).

BAREŠ, L. 1999. *The Shaft Tomb of Udjahorresnet at Abusir* (Prague: Karolinum Press).

— 2003. 'Relief Decoration in the Superstructures of the Late Period', *FS Altenmüller*: 11–15.

BAREŠ, L., K. SMOLÁRIKOVA and E. STROUHAL 2005. 'The Saite-Persian Cemetery at Abusir in 2003', *ZÄS* 132: 95–106.

BAREŠ, L. and E. STROUHAL 2000. 'The Shaft-tomb of Iufaa – Season of 1997/98', *ZÄS* 127: 5–14.

BARGUET, P. 1978. 'Remarques sur Quelques Scènes de la Salle du Sarcophage de Ramsès VI', *RdE* 30: 51–6.

BARSANTI, A. and G. MASPERO 1900a. 'Lex tombeaux de Psammétique et de Setariban', *ASAE* 1: 161–88.

— 1900b. 'Tombeau de Péténisis', *ASAE* 1: 230–61.

— 1900c. 'Tombeau de Zannehibou', *ASAE* 1: 262–82.

— 1901. 'Tombeau de Péténneit', *ASAE* 2: 97–111.

— 1904. 'Le tombeau de Hikaoumsaf', *ASAE* 5: 69–83.

BÁRTA, M. 1998. 'Serdab and Statue Placement in Private Tombs down to the Fourth Dynasty', *MDAIK* 54: 65–75.

— 1981. *Die Bedeutung der Pyramidentexte für den verstorbenen König* (Munich: Deutscher Kunstverlag).

— 2002. 'Sociology of the Minor Cemeteries during the Old Kingdom. A View from Abusir South', *ArchOr* 70: 291–300.

— 2003. 'Funerary rites and cults at Abusir South', *FS Altenmüller*: 17–30

BARTA, W. 1963. *Die Altägyptische Opferliste von der Frühzeit bis zur Griechisch-Römischen Epoche* (Berlin: B. Hessling).

BARTHELMESS, P. 1992. *Die Übergang ins Jenseits in den thebanischen Beamtengräbern der Ramessidenzeit* (Heidelberg: Orientverlag).

BARWIK, M. 2003. 'New data concerning the Third Intermediate Period cemetery in the Hatshepsut temple at Deir el-Bahari', *ThNec*: 122–30.

BASTA, M. 1966. 'Clearance of Some Tombs of the Late Period near the Serapeum at Saqqara' *ASAE* 59: 15–21.

— 1979. 'Excavations west of Kom Firin (1966–67)', *CdE* 54: 183–96.

BATES, O. 1917. *Ancient Egyptian Fishing* (Cambridge, MA: Harvard University).

BAUD, M. 1935. *Les Dessins Ebauchés de la nécropole Thébaine* (Cairo: IFAO).

—1997. 'Aux pieds de Djoser. Les mastabas entre fossé et enceinte de la partie nord du complexe funéraire', *Études Lauer*: 69–87.

BEAUX, N. 1997. 'Le mastaba de Ti à Saqqara', *Etudes sur l'Ancien Empire et la nécropole de Saqqara dédiées à Jean-Philippe Lauer*, C. Berger and B. Mathieu, eds (Montpelier: University Paul Valéry) 89–98.

BEINLICH-SEEBER, C. and A. G. SHEDID 1987. *Das Grab des Userhat (TT56)* (Mainz: Philip von Zabern).

BELL, M.R. 1985. 'Gurob tomb 605 and Mycenaean Chronology', *MelMokh* I (Cairo: IFAO): 61–86.

BELZONI, G. 1820. *Narrative of the Operations and Recent Discoveries in Egypt and Nubia* (London: John Murray).

BÉNÉDITE, G. 1894. *Tombeau de Neferhotpou, fils d'Amenemanit* (Cairo: IFAO)

— 1911. 'La tenderie dans la decoration murale des tombes civiles', *ZÄS* 48: 1–9.

BERLANDINI, J. 1979. 'La pyramide "ruinée" de Sakkara-nord et le roi Ikaouhor-Menkaouhor', *RdE* 31: 3–28.

— 1982. 'Les Tombes Amarniennes et d'Epoque Toutankhamon à Sakkara, Critères Stylistiques', *L'Ég* 1979 II: 195–12.

BERRILL, M. 1989. *Mummies, Masks and Mourners* (London: Hamish Hamilton).

BICKEL, S. and P. TALLET 1997. 'La nécropole saïte d'Héliopolis. Étude préliminaire', *BIFAO* 97: 67–90.

BIERBRIER, M.L. 1982. *The Tomb-Builders of the Pharaohs* (London: BMP).

— (ed.) 1997. *Portraits and Masks: Burial Customs in Roman Egypt* (London: British Museum).

BIETAK, M. 1996. *Avaris the Captial of the Hyksos* (London: British Museum).

BIETAK, M. and R. REISER-HASLAUER 1978, 1982. *Das Grab des Anch-Hor, Obersthofmeister der Gottesgemahlin Nitokris* (Mainz: Phillip von Zabern).

BINFORD, L.R. 1971. 'Mortuary practices: their study and their potential', in J. Brown (ed.), *Approaches to the Social Dimensions of Mortuary Practices* (Menasha WI: Society for American Archaeology): 6–29.

BISSING, F.W. 1897. 'Die Datirung des "Maket-Grabes"', *ZÄS* 34: 94–7.

— 1901. *La catacombe nouvellement decouverte de Kom el Chougafa* (Munich: J. B. Obernetter).

— 1905, 1911. *Die Mastaba des Gem-ni-kai*, 2vv. (Berlin: Alexander Duncker).

— 1915. 'Les tombeaux d'Assouan', *ASAE* 15: 1–14.

BLACKMAN, A. M. 1912. 'The Significance of Incense and Libations in Funerary and Temple Ritual', *ZÄS* 50: 69–75.

— 1916. 'The Ka-house and the serdab', *JEA* 3: 250–54.

BLACKMAN, A.M. and M. APTED 1914–1953. *The Rock Tombs of Meir*, 6vv. (London: EES).

BLACKMAN, W.S. 1922. 'Some Occurrences of the Corn-'Arusseh in Ancient Egyptian Tomb Paintings', *JEA* 8: 235–40.

BOCHI, P.A. 1994. 'Images of Time in Ancient Egyptian Art,' *JARCE* 31: 55–62.

— 1999. 'Death by Drama: The Ritual of Damnatio Memoriae', *GM* 171: 73–86.

BOLSHAKOV, A. 1991. 'The Old Kingdom Representations of Funeral Procession', *GM* 121: 31–54.

— 1994a. 'Hinting as a Method of Old Kingdom Tomb Decoration', *GM* 139: 9–33.

— 1994b. 'Addenda to "Hinting as a Method of Old Kingdom Tomb Decoration"', *GM* 143: 29–30.

BORCHARDT, L. 1897. 'Ein Ägyptisches Grab auf der Sinaihalbinsel', *ZÄS* 35: 112–15.

— 1898. 'Das Grab des Menes', *ZÄS* 36: 87–105.

— 1907. *Das Grabdenkmal des Königs Ne-user-re'* (Leipzig: Heinrichs').

— 1909. *Das Grabdenkmal des Königs Nefer ir-ka-re'* (Leipzig: Heinrichs').

— 1910. *Das Grabdenkmal des Königs S'aꜣhu-re'* (Leipzig: Heinrichs').

BORGHOUTS, J.F. 1978. *Ancient Egyptian Magical Texts* (Leiden: Brill).

— 1998. 'A Funerary Address to the High-priest Harmakhis', in L. H. Lesko (ed.), *Ancient Egyptian and Mediterranean Studies in Memory of William A. Ward*, (Providence: Brown University): 19–36.

BOURIANT, U. 1885. 'Les tombeaux d'Hiéraconpolis', in *Etudes archéologiques, linguistiques et historiques dediés a ... C. Leemans* (Leiden): 35–40.

— 1888. 'Les tombeaux d'Assouan', *RdT* 10: 181–98.

— 1894. 'Tombeau de Harmhabi', *MIFAO* 5: 413–34.

BOURRIAU, J.D. 1988. *Pharaohs and Mortals: Egyptian art in the Middle Kingdom* (Cambridge: University Press).

— 1991. 'Patterns of change in burial customs during the Middle Kingdom', *MKS*: 3–20.

BOUSSAC, H. 1896. *Le tombeau d'Anna* (Paris: E. Leroux).

BRACK, A. and A. 1977. *Das Grab des Tjanuni; Theben Nr. 74* (Mainz : Philip von Zabern).

— 1980. *Das Grab des Haremheb* (Mainz: Phillip von Zabern).

BRAND, P. 2000. *The Monuments of Seti I* (Leiden: Brill).

BRECCIA, E. 1922. *Alexandrea ad Aegyptum: a guide to the ancient and modern town, and to its Graeco-Roman Museum* (Bergamo: Instituto italiano d'arte grafiche).

BRESCIANI, E. 1983. *Tomba di Boccori: La Galleria di Pedineit, Vizir de Nectanebo I* (Pisa: Giardini).

BRESCIANI, E., M.C. BETRO, A. GIAMMARUSTI and C. LA TORRE 1988. *Tomba di Bakenrenef (L.24). Attivista del cantiere scuola* 1985–1987 (Pisa: Giardini).

BRESCIANI, E., S. AN-NAGGAR, S. PERNIGOTTO and F. SILVANO 1983. *La Galleria di Pedineit, visir di Nectanebo* (Pisa: Giardini).

BRESCIANI, E., S. PERNIGOTTI and M.O. GIANGERI SILVIS 1977. *La tomb di Ciennehebu, capo della flotta del Re* (Pisa: Giardini).

BREWER, D. and R. FRIEDMAN 1989. *Fish and Fishing in Ancient Egypt* (Warminster: Aris and Phillips).

BRINKS, J. 1979. *Die Entwicklung der königlichen Grabanlagen des Alten Reiches* (Hildesheim: Gerstenberg).

BRINKS, J. 1980. 'Mastaba', *LÄ* III: 1214–31.

BRISSAUD, P. 1987. *Cahiers de Tanis: Mission français des fouilles de Tanis* I (Paris: Editions Recherche sur les Civilisations).

— 1998. 'Les principaux résultats des fouilles récentes à Tanis (1987–1997)', in Brissaud and C. Zivie-Coche (eds.). *Tanis: travaux récents sur Tell Sân el-Hagar* (Paris: Éditions Noësis: 1998): 13–61.

BROCK, L.P. and R.L. SHAW 1997. 'The Royal Ontario Museum Epigraphic Project – Theban Tomb 89 Preliminary Report', *JARCE* 34: 167–78.

BRODRICK, M. and A. A. MORTON 1899. 'The tomb of Pepi Ankh (Khua), near Sharona', *PSBA* 21: 26–33.

BROVARSKI, R. 1984. 'Serdab', *LÄ* 5: 874–9.

— 2001. *The Sennedjemib Complex*, 2vv. (Boston: MFA).

BRUNNER, H. 1936. *Die Anlagen der ägyptischen Felsgräber bis zum Mittleren Reich* (Glückstadt and Hamburg: Augustin).

BRUNTON, G. 1920. *Lahun I: The Treasure* (London: BSAE).

— 1927–30. *Qau and Badari*, 3vv. (London: BSAE).

— 1937. *Mostagedda and the Tasian Culture* (London: Bernard Quaritch).

— 1947. 'The Burial of Pince Ptah-Shepses at Saqqara', *ASAE* 47: 125–37.

— 1948. *Matmar* (London: Bernard Quaritch).

BRUNTON, G. and G. CATON-THOMPSON 1928. *The Badarian Civilisation and Predynastic Remains near Badari* (London: BSAE).

BRUNTON, G. and R. ENGELBACH 1927. *Gurob* (London: BSAE).

BRUYÈRE, B. 1924–1953. *Rapport sur les Fouilles de Deir el Médineh* 1923–24ff. (Cairo: IFAO).

— 1952. *Tombes thébaines de Deir el Médineh à décoration monochrome* (Cairo: IFAO).

— 1956–7. 'Une nouvelle famille de prêtres de Montou, trouvée par Baraize à Deir el Bahri', *ASAE* 54: 11–33.

— 1959. *La Tombe no I de Sen-Nedjem à Deir El-Médineh* (Cairo: IFAO).

BRUYÈRE, B. and A. BATILLE 1936. 'Une tombe Gréco-Romaine de Deir el Médineh', *BIFAO* 36: 145–51.

BRUYÈRE, B. and C. KUENTZ 1926. *La tombe de Nakht-Min et la tombe d'Ari-Nefer* (Cairo: IFAO).

BRYAN, B. M. 1984. 'Evidence for Female Literacy from Theban Tombs of the New Kingdom', *BES* 6: 17–32.

— 1992. 'Designing the Cosmos: Temples and Temple Decoration', *Egypt's Dazzling Sun*, A. Kozloff and B. Bryan, eds (Cleveland: Cleveland Museum of Art) 73–115.

— 1996. 'The Disjunction Of Text And Image In Egyptian Art', *StudSimp*: 161–68.

— 1997. 'The Statue Program for the Mortuary Temple of Amenhotep III', in S. Quirke (ed.), *The Temple in Ancient Egypt* (London: BMP): 57–81.

— 2001. 'Painting techniques and artisan organization in the Tomb of Suemniwet, Theban Tomb 92', in W.V. Davies (ed.), *Colour and Painting in Ancient Egypt* (London: BMP): 63–72.

BUCHBERGER, H. 1983. 'Sexualität und Harfenspiel-Notizen zur "suxuellen" Konnotation der altägyptischen Ikonographie', *GM* 66: 11–44.

BUCHER, P. 1932. *Les Textes des tombes de Thoutmosis III et d'Aménophis II* (Cairo: IFAO).

CAILLAUD, F. 1823–27. *Voyage à Méroé …* (Paris: By the King's Permission at the Royal Press).

CALLENDER, V. 2002. 'A Contribution to the Burial of Women in the Old Kingdom', *ArchOr* 70: 301–8.

CALLENDER, V. and P. JANOSI 1997. 'The Tomb of Queen Khamerernebty II at Giza', *MDAIK* 53, 1–22.

CAPART, J., A.H. GARDENER and B. VAN DE WALLE 1936. 'New Light on the Ramesside Tomb Robberies', *JEA* 22: 169–93.

CARNARVON, Earl of, and H. CARTER 1912. *Five Years' Explorations at Thebes* (London: H. Frowde).

CARTER, H. 1916. 'Report on the Tomb of Zeser-ka-Ra Amen-hetep I, Discovered by the Earl of Carnarvon in 1914', *JEA* 3: 147–54.

— 1917a. 'A Tomb Prepared for Queen Hatshepsuit and Other Recent Discoveries at Thebes', *JEA* 4: 107–18.

— 1917b. 'A Tomb Prepared for Queen Hatshepsuit discovered by the Earl of Carnarvon', *ASAE* 16: 179–82.

CARTER H. and A.H. GARDINER 1917. 'The Tomb of Ramesses IV and the Turin Plan of a Royal Tomb', *JEA* 4: 130–58.

CARTER H. and A.C. MACE 1923–33. *The Tomb of Tut.ankh.Amen*, 3vv. (London: Cassell).

CASE, H.C. and J.C. PAYNE 1962. 'Tomb 100: the Decorated Tomb at Hierakonpolis', *JEA* 48: 5–18.

CASTEL, G. and D. MEEKS 1980. *Deir el-Médineh* 1970 (Cairo: IFAO).

CASTEL, G., L. PANTALACCI, and N. CHERPION 2001. *Le Mastaba de Khentika*, 1 (Cairo: IFAO).

CASTEL, G. and L. PANTALACCI 2005. *Les cimetières est et ouest du mastaba de Khentika, Oasis de Dakhla* (Cairo: IFAO).

CASTILLOS, J.J. 1982. *A Reappraisal of the Published Evidence on Egyptian Predynastic and Early Dynastic Cemeteries* (Toronto: Benben Publications).

— 1998. 'Tomb Size distribution in Egyptian Predynastic Cemeteries', *DE* 40:5 1–65.

CECIL, Lady William 1903. 'Report on the work done at Aswan', *ASAE* 4: 51–73.

— 1905. 'Report of work done at Aswan during the first months of 1904 by Lady William Cecil', *ASAE* 6: 273–83.

CENEVAL, J.-L. 1989. *Le mastaba* (Paris: Louvre).

CENTRE OF DOCUMENTATION 1980. *Le Ramesseum*, 11 vv. (Cairo: Centre of Documentation).

ČERNÝ, J. 1973a. *A Community of Workmen at Thebes in the Ramesside Period* (Cairo: IFAO).

— 1973b. *The Valley of the Kings* (Cairo: IFAO).

CHABAN, M. 1917. 'Le puits du général Ankh-uah-ab-Re-si-Niy à Saqqarah', *ASAE* 17: 177–82.

— 1920. 'Fouilles dans la nécropole de Saqqarah', *ASAE* 19: 208–15.

CHAPMAN, R., I. KINNES, and K. RANDSBORG (eds.) 1981. *The Archaeology of Death* (Cambridge: Cambridge University Press).

CHASSINAT, E. 1901. 'Une tombe inviolee de la XVIIIe dynastie decouverte aux environs de Medinet el-Gorab dans le Fayoûm', *BIFAO* 1: 225–34.

CHERPION, N. 1982. 'Autour de la tombe de Raour', *CdE* 114: 236–40.

— 1989. *Mastabas et hypogées d'ancien empire: le probleme de la datation* (Brussels: Conaissance de l'Egypte Ancienne).

— 1995. 'Survivances amarniennes dans la tombe d'Ipouy', *BIFAO* 95: 125–39.

CHERPION, N. et al. 1994. 'Le "cô̂ne d'onguent" gage de survie', *BIFAO*, 94: 79–106.

CHUGG, A. 2004/2005. *The Lost Tomb of Alexander the Great* (London, Richmond editions).

CLARKE, S, and R. ENGELBACH 1930. *Ancient Egyptian Masonry* (London: Lightning Source Inc).

CLEDAT, J. 1898. 'Le tombeau de la dame Amten', *Revue archéologique* 33: 15–20.

COLLINS, L. 1976. 'The Private Tombs of Thebes: Excavations by Sir Robert Mond 1905 and 1906', *JEA* 62: 18–40.

COLOGNE 1986. *Sen-nefer. Die Grabkammer des Bürgermeisters von Theben. Katalog der Sonderausstellung 1986 im Römisch-Germanischen Museum, Köln* (Mainz: Phillipp von Zabern).

COMMISSION DES MONUMENTS D'ÉGYPTE 1809–22. *Description de l'Égypte, ou Recueil des observations et des recherches qui ont été faites en Égypte pendent l'expédition de l'armée français: Antiquités (Planches)*, 9 + 10vv. (Paris: Imprimerie impériale).

COURY, R.M. 1992. 'The Politics of the Funeral: The Tomb of Saad Zaghlul', *JARCE* 29: 191–200.

COUR-MARTY, M-A. 1994. 'Les Textes des Pyramides témoignent du souci de normalisation des anciens Egyptiens', in *Homm. Leclant*, I: 123–40.

COVINGTON, L.D. 1906. 'Mastaba mount excavations', *ASAE* 6: 193–218.

CURTO, S. 1963. *Gli scavi italiani a el-Ghiza (1903)* (Rome: Aziende Tipographiche Eredi Dott. G. Bardi).

D'AURIA, S., P. LACOVARA, and C. ROEHRIG 1988. *Mummies & Magic: The Funerary Arts of Ancient Egypt* (Boston: Museum of Fine Arts).

DAOUD, K.A. 1998. 'The Herakleopolitan Stelae from the Memphite Necropolis', *P7ICE*: 303–8.

DARBY, W.J., P. GHALIOUNGUI, and L. GRIVETTI 1977. *Food: the Gift of Osiris* 1–2 (London: Academic).

DARESSY, G. 1900. 'Les Sépultures des Prêtres d'Ammon a Deir el-Bahari', *ASAE* I: 141–8.

— 1902a. 'Tombeau ptolémaique à Atfieh', *ASAE* 3: 160–80.

— 1902b. *Fouilles de la Vallée des Rois 1898–1899* (*CG*) (Cairo, IFAO).

— 1903. 'Tombe de Hor-Kheb a Saqqareh', *ASAE* 4: 76–83.

— 1917. 'Le mastaba de Khâ-f-khoufou à Gizeh', *ASAE* 16: 257–67.

DARESSY, G. and A. BARSANTI 1917. 'La nécropole des grands prêtres d'Heliopolis sous l'ancien empire', *ASAE* 16: 193–220.

DASZEWSKI, W.A. 1997. 'Mummy portraits from northern Egypt: The Necropolis in Marina el-Alamein', in Bierbrier (ed.) 1997: 59–65.

DAUMAS, F. 1964. 'Quelques remarques sur les représentations de pêche à la ligne sous l'Ancien Empire', *BIFAO* 62: 67–85.

DAVID, A.R. 1986. *The Pyramid Builders of Ancient Egypt* (London: Routledge & Kegan Paul).

DAVIES, B.G. 1999. *Who's Who at Deir el-Medina: a Prosopographical Study of the Royal Workmen's Commmunity* (Leiden: Nederlands Instituut voor het Nabije Oosten).

DAVIES, N. de G. 1900–1. *The mastaba of Ptahhetep and Akhethetep at Saqqareh*, 2vv. (London: EEF).

— 1901a. *The rock tombs of Sheikh Said* (London: EEF).

— 1901b. *The Mastaba of Ptahhotep and Akhethotep at Saqqareh*, 2vv. (London: EEF).

— 1902. *The rock tombs of Deir el Gebrawi*, 2vv. (London: EEF).

— 1903–08. *The rock tombs of El Amarna*, 6vv. (London: EEF).

— 1911. 'The rock-cut tombs of Sheikh Abd el Qurneh, at Thebes', *BMMA*.6: 53–59.

— 1913a. *Five Theban Tombs (being those of Mentuherkhepeshef, User, Daga, Nehemawäy and Tati)* (London: EEF)

— 1913b. 'The tomb of Senmen, brother of Senmut', *PSBA* 35: 282–5.

— 1915a. 'The Egyptian expedition, 1914–15: The work of the Robb de Peyster Tytus Memorial Fund', *BMMA*.10: 228–36.

— 1915b. 'The Tomb of Tetaky at Thebes (no. 15)', *JEA* 11: 10–18.

— 1917. *The tomb of Nakht at Thebes* (New York: MMA).

— 1920. *The tomb of Antefoker, vizier of Sesostris I, and of his wife, Senet (no. 60)* (London: EES).

— 1922–3. *The tomb of Puyemrê at Thebes*, 2vv. (New York: MMA).

— 1923a. *The Tombs of Two Officials of Tuthmosis IV, Nos. 75 & 90* (London: EES).

— 1923b. 'Akhenaten at Thebes', *JEA* 9: 132–45.

— 1925a. *The Tomb of Two Sculptors at Thebes* (New York: MMA).

— 1925b. 'The Tomb of Tetaky at Thebes', *JEA* 11: 10–18.

— 1927a. *Two Ramesside Tombs at Thebes* (New York: MMA).

— 1927b. *The Tomb of Nakht at Thebes* (New York: MMA).

— 1930. *The Tomb of Ken-Amun at Thebes* (New York: MMA).

— 1932. 'Tehuti: owner of tomb 110 at Thebes', *Stud. F.Ll.G*: 279–90.

— 1933a. *The Tomb of Nefer-hotep at Thebes* (New York: MMA).

— 1933b. *The Tombs of Menkheperrasonb, Amenmose and another. Nos. 86, 112, 42, 226* (London: EES).

— 1934. 'A High Place at Thebes', *Mélanges Maspero* I/1: 241–50 (Cairo: IFAO).

— 1935. *Paintings from the Tomb of Rekh-mi-Re' at Thebes* (New York: MMA).

— 1940. 'The Tomb of Amenmose, no. 89 at Thebes', *JEA* 26: 131–6.

— 1941. *The Tomb of the Vizier Ramose* (London: EES).

— 1943. *The Tomb of Rekh-mi-Re' at Thebes* (New York: MMA).

— 1948. *Seven Private Tombs at Thebes* (London: EES).

— 1949. 'Birds and Bats at Beni-Hasan', *JEA* 35: 13–20.

DAVIES, N. de G. and M. F. L. MACADAM 1957. *A Corpus of Inscribed Egyptian Funerary Cones* (Oxford: Oxford University Press).

DAVIES, N.M. 1938. 'Some Representations of Tombs from the Theban Necropolis', *JEA* 24: 25–40.

— 1942. 'Nubians in the Tomb of Amunedjeh', *JEA* 28: 50–52.

— 1944. 'A Scene of Worshipping Sacred Cows', *JEA* 30: 64.

— 1947. 'An Unusual Depiction of Rameside Funeral Rites', *JEA* 32: 69–70.

— 1963. *Private Tombs at Thebes IV* (Oxford: Griffith Institute).

DAVIES, N.M. and N. de G. DAVIES 1941a. 'The Tomb of Amenmose (N. 89) at Thebes', *JEA* 26: 131–36.

— 1941b. 'Syrians in the Tomb of Amunedjeh', *JEA* 27: 96–98.

DAVIES, N.M. and A.H. GARDINER 1915. *The Tomb of Amenemhat* (London: EEF).

— 1926. *The Tomb of Huy, Viceroy of Nubia in the Reign of Tut'ankhamun* (London: EES).

— 1936. *Ancient Egyptian Paintings* (Chicago: University Press).

DAVIES, W.V. 2003. 'Sobeknakht's Hidden Treasures', *British Museum Magazine* 46: 18–19.

DAVIES, W.V., A. EL-KHOULI, A.B. LLOYD and A.J. SPENCER 1984. *The Mastabas of Mereri and Wernu* (London: EES).

DAVIS, T.M. et al. 1904. *The Tomb of Thoutmôsis IV* (Westminster: Archibald Constable).

— 1906. *The Tomb of Hâtshopsîtû* (Westminster: Archibald Constable).

— 1907. *The Tomb of Iouiya and Touiyou* (Westminster: Archibald Constable).

— 1912. *The Tombs of Harmhabi and Touatânkhamanou* (Westminster: Archibald Constable).

DAVIS, W. 1989. *The Canonical Tradition in Ancient Egyptian Art* (New York: Cambridge University Press).

DAWSON, J. 2003. 'Conservation of the "Tombs of the Nobles": aspects of the past, issues for the present', *ThNec*: 210–17.

DAWSON, W.R., E.P. UPHILL and M.L. BIERBRIER 1995. *Who Was Who in Egyptology*, 3rd edition (London: EES).

DE BUCK, A. 1935–1961. *The Egyptian Coffin Texts*, 7vv. (Chicago: University Press).

DE GOROSTARZU, X. 1901. 'Lettre Sur Deux Tombeaux de Crocodiles', *ASAE* 2: 182–4.

DE MEULENAERE, H. and P. MACKAY 1977. *Mendes*, II (Warminster: Aris and Phillips).

DE MORGAN, J. 1895, 1903. *Fouilles à Dahchour* 2vv. (Vienna: Adolphe Holzhausen).

DEBONO, F. 1952. 'La Nécropole Prédynastique d'Héliopolis', *ASAE* 52: 625–52.

DECKER, W. 1992. *Sports and Games of Ancient Egypt* (Yale: Yale University Press).

— 1993. 'Le sport dans la décoration murale des tombes privées de l'Egypte pharaonique', *Spectacles sportifs et scéniques dans le monde Etrusco-Italique* (Rome: Ecole Française de Rome).

DENON, V. 1802. *Voyage dans la Basse et la Haute Egypte* (Paris).

DERCHAIN, P. 1962. *Rites Egyptiens*, I (Brussels: Fondation Egyptologique Reine Elisabeth).

— 1975. 'La Perruque et le Cristal', *SAK* 2: 55–74

— 1976. 'Symbols and Metaphors in Literature and Representations of Private Life', *Royal Anthropological Institute News* 15: 7–10.

DESROCHES-NOBLECOURT, C. 1982. 'Touy, Mère de Ramsès II, La Reine Tanedjmy et les Reliques de l'Expérience Amarnienne', *L'Ég* 1979 II: 227–43.

DEWACHTER, M. 1985. 'Nouvelles informations relatives à l'exploitation de la nécropole royale de Drah Aboul Neggah', *RdE* 36: 52–9.

DASZEWSKI, W.A. 1997. 'Mummy Portraits from Northern Egypt: The Necropolis in Marina el-Alamein', in Bierbrier (ed.) 1997: 59–65.

DOBREV, V. 1994. 'Observations sur quelques marques de la pyramide de Pépi Ier, *Homm. Leclant*, I: 147–58.

DODSON, A.M. 1987. 'The Tombs of the Kings of the Thirteenth Dynasty is the Memphite Necropolis', *ZÄS* 114: 36–45.

— 1988a. 'The Tombs of the Queens of the Middle Kingdom', *ZÄS* 115: 123–36.

— 1988b. 'The Tombs of the Kings of the Early Eighteenth Dynasty at Thebes', *ZÄS* 115: 110–23.

— 1988c. 'Egypt's first antiquarians?'. *Antiquity* 62/236: 513–7.

— 1991. *Egyptian Rock-cut Tombs* (Princes Risborough: Shire Publications)

— 1992a. 'Death after Death in the Valley of the Kings', *D&T*: 53–9.

— 1992b. 'On the Burial of Prince Ptahshepses', *GM* 129: 49–51.

— 1994. *The Canopic Equipment of the Kings of Egypt* (London: Kegan Paul International).

— 1996a. 'Mysterious Second Dynasty', *Kmt* 7:2: 19–31.

— 1996b. 'A canopic jar of Ramesses IV and the royal canopic equipment of the Ramesside Period', *GM* 152: 11–17.

— 1997/8. 'The So-Called Tomb of Osiris at Abydos', *Kmt* 8/4: 37–47.

— 1998. 'On The Threshold of Glory: The Third Dynasty', *Kmt* 9/2: 26–40.

— 1999. 'Protecting the Past: The First Century of The Egyptian Antiquities Service', *Kmt* 10/2: 80–84.

— 2000a. 'The Late Eighteenth Necropolis at Deir el-Medina and the Earliest 'Yellow' Coffin of the New Kingdom', *Deir el-Medina in the Third Milennium AD* (Laiden: Netherlands Institute).

— 2000b. *After the Pyramids* (London: Rubicon).

— 2000c. 'The Layer Pyramid at Zawiyet el-Aryan: Its Layout and Context', *JARCE* 38: 81–90.

— 2000d. 'The Eighteenth-Century Discovery of the Serapeum', *Kmt* 11:3, 48–53.

— 2003a. 'The Burial of Members of the Royal Family During the Eighteenth Dynasty', in *P8ICE*: 187–193.

— 2003b. 'The Tombs of the Royal Family of the Middle Kingdom'/'Las Tumbas de la Familia Real del Reino Medio', *Boletín de la Asociación Andaluza de Egiptologia* 1: 75–100.

— 2003c. *The Pyramids of Ancient Egypt* (London: New Holland).

— 2003d. 'The missing tombs of Tanis', in *70GMAE*: 95–97.

— 2003e. 'The lost tomb of Amenhotep I', in *70GMAE*: 80–83.

— forthcoming. 'The tombs of Ahmose I'.

DODSON, A.M. and J.J. JANSSEN 1989. 'A Theban Tomb and its Tenants', *JEA* 75: 125–38.

DONADONI ROVERI, A.M. 1969. *I sarcophagi egizi dalle origini alla fine dell' Antico Regno* (Rome: Università degli Studi di Roma).

— (ed.) 1988. *Egyptian Civilization: Religious Beliefs* (Turin: Instituto Bancario San Paolo di Torino).

DONADONI ROVERI, A.M., E. D'AMICONE, and E. LEOSPO 1994. *Gebelein. Il villaggio e la necropoli* (Turin: Museo Egizio).

DORET, E. 1994. 'Ankhtifi and the Description of his Tomb at Moalla', *FHK*: 79–86.

DORMAN, P.F. 1988. *The Monuments of Senenmut* (London: Kegan Paul International).

— 1991. *The Tombs of Senenmut: the Architecture and Decoration of Tombs 71 and 353* (New York: MMA).

— 1995. 'Two Tombs and One Owner', *Beamtennekropolen*: 141–54.

— 2003. 'Family burial and commemoration in the Theban necropolis', *ThNec*: 30–41.

DOYEN, F. 1998. 'La Figuration des Maisons Dans les Tombes Thebaines: Une Relecture de la Maison de Djehutynefer (TT104),' *P7ICE*: 345–55.

DREYER, G. 1993. 'Umm el-Qaab, 5/6. Vorbericht', *MDAIK* 49: 23–62.

— 1996. 'Umm el-Qaab, 7/8. Vorbericht', *MDAIK* 51: 11–81.

— 1998. *Umm el-Qaab I: Das prädynastische Königsgrab U-j und sein frühen Schriftzeugnisse* (Mainz: Philipp von Zabern).

— 2006. 'Report on the Season 2003/04 at the Tomb of Ninetjer in Saqqara (Causeway of Unas)', *ASAE* 80: 153–56.

DREYER, G. et al., 1988. 'Umm el-Qaab. Nachuntersuchungen im frühzeitlichen Königsfriedhof. 9/10. Vorbericht'. *MDAIK* 54: 77–168.

DRIOTON, E. 1954. 'Textes religieux de tombeaux Saïtes', *ASAE* 52: 105–28.

DRIOTON, E. and J.-Ph. LAUER 1951. 'Les tombes jumelées de Neferibrê-sa-Neith et de Ouahibrê-men' *ASAE* 51: 469–90.

DUELL, P. 1938. *The Mastaba of Mereruka*, 2vv. (Chicago: Oriental Institute).

DÜMICHEN, J. 1884–1894. *Der Grabpalast des Patuamenap in der thebanischen Nekropolis*, 3vv. (Leipzig: J. C. Hinrichs).

DUNAND, F., J.-L. HEIM, N. HENEIN and R. LICHTENBERG 1992. *Douch I: La necropole. Monographie des tombes 1 à 72* (Cairo: IFAO).

DUNHAM, D. 1921. 'The tomb of Dehuti-Nekht and his wife, about 2000 BC' *BMFA* 19: 43–6.

— 1950. *El-Kurru* (Boston: MFA).

— 1955. *Nuri* (Boston: MFA).

— 1958. *Royal Tombs at Meroe and Barkal* (Boston: MFA).

— 1963. *The West and South Cemeteries at Meroe* (Boston: MFA).

DUNHAM, D. and S.E. CHAPMAN 1952. *Decorated Chapels of the Meroitic Pyramids at Meroe and Barkal* (Boston: MFA).

DUNHAM, D. and W.K. SIMPSON 1974. *The Mastaba of Queen Mersyankh III* (Boston: MFA).

DZIOBEK, E. 1987. 'The Architectural Development of Theban Tombs in the Early Eighteenth Dynasty', *P&P*: 69–80.

— 1990. *Das Grab des Sobekhotep: Theben Nr. 63* (Mainz: Phillip von Zabern).

— 1992. *Das Grab des Ineni. Theban Nr. 81* (Mainz: Phillip von Zabern).

— 1994. *Die Gräber des Vezirs User-Amun. Theben Nr. 61 und 131* (Mainz: Phillip von Zabern).

— 1995. 'Theban Tombs as a Source for Historical and Biographical Evaluation: The Case of User-Amun,' *Beamtennekropolen*: 129–40.

— 1998. *Denkmäler des Vezirs User-Amun* (Heidelberg: Heidelberger Orintverlag).

DZIOBEK, E., Th. SCHNEYER and N. SEMMELBAUER 1992. *Eine ikonographische Datierungsmethode für thebanische Wandmalerein der 18. Dynastie* (Heidelberg: Orientverlag).

EATON-KRAUSS, M. 1984. *The Representations of Statuary in Private Tombs of the Old Kingdom* (Weisbaden: Otto Harrassowitz).

EBERS, G. 1887. *Egypt – Descriptive, historical and picturesque* (London: Cassell).

EDEL, E. 1967–1980. *Die Felsengräber der Qubbet el Hawa bei Assuan* 2vv. (Weisbaden: Otto Harrassowitz).

EDEL, E. and S. WENIG 1974. *Die Jahreszeitenreliefs aus dem Sonnenheiligtum des Königs Ne-user-Re* (Berlin: Staatliche Museen).

EDGAR, C.C. 1906. 'Tombs at Abou Billou', *ASAE* 7: 143–4.

— 1907. 'The Sarcophagus of an Unknown Queen', *ASAE* 8: 276–80.

EDINBURGH 1988. *Gold of the Pharaohs* (Edinburgh: City of Edinburgh Museums and Art Galleries).

EDWARDS, I.E.S. 1985. *The Pyramids of Egypt* (Harmondsworth: Penguin).

EGBERTS, A. 1995. *In Quest of Meaning: A Study of the Ancient Egyptian Rites of Consecrating the Meret-chests and Driving the Calves*, 2vv. (Leiden: Nederlands Instituut voor het Nabije Oosten).

EGGEBRECHT, A. 1973. *Schlachtungsbräuche im alten Ägypten und ihre Wiedergabe im Flachbild bis zum Ende des Mittleren Reiches* (Munich: Ludwig-Maximilians-Universität).

EIGNER, D. 1984. *Die monumentalen Grabbauten der Spätzeit in der Thebanischen Nekropole* (Vienna: Akademie der Wissenschaften).

EL-ALFI, M. 1990. 'The tomb of Nikaankh at Tihna: Frasier Tomb n. 2', *DE* 16: 35–42.

EL-BIALY, M. 1996. 'An Unrecorded Tomb Discovered in Qurnet Murai', *Kmt* 7/3: 69–71.

EL-DALY, O. 2005. *Egyptology: The Missing Millennium. Ancient Egypt in Medieval Arabic Writings* (London: UCL Press).

EL-DIN, M. 1994. 'Discovery of a Tomb of the Late Old Kingdom below the Rock Tombs of Qubbet el-Hawa, Aswan', *MDAIK* 50: 31–4.

EL-FIKEY, S.A. 1980. *The Tomb of the Vizier Re'wer at Saqqara* (Warminster: Aris and Phillips).

EL-GHANDOUR, M. 1997. 'Report on Work at Saqqara South of the New Kingdom Cemetery', *GM* 161: 5–25.

EL-GHANDOUR, M. and N. ALEXANIAN 2005. 'An Old Kingdom Cemetery in Southern Dahshur', *MDAIK* 61: 191–206.

EL-HEGAZY, A.A. and M. TOSI 1983. *A Theban Private Tomb No. 295* (Mainz: Phillip von Zabern).

EL-KHOULY, A. and G.T. MARTIN 1987. *Excavations in the Royal Necropolis at El-'Amarna 1984* (SASAE 33) (Cairo: EAO).

EL-KHOULY, A. and N. KANAWATI 1989. *Quseir el-Amarna. The Tombs of Pepy-ankh and Khewen-wekh* (Sydney: Australian Centre for Egyptology).

— 1990. *The Old Kingdom Tombs of el-Hammamiya* (Sydney: Australian Centre for Egyptology)

EL-SAADY, H. 1996. *Tomb of Amenemhab, no. 44 at Qurnah: the Tomb-chapel of a Priest Carrying the Shrine of Amun* (Warminster: Aris and Phillips).

EL-SABBAHY, A.-F. 1993. 'Blocks from the tomb of Shed-Abed at Saqqara', *JEA* 79: 243–47.

EL-SAWI, A, and F. GOMAA. 1993. *Das Grab des Panehsi, Gottesvater von Heliopolis in Mataryia*. Wiesbanden: Harrassowitz.

EL-SADEEK, W. 1984. *Twenty-sixth Dynasty Necropolis at Giza* (Vienna: Institut für Afrikanistik und Ägyptologie).

EL-SAWI, A. and F. GOMÁA 1993. *Das Grab des Panehsi, Gottesvaters von Heliopolis in Matariya* (Weisbaden: Otto Harrassowitz).

EMERY, W.B. 1938. *The Tomb of Hemaka* (Cairo: IFAO).

— 1939. *Hor Aha* (Cairo: IFAO).

— 1949–58. *Great Tombs of the First Dynasty*, 3vv. (Cairo: IFAO/London: EES).

— 1961. *Archaic Egypt* (Harmondsworth: Penguin).

— 1962. *A Funerary Repast in an Egyptian Tomb of the Archaic Period* (Leiden: Nederlands Instituut voor het Nabije Oosten).

— 1968. 'Tomb 3070 at Saqqara', *JEA* 54: 11–13.

EMPEREUR, J.-Y. 1998. *Alexandria Rediscovered* (London: BMP).

— 1995. *A Short Guide to The Catacombs of Kom el Shoqafa Alexandria* (Alexandria: Sarapis).

— (ed.) 2003. *Nécropolis*, 3vv. (Cairo: IFAO).

ENGELBACH, R. 1915. *Riqqeh and Memphis VI* (London: ERA).

— 1923. *Harageh* (London: BSAE).

— 1924. 'Saite Tomb Discovered at Beni Hasan', *ASAE* 24: 159–60

ENGELMAN-VON CARNAP, B. 1998. 'Zur zeitlichen Einordnung der Dekoration thebanischer Privatgräber der 18. Dynastie anhand des Fisch- und Vogelfang-Bildes', *Stat.*: 247–62.

ENGLUND, G. (ed.) 1987. *The Religion of the Ancient Egyptians. Cognitive Structures and Popular Expressions* (Uppsala: Boreas).

EPIGRAPHIC SURVEY 1930–69. *Medinet Habu*, 8vv. (Chicago: University Press).

— 1980. *The Tomb of Kheruef, Theban Tomb 192* (Chicago: Oriental Institute).

ÉPRON, L. and F. DAUMAS 1939. *Le Tombeau de Ti*, I (Cairo: IFAO).

ERMAN, A. 1895. 'Aus dem Grabe eines Hohenpriesters von Memphis', *ZÄS* 33: 18–24.

EYRE, C.J. 1987. 'Work and the Organisation of Work in the New Kingdom', *Labor in the Ancient Near East*, M. A. Powell, ed (New Haven: American Oriental Society) 5–47, 167–22.

FAKHRY, A. 1951. *The necropolis of el-Bagawat in Kharga Oasis* (Cairo: Government Press).

— 1959. *The Monuments of Sneferu at Dahshur* 1–2 (Cairo: General Organization for Government Printing).

— 1961/1969. *The Pyramids* (Chicago: Chicago University Press).

— 1973–74. *The Oases of Egypt*, 2vv. (Cairo: American University in Cairo Press).

FARAG, N. and Z. ISKANDER 1971. *The Discovery of Neferwptah* (Cairo: General Organization for Government Printing Offices)

FAULKNER, R.O. 1969. *The Ancient Egyptian Pyramid Texts* (Oxford: Griffith Institute).

— 1973–8. *The Ancient Egyptian Coffin Texts*, 3vv. (Warminster: Aris and Phillips).

— 1985. *The Ancient Egyptian Book of the Dead* (London: BMP).

FEDAK, J. 1990. *Monumental Tombs of the Hellenistic Age* (Toronto: University of Toronto Press).

FEKRI, M., A.-M. LOYRETTE, et al. 1998. 'Vallée des Reines: la tombe VdR 34 d'une reine inconnue et le Puits VdR 87', *Memnonia* IX: 121–38.

FEUCHT, E. 1985. *Das Grab des Nefersecheru (TT296)* (Mainz: Phillip von Zabern).

— 1992. 'Fishing and Fowling with the Spear and the Throw-stick Reconsidered', *IHE*: 157–69.

FIORE-MAROCHETTI, E. 1995. 'On the Design, Symbolism, and Dating of some XIIth Dynasty Tomb Superstructures' *GM* 144: 43–52.

FIRTH, C.M. 1929. 'Excvations of the Department of Antiquities at Saqqara', *ASAE* 29: 64–70.

FIRTH, C.M. and B. GUNN 1926. *The Teti Pyramid Cemeteries* (Cairo: IFAO).

FIRTH, C.M. and J.E. QUIBELL 1935. *The Step Pyramid* (Cairo: IFAO).

FISCHER, H.G. 1959. 'A scribe of the army in a Saqqara mastaba of the early fifth dynasty', *JNES* 18: 233–72.

— 1968. *Ancient Egyptian Representations of Turtles* (New York: MMA).

— 1968. *Dendera in the Third Millennium BC down to the Theban Domination of Upper Egypt* (Locust Valley: Augustin).

— 1981. 'Notes on Two Tomb Chapels at Giza', *JEA* 67: 166–68.

— 1996. *The Tomb of 'Ip at el Saff* (New York: MMA).

— 1997a. 'Quelques particuliers enterrés a Saqqara', *Etudes Lauer*: 177–89.

— 1997b. *Egyptian Titles of the Middle Kingdom. A Supplement to Wm. Ward's Index*, 2nd ed (New York: MMA).

FITZENREITER, M. 1995. 'Totenverehrung und soziale Repräsentation im thebanischen Beamtengrab der 18. Dynastie', *SAK* 22: 95–130.

FORBES, D.C. 1999. *Tombs; Treasures; Mummies: Seven Great Discoveries of Egyptian Archaeology* (San Francisco: Kmt Communications,).

FORMAN, W. and S. QUIRKE 1996. *Hieroglyphs and the afterlife in Ancient Egypt* (Norman: University of Oklahoma).

FRANKE, D. 1991. 'The Career of Khnumhotep III of Beni Hasan and the so-called "Decline of the Nomarchs"', *MKS*: 51–67.

FRANKFORT, H. 1930. 'The cemeteries of Abydos: work of the season 1925–26', *JEA* 16: 213–19.

FRANKFORT, H., A. DE BUCK and B. GUNN 1933. *The Cenotaph of Seti I at Abydos*, 2vv. (London: EES).

FRASER, G. 1902. 'The Early Tombs at Tehneh', *ASAE* 3: 67–76.

FRASER, P.M. 1972. *Ptolemaic Alexandria*, 3vv. (Oxford: University Press).

FREED, R.E. 2000. 'Observations on the dating and decoration of the tombs of Ihy and Hetep at Saqqara', *AbSaq*2000: 207–14.

FRIEDMAN, F.D. 1996. 'Notions of Cosmos in the Step Pyramid Complex', StudSimp: 337–51.

FRITZ, U. 2004. *Typologie der Mastabagräber des Alten Reiches: Strukturelle Analyse eines Altägyptsches Grabtyps* (Berlin: Achet Verlag – Dr. Norbert Dürring).

GABALLA, G.A. 1977. *The Memphite Tomb-Chapel of Mose* (Warminster: Aris and Phillips).

GABOLDE, L. et al. 1994. 'Le "Tombeau Suspendu" de la "Vallée de l'Aigle"', *BIFAO* 94: 173–259.

GABRA, S. 1932. 'Rapport Préliminaire sur les fouilles de l'université égyptienne à Touna (Hermopolis Ouest)', *ASAE* 32: 56–77.

— 1939. 'Fouilles de l'Université "Fouad el Awal", à Touna el-Gebel (Hermopolis Ouest)', *ASAE* 39: 483–527.

— 1971. *Chez les Derniers Adorateurs du Trismegiste* (Cairo: al-Hayah al-Misriyah al-Ammah).

GABRA, S. and E. DRIOTON 1954. *Peintures à fresques et scenes peintes à Hermopolis-Ouest* (Touna el-Gebel) (Cairo: IFAO).

GAILLARD, C. 1923. *Recherches sur les poissons représentés dans quelques tombeaux égyptiens de l'ancien empire* (Cairo: IFAO).

GALAN, J.M. 1994. 'Bullfight scenes in Ancient Egyptian tombs', *JEA* 80: 81–96.

GARDINER, A.H. 1910. 'The tomb of Amenemhet, high-priest of Amon', *ZÄS* 47: 87–99.

— 1917. 'The tomb of a much-travelled Theban official', *JEA* 4: 28–38.

— 1935. *The Attitude of the Ancient Egyptians to Death and the Dead* (Cambridge: University Press).

— 1955. 'A Unique Funerary Liturgy', *JEA* 41: 9–17.

— 1957. *Egyptian Grammar*, 3rd edition (Oxford: Clarendon Press).

GARDINER, A.H. and A.E.P. WEIGALL 1913. *A Topographical Catalogue of the Private Tombs of Thebes* (London: B. Quaritch).

GARDINER, A.H. and K. SETHE 1928. *Egyptian Letters to the Dead* (London: Egypt Exploration Society).

GARDINER, H.M. 1983. 'Concerning some Tomb Scenes from El-Bersha', *GM* 64: 19–21.

GARNOT, J. 1938. *L'Appel aux Vivants dans les Textes Funéraires Égyptiens des Origines á la Fin de l'Ancien Empire* (Cairo: Institut Français d'Archéologie Oriental).

GARSTANG, J. 1901. *El Arábah* (London: Egyptian Research Account).

— 1903. *Mahâsna and Bêt Khallâf* (London: Egyptian Research Account).

— 1904 *Report of excavations at Reqaqnah 1901–2. Tombs of the third Egyptian dynasty at Raqaqnah and Bet Khallaf* (Westminster: Constable).

— 1907. *The Burial Customs of Ancient Egypt* (London: Constable).

— 1909. 'Excavations at Abydos 1909', *LAAA* 5: 107–9.

GASM EL SEED, A.A. 1985. 'La Tombe de Tanoutamon à El Kurru (KU. 16)', *RdE* 36: 67–72.

GAUTHIER, H. 1921. 'Un tombeau de Tell Moqdam', *ASAE* 21: 21–7.

— 1927. 'Une tombe d'époque Saïte à Héliopolis', *ASAE* 27: 1–18.

— 1928. 'Un vice-roi d'Éthiopie enseveli à Bubastis', *ASAE* 28: 129–37.

— 1932. 'Une tombe de la XIXe dynastie à Qantir (Delta)', *ASAE* 32: 115–28.

— 1933. 'Découvertes recentes dans la nécropole Saïte à Héliopolis', *ASAE* 33: 27–53.

GAUTIER, J. and G. JÉQUIER 1902. *Memoire sur les fouilles de Licht* (Cairo: IFAO).

GIDDY, L. 1992. *The Anubieion at Saqqara*, 2 (London: EES).

GNIRS, A. M. 1995. 'Das Pfeilerdekorationsprogramm im Grab des Meri, Theben Nr. 95: Ein Beitrag zu den Totenkultpraktiken der 18. Dynastie', *Beamtennekropolen*: 233–54.

GNIRS, A. M., E. GROTHE and H. GUKSCH 1997, 'Zweiter Vorbericht über die Aufnahme und Publication von Gräbern der 18. Dynastie der thebanischen Beamtennekropole', *MDAIK* 53: 57–84.

GOEDICKE, H. 1955. 'The Egyptian Idea of Passing from Life to Death', *Orientalia* 24: 225–39.

— 1970. *Die privaten Rechtsinschriften aus dem Alten Reich* (Vienna: Verlag Notring).

— 1971. *Re-used Blocks from the Pyramid of Amenemhat I at Lisht* (New York: MMA).

— 1988. 'The High Price of Burial', *JARCE* 25: 195–99.

GOHARY, S. 1991. 'The Tomb-Chapel of the Royal Scribe Amenemone at Saqqara', *BIFAO* 91: 195–205.

GOLVIN, J.-C. and R. VERGNIEUX 1985 'Etude des techniques de constructions dans l'Egypte ancienne', *MelMokh* I: 323–38.

GOMAÀ, F. and El-S. HEGAZY 2001. *Die neuentdeckte Nekropole von Athribis* (Weisbaden: Harrassowitz).

GÖRSDORF, J., G. DREYER and U. HARTUNG 1998. 'C-14 Dating Results of the Archaic Royal Necropolis Umm el-Qaab at Abydos', *MDAIK* 54: 169–76.

GOYON, G. 1987. *La découverte des trésors de Tanis* (Paris: Perséa).

GOYON, J-C. 1972. *Rituels Funéraires de l'Ancienne Egypte* (Paris: Cerf).

GOYON, J-C. et al. 1998. 'Le prêtre 'purificcateur d'avan d'Amon' à la fin du Nouvel Empire: à propos des fragments du tombeau de Khâemipet, ancêtre d'Iymiseba', *Memnonia* IX: 139–54.

GRAEFE, E. 1990. *Das Grab des Ibi, Obervermogenverwalters der Gottesgemahlin des Amun (thebanisches Grab Nr. 36)* (Brussels: Brepols).

— 2003a. *Das Grab des Padihorresnet, Obervermögenverwalters der Gottesgemahlin des Amun (thebanisches Grab Nr. 196)* (Brussels: Brepols).

— 2003b. 'The Royal Cache and the Tomb Robberies', *ThNec*: 74–82.

— 2005. 'Der Hügel (q3y) der Inhapi, der in der Heilige Ort ist, in dem Amenhotep ruht', *MDAIK* 61: 207–9.

GRAJETZKI, W. 2003. *Burial Customs in Ancient Egypt: Life in Death for Rich and Poor* (London: Duckworth).

GREENER, L. 1966. *The Discovery of Egypt* (London: Cassell).

GRENFELL, B.P. and A.S. HUNT 1900–1. 'Excavations in the Fayûm', *EEF AR* 1900–1901: 4–7.

— 1901–2. 'Excavations in the Fayûm and at El Hibeh', *EEF AR* 1901–2: 2–5.

— 1903–4. 'Excavations at Oxyrhnchus', *EEF AR* 1903–4: 14–7.

GRENFELL, B.P. and D.G. HOGARTH 1900. *Fayum Towns and their Papyri* (London: EEF).

GREENLEES, T.H. 1923. 'An Unusual Tomb Scene from Dira 'abu'l-Nega' *JEA* 9: 131.

GRIFFITHS, J.G. 1980. *The Origins of Osiris and his Cult* (Leiden: Brill).

GRIFFITHS, J.G. and L. TROY 1993. 'Creating a God: the Mummification Ritual', *BACE* 4: 55–56.

GRUNDLACH, R., et al. 1988. *Sennefer: Die Grabkammer des Bürgermeisters von Theben* (Hildesheim: Römer und Pelizaeus Museum/Mainz: Verlag Phillip von Zabern).

GUILHOU, N. 1993. 'La mutilation rituelle du veau dans les scènes de funérailles au Nouvel Empire' *BIFAO* 93: 277–98.

— 1997. 'Les parties du corps humain dans la pyramide d'Ounas, lecture rituelle et valeur symbolique', *Etudes Lauer*: 221–31.

GUILMANT, F. 1907. *Le Tombeau de Ramsès IX* (Cairo: IFAO).

GUIMER-SORBETS, A.-M. and M. SEIF EL-DIN. 'Les Peintures de la Nécropole de Kom el-Chougafa à Alexandrie, Éléments de Méthode pour la Lecture Iconographique et l'Interprétation du Stile "Bilingue"', *La peinture funéraire antique*. Barbet, A. 2001 (Paris: Errance), 129–36

GUKSCH, H. 1978. *Das Grab des Benja gen. Paheqamen, Theben Nr. 343* (Mainz: Phillip von Zabern).

— 1982. 'Das Grab des Benja', *MDAIK* 38: 195–99.

— 1994. *Königsdienst. Zur Selbstdarstellung der Beamten in der 18. Dynastie*, Vol. 11, (Heidelberger: Orientverlag).

— 1995. *Die Gräber des Nacht-Min und Men-cheper-Ra-seneb. Theben Nr. 87 und 79* (Mainz: Phillip von Zabern).

GUKSCH, H., C. SEEBER and A.G. SHEDID 1982. 'Vorbericht über die weitere Aufnahme und Publikation von Gräbern der thebanischen Beamtennekropole', *MDAIK* 38: 413–17.

GUNDLACH, R. 1982. 'Zum Text- und Bildrpogramm Agyptischer Felstempel', *L'Ég* 1979: 105–09.

HABACHI, L. 1939. 'A First Dynasty Cemetery at Abydos', *ASAE* 39: 767–81.

— 1955. 'Clearance of the Tomb of Kheruef at Thebes, 1957–58', *ASAE* 55: 325–50.

— 1957. *Tell Basta* (Cairo: IFAO).

— 1969. 'La reine Touy, femme de Séthi I et ses proches parents inconnus', *RdE* 21: 27–47.

HABACHI, L.. and P. ANUS 1977. *Le tombeau de Naÿ à Gournet Mar'ei* (no 271) (Cairo: IFAO).

HAENY, G. (ed.), 1981 *Untersuchungen im Totentempel Amenophis' III* (Weisbaden: Otto Harrasowitz).

— 1998. 'New Kingdom «Mortuary Temples» and «Mansions of Millions of Years»', *TAE*: 86–126.

HAIKAL, F. 1985. 'Preliminary Studies on the Tomb of Thay in Thebes: The Hymn to the Light', *MelMokh*: 361–72.

HAMADA, A. 1935. 'A sarcophagus from Mit-Rahîna', *ASAE* 35: 122–31.

— 1937a. 'The Clearance of a Tomb Found at Al-Fostât, 1936', *ASAE* 37: 58–70.

— 1937b. 'Tomb of Pawen-Hatef at Al-Fostât', *ASAE* 37: 135–42.

— 1938. 'Une troisième tombe à el-Foustât', *ASAE* 38: 135–42.

HANDOUSSA, T. 1988. 'Fish Offering in the Old Kingdom', *MDAIK* 44: 105–09.

HARER, W.B. Jr., 1985. 'Pharmacological and Biological Properties of the Egyptian Lotus,' *JARCE* 22: 49–54.

HARI, R. 1985. *La tombe du père divin Neferhotep (TT50)* (Geneva: Editions de Belles Lettres).

HARING, B.J. 1997. *Divine Households, Administrative and Economic Aspects of the New Kingdom Royal Memorial Temples in Western Thebes* (Leiden: Nederlands Instituut voor het Nabije Oosten).

HARPUR, Y. 1987. *Decoration of Private Tombs in the Old Kingdom* (London: Kegan Paul International).

— 2001. *The Tombs of Nefermaat and Rahotep at Maidum: Discovery, Destruction and Reconstruction* (Oxford: Oxford Expedition to Egypt).

HARRELL, J.A. and T.M. BOWN 1995. 'An Old Kingdom basalt quarry at Widan el-Faras and the quarry road to Lake Moeris in the Fayum, Egypt.' *JARCE* 32: 71–91.

HARTWIG, M. 2000. *Institutional Patronage and Social Commemoration in Theban Tomb Painting during the Reigns of Thutmose IV and Amenhotep III* (Ann Arbor: UMI).

HARVEY, J. 2001. *Wooden Statues of the Old Kingdom: a Typological Study* (Leiden: Brill).

HARVEY, S. 1994: 'Monuments of Ahmose at Abydos', *EgArch* 4: 3–5.

HASEGAWA, S. 2003. 'The New Kingdom Necropolis at Dahshur', *P8ICE* I: 229–33.

HASSAN, S. 1932–60. *Excavations at Giza*, 10vv. (Oxford: University Press/Cairo: Government Press).

— 1975. *Excavations at Saqqara, 1937–1938*, 3vv. (Cairo: ASAE).

— 1975. *Mastabas of Princess Hemet-R' and others* (Cairo: General Organisation for Government Printing Offices).

HASSANEIN, F. and M. NELSON. 1976. *La Tombe du Prince Amon-(her)-khepchef* (Cairo: Centre d'Etude et de Documentation sur l'Ancienne Egypte).

HAUSER, W. 1932. 'The Christian necropolis in Khargeh Oasis', *BMMA* 27, Part II: 38–50.

HAWASS, Z. 1998. 'Pyramid Construction. New Evidence Discovered in Giza', *Stat*: 53–62.

— 2000a. *Valley of the Golden Mummies* (London: Virgin/New York: Abrams).

— 2000b. 'Finding Pharaoh's Vizier: More Secrets from the Valley of the Golden Mummies', *Egypt Revealed* 1: 26–35.

— 2002. *Hidden Treasures of the Egyptian Museum* (Cairo: AUC Press).

— 2003. *Secrets from the Sand: my search for Egypt's past* (London: Thames & Hudson/New York: Abrams).

— (ed). 2003. *The Treasures of the Pyramids* (Cairo: AUC Press).

— 2006. *The Royal Tombs of Egypt. The Art of Thebes Revealed* (London and New York: Thames & Hudson).

— 2007. 'The discovery of the Osiris Shaft at Giza', In Z.A. Hawass and J. Richards, *The Archaeology and Art of Ancient Egypt: Essays in Honor of David B. O'Connor* (Cairo: Conseil Suprême des Antiquités de l'Égypte): I, 379-397

HAWASS, Z. and M. VERNER. 1996. 'Newly Discovered Blocks from the Causeway of Sahure', *MDAIK* 52: 177–86.

HAYES, W.C. 1935a. 'The Tomb of Nefer-khewet and his Family', *BMMA* 30, Part II: 17–36.

— 1935b. *Royal Sarcophagi of the XVIII Dynasty* (Princeton: University Press).

— 1937. *The texts from the Mastabeh of Senwosret-'ankh at Lisht* (New York: MMA).

— 1953, 1959. *Scepter of Egypt*, I, II (Cambridge, MA: Harvard University Press).

HELCK, W. 1962. 'Sociale Stellung und Grablage', *JESHO* 5: 225–43.

— 1996. 'Ein verlorenes Grab in Theben-West: TT145 des Offiziers Neb-Amun unter Thutmosis III', *Antike Welt* 27: 73–85.

HENDRICKX, S. 1993. 'Status Repoprt on the Excavation of the Old Kingdom Rock Tombs at Elkab', *A6CIE*: I, 255–57.

HODEL-HOENES, S. 2000. *Life and Death in Ancient Egypt* (Ithaca: Cornell University).

HOFFMAN, M.A. 1979. *Egypt Before the Pharaohs* (London: Routledge and Kegan Paul).

HOFFMEIER, J.K. 1975. 'Hunting Desert Game with the Bow: A Brief Examination', *JSSEA* 6.2: 8–13.

— 1991. 'The Coffins of the Middle Kingdom: The Residence and the Regions', *MKS*: 69–86.

HOFMAN, E. and K.-J. SEYFRIED 1995. *Das Grab der Neferrenpet gen. Kenro* (TT178) (Mainz: Phillip von Zabern).

HOGARTH, D.G. and E.F. BENSON 1895. *Report on Prospects of Research in Alexandria* (London: Society for the Promotion of Hellenic Studies).

HÖLSCHER, U. 1939. *The Excavation of Medinet Habu, II, The Temples of the Eighteenth Dynasty* (Chicago: University Press).

— 1941–51. *The Excavation of Medinet Habu, III–IV, The Mortuary Temple of Ramses III* (Chicago: University Press).

— 1954. *The Excavation of Medinet Habu, V: Post-Ramessid Remains* (Chicago: University Press).

HOPE, C.A. 1988. *Gold of the Pharaohs* (Victoria: International Cultural Corporation of Australia).

HORNUNG, E. 1971 *Das Grab des Haremhab im Tal der Könige* (Bern: Franke Verlag).

— 1975. 'Das Grab Thutmosis' II', *RdE* 27: 125–31.

— 1983. *Conceptions of God in Ancient Egypt* (London: Routledge and Kegan Paul).

— 1990a. *Valley of the Kings: Horizon of Eternity* (New York: Timken).

— 1990b *Zwei ramessidischen Königsgräber: Ramses IV. und Ramses VII* (Mainz: Phillip von Zabern,).

— 1991 *The Tomb of Pharaoh Seti I/Das Grab Sethos' I* (Zurich and Munich: Artemis).

— 1992a. *Idea into Image. Essays on Ancient Egyptian Thought*. E. Bredeck, trans (New York: Timken).

— 1992b. 'Zur Struktur des ägyptischen Jenseitsglaubens', *ZÄS* 119: 124–30.

— 1995. 'Studies on the Decoration of the Tomb of Seti I', *VSK*: 70–3.

— 1999. *The Ancient Egyptian Books of the Afterlife*, (Ithaca: Cornell University).

HÖLZL, C. 1993. 'The Rock-tombs of Beni Hasan: Architecture and Sequence', *A6CIE*: I, 279–83.

IKRAM, S. 1991. 'Animal Mating Motifs in Tombs of the Old Kingdom', *GM* 124: 511–61.

— 1995. *Choice Cuts: Meat Production in Ancient Egypt* (Leiden: Peeters).

— 2000. 'The Pet Gazelle of One of the Ladies of the Pinudjem Family', *Kmt* 11/2: 58–61.

— 2001. 'The Iconography of the Hyena in Ancient Egypt', *MDAIK* 57: 127–40.

— 2003a. *Death and Burial in Ancient Egypt* (London: Pearson).

— 2003b. 'Hunting Hyenas in the Middle Kingdom: the Appropriation of a Royal Image?', in *Homm. Haikal*: 141–48.

— (ed.), 2004. *Divine Creatures: animal mummies in ancient Egypt* (Cairo: American University in Cairo Press).

IKRAM, S. and A.M. DODSON 1998. *The Mummy in Ancient Egypt: Equipment for Eternity* (London and New York: Thames & Hudson; Cairo: American University in Cairo Press).

JACQUET-GORDON, H.K. 1962. *Les noms des domaines funéraires sous l'Ancien Empire* (Cairo: IFAO).

JAMES, T.G.H. 1997 ''The Very Best Artist', *ChSeers*: 164–73.

— 2002. *Ramesses II* (Vercelli: White Star).

— (ed.) 1982. *Excavating in Egypt. The Egypt Exploration Society* 1882–1982 (London: BMP).

JAMES, T.G.H. and M.A. APTED 1953. *The Mastaba of Khentika called Ikhekhi* (London: EES).

JANOSÍ, P. 1992a. 'Das Pyramidion der Pyramide G III-a und einige Bemerkungen zu den Pyramidenspitzen des Alten Reiches', *IHE*: 301–08.

— 1992b. 'The Queens of the Old Kingdom and their Tombs', *Bulletin of the Australian Centre for Egyptology* 3: 51–57.

— 1994a. 'Ezbet Helmi. Bericht über die ersten drei Grabungskampagnen 1989–1991', *Ägypten und Levante* 4: 20–38.

— 1994b. 'Totenopferraum und Scheintür in den Pyramidentempeln des Alten Reiches', in R. Gundlach and M. Rochholz (eds.), *Ägyptische Tempel - Struktur, Funktion und Programm* (Hildesheim: Gerstenberg Verlag): 143–63.

— 1996a. *Die Pyramidenanlagen der Königinnen: Untersuchungen zu einem Grabtyp des Alten und Mittleren Reiches* (Vienna: Akademie der Wissenschaften).

— 1996b. 'Die Grabanlagen der Königin Hetepheres II.', *ZÄS* 123: 46–62.

— 1997. *Österreich vor den Pyramiden: die Grabungen Hermann Junkers im Auftrag der Österreich Akademie der Wissenschaften bei den grossen Pyramiden in Giza* (Vienna: Akademie der Wissenschaften).

— 2000. '"Im Schatten" der Pyramiden – Die Mastabas in Abusir. Einige Beobachtungen um Grabbau der 5. Dynastie', *AbSaq* 2000: 445–66.

JANOSÍ, P. and Di. ARNOLD 1986. 'Säule', *LÄ* V: 343–48.

JANSEN-WINKELN, K. 1987. 'Thronname und Begräbnis Takeloths I', *VA* 3 (), 253–8.

— 1997. 'Eine Grabübernahme in der 30. Dynastie', *JEA* 83: 169–78.

JANSSEN, J.J. 1975. *Commodity Prices from the Ramessid Period* (Leiden: E.J. Brill).

— 1997. *Village Varia* (Leiden: Nederlands Instituut voor het Nabije Oosten).

JANSSEN, J.J. and P.W. PESTMAN 1968. 'Burial and Inheritance in the Community of Workmen at Thebes', *Journal of the Economic and Social History of the Orient* 11: 137–70.

JARITZ, H. 1994. 'What Petrie Missed', *EgArch* 5: 14–16.

JAROß-DECKERT, B. 1984. *Das Grab des Jnj-jtj.f. Die Wandmalerein der 11. Dynastie* (Mainz: Phillip von Zabern).

JEFFRIES, D.G. 1985. *The Survey of Memphis I* (London: EES).

JEFFRIES, D.G. and A. TAVARES 1994. 'The Historic Landscape of Early Dyanstic Memphis', *MDAIK* 50: 143–73.

JÉQUIER, G. 1928. *Le Pyramide d'Oudjebten* (Cairo: IFAO).

— 1929. *Tombeaux de particuliers contemporains de Pepi II* (Cairo: IFAO).

— 1933. *Les Pyramides des Reines Neit et Apouit* (Cairo: IFAO).

— 1936–40. *Le monument funéraire de Pepi II*, vv. 1–3 (Cairo: IFAO).

— 1938. *Deux pyramides du Moyen Empire* (Cairo: IFAO).

— 1940. *Douze ans de fouilles dans la Nécropole Memphite* (Neuchâtel: Secrétariat de l'université).

JONES, O. and J. GOURY 1843. *Views on the Nile* (London: Graves).

JUNKER, H. 1914. 'The Austrian Excavations 1914', *JEA* 1: 250–53.

— 1928. 'Die Stele des Hofarztes 'Irj', *ZÄS* 63: 53–70.

1929–1955. *Grahungen auf dem Friedhof des Alten Reiches bei den Pyramiden von Giza*, 12vv. (Vienna and Leipzig: Hölder-Pichlek Tempsky).

— 1940. 'Der Tanz der Mww und das Butische Begräbnis im Alten Reich', *MDAIK* 9: 1–39.

KAISER, W. 'Zu den Königsgräbern der 2. Dynastie in Sakkara und Abydos', *Essays Goedicke*: 113–23.

KAISER, W,. and G. DREYER 1982. 'Umm el-Qaab, 2. Vorbericht', *MDAIK* 38: 211–69.

KÁKOSY, L. 1982. 'Temples and Funerary Beliefs in the Graeco-Roman Epoch', *L'Ég* 1979: 117–27.

— 1994. 'Ninth preliminary report on the Hungarian excavation in Thebes; Tomb No. 32', *Acta Archaeologica Academiae Scientiarum Hungaricae* 46: 21–31.

— 1997. 'Funerary Beliefs in the Late New Kingdom', in *L'impero rameside: Convegno Donadoni* (Rome: Quaderno): 95–99.

KÁKOSY, L., T.A. BÁCS, Z. BARTOS, Z.I. FÁBIÁN and E. GAÁL 2004. *The Mortuary Monument of Djehutymes* (TT 32) (Budapest: Archaeolingua Alapítvány).

KÁKOSY, L. and G. SCHREIBER, 'Use and re-use. An overview of the post-Ramesside burials in TT 32', *FS Altenmüller*: 203–9.

KAMAL, A. 1902. 'Exploration dans la Province de Siout', *ASAE* 3: 32–7.

— 1916. 'Fouilles à Deir Dronka et à Assiout (1913–1914)', *ASAE* 16: 65–114.

KAMPP, F. 1994. 'Vierter Vorbericht über die Arbeiten des Agyptologischen Instituts der Universität Heidelberg in thebanischen Gräbern der Ramessidenzeit', *MDAIK* 50: 175–88.

— 1996. *Die thebanische Nekropole: zum Wandel des Grabgedankens von der XVIII.*

bis zur XX. Dynastie, 2vv. (Mainz: Phillipp von Zabern).

KAMPP-SEYFRIED, F. 2003. 'The Theban Necropolis: an overview of topography and tomb development from the Middle Kingdom to the Ramesside period', *ThNec*: 2–10.

KAMRIN, J. 1999. *The Cosmos of Khnumhotp II at Beni Hasan* (London: Kegan Paul International).

KANAWATI, N. 1977. *The Egyptian Administration in the Old Kingdom* (Warminster: Aris and Phillips).

— 1980–1992. *The Rock Tombs of el-Hawawish: the Cemetery of Akhmim*, 10vv. (Sydney: Australian Centre for Egyptology).

— 1981. 'The Living and the Dead in Old Kingdom Tomb Scenes', *SAK* 9: 213–25.

— 1993–1995. *The Tombs of El-Hagarsa*, 3vv. (Sydney: Australian Centre for Egyptology).

— 2001. *The Tomb and Beyond: Burial Customs of Ancient Egyptian Officials* (Warminster: Aris and Phillips).

— 2005. *Deir el-Gebrawi* I: *The Northern Cliff* (Oxford: Aris and Phillips).

KANAWATI, N. and M. ABDER-RAZIQ 1999. *The Teti Cemetery at Saqqara*, 5 (Warminster: Aris and Phillips).

KANAWATI, N., A. EL-KHOULI, A. MCFARLANE and N.V. MAKSOUD 1984–88. *Excavations North west of Teti's Pyramid* (Sydney: Australian Centre for Egyptology).

KANAWATI, N. and A. HASSAN 1996, 1997. *The Teti Cemetery at Saqqara*, 2vv. (Sydney: Australian Centre for Egyptology).

KANAWATI, N. and A. MCFARLANE 1993. *Deshasha. The Tombs of Inti, Shedu and others* (Sydney: Australian Centre for Egyptology).

KANAWATI, N. and R. SCANNELL 1988. *A Mountain Speaks: the First Australian Excavation in Egypt* (Sydney: Australian Centre for Egyptology).

KANTOR, H.J. 1960. 'A Fragment of Relief from the Tomb of Mentuemhat at Thebes (No. 34)', *JNES* 19: 213–16.

KAPLONY, P. 1976. *Studien zum Grab des Methethi* (Bern: Abegg-Stiftung).

KELLER, C.A. 1991. 'Royal Painters: Deir el-Medina in Dynasty XIX', in E. Bleiberg and R. Freed (eds.), *Fragments of a Shattered Visage: The Proceedcings of the International Symposium of Ramesses the Great* (Memphis: Memphis State University): 50–86.

KEMP, B.J. 1966. 'Abydos and the Royal Tombs of the First Dynasty', *JEA* 52: 13–22.

— 1967. 'The Egyptian First Dynasty Royal Cemetery', *Antiquity* 41: 22–32.

— 1973. 'Photographs of the Decorated Tomb at Hierakonpolis', *JEA* 59: 36–43.

— 2006. *Ancient Egypt: Anatomy of a Civilisation*, 2nd edition (London: Routledge).

KEMP, B.J. and R.S. MERRILLEES 1980. *Minoan Pottery in Second Millennium Egypt* (Mainz: Phillipp von zabern).

KENDALL, T. 1978. *Passing through the netherworld. The Meaning and Play of Senet, and Ancient Egyptian Funerary Game* (Boston: Boston Museum of Fine Art and The Kirk Game Company).

— 1981. 'An unusual rock-cut tomb at Giza', in W.K. Simpson and W. M. Davis (eds.), *Studies in Ancient Egypt, the Aegean, and the Sudan* (Boston: Museum of Fine Arts) 104–14.

KESSLER, D. 1986. 'Tuna', LÄ 6: 797–804.

— 1987. 'Zur Bedeutung der Szenen des täglichen lebens in den Privatgräbern', *ZÄS* 114: 59–88.

— 1989. *Die Heiligen Tiere und der König* (Wiesbaden: Otto Harrassowitz).

— 1990. 'Zur Bedeutung der Szenen des täglichen lebens in den Privatgräbern', *ZÄS* 117: 21–43.

KITCHEN, K.A. 1979. 'Memphite tomb-chapels in the New Kingdom and later', *FS Edel*: 272–84.

KLEBS, L. 1915. *Die Reliefs und Malereien des alten Reiches* (Heidelberg: Carl Winters Universitätsbuchhandlung).

— 1922. *Die Reliefs und Malereien des mittleren Reiches* (Heidelberg: Carl Winters Universitätsbuchhandlung).

— 1934. *Die Reliefs und Malereien des neuen Reiches* (Heidelberg: Carl Winters Universitätsbuchhandlung).

KLEMM, R. and D. D. 1993. *Steine und Steinbrüche im Alten-Agypten* (Berlin: Springer).

KONDO, J. 1992. 'A Preliminary Report on the Re-clearance of the Tomb of Amenophis III', *ATut*, 41–54.

— 1995. 'The Re-clearance of Tombs WV22 and WVA in the Western Valley of the Kings', *VSK*: 25–33.

KOZLOFF, A.P. 1979. 'A Study of the painters of the Tomb of Menna, No. 69', *A1ICE*: 395–402.

KOZLOFF, A. and B.M. BRYAN 1992. *Egypt's Dazzling Sun: Amenhotep III and his World* (Cleveland, OH: Cleveland Museum of Art/Indiana University Press).

KRAUSS, R. 1994. 'Tilgungen und Korrekturen auf Senenmuts Denkmälern: Berlin 2066 und 2096', *JARCE* 31: 49–54.

— 1996. 'The Length of Sneferu's Reign and How Long it Took to Build the "Red Pyramid"', *JEA* 82: 43–50.

KUBISH, S. 2000. 'Die Stelen der 1. Zwischenzeit aus Gebelein', *MDAIK* 56: 239–65.

KUENY, G. 1950. 'Scenes apicoles dans l'ancienne Egypte', *JNES* 9: 84–93.

KUHLMANN, K.P. and W. SCHENKEL 1983. *Das Grab des Ibi, Obergutsverwalters der Gottesgemahlin des Amun* (Thebanisches Grab Nr. 36) (Mainz: Phillipp von Zabern).

KURTZ, D. C. and J. BOARDMAN 1971. *Greek Burial Customs* (London: Thames & Hudson).

LABOURY, D. 1997. 'Une relecture de la tombe de Nakht', in Tefnin (ed.), 1997: 49–81.

LABROUSSE, A. 1994. 'Les reines de Teti, Khouit et Ipout I, rechercehes architecturales', *Homm. Leclant*: 231–44.

— 1996–2000. *L'architecture des pyramides à textes*, 2vv. (Cairo: IFAO).

— 1999. *Les pyramides des reines. Une nouvelle nécropole à Saqqâra* (Paris: Hazen).

LABROUSSE, A. and A. MOUSSA 1996. *Le Temple d'Accueil du Complexe Funéraire du Roi Ounas* (Cairo: IFAO).

LACAU, P. 1913. 'Suppressions et modifications de signes dans les textes funéraires', *ZÄS* 51: 1–64.

LACOVARA, P. and B. T. TROPE 2001. *The Realm of Osiris*. (Atlanta: Michael Carlos Museum).

LANSING, A. 1917. 'The Egyptian Expedition 1916–16', *BMMA* 12, Pt.II: 7–26.

— 1920. 'The Egyptian Expedition 1918–20', *BMMA* 15, Pt.II: 4–12.

— 1924. 'The Museum's Excavations at Lisht', *BMMA* 19, Pt. II: 33–43.

— 1933. 'The Egyptian Expedition', *BMMA* 29, Pt. II: 4–38.

LANSING, A. and W.C. HAYES 1937. 'The Egyptian Expedition 1935–36', *BMMA* 32 Supp: 4–39.

LAPP, G. 1986. *Die Opferformel des Alten Reiches unter Berücksichtigung einiger später Formen* (Munich: Philipp von Zabern)

— 1993. *Typologie der Särge und Sargkammern von der 6. bis* 13. *Dynastie* (Heidelberg: Orientverlag).

LAUER, J.-Ph. 1954. 'La structre de la tombe de Hor à Saqqarah (XXVIe Dynastie), *ASAE* 52: 133–6.

— 1976. *Saqqara, Royal Necropolis of Memphis* (London: Thames & Hudson).

— 1993. 'Sur l'emploi et le role de la couleur aux monuments du complexe du roi Djoser', *RdE* 44: 75–80.

LAUER, J.-Ph. and P. LACAU 1936–1961. *La pyramide a degrees*, 5vv. (Cairo: IFAO).

LEAHY, A. 1989. 'A Protective Measure at Abydos', *JEA* 75: 41–60.

— 1990. 'Abydos in the Libyan Period', in A. Leahy (ed.), *Libya and Egypt c.* 1300–750 *BC* (London: SOAS): 155–200.

— 1994. 'Kushite Monuments at Abydos', *UReed*: 171–92.

LEBLANC, C. 1989. *Ta Set Neferou: une nécropole de Thebes-Ouest et son histoire* I (Cairo: Nubar).

— 1997a. 'The Tomb of Ramesses II and the Remains of his Funerary Treasure', *EgArch* 10: 11–13.

— 1997b. 'Quelques réflexions sur le programme iconographique et la fonction des temples de "Millions d'Années"', *Memnonia* 8: 93–105.

LECLANT, J. 1951. 'Le role du lait et de l'allaitement d'apres les Textes des Pyramides', *JNES* 10: 123–27.

— 1961. *Montuemhat, Quatrième Prophète d'Amon*, Prince de Ville (Cairo: IFAO).

LEFÉBURE, E. 1889. *Les hypogées royaux de Thebes*, II (Paris: E. Leroux).

LEFEBVRE, G. 1922. 'Légendes de Scènes Agricoles au Tombeau de Petosiris', *RecChamp*: 75–92.

— 1923–4. *Le tombeau de Petosiris*, 3vv. (Cairo: IFAO).

LEHNER, M. 1985. *The Pyramid Tomb of Hetep-heres and the Satellite Pyramid of Khufu* (Mainz: Philipp von Zabern).

— 1997. *The Complete Pyramids* (London and New York: Thames & Hudson; Cairo: American University in Cairo Press).

— 2002. 'The Pyramid Age Settlement of the Southern Mount at Giza', *JARCE* 39: 27–74.

LEPROHON, R. J. 1994. 'The Sixth Dynasty False Door of the Priestess of Hathor Irti', *JARCE* 31: 41–8.

LEPSIUS, C.R. 1842. *Auswahl der wichtigsten Urkunden des ægyptischen Alterthums* (Leipzig: G. Wigand).

— 1849–59. *Denkmaeler aus Aegypten und Aethiopien*, 6vv. (Berlin/Leipzig: Nicolaische Buchhandlung).

— 1897. *Denkmaeler aus Aegypten und Aethiopien*, Text, ed. E. Naville, L. Borchardt and K. Sethe (Leipzig: J.C. Hinrichs).

LESKO, B. 1969. 'Royal mortuary suites of the Egyptian New Kingdom', *AJA* 73: 453–58.

— 1971–1972. 'Three Reliefs from the Tomb of Mentuemhat', *JARCE* 9: 85–8.

LESKO, L. H. 1977. *The Ancient Egyptian Book of Two Ways* (Berkeley: University of California).

— (ed.) 1994. *Pharaoh's Workers* (Ithaca, NY: Cornell University Press).

LEXA, F. 1925. *La Magie dans l'Egypte Antique* (Paris: P. Geuthner).

LICHTHEIM, M. 1973, 1976, 1980. *Ancient Egyptian Literature*, 3vv. (Berkeley: University of California Press).

— 1988. *Ancient Egyptian Autobiographies* (Freiburg: Orbis biblicus et orientalis universitatsverlag).

LIEBOWITZ, H.A. 1967. 'Horses in New Kingdom Art and the Date of an Ivory from Megiddo', *JARCE* 7: 129–34.

LILYQUIST, C. 1979. 'A Note on the Date of Senebtisi and other Middle Kingdom Groups', *Serapis* 5: 27–8.

— 1974. 'Early Middle Kingdom Tombs at Mitrahina', *JARCE* 11: 27–30.

— 1988. 'The Gold Bowl Naming General Djehuty: A Study of Objects and Early Egyptology', *MMJ* 23: 5–68.

— 2003. *The Tomb of Three Foreign Wives of Tuthmosis III* (New York: MMA).

LLOYD, A.B. 1976. *Herodotus, Book II, Commentary* 1–98 (Leiden: Brill).

— 1989. 'Psychology and Society in the Ancient Egyptian Cult of the Dead', *Religion and Philosophy in Ancient Egypt* (New Haven: Yale University).

LLOYD, A.B., A.J. SPENCER and A. EL-KHOULI 1990. *The Mastabas of Meru, Semdenti, Khui and others* (Lonodn: EES).

LOAT, L. 1905. Gurob (London: ERA).

— 1914. 'The Ibis Cemetery at Abydos', *JEA* 1: 40.

— 1923. 'A Sixth Dynasty cemetery at Abydos', *JEA* 9: 161–3.

LOYRETTE, A.-M. 1997. 'Les Tombes de la Vallée des Trois Puits, à Thèbes-Ouest', *Memnonia VIII*: 177–95.

LOYRETTE, A.-M. and S. MOHAMMED SAYED. 1992–93. 'La tombe d'une princesse anonyme (N. 36) de la Vallée des Reines', *ASAE* 72: 119–32.

LUCAS, A. and J.R. HARRIS 1962. *Ancient Egyptian Materials and Industries*, 4th edition (London: Hutchinson).

LULL, J. 2002. *Las tumbas reales egipcias del Tercer Período Intermedio* (dinastías XXI–XXV) (Oxford: Archaeopress).

LUSTIG, J. 1997. 'Kinship, Gender and Age in Middle Kingdom Tomb Scenes and Texts', in J. Lustig (ed.), *Anthropology and Egyptology: A Developing Dialogue* (Sheffield: Sheffield Academic Press) 43–65.

LYTHGOE, A.M. 1907. 'Egyptian Expedition', *BMMA* 2: 163–69.

— 1908. 'The Oasis of Kharga', *BMMA* 3: 203–08.

MACE, A.C. 1914. 'Excavations at the North Pyramid of Lisht', *BMMA* 9: 207–22.

— 1921. 'Excavations at Lisht', *BMMA* 16 Part II: 5–19.

MACE, A.C. and H.E. WINLOCK 1916. *The Tomb of Senebtisi at Lisht* (New York: MMA).

MACKAY, E. 1916. 'Note on a New Tomb (No. 260) at Drah Abu'lNaga, Thebes', *JEA* 3: 125–26.

— 1917. 'Proportion Squares on Tomb Walls in the Theban Necropolis', *JEA* 4: 74–85.

— 1920a. 'On the Use of Beeswax and Resin as Varnishes in Theban Tombs', *Ancient Egypt* 2: 35–8.

— 1920b. 'Kheker Friezes', *Ancient Egypt* 4: 111–22.

MACKAY, E., L. HARDING and W.M.F. PETRIE 1929. *Bahrein and Hemamieh* (London: BSAE).

MACRAMALLAH, R. 1935. *Le mastaba d'Idout* (Cairo: IFAO).

MAHMOUD, A. 1999. 'Ii-neferti, a Poor Woman', *MDAIK* 55: 315–23.

MALEK, J. 1982. 'Nekropolen. Late Period', *LÄ* IV: 440–9.

— 1985. 'Sais', *LÄ* VI: 355–8.

— 1993. *The Cat in Ancient Egypt* (London: British Museum).

— 1994. 'King Merykare and his Pyramid', in Homm. *Leclant*, I: 203–14.

MANLEY, B. 1988. 'Tomb 39 and The Sacred Land', *JACF* 2: 41–57.

— (ed.) 2003. *Seventy Mysteries of Ancient Egypt* (London and New York: Thames & Hudson).

MANNICHE, L. 1986. 'The Tomb of Nakht, The Gardener, at Thebes (No. 161), as copied by Robert Hay,' *JEA* 72: 55–78.

— 1987. *City of the Dead/The Tombs of the Nobles at Luxor* (London: BMP; Cairo: American University in Cairo Press).

—1988a. *Lost Tombs: a Study of Certain Eighteenth Dynasty Monuments in the Theban Necropolis* (London: Kegan Paul International).

—1988b. *The Wall Decoration of three Theban Tombs* (TT77, 175 and 249) (Copenhagen: Carten Niebuhr Institute).

— 1997. 'Reflections on the Banquet Scene', in R. Tefnin (ed.), *La Peinture Egyptienne Ancienne* (Brussels: Fondation Égyptologique Reine Elisabeth): 29–36.

— 2003. 'The so-called scenes of daily life in the private tombs of the Eighteenth Dynasty: an overview', *ThNec*: 42–45.

MANNING, S. 1887. *The Land of the Pharaohs* (London: Religious Tract Society).

MANUELIAN, P.D. 1983. 'Prolegomena zur Untersuchung saitischer "Kopien"', *SAK* 10: 221–45.

— 1985. 'Two fragments of relief and a new model for the tomb of Montuemhat at Thebes', *JEA* 71: 98–121.

—1988. Review of Eigner 1984, *JNES* 47: 297–304.

—1994a. *Living in the Past: Studies in Archaism of the Egyptian Twenty-Sixth Dynasty* (London: Kegan Paul International).

—1994b. 'The Giza Mastaba Niche and Full Frontal Figure of Redi-nes in the Museum of Fine Arts, Boston', *FHK*: 55–78.

— 1996. 'Presenting the Scroll: Papyrus Documents in Tomb Scenes of the Old Kingdom', *StudSimp*: 561–88.

— 1999. 'A Case of Prefabrication? The False Door of Inti', *JARCE* 35: 115–128.

MARAGIOGLIO, V. and C.A. RINALDI 1964–77, *L'architettura delle Piramidi Menfite*, II–VIII (Rapallo: Officine Grafiche Canessa).

MARAITE, E. 1992. 'Le Cone de Parfum dans l'Ancienne Egypte', in, C. Obsomer and A-L. Oosthoek (eds.), *Amosiadès* (Louvain-la-Neuve: Catholic University of Louvain): 213–19.

MARIETTE, A. 1857. *Le Sérapeum de Memphis* (Paris: Gide).

—1869–80. *Abydos*, 2vv. (Paris: Franck).

—1872–89. *Monuments divers recuillis en Égypte et en Nubie* (Paris: F. Vieweg).

—1882. *Le Sérapeum de Memphis*, I (Paris: F. Vieweg).

—1884–5. *Les mastabas de l'ancien empire* (Paris: F. Vieweg).

MAROCHETTI, E.F. 1993. 'Variations of the mastaba tomb during the Middle Kingdom', *A6CIE* II: 121–27.

MARTIN, G.T. 1974, 1989. *The Royal Tomb at el-'Amarna I, II* (London: EES).

— 1979. *The Tomb of Hetepka and other Reliefs and Inscriptions from the Sacred Animal Necropolis at North Saqqara* (London: EES).

— 1981. *The Sacred Animal Necropolis at North Saqqara: the Southern Dependencies of the Main Temple Complex* (London: EES).

— 1982. 'Queen Mutnodjmet at Memphis and El-'Amarna', *L'Ég* 1979 II: 275–8.

— 1985. *The Tomb Chapels of Paser and Ra'ia at Saqqara* (London: EES).

— 1986. 'Shabtis of Private Persons in the Amarna Period', *MDAIK* 42: 109–29.

— 1987. *Corpus of Reliefs of the New Kingdom from the Memphite Necropolis and Lower Egypt*, I (London: Kegan Paul International).

— 1991. *The Hidden Tombs of Memphis* (London and New York: Thames & Hudson).

—1997a. '"Covington's Tomb" and Related Early Monuments at Gîza', *Études Lauer*: 279–88.

— 1997b. *The Tomb of Tia and Tia: a Royal Monument of the Ramesside Period in the Memphite Necropolis* (London: EES).

MARTIN, G.T., J. VAN DIJK, M.J. RAVEN, B.G. ASTON, D.A. ASTON, E. STROUHAL and L. HORÁÁKOVÁ 2001. *The Tombs of Three Memphite Officials: Ramose, Khay and Pabes* (London: EES).

MARTIN, G.T. and H.D. SCHNEIDER 1989, 1996. *The Memphite Tomb of Horemheb, Commander-in-Chief of Tut'ankhamūn*, 2vv. (London: EES).

MASPERO, G. 1885. *Trois années de fouilles dans les tombeauz de Thebes et Memphis* (Paris).

— 1889. *Les momies royales de Déir el-Baharî* (Cairo: IFAO).

MASPERO, G. and E. BRUGSCH 1881. *La trouvaille de Deir el-Bahari* (Cairo: F. Mourès & Cie.).

MATHIESON, I., E. BETTLES, J. CLARKE, C. DUHIG, S. IKRAM, L. MAGUIRE, S. QUIE and A. TAVARES 1997. 'The National Museums of Scotland Saqqara Survey Project 1993–1995', *JEA* 83: 17–53.

MATHIESON, I., E. BETTLES, S. DAVIES and H.S. SMITH 1995. 'A Stela of the Persian Period from Saqqara', *JEA* 81: 23–41.

MATHIESON, I.J. and A. TAVARES 1993. 'Preliminary Report of the National Museums of Scotland Saqqara Survey Project', *JEA* 79: 17–31.

MATHIEU, B. 1997. 'La fonction du serdab dans la pyramide d'Ounas', *Etudes Lauer*: 289–304.

MAYSTRE, C. 1936. *La tombe de Nebenmât* (no 219) (Cairo: IFAO).

— 1939. 'Le Tombeau de Ramsès II', *BIFAO* 38: 183–90.

MCDONALD, J. 1996. *House of Eternity: the Tomb of Nefertari* (Los Angeles: The Getty Conservation Institute and the J. Paul Getty Museum).

MCDOWELL, A. 1999/2001. *Village Life in Ancient Egypt* (Oxford: OUP).

MENDELSSHON, K. 1974. *The Mystery of the Pyramids* (London: Thames & Hudson).

MEKHITARIAN, A. 1954. *Egyptian Painting* (Geneva: Skira).

— 1994. *La misère des tombes thebaines* (Brussels: Fondation Égytologique Reine Élisabeth).

MENU, B. 1994. 'Le tombeau de Pétosiris', *BIFAO* 94: 311–29.

MESKELL, L. 1999. *Archaeologies of Social Life* (Oxford: Blackwell).

— 2002. *Private Life in New Kingdom Egypt* (Princeton: Princeton University Press).

METROPOLITAN MUSEUM OF ART 1999. *Egyptian Art in the Age of the Pyramids* (New York: Metropolitan Museum of Art).

MICHALOWSKI, K., C. DESROCHES, J. de LINAGE and J. MANTEUFFEL 1950. *Tell Edfou 1939* (Cairo: IFAO).

MICHALOWSKI, K., J. de LINAGE, J. MANTEUFFEL, and J. SAINTE FARE GARNOT 1938. *Tell Edfou 1938* (Cairo: IFAO).

MIDANT-REYNES, B., E. CRUBÉZY and T. JANIN 1996. 'The Predynastic Site of Adaima', *Egyptian Archaeology* 9: 13–15.

MILDE, H. 1988. 'It is All in the Game', *FSR*: 89–95.

— 1994. '"Going out into the Day" Ancient Egyptian Beliefs and Practices concerning Death', in J. M. Bremer, Th. P. J. van den Hout, R. Peters (eds.), *Hidden Futures: Death and Immortality in Ancient Egypt, Anatolia, the Clasical, Biblical and Arabic-Islamic World*, (Amsterdam: Amsterdam University Press): 15–36.

MILLET, N. B. 1981. 'The Reserve Heads of the Old Kingdom', in W.K. Simpson and W. M. Davis (eds), *Studies in Ancient Egypt, the Aegean, and the Sudan: Essays in Honor of Dows Dunham on the Occasion of his 90th Birthday*, June 1, 1980 (Boston: MFA).

MINAULT-GOUT, A. and P. DELEUZE 1992. Balat II. *Le mastaba d'Ima-Pépi* (Cairo: IFAO).

MOHR, H.T. 1943. *The Mastaba of Hetep-Her-Akhti* (Leiden: E. J. Brill).

MÖLLER, G. and A. SCHARFF 1926. *Die archaeologischen Ergebnisse des vorgeschichtlichen Gräberfelds von Abusir el-Meleq* (Leipzig: Heinrichs').

MOND, R. 1905. 'Report of work in the necropolis of Thebes during the winter of 1903–1904', *ASAE* 6: 65–96.

MOND, R. and O.H. MYERS 1934. *The Bucheum*, 3vv. (London: EES).

MOND, R. and W.B. EMERY 1929. 'The burial shaft of the tomb of Amenemhat', *LAAA* 16: 49–74.

MONNET-SALEH, J. 1987. 'Remarques sur les representations de la peinture d'Hierakonpolis (tombe No 100)', *JEA* 73: 51–58.

MONTET, P. 1913. 'La fabrication du vin dans les tombeaux antéreurs au Nouvel Empire', *RecTrav* 35: 117–24.

— 1925. *Les scènes de la vie privée dans les tombeaux égyptiens de l'Ancien Empire* (Strasbourg: Alsacienne).

— 1928–36. 'Les tombeaux le Siout et de Deir Rifeh', *Kêmi* 1: 53–68; 3: 45–111; 6: 131–63.

— 1938. 'Tombeaux de la Ière et de la IV dynasties à Abou-Roach', *Kêmi* 7: 45–111.

— 1947. *La nécropole royale de Tanis* I: *Les constructions et le tombeau de Osorkon II à Tanis* (Paris).

— 1951. *La nécropole royale de Tanis* II: *Les constructions et le tombeau de Psousennes à Tanis* (Paris).

— 1960. *La nécropole royale de Tanis* III. *Les constructions et le tombeau de Chéchanq III à Tanis* (Paris).

MONTSERRAT, D. and L. MESKELL 1997. 'Mortuary Archaeology and Religious Landscape at Graeco-Roman Deir el-Medina', *JEA* 83: 179–97.

MORGANSTEIN, M. E. and C. A. REDMONT 1998. 'Mudbrick Typology, Sources, and Sedimentology Composition: A Case Study from Tell el-Muqdam, Egyptian Delta', *JARCE* 35: 129–46.

MORRIS, I. 1992. *Death-Ritual and Social Structure in Classical Antiquity* (Cambridge: University Press).

MORSCHAUSER, S. 1991. *Threat-Formulae in Ancient Egypt: A Study of the History, Structure and Use of Threats and Curses in Ancient Egypt* (Baltimore: Halgo).

MOSJOV, B. 2002. 'The Ancient Egyptian underworld In The Tomb Of Sety I', in R. Stock (ed.), *Massachusetts Review: Egypt, Winter* 2001–2002,: 489–506.

MOSS, R. 1933. 'An Unpublished Rock-Tomb at Asyut', *JEA* 19: 33.

MOSTAFA, D.M. 1989. 'The Role of the Djed-Pillar in New Kingdom Tombs', *GM* 109: 41–51.

— 2000. 'Remarks on the architectural development in the necropolis of Deir el-Medina', *Memnonia* XI: 209–225.

MOSTAFA, M.F. 1995. *Das Grab des Neferhotep und des Meh (TT257)* (Mainz: Phillipp von Zabern).

MOUSSA, A. and H. ALTENMÜLLER 1977. *Das Grab des Nianchchnum und Chnumhotep* (Mainz: Phillip von Zabern).

MOUSSA, A. and F. JUNGE 1975. *Two Tombs of Craftsmen* (Mainz: Philipp von Zabern).

MUHAMMED, A.-Q. 1966a. *The Development of the Funerary Beliefs and Practices Displayed in the Private Tombs of the New Kingdom at Thebes* (Cairo: General Organisation for Government Printing).

— 1966b. *Two Theban Tombs: Kyky and Bak-en-amun* (Cairo: General Organisation for Government Printing).

— 1987. 'An Ibis Catacomb at Abu-Kir', *ASAE* 66: 121–3.

MÜLLER, C. 1975. 'Anruf an Lebende', *LÄ* I: 293–99.

— 1984. 'Salbkegel', *LÄ* V: 366–67.

MÜLLER, H.W. 1940. *Die Felsengräber der Fürsten von Elephantine* (Glückstadt: Augustin).

MÜLLER, I. 1974. 'Die Ausgestaltung der Kultkammern in den Gräbern des Alten Reiches in Giza und Saqqara', *Forschungen und Berichte Staaatliche Museen zu Berlin* 16: 79–96.

MÜLLER, M. 1993. 'Iconography: basic problems of the classification of scenes', *A6 CIE*: II, 337–45.

MUNRO, P. 1973. *Die spätägyptischen Totelstelen* (Glückstadt: Augustin).

— 1983. 'Das Unas-Friedhof in Saqqara', *SAK* 10: 278–82.

— 1993a. *Der Unas-Friedhof Nord-West I* (Mainz: Phillipp von Zabern).

— 1993b 'Report on the work of the Joint Archaeological Mission free University of Berlin/University of Hannover during their 12th Campaign (15th March until 14th May, 1992) at Saqqâra', *DE* 26: 47–58.

MURNANE, W.J. 1980. *United with Eternity: a Concise Guide to the Monuments of Medinet Habu* (Cairo: American University in Cairo Press).

MURRAY, M.A. 1904–5. *Saqqara Mastabas* (London: Egyptian Research Account).

— 1910. *The Tomb of Two Brothers* (Manchester: Sherratt and Hughes/London: Dulau and Co.).

MYERS, O. H. and H. W. FAIRMAN 1931. 'Excavations at Armant, 1929–31', *JEA* 17: 223–32.

MYŚLIWIEC, K. 1985. *Eighteenth Dynasty Before the Amarna Period* (Leiden: E. J. Brill).

NAGEL, G. 1929. *Rapport sur les fouilles de Deir el-Médineh (nord)* (Cairo: IFAO).

NASR, M. 1993. 'The Theban Tomb 260 of User', *SAK* 20: 173–202.

— 1997. 'The Excavations of the tomb of Montuemhat at Thebes', *Memnonia* VIII: 211–23.

NAVILLE, E. 1894–5. 'The Excavation at Deir el Bahari during the winter, 1894–95', *EEFAR* 1894–1895: 33–37.

— 1896–1900. *The Temple of Deir el-Bahari*, 6vv. (London: EEF).

— 1914. *The Cemeteries of Abydos* I (London: EEF).

NAVILLE, E. and H.R. HALL 1907–1913. *The XIth Dynasty Temple at Deir el-Bahari*, 3vv. (London: EEF).

NEGM, M. 1997. *The Tomb of Simut Called Kyky* (Warminster: Aris and Phillips).

NELSON, M. 2003. 'The Ramesseum Necropolis', *ThNec*: 88–94.

NEUGEBAUER, O. and R. PARKER 1969. *Egyptian Astronomical Texts*, 2vv. (Providence: Brown University).

NEWBERRY, P.E. and F.Ll. GRIFFITH 1893–4. *Beni Hasan*, 4vv. (London: EEF).

— 1894–5. *El-Bersheh*, 2vv. (London: EES).

NICHOLSON, P.T. 1996. 'The North Ibis Catacomb at North Saqqara', *EArch* 9: 16–17.

— 1999. 'The North Ibis Catacomb at Saqqara: "The Tomb of the Birds"', *StudSmith*: 209–14.

NIWINSKI, A. 1983. 'Sarg NR-SpZt', *LÄ* 5: 434–68.

— 1988a. *21st Dynasty Coffins from Thebes: Chronological and Typological Studies* (Mainz: Philipp von Zabern).

— 1988b. 'Relativity in Iconography', *FSR*: 96–104.

NORDEN, F. L. 1757. *Travels in Egypt and Nubia* (London).

NORTHAMPTON, Fifth Marquess of, W. SPIEGELBERG and P.E. NEWBERRY 1908. *Report on Some Excavations in the Theban Necropolis during the Winter of 1898–9* (London: Constable).

NUNN, J.F. 1996. *Ancient Egyptian Medicine* (London: British Museum).

O'CONNOR, D. et al. 1985. 'The "Cenotaphs" of the Middle Kingdom at Abydos', *MelMokh* II: 161–77.

— 1989. 'New Funerary Enclosures (Talbezirke) of the Early Dynastic Period at Abydos', *JARCE* 26: 62–71.

— 1996. 'Sexuality, Statuary and the afterlife: Scenes in the Tomb-chapel of Pepyankh', *StudSimp*: 621–33.

— 2003. 'Abydos: the last royal pyramid?', in *70 GMAE*: 75–79.

O'CONNOR, D. and CLINE, E. H. 1998. *Amenhotep III: perspectives on his reign* (Ann Arbor: University of Michigan Press).

O'CONNOR, D. and D. CRAIG PATCH 2001. 'Sacred Sands: Exploring the tombs and temples of Ancient Abydos', *Archaeology* 54/3: 42–9.

OCKINGA, B.G. 1997. *A Tomb from the Reign of Tutankhamun at Akhmim* (Warminster: Aris and Phillips).

— 2000. 'The Saqqara tomb of the Overseer of Craftsmen and Chief Goldworker, Amenemone', *AbSaq2000*: 121–32.

OCKINGA, B.G. and Y. AL-MASRI 1990. *Two Ramesside Tombs at El-Mashayikh* (Sydney: Ancient History Documentary Research Centre).

OSING, J. 1977. *Der Tempel Sethos' I. in Gurna* (Mainz: Philipp von Zabern, 1977).

— 1992. *Das Grab des Nefersecheru in Zawiyet Sultan* (Mainz: Phillipp von Zabern).

OTTO, E. 1952. *Topographie des thebanischen Gaues* (Leipzig: Heinrichs).

— 1960. *Das ägyptische Mundöffnungsritual* (Wiesbaden: Otto Harrassowitz).

OWEN, G. and B. KEMP 1994. 'Craftsmen's work patterns in unfinished tombs at Amarna', *CAJ* 4: 121–29.

PADRO, J., M. HAMZA, M. ERROUX-MORFIN, E. SUBIAS, H. IBRAHIM, L. M. GONZÁLVEZ and T. MASCORT 1998. 'Fouilles archéologiques à Oxyrhynchos, 1992–1994', in *P7ICE*: 135–6.

PALEOLOGICAL ASSOCIATION OF JAPAN 1997. *Akoris. Report of the Excavations at Akoris in Middle Egypt 1981–1992*, 2vv. (Kyoto: Koyo Shobo).

PANTALACCI L. and BERGER EL-NAGGAR, C. (eds) 2005. *Des Neferkare aux Montouhotep* (Lyon: Maison de l'Orient et de la Mediterranée).

PARKER, R. A. 1950. *The Calendars of Ancient Egypt* (Chicago: University of Chicago).

PARKINSON, R. and S. QUIRKE 1992. 'The Coffin of Prince Herunefer and the Early History of the Book of the Dead', in A.B. Lloyd (ed.), *Studies in Pharaonic Religion and Society in Honour of J. Gwyn Griffiths* (London: Egypt Exploration Society): 37–51.

PARLASCA, K. 1966. *Mumienporträts und verwandte Denkmäler* (Wiesbaden: DAI).

PASSALACQUA, J. 1826. *Catalogue raisonné et historique des antiquités découvertes en Égypte par M. Jph Passalacqua de Trieste …* (Paris: A la Galerie d'antiquités égyptiennes).

PAYNE, J.C. 1973. 'Tomb 100: The Decorated Tomb at Hierakonpolis Confirmed', *JEA* 59: 31–35.

PEET, T.E. 1930. *The Great Tomb Robberies of the Twentieth Egyptian Dynasty*, 2 vv. (Oxford: University Press).

PEET, T.E. et al. 1913–14. *The Cemeteries of Abydos*, 3vv. (London: EEF).

PERIZONIUS, R. et al. 1993. 'Monkey Mummies and North Saqqara', *Bulletin of the Egypt Exploration Society* 3: 31–3.

PERZ-DIE, M. del C. and P. VERNUS 1992. *Excavaciones en Ehnesaya El Medina (Heracleópolis Magna) I* (Madrid: Ministerio de Cultura).

PETRIE, W.M.F. 1883. *The Pyramids and Temples of Gizeh* (London: Field and Tuer).

— 1889. *Hawara, Biahmu and Arsinoe* (London: Field and Tuer).

— 1891. *Illahun, Kahun and Gorub. 1889–90* (London: David Nutt).

— 1892. *Medum* (London: D. Nutt).

— 1896. *Naqada and Ballas 1895* (London).

— 1897. *Six Temples at Thebes 1896* (London, B. Quartitch).

— 1898. *Deshasheh* (London: EEF).

— 1900. *Dendereh* (London: EEF).

— 1901a. *The Royal Tombs of the Earliest Dynasties*, 2vv. (London: EEF).

— 1901b. *Diospolis Parva the Cemeteries of Abadiyeh and Hu 1898–9* (London: EEF).

— 1904. *Ehnasya* (London: EEF).

— 1908. *Athribis* (London: BSAE).

— 1909. *Qurneh* (London: ERA)

— 1911. *Roman Portraits and Memphis (IV)* (London: BSAE).

— 1912. *The Labyrinth, Gerzeh and Mazghuneh* (London: BSAE).

— 1913. *Tarkhan I and Memphis V* (London: BSAE).

— 1914. *Tarkhan II* (London: BSAE).

— 1915. *Heliopolis Kafr Ammar and Shurafa* (London: BSAE).

PETRIE, W.M.F. et al. 1902–3. *Abydos I, II* (London: EEF).

— 1910. *Meydum and Memphis (III)* (London: ERA).

— 1915. *Heliopolis, Kafr Ammar and Shurafa* (London: BSAE).

— 1923. *Lahun II* (London: BSAE).

— 1925. *The Tombs of the Courtiers and Oxyrhynkhos* (London: BSAE).

— 1930. *Antaeopolis: the Tombs of Qau* (London: BSAE).

PHILLIPS, J. 1992 'Tomb-robbers and their Booty in Ancient Egypt', *D&T*: 157–92.

PIACENTINI, P. and C. ORSENIGO 2005. *La Valle dei Re Riscoperta: I giornali di scavo di Victor Loret (1898–1899) e altri inediti* (Milan: Skira/Università degli Studi di Milano).

PIANKOFF, A. 1954. *The Tomb of Ramesses VI* (New York: Bollingen).

— 1955. *The Shrines of Tut-Ankh-Amon* (New York: Bollingen).

— 1958. 'Les peintures dans le tombe du rois Ai', *MDAIK* 16 (1958), 247–51.

— 1974. *The Wandering of the Soul* (Princeton: Princeton University Press).

PINCH, G. 1994. *Magic in Ancient Egypt* (London: British Museum).

POCOCKE, R. 1743–45. *A Description of the East, and some other countries*, 2vv. (London: Bowyer).

PODZORSKI, P. 1990. *Their Bones Shall Not Perish* (New Malden, Surrey: Sia).

POLZ, D. 1987. 'Excavation and Recording of a Theban Tomb. Some Remarks on Recording Methods', *P&P*: 119–140.

— 1995a. 'Bericht über die 4. und 5. Grabungskampagne in der Nekropole von Dra' Abu el-Naga/Theben-West', *MDAIK* 51: 207–25.

— 1995b. 'Excavations in Dra Abu el-Naga', *EgArch* 7: 6–8.

— 1995c. 'The Location of the Tomb of Amenhotep I: A Reconsideration', *VSK*, 8–21.

— 1997a. *Das Grab des Hui and des Kel: Theban Nr. 54* (Mainz: Phillipp von Zabern).

— 1997b. 'An Architect's Sketch from the Theban Necropolis', *MDAIK* 53: 233–240.

— 2003b. 'The pyramid-tomb of king Nub-Kheper-Ra Intef in Dra' Abu el-Naga', *EArch* 22: 12–15.

POLZ, D. and A. SEILER 2003. *Die Pyramidenanlage des Königs Nub-Cheper-Re Intef in Dra' Abu el-Naga* (Mainz: Philipp von Zabern).

PORTER B. and R.B. MOSS 1960; 1972; 1974–81; 1934; 1937; 1939; 1952; 1999ff. *Topographical Bibliography of Ancient Egyptian Hieroglyphic Texts, Reliefs and Paintings*: I², *The Theban Necropolis*; II², *Theban Temples*; III², *Memphis*; IV, *Lower and Middle Egypt*; V, *Upper Egypt: Sites*; VI, *Upper Egypt: Chief Temples (excl. Thebes)*; VII, *Nubia, Deserts, and Outside Egypt*; VIII, *Objects of Provenance Not Known*, by J. Malek (Oxford: Clarendon Press/Griffith Institute).

PRISSE D'AVENNES, E. 1868–79. *Atlas d'histoire de l'art égyptien* (Paris: Bertrand).

PUSCH, E.B. 1984. 'Senet', *LA* V: 851–56.

QUIBELL, A. 1925. *The Tombs of Sakkara* (Cairo: Church Missionary Society).

QUIBELL, J.E. 1898a. *The Ramesseum* (London).

— 1898b. *El Kab* (London: ERA).

— 1907. *Excavations at Saqqara 1905–06* (Cairo: IFAO).

— 1908a. *Excavations at Saqqara 1906–07* (Cairo: IFAO).

— 1908b. *Tomb of Yuaa and Thuiu (CG)* (Cairo: IFAO).

— 1909. *Excavations at Saqqara 1907–08* (Cairo: IFAO).

— 1913. *Excavations at Saqqara (1911–12). The tomb of Hesy* (Cairo: IFAO).

— 1923. *Excavations at Saqqara 1912–14* (Cairo: IFAO).

QUIBELL, J.E. and F.W. GREEN 1900–02. *Hierakonpolis*, 2vv. (London: ERA).

QUIBELL, J.E. and A.G.K. HAYTER 1927. *Teti Pyramid, north side* (Cairo: IFAO).

QUIRKE, S. 1992. *Ancient Egyptian Religion* (London: BMP).

RACHEWILTZ, B. DE. 1960. *The Rock Tomb of Irw-k3-pth* (Leiden: Brill).

RADWAN, A. 1969. *Die Darstellungen des regierenden Königs und seiner Familienangehörigen in den Privatgräbern der 18. Dynastie* (Berlin: Verlag Bruno Hessling).

— 1995. 'Recent Excavations of the Cairo University at Abusir: A Cemetery of the 1st Dynasty', in D. Kessler and R. Schulz (eds.), *Gedenkschrift für Winfried Barta* (Berlin: Peter Land): 311–15.

RAMMANT-PEETERS, A. 1983. *Les pyramidions égyptiens du nouvel empire* (Louvain: Peeters).

RANDALL-MACIVER D. and A.C. MACE 1902. *El Amrah and Abydos* (London: EEF).

RANSOM-WILLIANS, C. 1932. *The Decoration of the Tomb of Per-neb* (New York: Metropolitan Museum of Art).

RAUE, D. 1995. 'Zum memphitischen Privatgrab im Neuen Reich', *MDAIK* 51: 255–68.

RAVEN, M. 1991. *The Tomb of Iurudef, a Memphite Official in the Reign of Ramesses II* (London: EES).

— 1994. 'A sarcophagus for Queen Tiye and other fragments from the Royal Tomb at El-Amarna', *OMRO* 74: 7–20.

— 2002. 'The tomb of Meryneith at Saqqara', *EgArch* 20: 26–8.

— 2006. 'Feldarbeit in der Nekropole des Neuen Reiches in Sakkara: Ergenisse der niederländischen Grabungskampagnen 1999–2006', *Sokar: Das ägyptische Pyramidzeitalter* 13: 58–67.

REDFORD, D.B. 2004. *Excavations at Mendes I: The Royal Necropolis* (Leiden and Boston, Brill).

REDFORD, S. and D. 1994. *The Tomb of Re'a (TT201)* (Toronto: Akhenaten Temple Project).

REDFORD, S. 1996. 'Preliminary Report on the Work in the Tomb of Parennefer – T T 188', *Memnonia* VII: 227–34.

REEVES, C.N. 1990a. *Valley of the Kings: the decline of a royal necropolis* (London: Kegan Paul International).

— 1990b. *The Complete Tutankhamun* (London and New York: Thames & Hudson; Cairo: American University in Cairo Press).

— 2000. *Ancient Egypt: the Great Discoveries. A Year-by-Year Chronicle* (London and New York: Thames & Hudson).

— 2003. 'On some queens' tombs of the Eighteenth Dynasty', *ThNec*: 69–73.

REEVES, C.N. and R. WILKINSON 1996. *The Complete Valley of the Kings* (London and New York: Thames & Hudson; Cairo: American University in Cairo Press).

REFAI, H. 1998. 'Die Besätigung im Fest zur volle der Thebanischen Feste bei der erneuerung der Konigsmacht', *Memnonia* XI: 181–89.

REISNER, G.A. 1918. 'The Tomb of Hepzefa, Nomarch of Siut', *JEA* 5: 79–98.

— 1932. *A Provincial Cemetery of the Pyramid Age; Naga-ed-Dêr III* (Berkeley and Los Angeles: University of California Press).

— 1936. *The Development of the Egyptian Tomb Down to the Accession of Cheops* (Oxford: University Press/Cambridge, MA: Harvard University Press).

— 1942. *A History of the Giza Necropolis*, I (Cambridge, MA: Harvard University Press).

REISNER, G.A. and A.C. MACE 1908–9. *The Early Dynastic Cemeteries of Naga-ed-Dêr* (Leipzig: J.C. Heinrichs).

RHIND, A.H. 1862. *Thebes: its Tombs and their Tenants* (London: John Murray).

RICHARDS, J.E. 1997. 'Ancient Egyptian Mortuary Practice and the Study of Socioeconomic Differentiation', in J. Lustig (ed.), *Anthropology and Egyptology: A Developing Dialogue* (Sheffield: Sheffield Academic Press) 32–42.

— 2001. 'Quest for Weni the Elder', *Archaeology* 54/3: 48–9.

— 2002. 'Text and Context in late Old Kingdom Egypt: The Archaeology and Historiography of Weni the Elder', *JARCE* 39: 75–102.

— 2003. 'The Abydos Cemeteries in the Late Old Kingdom', *P8ICE* I: 400–07.

— 2004. *Society and Death in Middle Kingdom Egypt* (Cambridge: Cambridge University Press).

RICKE, H. 1939. *Der Totentempel Thutmoses' III. Baugeschichtliche Untersuchungen* (Cairo: Selbstverlag).

RIGGS, C. 2006. *The Beautiful Burial in Roman Egypt: Art, Identity, and Funerary Religion.* Oxford, Oxford University Press.

RITNER, R.K. 1993. *The Mechanics of Ancient Egyptian Magical Practice* (Chicago: Oriental Institute/University of Chicago).

RIEFSTAHL, E. 1956. 'Two Hairdressers of the Eleventh Dynasty', *JNES* 15: 10–17.

ROBINS, G. 1988. 'Ancient Egyptian Sexuality', *DE* 11: 61–72.

— 1990. *Beyond the Pyramids: Egyptian regional art from the Museo Egizio, Turin* (Atlanta: Emory University Museum).

— 1991. 'Composition and the Artist's Squared Grid', *JARCE* 28: 41–54.

— 1994. *Proportions and Style in Ancient Egyptian Art* (London: Thames & Hudson/Austin TX: University of Texas Press).

— 1997. *The Art of Ancient Egypt* (London: BMP).

ROBINS, G. and C. SHUTE 1987. *The Rhind Mathematical Papyrus* (London: British Museum).

ROCCATI, A. 1996. 'The Activities of the Italian Archaeological Mission in Egypt', *Memnonia* 8: 241–44.

ROEHRIG, C.H. 1995a. 'Gates to the underworld: The Appearance of Wooden Doors in the Royal Tombs in the Valley of the Kings', *VSK*, 82–107.

— 1995b. 'The Early Middle Kingdom Cemeteries At Thebes And The Tomb Of Djari', *Beamtennekropolen*: 255–70.

ROMANO, J.F. 1990. *Death, Burial, and afterlife in Ancient Egypt* (Pittsburgh: Carnegie Museum of Natural History).

ROMANO, J.F. and G. ROBINS 1994. 'A Painted Fragment from the Tomb of *D'w* at Deir el Gebrawi', *JARCE* 31: 21–32.

ROMER, J. 1974. 'Tuthmosis I and the Bibân el-Molûk: some Chronological Considerations', *JEA* 60: 119–33.

—1975. 'The Tomb of Tuthmosis III', *MDAIK* 31: 315–48.

—1976. 'Royal Tombs of the Early Eighteenth Dynasty', *MDAIK* 32: 191–206.

—1981. *Valley of the Kings* (London: Michael Joseph).

— 1984. *Ancient Lives: The Story of the Pharaoh's Tombmakers* (London: Weedenfield & Nicholson).

— 1994. 'Who Made the Private Tombs of Thebes?', *Essays Goedicke*: 211–32.

ROSE, J. 2000. *Tomb KV39: a double archaeological enigma* (Bristol: Western Academic & Specialist Press).

ROSELLINI, I. 1832–44. *I monument dell'Egitto e della Nubia*, 11vv. (Pisa: Proesso N. Capurro).

ROSSI, C. 2004. *Architecture and Mathematics in Ancient Egypt* (Cambridge: Cambridge University Press).

ROSSI, C. and S. IKRAM 2004. 'North Kharga Oasis Survey 2001–2002 Preliminary Report: Ain Gib and Qasr el-Sumayra', *MDAIK* 62.

ROSTEM, O. 1943. 'Note on the method of lowering the lid of the sarcophagus in a Saite tomb of Saqqara', *ASAE* 43: 351–56.

ROTH, A.M. 1992. 'The *pss-kf* and the 'Opening of the Mouth': A Ritual of Birth and Rebirth', *JEA* 78: 57–80.

— 1993. 'Social Change in the Fourth Dynasty: The Spatial Organization of Pyramids, Tombs, and Cemeteries', *JARCE* 30: 33–56.

— 1994. 'The Practical Economics of Tomb-Building in the Old Kingdom: A Visit to the Necropolis in a Carrying Chair', *FHK*: 227–40.

— 1995. *A Cemetery of Palace Attendants, including G 2084–2099, 2230+2231* (Boston: MFA).

— 1998. 'The Organization of Royal Cemeteries at Saqqara in the Old Kingdom', *JARCE* 25: 201–14.

ROULIN, G. 1998. 'Les tombes royales de Tanis: Analyse du programme decoratif', in P. Brissaud and C. Zivie-Coche (eds.), *Tanis: travaux récents sur le Tell Sân el-Hagar* (Paris: Éditions Noêsis): 193–275.

ROWE, A. 1938. 'New light on objects belonging to the Generals Potasimito and Amasis in the Egyptian Museum', *ASAE* 38: 157–95.

RUSSMAN, E.R. 1994. 'Relief Decoration in the Tomb of Mentuemhat (TT34)', *JARCE* 31: 1–19.

— 1995. 'The Motif of Bound Papyrus Plants and the Decorative Program in Mentuemhat's First Court', *JARCE* 32: 117–26.

— 1997. 'Mentuemhat's Kushite Wife (Further Remarks on the Decoration of the Tomb of Mentuemhat, 2)', *JARCE* 34: 21–40.

RYAN, D.P. 1992. 'Some observations concerning uninscribed tombs in the Valley of the Kings', *ATut*: 21–27.

RZEPKA, S. 1995. 'Some Remarks on the Rock-cut Group-Statues in the Old Kingdom', *SAK* 22: 227–36.

SAAD, Z.Y. 1942. 'Preliminary Report on the Royal Excavations at Saqqara', *ASAE* 41: 381–409.

— 1947. *Royal Excavations at Saqqara and Helwan* (Cairo: IFAO).

— 1957. *Ceiling Stelae in the Second Dynasty Tombs from the Excavations at Helwan* (SASAE 21) (Cairo: IFAO).

SAAD, Z.Y. and J.F. AUTRY 1969. *The Excavations at Helwan* (Norman: University of Oklahoma Press).

SAKURAI, K., S. YOSHIMURA and J. KONDO (eds) 1988. *Comparitive Studies of Noble Tombs in the Theban Necropolis (Tomb Nos. 8, 38, 39, 48, 50, 54, 57, 63, 64, 66, 74, 78, 89, 90, 91, 107, 120, 139, 147, 151, 181, 201, 253, 295)* (Tokyo: Waseda University).

SALEH, M. 1977. *Three Old Kingdom Tombs at Thebes* (Mainz: Philipp von Zabern).

SALEH, M. and H. SOUROUZIAN 1987. *The Egyptan Museum Cairo: Official Catalogue* (Mainz/Cairo: Philipp von Zabern).

SAMIVEL and M. AUDRAIN 1955. *The Glory of Egypt* (London: Thames & Hudson).

SANDYS, G. 1615. *A Relation of a Journey begun An. Dom. 1610* (London: W. Barrett).

SÄVE-SÖDERBERGH, T. 1953. *On Egyptian Representations of Hippopotamus Hunting as a Religious Motive* (Uppsala: Horae Soederblomianae).

— 1957. *Four Eighteenth Dynasty Tombs* (Oxford: Griffith Institute).

— 1958. 'Eine Gastmahlsszene im rabe des Schatzhausvorrstehers Djehuti (TT11)', *MDAIK* 16: 290ff.

— 1994. *Old Kingdom Cemetery at Hamra Dom (El-Qasr wa es-Saiyad)* (Stockholm: Royal Academy of Letters, History and Antiquities).

SÄVE-SÖDERBERGH, T. and L. TROY (eds.) 1991. *New Kingdom Pharaonic Sites* (Stockholm: Scandinavian Joint Expedition to Sudanese Nubia).

SCHADEN, O.J. 1979. 'Preliminary Report on the Re-clearance of Tomb 25 in the Western Valley of the Kings (WV-25)', *ASAE* 63: 161–8.

— 1984. 'Clearance of the tomb of King Ay (WV-23)', *JARCE* 21: 39–64.

— 1995. 'Some Observations on the Tomb of Amenmesse (KV-10)', *Essays Goedicke*: 243–54.

— 2004. 'KV-10: Amenmesse 2000', *ASAE* 78: 129–48.

— 2007. 'A KV-63 Update', *Kmt* 18⅟.

SCHÄFER, H. 1908. *Priestergräber und andere Grabfunde von Ende des Alten Reiches bis zur grieschenischen Zeit vom Totentempel des Ne-user-re* (Leipzig: J.C. Hinrichs).

— 1986. *Principles of Egyptian Art* (Oxford: Griffith Institute).

SCHENKEL, W. and F. GOMAÀ 2004. *Scharuna I: Der Grabungsplatz. Die Nekropole: Gräber aus der Alten-Reichs-Nekropole*, 2vv. (Mainz: Philpp von Zabern).

SCHIAPARELLI, E. 1924. *Esplorazione della 'Valle delle Regine' nella necropoli di Tebe* (Turin: Museum of Antiquities)

— 1927. *La Tomba Intatta dell'Architetto Cho Nella Necropoli di Tebe* (Turin: Museum of Antiquities).

SCHIFF GIORGINI. M. 1981. *Soleb*, II, *Les Necropoles* (Florence: Sansoni).

SCHMIDT, H.C. and J. WILLEITNER 1994. *Nefertari: Gemahlin Ramses' II* (Mainz: Philipp von Zabern).

SCHMIDT, V. 1919. *Levende og døde i det gamle Ægypten: Album til ordnung af Sarkofager, Mumiekister, Mumiehylstre o. lign* (Copenhagen: J. Frimots Forlag).

SCHNEIDER, H.D. 1977. *Shabtis*, 3vv. (Leiden: National Museum of Antiquities).

SCHOTT, S. 1953. *Das schöne Fest vom Wüstentale: Festbräuche einer Totenstadt* (Mainz: Steiner).

— 1957. *Wall Scenes from the Mortuary Chapel of the Mayor Paser at Medinet Habu* (Chicago: University of Chicago).

SCHULMAN, A.R. 1982. 'The Iconographic Theme: "Opening of the Mouth" on Stelae', *JARCE* 21: 169–96.

— 1985. 'A Birth (?) Scene from Memphis', *JARCE* 22: 97–104.

SEEHER, J. 1999. 'Siebzehn Gefäße aus der Grabung des Fouad I Desert Institute in der prädynastischen Nekropole von Heliopolis, 1950,' *MDAIK* 55: 427–33.

SEELE, K.C. 1959. *The Tomb of Tjanefer at Thebes* (Chicago: Oriental Institute).

SEIDLMAYER, S.J. 1990. *Gräberfelder aus dem Übergang vom Alten zum Mittleren Reich* (Heidenberg: Heidelberger Orientverlag).

— 1997. 'Stil und Statistik. Die Datierung dekorierter Gräber des Alten Reiches-ein Problem der Methode', in J. Müller and A. Zimmerman (eds.), *Archäologie und Korrespondenzanalyse: Beispiele, Fragen, Perspectiven* (Espelkamp: Marie Leidorf): 17–51.

SERGENT, F. 1986. *Momies Bovines de l'Egypte Ancienne* (Paris: L'École Pratique des Hautes Etudes).

SETTGAST, J. 1963. *Untersuchungen zu altägyptischen Bestattungsdarstellungen* (Glückstadt: Augustin).

SEYFRIED, K.-J. 1987. 'Entwicklung in der Grabarchitektur des Neuen Reiches als eine weitere Quelle für Theologische Konzeptionen der Ramessidenzeit', *P&P*: 219–53.

— 1990. *Das Grab des Amonmose (TT373)* (Mainz: Phillipp von Zabern).

— 1991. *Das Grab des Paenkhemenu (TT68) und die Anlage TT227* (Mainz: Phillipp von Zabern).

— 1995. *Das Grab des Djehutiemhab, TT194* (Mainz: Phillipp von Zabern).

— 1998. 'Kammern, Nischen und Passagen in Felsgräbern des Neuen Reiches', *Stat*: 387–406.

— 2003. 'Reminiscences of the 'Butic burial' in Theban tombs of the New Kingdom', *ThNec*: 61–68.

SHAFER, B (ed.) 1997. *Temples of Ancient Egypt* (Ithaca: Cornell University Press).

SHARAWI, G. and Y. HARPUR. 1988. 'Reliefs from Various Tombs at Saqqara', *JEA* 74: 57–67.

SHAW, I (ed.) 2000. *The Oxford History of Ancient Egypt* (Oxford: Cambridge University).

SHAW, I. and P.T. NICHOLSON (eds.) 2000. *Ancient Egyptian Materials and Technology* (Cambridge: Cambridge University Press).

SHEDID, A.G. 1988. *Stil der Grabmalereien in der Amenophis' II. Untersucht an den thebanischen Gräbern Nr. 104 und Nr. 80* (Mainz: Phillipp von Zabern).

— 1991. *Das Grab des Nacht. Kunst und Geschichte eines Beamtengrabes der 18. Dynastie in Theben-West* (Mainz: Phillipp von Zabern).

— 1994a. *Die Felsengräber von Beni Hasan in Mittelägypten* (Mainz: Phillipp von Zabern).

— 1994b. *Das Grab des Sennedjem. Ein Kunstlergrab der 19. Dynastie in Deir el-Medineh* (Mainz: Phillipp von Zabern).

SHEIKHOSLAMI, C. M. 2003. 'The burials of priests of Montu at Deir el-Bahari in the Theban necropolis', *ThNec*: 131–37.

SHORTER, A. W. 1930. 'The Tomb of Aahmose Supervisor of the Mysteries of the House of the Morning', *JEA* 16: 54–62.

SIEBELS, R. 1996. 'The Wearing of Sandals in Old Kingdom Tomb Decoration', *BACE* 7: 75–88.

SILVERMAN, D. 1969. 'Pygmies and Dwarves in the Old Kingdom', *Serapis* I: 53–62.

— 1988. *The Tomb Chamber of Hsw the Elder: the Inscribed Material at Kom el-Hisn* (Winona Lake: Eisenbraum's).

— 2000. 'Middle Kingdom tombs in the Teti pyramid cemetery', *AbSaq*2000: 259–82.

SIMPSON, C. 2003. 'Modern Qurna – pieces of an historical jigsaw', *ThNec*: 244–9.

SIMPSON, W.K. 1963. *Heka-nefer, and the dynastic material from Toshka and Arminna* (New Haven: Peabody Museum/Philadelphia: University Museum).

— 1974. *The Terrace of the Great God at Abydos* (New Haven: Peabody Museum/Philadelphia: University Museum).

— 1976a. *The Mastabas of Qar and Idu G 7101 and 7102* (Boston: MFA).

— 1976b *The Offering Chapel of Sekhem-ankh-ptah in the Museum of Fine Arts, Boston* (Boston: MFA).

— 1978. *The Mastabas of Kawab, Khafkhufu I and II. G 7110–20, 7130–40 and 7150 and Subsidiary Mastabas of Street 7100* (Boston: MFA).

— 1979. 'Topographical notes on Giza mastabas', *FS Edel*: 489–99.

— 1980. *Mastabas of the Western Cemetery, I: Sekhemka (G 1029); Tjetu I (G 2001); Iasen (G 2196); Penmeru (G 2197); Hagy, Nefertjenet and Nimesti (G 2337X, 2343, 2366)* (Boston: MFA).

— 1988. 'Lepsius Pyramid LV at Dahshur: the Mastaba of Si-Ese, Vizier of Amenemhet II', *Pyr. Stud.*: 57–60.

— 1992. *The Offering Chapel of Kayemnofret in the Museum of Fine Arts, Boston* (Boston: MFA).

SIST, L. 1993a. 'Le figurazione della Tomba TT27', *Vicino Oriente* 9 (Rome): 15–54.

— 1993b. 'The Reliefs of Tomb n. 27 at the Asasif', *A6CIE*: II, 485–90.

SMITH, M. 1994. 'Budge at Akhmim, January 1896', in *UReed*: 293–303.

SMITH, S.T. 1992. 'Intact Tombs of the Seventeenth and Eighteenth Dynasties from Thebes and the New Kingdom Burial System', *MDAIK* 48: 193–31.

SMITH, W.S. 1949. *History of Egyptian Sculpture and Painting in the Old Kingdom*, 2nd edition (Oxford: University Press).

— 1951. 'Paintings of the Egyptian Middle Kingdom at Bersheh', *AJA* 55: 321–32.

— 1957. 'A Painting in the Assiut Tomb of Hepzefa', *MDAIK* 15: 221–24.

— 1964. 'Birds and Insects', *BMFA* 62: 145.

— 1981. *The Art and Architecture of Ancient Egypt*, rev. W.K. Simpson (Harmondsworth: Penguin)

SMOLÁRIKOVÁ, J. 2000. 'The Greek cemetery at Abusir', *AbSaq*2000: 67–72.

SOTTAS, H. 1913. *La Preservation de la propriété funeraire dans l'ancienne Égypte* (Paris: Édouard Champion).

SOUKIASSIAN, G. 1982. 'Textes des Pyramides et Formules Apparentées: Remarques à Propos des Tombes Saites', *L'Ég* 1979 II: 55–61.

SOUROUZIAN, H. 1989. *Les Monuments du roi Merenptah* (Mainz: Philipp von Zabern).

SPANEL, D. 1989. 'The Herakleopolitan Tombs of Kheti I and Kheti II at Asyut', *Orientalia* 58: 301–14.

SPENCER, A.J. 1974. 'Researches on the Topography of North Saqqara', *Orientalia* 43.1: 1–11.

— 1979. *Brick Architecture in Ancient Egypt* (Warminster: Aris and Phillips).

— 1982. *Death in Ancient Egypt* (Harmondsworth: Penguin).

— 1993. 'A Cemetery of the First Intermediate Period at El-Ashmunein', *A6CIE*: I, 573–78.

— 2001. 'An elite cemetery at Tell el-Balamun', *EArch* 18: 18–20.

— 2004. *Excavations at Tell el-Balamun 1999–2001* (London: BMP).

— (ed.) 1993 *Early Egypt: the Rise of Civilisation in the Nile Valley* (London: BMP).

STADELMANN, R. 1969. 'Šwt-R'w als Kultsätte des Sonnengottes im Neuen Reich', *MDAIK* 25: 159–78.

— 1971. 'Das Grab in Tempelhof. Der Typus des Königsgrabes in der Spätzeit', *MDAIK* 27: 111–23.

— 1986. 'Totentempel III', *LÄ* VI: 706–11.

— 1991. *Die ägyptischen Pyramiden* (Mainz: Philipp von Zabern).

STADELMANN, R. and N. ALEXANIAN 1998. 'Die Friedhöfe der Alten und Mittleren Reiches in Dahschur', *MDAIK* 54: 291–317.

STECKEWEH, H. 1936. *Die Fürstengräber von Qaw* (Leipzig: Heinrichs).

STEINDORFF, G. 1913. *Das Grab des Ti* (Leipzig: Heinrichs).

— 1937. *Aniba* II, 2vv. (Glückstadt: Augustin).

STEINDORFF, G. and W. WOLF 1936. *Die thebanische Gräberwelt* (Glückstadt: Augustin).

STIERLIN, H. and C. ZIEGLER 1987. *Tanis: Trésors des pharaons* (Fribourg: Seuil).

STÖRK, L. 1977 'Erotik.' *LÄ* II: 4–11

STRUDWICK, N. 1985. *The Administration of Egypt in the Old Kingdom* (London: Kegan Paul International).

— 1994. 'Change and Continuity at Thebes. The Private Tomb after Akhenaten', *UReed*: 321–36.

— 1995. 'The Population of Thebes in the New Kingdom: Some Preliminary Thoughts', *Beamtennekropolen*: 97–106.

— 1996. *The Tombs of Amenhotep, Khnummose and Amunmose at Thebes: nos. 294, 253 and 254* (Oxford: Griffith Institute).

— 2001. 'The Tomb of Sennefri at Thebes', *EArch* 18: 6–8.

— 2003. 'Some aspects of the archaeology of the Theban necropolis in the Ptolemaic and Roman periods', *ThNec*: 167—88.

STRUDWICK, N. and H. 1997. 'The House of Amenmose in Theban Tomb 254', in Tefnin (ed.) 1997: 37–47.

— 1999. *Thebes in Egypt* (London: BMP; Ithaca: Cornell University).

STROUHAL, E. and L. BAREŠ 1993. *Secondary Cemetery in the Mastaba of Ptahshepses at Abusir* (Prague: Charles University).

STUART, H.W.V. 1879. *Nile Gleanings* (London: John Murray).

SWELIM, N. 1983. *Some Problems on the History of the Third Dynasty* (Alexandria: The Archaeological Society of Alexandria).

— 1987. *The Brick Pyramid at Abu Rowash, Number 'I' by Lepsius: a preliminary study* (Alexandria: The Archaeological Society of Alexandria).

— 1994. 'Pyramid Research from the Archaic to the Second Intermediate Period: Lists, Catalogues and Objectives', *Homm. Leclant*, 1: 337–50.

SWELIM, N. and A. DODSON 1998. 'On the Pyramid of Ameny-Qemau and its Canopic Equipment', *MDAIK* 54: 319–34.

TAWFIK, S. 1991. 'Recently Excavated Ramesside Tombs at Saqqara. 1. Archiecture', *MDAIK* 47: 403–9.

TAWFIK, T.S. 2003. 'The Extent of the New Kingdom Cemetery in the Memphite Necropolis', *P8ICE* I: 508–13.

TAYLOR, J.H. 1989. *Egyptian Coffins* (Princes Risborough: Shire Publications).

— 1992. 'Aspects of the History of the Valley of the Kings in the Third Intermediate Period', *ATut*: 186–206.

— 2001. *Death and the afterlife in Ancient Egypt* (London: BMP).

TEFNIN, R. 1987. 'Discours et iconicité dans l'art égyptien', *GM* 79: 55–72.

— 1991. 'Eléments pour une sémiologie de l'image Égyptienne,' *CdE* 66: 60–88.

— (ed.) 1997. *La Peinture Egyptienne Ancienne* (Brussels: Fondation Égyptologique Reine Élisabeth).

THOMAS, E. 1963. 'The Four Niches and Amuletic Figures in Theban Royal Tombs', *JARCE* 3: 71–8.

— 1966. *The Royal Necropoleis of Thebes* (Princeton: privately printed).

— 1978. 'The 'Well' in the Kings' Tombs of Biban el-Moluk', *JEA* 1978: 80–83.

— 1979. 'The *k3y* of Inhapy', *JARCE* 16: 85–92.

— 1980. 'The Tomb of Queen Ahmose(?) Merytamen, Theban Tomb 320', *Serapis* 6: 171–81.

THOMAS, N. (ed.) 1996. *The American Discovery of Ancient Egypt* (Los Angeles: Los Angeles County Museum of Art).

THOMPSON, S.E. 1998. 'The Significance of Anointing in Ancient Egyptian Funerary Beliefs', in L. H. Lesko (ed.), *Ancient Egyptian and Mediterranean Studies in Memory of William A. Ward* (Providence: Brown University): 229–43.

TIRADRITTI, F. 1998. 'Three Years of Researches in the Tomb of Harwa', *EArch* 13: 3–6.

— 2004. 'Archaeological Activities of the Museum of Milan in the Tomb of Harwa (TT 37)', *ASAE* 78: 161–198.

TKACZOW, B. 1993. *Topography of Ancient Alexandria (An Archaeological Map)* (Warsaw: Polish Academy of Sciences).

TODA, E. 1887. 'Son Notém en Tebas. Inventario y textos de un sepulcro egipcio de la xx dinastia', *Boletin Real academia de la historia* 10: 91–148.

— 1920. 'La découverte et l'inventaire du tombeau de Sen-Nezem', *ASAE* 20: 145–58.

TOOLEY, A.M.J. 1995. *Egyptian Models and Scenes* (Princes Risborough: Shire).

TOYNBEE, J.M.C. 1971. *Death and Burial in the Roman World* (London: Thames & Hudson).

TRIGGER, B.R. 1969. 'The Royal tombs at Qustul and Ballana and their Meroitic Antecedents', *JEA* 55: 117–28.

TRIGGER, B.G., B.J. KEMP, D. O'CONNOR and A. B. LLOYD 1983. *Ancient Egypt: A Social History* (Cambridge: Cambridge University).

TYLOR, J.J. 1896. *The Tomb of Sebeknekht* (London: Quaritch).

TYLOR, J.J. and F.Ll. GRIFFITH 1894. *The Tomb of Paheri at El-Kab* (London: EEF).

UCHIDA, S. 1993. 'The Destruction of Tomb Reliefs in the Old Kingdom. An

Aspect of the Tomb Violation', *Orient* (Tokyo) 29: 77–92.

UPHILL, E.P. 1992. 'Where were the Funerary Temples of the New Kingdom Queens?', *A6CIE*, I: 613–18.

— 2000. *Pharaoh's Gateway to Eternity: The Hawara Labyrinth of King Amenemhat III* (London and New York: KPI)

VALBELLE, D. 1975. *La Tombe de Hay à Deir el-Médineh (no 267)* (Cairo: IFAO).

— 1985. *«Les ouvriers de la tombe»: Deir el-Médineh à l'époque Ramesside* (Cairo: IFAO).

VALLOGGIA, M. 1986. *Balat I. Le mastaba de Medou-Nefer* (Cairo: IFAO).

— 1986. *Balat IV. Le monument funéraire d'Ima-Pepy/Ima-Meryrê* (Cairo: IFAO).

VAN DE WALLE, B. 1930. *Le Mastaba de Neferirtenef* (Brussels: Fondation Egyptologique Reine Elisabeth).

— 1978. *La chapelle funéraire de Neferirtenef* (Brussels: Musées Royaux d'Art et d'Histoire).

— 1981. *Wall Scenes from the Tomb of Amenhotep (Huy), Governor of the Bahria Oasis* (San Antonio: Van Siclen Books).

VAN DEN BRINK, E.C. 1982. *Tombs and Burial Customs at Tell el-Daba* (Vienna: Austrian Archaeological Institut in Cairo).

VAN DIJK, J. 1988. 'The Development of the Memphite Necropolis in the Post-Amarna Period', in Zivie (ed.) 1988: 37–46.

— 1993 *The New Kingdom Necropolis of Memphis. Historical and Iconographical Studies*, (Groningen: Proefschrift Rijksuniversiteit Groningen).

VAN SICLEN, C.C. 1980. 'The Temple of Meniset at Thebes', *Serapis* 6: 183–207.

VAN WALSEM, R. 1998. 'The Interpretation of Iconographic Programmes in Old Kingdom Elite Tombs of the Memphite Area. Methodological and Theoretical (Re)Considerations', *P7ICE*: 1205–1213.

— 2003. 'The Tomb of Meryneith at Saqqara, Results of the Dutch Mission 2001–2003', *Bulletin of the Australian Centre for Egyptology* 14: 117–34.

— 2005. *The Iconography of Old Kingdom Elite Tombs* (Leuven: Peeters).

VANDERSLEYEN, C. 1975. 'Le sens symbolique des puits funéraires dans l'Egypte ancienne', *CdE* 50/99–100: 151–57.

— 1993. 'Les scènes de lamentation des chambres alpha et gamma dans la tombe d'Akhénaton' *RdE* 44: 192–94.

— 1995. 'Who Was the First King in the Valley of the Kings?', *VSK*: 22–24.

VANDIER, J. 1935. *La tombe de Nefer-Abou* (Cairo: IFAO).

— 1950. *Mo'alla. La tombe d'Ankhtifi et la tombe de Sébekhotep*. Cairo: IFAO.

— 1952–78. *Manuel d'Archéologie Égyptienne*, 6vv. (Paris: A. et J. Picard).

VANDIER, J. and G. JOURDAIN 1939. *Deux tombes de Deir el-Médineh* (Cairo: IFAO).

VANEK, S. 1989. 'Marshland scenes in the private tombs of the Eighteebnth Dynasty', in *The Archaeology, Geography and History of the Delta*, (Oxford: DE Publications), 311–22.

VARILLE, A. 1968. *Inscriptions concernant l'arcitecte Amenhotep fils de Hapou* (CAIRO: IFAO).

VENIT, M.S. 1988. 'The Painted Tomb from Wardian and the Decoration of Alexandrian Tombs', *JARCE* 25: 71–91

— 2001 'Style, Substance, and the Efficacy of the Image in Tomb Painting of Roman Alexandria', in *La peinture funéraire antique*, Barbet, A. (Paris: Errance), 137–42.

— 2002. *Monumental Tombs of Ancient Alexandria: The Theater of the Dead* (Cambridge: Cambridge University Press).

VENTURA, R. 1986. *Living in a City of the Dead*. Freiburg (Schweiz: University Publishers).

— 1988. 'The Largest Project for a Royal Tomb in the Valley of the Kings', *JEA* 74: 137–56.

VERCOUTTER, J. 1975. *Mirgissa* II: *les nécropoles* (Paris: Direction générale des relations culturelles, scientifiques et techniques).

VERCOUTTER, J. and N.H. HENEIN 1986. *Le Mastaba de Medou-Nefer* (Cairo: IFAO).

VERHOEVEN, U. 1984. Grillen, Kochen, Backen im Alltag und im Ritual Altagyptens (Brussels: Fondation Egyptologique Reine Elisabeth).

VERNER, M. 1977a, 1986. *The Mastaba of Ptahshepses* (Prague: Charles University).

— 1993. 'The mastaba of Kaaper', *ZÄS* 120: 84–105.

— 1994. *Forgotten Pharaohs, Lost Pyramids* (Prague: Akademia/Skodaexport).

— 1995. 'An Early Old Kingdom Cemetery at Abusir' *ZÄS* 122: 78–91.

— 2001. *The Pyramids* (London: Atlantic/New York: Grove Press).

— 2002. *The Realm of Osiris* (Cairo: American University in Cairo Press).

VERNUS. P. 1976. 'Inscriptions de la troisième période intermédiare (II)', *BIFAO* 75: 67–72.

VIREY, P. 1891 *Sept tombeaux Thébains de la XVIIIe dynastie* (Cairo: IFAO).

VON BISSING, F. L., L. BORCHARDT, and H. KEES 1905–28. *Das Re-Heiligtum des Königs Ne-woser-re* (Rathures) (Leipzig. J. C. Hinrichs).

VON DRIESCH, A., D. KESSLER, F. STEINMANN, V. BERTEAUX and J. PETERS 2005. 'Mummified, Deified and Buried at Hermopolis Magna – the Sacred Birds from Tuna el-Gebel, Middle Egypt', *Ägypten und Levant* 15: 203–241.

VÖRÖS, G. 1998. *The Temple on the Pyramid of Thebes: Hungarian Excavations on Thoth Hill at the Temple of Pharaoh Montuhotep Sankhkara 1995–1998* (Budapest: Szazszorszep Kiado es Nyomda).

VYSE, R.W.H. 1840. *Operations carried on at the Pyramids of Gizeh in* 1837, 3vv. (London: James Fraser).

WACHSMANN, S. 1987. *Aegeans in the Theban Tombs* (Leuven: Peeters).

WALKER, S. and M.L.BIERBRIER 1997. *Ancient Faces: Mummy Portraits from Roman Egypt* (London: BMP).

WARD, C. 2000. *Sacred and Secular: Ancient Egyptian Ships and Boats* (Philadelphia: University Museum).

WARD, W. A. 1983. 'The Date of the Reused False Door of *Nfrtm-m-sa.f*', *JEA* 70: 87–91.

WARMENBOL, E. and L. DELVAUX 1999. 'La Tombe de Basa (TT389)', l'Assasif et le Description de l'Egypte', *MDAIK* 55: 435–43.

WEEKS, K.R. 1994. *Mastabas of Cemetery G 6000: including G 6010 (Naferbauptah); G 6020 (Iymery); G 3060 (Ity); G 6040 (Shepseskafankh)* (Boston: MFA).

— 1998. *The Lost Tomb: the Greatest Discovery in the Valley of the Kings since Tutankhamun* (London: Wiedenfeld and Nicolson).

— 2000a. *KV5: A Preliminary Report* (Cairo: AUC Press).

— (ed.) 2000b. *Atlas of the Valley of the Kings* (Cairo: AUC Press).

— (ed.) 2001. *Valley of the Kings* (Vercelli: White Star).

— 2003. 'The Sycomore Fig', in *Homm. Haikal*: 205–314.

WEILL, R., Mme TONY-REVILLON and M. PILLET 1958. *Dara: campaignes de 1946–1948* (Cairo: Organisme Générale des Imprimeries Gouvernementales).

WERBROUCK, M. 1934. 'L'oiseau dans les tombes thébaines', *Mélanges Maspero* I, 21–25 (Cairo: IFAO).

— 1938. *Les pleureuses dans l'Egypte ancienne* (Brussels: Fondation Reine Élisabeth).

— 1949. *Le Temple d'Hatshepsut à Deir el Bahari* (Brussels: Fondation Reine Élisabeth).

WESTENDORF, W. 1967. 'Bemerkungen zur "Kammer der Wiedergeburt" im Tutankhamungrab', *ZÄS* 94: 139–50.

WETTENGEL, W. 1994. 'Die Sargkammer des Sennedjem. Arbeiten an der Kopie eines altägyptischen Grabes' *Antike Welt* 25: 172–74.

WILD, H. 1953, 1966. *Le tombeau de Ti*, II, III (Cairo: IFAO).

— 1961. 'Observations sur quelques Scènes du Tombeau de Ti et Leur Enchainement', *Mélanges Mariette*, J. Garnot, ed. Cairo: IFAO, 177–97.

— 1979. *La tombe de Néferhotep (I) et Nef.néfer à Deir el-Médina [No.6] et autres documents les concernant*, II (Cairo: IFAO).

WILKINSON, A. 1998. *The Garden in Ancient Egypt* (London: Rubicon).

— 1994. 'Landscapes for Funeral Rituals in Dynastic Times', *UReed*: 391–401.

WILKINSON, J.G. 1835. *The Topography of Thebes and general view of Egypt* (London: John Murray).

— 1878. *Manners and Customs of the Ancient Egyptians* (London: J. Murray).

WILKINSON, R.H. 1993 'The Paths of Re: symbolism in the royal tombs of Wadi Biban el Moluk', *Kmt* 4/3: 42–51.

— 1994. 'Symbolic Orientation and Alignment in New Kingdom Royal Tombs and their Decoration', *JARCE* 31: 79–86.

— 1995. 'Symbolic Orientation and Alignment in New Kingdom Royal Tombs', *VSK*: 74–81.

— 2000. *The Complete Temples of Ancient Egypt* (London and New York: Thames & Hudson; Cairo: American University in Cario Press).

— 2003. *The Complete Gods and Goddesses of Ancient Egypt* (London and New York: Thames & Hudson; Cairo: American University in Cario Press).

WILLEMS, H. 1988. *Chests of Life* (Leiden: Ex Orient Lux).

WILSON, H. 1990. 'Sycamore and fig', *DE* 18: 71–82.

WILSON, J.A. 1944. 'Funeral Services in the Egyptian Old Kingdom', *JNES* 3: 201–18.

WINLOCK, H.E. 1922. 'The Egyptian Expedition 1921–22', *BMMA* 17, Pt.II: 19–48.

— 1923. 'The Egyptian Expedition 1922–23', *BMMA* 18, Pt.II: 11–39.

— 1924a. 'The Tombs of the Kings of the Seventeenth Dynasty at Thebes', *JEA* 10: 217–77.

— 1924b. 'The Egyptian Expedition 1923–24', *BMMA* 19, Pt.II: 5–32.

— 1926. 'The Egyptian Expedition 1924–25', *BMMA* 21, Pt.II: 5–32.

— 1930. 'The Egyptian Expedition 1929–30', *BMMA* 25, Pt.II: 3–28.

— 1932. *The Tomb of Queen Meryet-Amun at Thebes* (New York: MMA).

— 1942. *Excavations at Deir el Bahri 1911–1931* (New York: Macmillan).

— 1945. *The Slain Soldiers of Neb-Hepet-Re Mentu-Hotpe* (New York: MMA).

— 1947 *The Rise and Fall of the Middle Kingdom in Thebes* (New York: Macmillan,).

— 1948. *The Treasure of Three Egyptian Princesses* (New York: MMA).

— 1955. *Models of Daily Life in Ancient Egypt* (Cambridge MA: Harvard University).

WOOD, W. 1978. 'A Reconstruction of the Reliefs of Hesy-Re', *JARCE* 15: 9–24.

— 1987. 'The Archaic Stone Tombs at Helwan', *JEA* 73: 59–70.

WORSHAM, C.E. 1979. 'A Reinterpretation of the So-called Bread Loaves in Egyptian Offering Scenes', *JARCE* 16: 7–10.

WRESZINSKI, W. et al. 1923–1942. *Atlas zur altägyptischen Kulturgeschichte*, 3vv. (Leipzig: Heinrichs').

YACOUB, F. 1981. 'The Archaic Tombs at Tura el-Asmant', *ASAE* 64: 159–61.

— 1988. 'Excavations at Tura el-Asmant from the Old Kingdom till the Greco-Roman Period, Seasons 1965–66', *ASAE* 67: 193–211.

YEIVIN, S. 1926. 'The Mond Excavations at Luxor, Season 1924–25', *LAAA* 13: 3–16.

YOSHIMURA, S. and S. HASEGAWA 2000. 'The New Kingdom necropolis at Dahshur', *AbSaq* 2000: 145–60.

YOSHIMURA, S., N. KAWAI and H. KASHIWAGI 2005. 'A Sacred Hillside at Northwest Saqqara: A Preliminary Report on the Excavations 2001–2003', *MDAIK* 61: 361–402.

YOSHIMURA S. and J. KONDO 1995 'Excavations at the tomb of Amenophis III', *EgArch* 7: 17–18.

YOYOTTE, J. 1958. 'The Tomb of a Prince Ramesses in the Valley of the Queens', *JEA* 44: 26–30.

ZANDEE, J. 1960. *Death as an Enemy According to Ancient Egyptian Conceptions* (Leiden: Brill).

ZIEGLER, Ch. 1981. 'La tombe de Sennefer à Deir el-Medineh', *Une siècle de fouilles Françaises en Égypte*, 1880–1980 (Paris: Musée du Louvre): 213–17.

— 1993. *Le Mastaba d'Akhethetep* (Paris: Réunion des musées nationaux).

ZIVIE, A.-P. 1979. *La tombe de Pached à Deir el-Médineh (no 3)* (Cairo: IFAO).

— 1983a. 'Les tombes de la falaise du Bebasteion a Saqqara', *Le Courrier du CNRS* 49: 37–44.

— 1983b. 'Trois saisons a Saqqarah: les tombeaux du Bubasteion', *BSFE* 98: 40ff.

— 1990. *Decouverte à Saqqarah. Le vizir oublié* (Paris).

— 2000a. 'La résurrection des hypogées du Nouvel Empire à Saqqara', *AbSaq* 2000: 173–92.

— [2000]. 'Les surprises de Saqqara: Découvertes et perspectives nouvelles sur le régne d'Amenhotep III', in *Amen-hotep III y su tiempo: I Jornadas Temáticas* (Madrid): 17–36.

— (ed.) 1988. *Memphis et ses nécropoles au Nouvel Empire* (Paris: Centre National de la Recherche Scientifique).

ZIVIE-COCHE, C. 1991. *Giza Au Premier Millenaire, autour du Temple D'Isis Dame des Pyramides* (Boston: Museum of Fine Arts).

— 1997. 'Un sarcophage tardif à Saqqâra', *Études Lauer*: 491–4.

ZONHOVEN, L.M.J. 1979. 'The Inspection of a Tomb at Deir el-Medina', *JEA* 65: 89–98.

Sources of Illustrations

a=above, b=below, l=left, r=right

akg-images/Hervé Champollion 301, 302, XVII
akg-images/François Guénet VI, XXVI
akg-images/Andrea Jemolo 114
akg-images/Erich Lessing 96, 193, II, VIII, XIV, XVIII
akg-images/Robert O'Dea 43b
E. Amélineau, *Le Tombeau d'Osiris*, 1899 65
Ladeslav Bares 283ar
A.M. Blackman, *The Rock Tombs of Meir*, 1914 89b
Museum of Fine Arts, Boston 70a
Bristol City Museum and Art Gallery 60
Costa, Cairo 289
DAI, Cairo 135r, 137, 208a
Egyptian Museum, Cairo 23, 38, 229a, XIII
Service des Antiquités, Cairo 117, 121, 155
Oriental Institute, University of Chicago 21, 119b
© Stephane Compoint XII, XXVIII
Ny Carlsberg Glyptotek, Copenhagen 152r, 188
Corbis 64
© The Art Archive/Corbis V
© Yann Arthus-Bertrand/Corbis 153
© Ron Watts/Corbis XXVII
Martin R. Davies 13, 16, 52, 55b, 86, 99al, 122, 150b, 222a, 226r, 227, 257b, 26bl, 263b, 264, 266
N. de Garies Davies, *The Tomb of Nakht*, 1917 67
N. de Garies Davies, *The Mastaba of Ptah-hotep*, 1900 113
N. de Garies Davies, *The Tomb of Queen Tiye*, 1910 66
J. De Morgan, *Fouilles à Dahchour*, 1895 15r
V. Denon, *Voyage*, 1802 187b
Description de l'Egypte, 1809-22 55a, 59b
Aidan Dodson 15l, 28-29, 32, 39a, 43a, 53, 54, 55c, 90, 115, 127, 135al, 139b, 144a, 149a, 149b, 150a, 154c, 154br, 157a, 157c, 157br, 158al, 158ar, 158br, 173, 175b, 178b, 179al, 179bl, 180a, 183, 192r, 194, 195c, 197ar, 207, 208b, 214, 215a, 216bl, 222b, 230, 243ar, 247b, 253, 270, 271b, 274a, 275a, 275b, 276l, 276ar, 278a, 280a, 280b, 281, 284, 287ar, 288b, 290a, 290b, 292br, 293, 294, 301, 303a, 303b
Francis Dzikowski 12, 19, 22a, 44b, 46, 111a, 112, 125, 131, 211, 220, 221, 224br, 246, 254, 258-9, XI, XIX
Egypt Exploration Fund 229b
W. Emery, *Archaic Egypt*, 1961 138
Firth and Gunn, *Excavations at Saqqara*, 1926 182
Joann Fletcher 216a
Laura Foos, courtesy of Stephen P. Harvey 210a
John Freeman 231a
John Wilkinson Gardner 118
© The J. Paul Getty Trust [1992]. All rights reserved. Photo Guillermo Aldana XXIII
Giraudon 87
Heidi Grassley © Thames & Hudson Ltd. 10, 25a, 99c, 170a, 177r, 248a
Leslie Grinsell (courtesy Bristol City Museum and Art Gallery) 160a, 198, 205bl
Dyan Hilton 40b, 156, 215b, 217c, 219, 279, 299br, 300ar
Hirmer Verlag 9, 76, 89a, 119a, 132, 143b, 177l, 213, 218a, 247a, 249a
Salima Ikram 30a, 39b, 40a, 42, 45l, 49, 50l, 51, 56, 68, 74, 79, 80, 883l, 3r, 84, 95a, 97, 98, 111b, 135b, 170bl, 201b, 212al, 231b, 243b, 250, 251, 295, 296, 298, III
Andrea Jemolo 78b, 95b, VII, XV, XXI, XXIV, XXV
Jean-Philippe Lauer 146l, 175a

Rijksmuseum van Oudheden, Leiden 244
Lepsius, *Denkmäler aus Aegypten und Aethiopien*, 1849-59 11, 31, 61, 78a, 142, 187c, 283b
Jürgen Liepe 191, IV, XVI
British Museum, London 8, 18, 57b, 93, 134, 190a, IX
Petrie Museum, University College, London 63b
William MacQuitty 130
S. Manning, *The Land of the Pharaohs*, 1887 63a
P. Montet, *Fouilles de Tanis*, 1947 71
Naville and Hall, *The XIth Dynasty Temple at Deir el-Bahri*, 1907-1913 190b
The Metropolitan Museum of Art, New York 92, 174a
P. Newberry, *Beni Hasan*, 1893 186, 201a
F. L. Norden, *Travels through Egypt and Nubia*, 1757 59a
© Copyright Griffith Institute, Oxford 70b, 245b
W.F. Petrie, E. Mackay & G. Wainwright, *Meidum and Memphis*, 1910 45r
W.F. Petrie, *Athribis*, 1908 297
Jackie Phillips 277
R. Pococke, *A Description of the East and some other countries*, 1743 58b
J.E. Quibell, *The Tomb of Hesy*, 1913 145
J.E. Quibell and A.G.K. Hayter, *Excavations at Saqqara*, 1927 241
J.E. Quibell, *The Ramasseum*, 1898 275
Copyright: 2004, www.reconstructions.org. Organizational authors: The Metropolitan Museum of Art and www.reconstructions.org, Dieter Arnold (Supervising Archaeologist), David Johnson (Digital Architect) 199b
John G. Ross 129, 147a
G. Sandys, *A Relation of a Journey...*, 1615 58a
E. Schiaparelli, *Tomba Intatta dell'Architetto Cha*, 1927 24, 218b
Albert Shoucair 77, 100, 109, 178a, X
H.W.V. Stuart, *Nile Gleanings concerning the ethnology, history and art of ancient Egypt*, 1879 62
© Theban Mapping Project 47, 50r, 260, XX, XXII
Guido Alberto Rossi/Tips Images 189
Vyse & Perring, *Operations Carried on at the Pyramids of Gizeh*, 1840 160b
Jim Wearing 200
Werner Forman Archive 128, 267, I
Milan Zemina 73

DRAWINGS

Ian Bott 245a
Violane Chauvet 120
Violane Chauvet/Aidan Dodson 14
Robin Cook 27
Garth Denning 224bl
Aidan Dodson 22b, 30b, 126, 136, 140a, 140b, 141a, 141b, 144b, 146ar, 148, 151, 152bl, 154a, 154bl, 169r, 174b, 176a, 176b, 179r, 180b, 181l, 181r, 187a, 192l, 195al, 195ar, 197al, 197c, 199a, 202, 204, 205c, 205bc, 205br, 210b, 212ar, 216br, 217br, 223, 225l, 225r, 242, 243al, 252, 256, 263a, 264, 271a, 272, 278b, 282al, 282ar, 283al, 285b, 286al, 286ac, 287al, 291, 292bl, 299bl, 300al
Aidan Dodson after Drioton and Lauer 1951, 286ar
Christine End,after Jéquier 1936-40 170br, 172l, 172r
Dyan Hilton 17, 57a
Salima Ikram 82
Drazen Tomic 81, 139a
Philip Winton 25b, 37, 44a, 61a, 143a, 147b, 169l, 171, 196, 203, 232, 248b, 249b, 257a, 285a

hunting, scenes of 78, 86–90, 98–99
Hussein, Abdelsalam (d.1949) 72
Huy (S2735) 232
Huy (TT14) 124
Huy (TT40): see Amenhotep-Huy
Huy iv (TT339) 269
Huya (TA1) 229, 232
Hyksos 207, 209

Iarti (Saqqara) 185
Iaru, Fields of 13, 15, 17–18, 85, 118, 228,
    250, 262, 268–9, 274, pl. V
Ibi (DG8) 126
Ibi (TT36) 52, 220, 279
Idi (Abydos) 183
Idu (Dendara) 183
Idu (G7102) 127, 156, 176, 177
Idut (Saqqara) 184
Ihy (Saqqara) 197, 202, 206
Imbaba 324–25, map I[27]
Imhotep (S3518?) 27, 28, 142, 145–46,
    148
Imiseba (TT65) 124, 127, 253
Inemhes (Saqqara) 292
Ineni (TT81) 8, 116, 215, 219
Inherkhau ii (TT359) 16, 266, 269
Inpy (Lahun 620) 197–98, 205
Inti (Deshasha 1) 179
INYOTEF I (El-Tarif Saff Dawaba)
    186–87
INYOTEF II (El-Tarif Saff el-Qisasiya)
    99, 187
INYOTEF III (El-Tarif Saff el-Bagar)
    186–87
INYOTEF V (Dra Abu'l-Naga) 208
INYOTEF VI (Dra Abu'l-Naga) 208
Inyotef (TT155) 51, 99, 219
Inyotef (TT164) 88, 219
Inyotef (TT386) 279
Inyotefiqer (TT60/Lisht 400) 52, 56,
    86, 126, 198, 200
Inyotefiqer ii (Dendara) 193–94
Ipay (Dahshur) 242
Ipi (SQ75) 206
Ipi (Saqqara-South) 114
Ipiy (Riqqa F201) 246
Ipuia (S2730) 241
Ipuky (TT181) 126
Iput II (Saqqara-South) 171, 182
Ipuy (TT217) 92, 120, 253
Irahor (LS23) 286, 287
Irtuharerau (Abydos G57) 289, 292
Irukaptah-Khenu 80, 156
Irynefer (TT290) 268, 269
ISESI (Saqqara L.XXXVII) 72, 158,
    169–70, 174
Isetirdis (Saqqara) 292
Isis (goddess) 17–18, 120, 224, 260, 266,
    270–71, 268–69, 301–02, pl. III, XX
Isis A 224
Iskander, Zaki (1916–1979) 72
Istabl Antar 324–25, map I[70]
Itet (Meidum 16) 152
Iteti-Ankhiris (Saqqara D63) 177
Iti (Gebelein) 96
Iti (G6030) 173
Iufaa (Abu Sir) 72, 73, 282–84, 287
Iuput A (Abydos) 275

Iuu (Abydos) 183
Iymery (Gebel el-Teir) 156

Jenni, Hanna 74
Jéquier, Gustave (1868–1946) 71
jewelry-production 109–10
Junker, Hermann (1877–1962) 69

ka 16, 127, 176–77, 245, pl. III
Kaemankh (G4561) 182, 183, 194
Kafr Ammar 324–25, map I[44]
Kagemeni (Saqqara LS10) 48, 65, 77,
    100, 180, 181–84
Kaha (Saqqara) 178, 184, 197
Kakerenptah (G7721) 127, 156
Kamal, Ahmed (1851–1923) 69
Kama(ma) (Leontopolis) 275
Kanawati, Naguib 74
Kanefer (Saqqara) 292
Kaninisut i (G2155) 52
Karabasaken (TT391) 279
Karakhamun (TT223) 279
Karanis/Kom Ushim 297
Karnak 43, 220, pl. I
Kasa i (TT10B) 269
Kawab (G7110+7120) 154
Kemsit (TT308) 194
KHABA (Zawiyet-el-Aryan L.XIV) 148
Kha (TT8) 11, 24, 69, 96, 218, 228
Khabaukhnum Biu (Saqqara-South
    MXIV) 184
Khabausokar (S3073) 145, 146, 151
Khabekhnet i (TT2) 266, 268
Khaemhat (TT57) 91, 219, 221
Khaemopet (TT105) 255
Khaemopet (TT272) 124
Khaemteri i (TT220) 266, 269
Khaemwaset C 56
Khaemwaset (TT261) 120
KHAFRE (Giza L.VIII) 42, 60, 144, 151,
    153, 156, 158, 160, 291
Khaled, Lotfi 74
Kharga Oasis 75, 295, 298. 303–04,
    324–25, map I[150]
KHASEKHEMWY (Umm el-Qaab V)
    135, 139–42, 149
Khawy ii (TT214) 269
Khedebneithirbinet II 61, 292
khekher-frieze 50, 124–26, 142
KHENDJER (Saqqara-South L.XLIV)
    71
Khentika (Balat III) 182–83
Khentika-Ikhekhi (Saqqara) 131, 185
Khentkaues I (LG100) 32, 156
Khentysehnetjer: see Anubis
Khenuka (Tihna 14) 176
Khenut (Saqqara) 177, 179
Kheperre (G7757) 287, 296
Kheruef (TT192) 28, 113, 119, 217, 219,
    221, 228, 230, 279
Khety (BH-XVII) pl. V
Khety (TT311) 192, 194
Khnemet (Dahshur) 64
Khnemu (Saqqara-South OII) 185
Khnum 16–17
Khnumemheb (TT26) 128
Khnumenti (G2374) 174–75

Khnumhotep (Dahshur 2) 198, 199, 205
Khnumhotep (Saqqara) 72, 84, 95, 113
Khnumhotep i (BH-XIV) 199
Khnumhotep iii (BH-III) 11, 88, 126,
    186, 199, 200; pl. XVIII
Khokha: see Thebes-West
Khonsu (god) 210
Khonsu (TT31) 127
Khonsumose (TT30) 127
Khubawy (Saqqara) 185
KHUFU (L.IV) 23, 149–51, 153–54, 159,
    291
Khunes (Zawiyet Sultan 2) 179
Khunes (QH34) 324–25, map I[127]
Köhler, Christiana 71
Kom Abu Billo 324–25, map I[20]
Kom Ausim (Letopolis) 324–25, map
    I[24]
Kom el-Ahmar Sawaris 324–25, map
    I[63]
Kom el-Hisn 324–25, map I[15]
Kom el-Kharaba el-Kebir (Philadelphia)
    324–25, map I[49]
Kom el-Shugafa: see Alexandria
Kom Firin 324–25, map I[14]
Kom Ombo 324–25, map I[126]
Kom Ushim: see Karanis
Koshtemna 324–25, map I[129]

Lahun 41–42, 53–54, 198, 324–25, map
    I[52]; tombs 620 (Inpy) 197–98, 205;
    L.LXVI (SENWOSRET II) 41–42,
    195, 197, 203
Lauer, Jean-Philippe (1902–2001) 72
leatherworking, scenes of 110, 112
Lehner, Mark 75
Leiden University 72
Leiden, National Museum of
    Antiquities 72; objects: AMT.1-35
    232; H.III.CCCC 244
Leontopolis (Tell Moqdam) 275,
    324–25, map I[16]
Lepsius, Karl Richard (1810–1884) 61
Lisht 70–71, 196, 324–25, map I[43];
    tombs: 372 (Rehudjersen) 196; 378
    202; 400 (Inyotefiqer) 196; 493 202;
    L.LX (AMENEMHAT I) 194, 201;
    L.LXI (SENWOSRET I) 71, 194–96,
    201–02; Mastaba du Nord 202;
    Mentuhotep 197; Sehetepibre-ankh
    196; Senwosret 197; Senwosret-ankh
    196–97, 202–03, 206
London, British Museum, objects: EA10
    290; EA23 57; EA478 208; EA9901
    18; EA1397 190; EA32751 134;
    EA37983 96; ; EA37984 8; EA37986
    pl. IX
Loret, Victor (1859–1946) 65
Lucas, Paul (1664–1737) 58
Luxor 58, 212, pl. I

Maadi 324–25, map I[30]
maat (concept) 13, 17, 77, 88, 90–91, 96,
    112, 174
Maat (goddess) 12, 120, 260, 269, 284
Mahu (Saqqara) 52
Maihirpri (KV36) 65, 225
Manniche, Lise 75, 124

Mariette, Auguste (1821–1881) 61–62
Marina el-Alamein 30, 75, 298, 303,
    324–25, map I[12]
Martin, Geoffrey T. 66, 74
Maru Bebi (Saqqara) 184
Maspero, Gaston (1846–1916) 62–63,
    65–66, 69
Matariya (Heliopolis) 324–25, map I[25]
Mathieson, Ian 72
Matmar 71, 324–25, map I[86]
May (TA14) 230
May (TT338) 69
Maya (LS27) 72, 99, 242, 243, 245
Maya (Saqqara I.20) 73, 242
Mazghuna 324–25, map I[41]
Medinet Habu: see Thebes-West
Mehytenweskhet C 278, 285
Meidum 43, 45, 158, 324–25, map I[47];
    tombs: 6 (Rahotep A) 152, 158, pl.
    XVI; 16 (Nefermaat A) 151–52, 153,
    158; 17 ([...]) 37, 158; L.LXV
    (SENEFERU) 43, 148–49, 151, 157,
    158
Meir 100, 180, 324–25, map I[77];
    tombs: A2 (Pepyankh-Henikem) 121;
    A3 (Ukhhotep-son-of-Iam) 206; A4
    (Hepi-kem) 182, 183; B1 (Senbi) 89,
    200; B2 (Ukhhotep-son-of-Senbi)
    200; B4 (Ukhhotep-son-of-
    Ukhhotep & Mersy) 200; C1
    (Ukhhotep-son-of-Ukhhotep &
    Heny) 126; D2 (Pepyankh-heryib-
    Neferka) 183
Meketre (TT280) 191, 193
Mekhu (QH25) 176, 179, 180
Memnon, Colossi of: see Thebes-West
Memphis/Mit Rahina 38, 72, 142, 275,
    276, 324–25, map I[35]; tombs:
    Shoshenq D 275, 276; Tjaisetenimu
    289
Menankh-Pepy (Dendara) 183
Mendes (Tell Ruba) 182, 324–25, map
    I[6]; tomb of Naefarud I 75, 289, 291
Menena (TT69) 51, 52, 115, 219, 222
Meni (Dendara) 180, 181
Menib (G7249) 52
MENKAUHOR (Saqqara L.XXIX) 158
MENKAURE (Giza L.IX) 24, 32, 43,
    151, 154, 156, 158, 160
Menkheperresonbe (TT86 & TT112)
    26, 51, 99, 118, 120
Mentu, Priests of (Deir el-Bahari) 61
Mentuemhat (TT34) 9, 52, 128, 261,
    279, 284–85, pl. XXV
Mentuhirkopshef (TT20) 123
MENTUHOTEP II (DBXI.14) 189–91,
    194, 211, 268
MENTUHOTEP III (TT281?) 189,
    191–92
MENTUHOTEP IV 192
Mentuhotep (Lisht) 197
Mentuiywy (TT172) 120
Mentusebaef (Sheikh Abd el-Qurna)
    61, 279
MERENPTAH (KV8) 129, 248, 260
Mereri (Dendara) 181, 182
Mereri (Saqqara) 185
Mereruka (Saqqara) 43, 48, 65, 78, 83,